Cultural Contact and Linguistic Relativity
among the Indians of Northwestern California

Cultural Contact and Linguistic Relativity among the Indians of Northwestern California

SEAN O'NEILL

University of Oklahoma Press : Norman

Library of Congress Cataloging-in-Publication Data

O'Neill, Sean, 1969–
    Cultural contact and linguistic relativity among the Indians of northwestern California /
Sean O'Neill.
        p.   cm.
    Includes bibliographical references and index.
    ISBN 978-0-8061-3922-7 (hardcover : alk. paper) 1. Indians of North America—
California, Northern—Languages. 2. Anthropological linguistics—California, Northern.
I. Title.
    PM501.C2054   2008
    497'.0979—dc22

                                                        2007035710

1 2 3 4 5 6 7 8 9 10

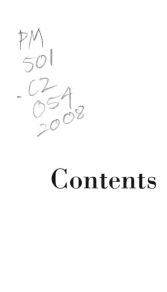

Contents

CONTENTS

Illustrations

TABLES

Preface

This book focuses on the traditional language and culture of northwestern California as reflected in the social worlds of three neighboring speech communities: Hupa, Yurok, and Karuk. One of the primary goals of this book is to assess the long-term effects of social contact among speakers of diverse languages. Convergence is certainly a predictable outcome of this ongoing interaction. However, there is also evidence that long-standing contact has, in some cases, produced increasing opposition among the linguistic groups of northwestern California, perhaps partly as a reflection of various reactions to a common theme or cultural element. Once set into motion, these differences serve as markers of identity, setting the neighboring communities apart in publicly accentuated ways while opening the door to both linguistic and cultural relativity at the local level. In contrast, where convergence is evident, one can see that the speakers have settled on a common cultural outlook, providing evidence of a broader relationship between language and worldview, one that operates at the regional, rather than the strictly local, level.

Throughout this book, my reference is primarily to the traditional culture of the region as it existed from the time of contact with Americans during the late 1840s into the early twentieth century. By the late nineteenth century, government policies had begun to seriously disrupt the traditional way of life, and few people in the early twentieth century were still practicing the traditional hunting-and-gathering mode of subsistence (see Keeling 1992:27–32 and Buckley 2002:7–12). Similar measures were taken to eradicate the languages, and for decades children were frequently sent to boarding schools, where the transmission of languages from generation to generation could be more or less permanently broken (see Hinton 1994:173–79). However, many aspects of the traditional culture—especially folklore, religion, and storytelling—continue to play a part in the daily lives of the Hupa, Yurok, and Karuk Tribes, so I hesitate to couch my statements about the culture purely in the past. In addition, the Hupa, Yurok, and Karuk languages are all currently undergoing revitalization (see Hinton 1994:235–47), with many new speakers cropping up in the present generation; to speak of any one of the languages as if it were a thing of the past is thus deeply inappropriate. In short, the language and culture were never truly lost, and both continue to undergo revitalization, so I use the present tense in reference to both throughout this book.

My approach to the principle of linguistic relativity draws heavily on the works of Boas, Sapir, and Whorf, who all argued for the role of language in guiding human perception, especially in the culturally charged settings of everyday life. Although current discussions of linguistic relativity concentrate heavily on psycholinguistic experiments with subjects in the laboratory, the original architects of this school of thought, especially Sapir and Whorf, focused on controlled comparisons between contrasting linguistic traditions and related patterns of behavior in society, often with an eye to the historical impact of cultural categories on the evolution of language (see Sapir 1921:147–70 and Whorf 1956:134–59). Taking the Hupa, Yurok, and Karuk languages as a case study, this book demonstrates the importance of language in conveying pervasive cultural ideologies, such as those associated with mythology, religion, folklore, and geographical systems of spatial orientation.

Part I serves as an introduction to the concept of linguistic relativity. Reflecting the localized nature of language, each of the later sections of this book addresses the comparative status of conceptual categories within a series of domains. Part II examines the comparative status of spatial concepts in the area's linguistic and cultural systems. Part III focuses on the semantics of time, specifically, the comparative representation of parallel mythic epochs in each of the linguistic traditions. Part IV explores general issues of taxonomy and vocabulary. Finally, Part V reexamines the question of linguistic drift in light of the evidence introduced in the preceding chapters, weighing the cases for both convergent and divergent historical trends.

Acknowledgments

The intellectual diversity of our species throughout the ages has intrigued me for as long as I can remember. The present work, which represents my own attempt to grapple with this difficult but perennial problem, has been influenced and facilitated by many others.

First, I would like to thank Aram Yengoyan, my mentor at the University of California at Davis, for wisely pointing me in the direction of linguistics, though my first ambitions in this field lay in the realms of phenomenology and comparative psychology. Never content with simple answers to questions regarding complexities of human social life, Yengoyan pushed me in the direction of comparative linguistics when I was happy to work within the confines of a single linguistic tradition, namely, the comfortable, though respectably intricate, world of Hupa language and culture.

Next, I would like to thank Victor Golla for first training me as a linguist and then accepting me as his apprentice within the realm of Athabaskan linguistics. Without this training, I would have never been able to enter the majestic universe of Hupa linguistics, nor would I have ever gained an appreciation of the joys and sublime insight that meticulous linguistic research can afford.

Finally, I would also like to thank Martha Macri, of the Department of Native American Studies at the University of California at Davis, for her quiet encouragement and support over the years, without which I would have gotten nowhere.

I also owe an enormous debt of gratitude to several reviewers who have offered me many insightful criticisms and suggestions for revisions. First, I would like to thank William Bright, who first checked the manuscript for technical soundness of the Karuk analysis, then asked for clarification on several key points relating to recent work on linguistic relativity. I am also grateful to a second and anonymous reviewer who requested that I expand my general argument by incorporating recent literature on language contact, sociolinguistics, and cognitive linguistics, as well as language ideologies. Though these topics were indeed central to my thinking all along, I had not realized how much of my argument was merely implicit in the original dissertation. In the end, it was very rewarding to take the time to spell out the larger theoretical implications for the fields of anthropology and linguistics. I would also like to thank Jane Hill for asking me to clarify some of the theoretical sections on language contact and linguistic relativity and for providing further background on William Bright's Karuk fieldwork following his untimely death in the fall of 2006. The insights of all the reviewers have been critical to the development of this book, so I am enormously grateful for the comments I received. My copy editor, Sally Bennett, pored over the manuscript with great care and spared me a number of potential inconsistencies, and so I owe a debt of gratitude to her as well. Finally, I would like to thank Andrew Garrett of the University of California–Berkeley, who was kind enough to offer his expert advice on some aspects of the Yurok analysis.

My research on this project has been supported by generous grants from a number of sponsors, without which I would never have been able to complete this ambitious and time-consuming study. First, I must express my gratitude to the Wenner-Gren Foundation for offering me my first research grant (#6248), which supported my fieldwork throughout the 1998 calendar year. Second, I would like to thank the National Science Foundation for supporting further fieldwork in 1999 (BSN #9810666), while also providing a computer for analyzing the comparative, cross-linguistic database I was able to assemble, combining texts, grammar, and lexicon in all three languages. Next, I would like to thank the American Philosophical Society for providing further funds for travel, without which I would not have been able to afford my many return visits to Hoopa Valley for the purpose of carrying out follow-up research. In addition, I would like to thank the University of Oklahoma for offering me a Junior Faculty Research Fellowship over the summer of 2003, which granted me the time to supplement the volume with several additional chapters not included in the dissertation. Earlier in the writing process, I also benefited from the commentary of my colleagues at the University of Oklahoma, especially Morris Foster, Circe Sturm, Jason Jackson, Alex Dent, and Patricia Gilman. I would like to extend my gratitude to the Department of Anthropology and the College of Arts and Sciences at the University of Oklahoma for kindly providing a subvention to defray some of the costs associated with this publication. Finally, I would like to thank Alessandra Jacobi Tamulevich, acquisitions editor at the University of Oklahoma Press, for encouraging me to publish this book and for responding with enthusiasm to my many questions along the way.

Earlier versions of some sections of this book appeared in "Northwest California Ethnolinguistics: A Study in Drift," *Proceedings of the 50th Anniversary Celebration of the Survey of California and Other Indian Languages*, edited by Lisa Conathan and Teresa McFarland, pp. 64–88, reprinted with the permission of the Department of Linguistics, University of California, Berkeley. These sections are as follows: "Fundamental Aspects of the Languages" (chapter 1); "Verbal Paradigms," "Double Directional Expressions," "Directional versus Non-Directional Verbs," and "Overlap with Temporal Marking" (chapter 4); "Temporal Structure in Oral Literature" (chapter 7); "Grammatical Patterning in Northwestern California" (chapter 8); and "Maintaining Linguistic Difference" (chapter 11). Two sections of chapter 2 ("Vocabulary and Linguistic Relativity" and "Narrative Texts, Language Use, and Linguistic Relativity") and an earlier version of chapter 9 appeared as "Mythic and Poetic Dimensions of Speech in Northwestern California: From Cultural Vocabulary to Linguistic Relativity," *Anthropological Linguistics* 48 (4): 305–34, reprinted with the permission of the publisher.

My wife, Misha Klein, and my son, Theo, have made it all worthwhile. I would also like to thank my mother, Judith Riis, and my uncle, Jim Riis, for a lifetime of stimulating conversations. It was my father who originally encouraged my interest in philosophy, linguistics, and anthropology, so I must thank him as well.

Finally, let me offer the following sincere wish: May the native languages of northwestern California continue to be spoken forever. This book is dedicated to JJ and the other elders, now deceased, who first taught me about northwestern California.

All proceeds from this book are being donated to the Advocates for Indigenous California Language Survival (AICLS), so that future generations will have the opportunity to continue learning these languages.

Guide to the Orthographies

All of the Hupa, Yurok, and Karuk words in this volume are written in phonemic scripts loosely based on those published in the major grammatical treatments of these languages. The Hupa script follows Sapir 2001, while the Karuk and Yurok orthographies are based on the systems presented in Bright 1957 and Robins 1958, respectively. Where possible, rough English equivalents are given in the descriptions below, with exact values, represented by the International Phonetic Alphabet (IPA), in brackets. Some letters represent sounds also found in English, including *h, m, n, l, w,* and *y*. Other letters represent nearly the same sounds in Hupa, Yurok, and Karuk, including the following characters:

ʔ   [ʔ] a glottal stop, the sound in the middle of English *uh-oh*

k   generally aspirated [kʰ] in Yurok, as in English *kin*; unaspirated [k] in Karuk, as in English *skin*

ł   [ɬ] a voiceless lateral fricative, like the voiceless *l* in English *clean*, but with more audible friction; like Welsh double *ll*, as in *Lloyd*

p   generally aspirated [pʰ] in Yurok, as in English *pun*; unaspirated [p] in Karuk, as in English *spoon*

s   [s] in Hupa, as in English *sing*; slightly retroflex [ʂ] in Yurok and Karuk, with the tip of the tongue turned back slightly creating a sound that is between English *s* and *sh*, as in *sign* and *shine*

š   [ʃ] English *ship*

t   aspirated [tʰ] in Hupa and Yurok, as in English *top*; unaspirated [t] in Karuk, as in English *stop*

t'   [t'] articulated in the same place as English *tip*, though pronounced with a sharp, popping sound, called glottalization

x   [x] like German *ch* in *Bach*

LANGUAGE SPECIFIC SOUNDS

Many of the sounds do not have close equivalents in the neighboring languages, even in cases where similar or identical phonemic characters are used. The language-specific characters and values are given below, with their IPA equivalents in brackets.

HUPA

a   generally [ɒ] as in English *father*, except when short, where the value is usually reduced to [ʌ] like English *u* in *but*; always [ɒ] before *h* or *ʔ*, even when short

c   [tsʰ] like English *ts* in *hats*

c'   [ts'] like English *ts*, though with sharp, popping sound, called glottalization

čʷ   [tʃʷ] like English *ch* in *church*, though with tightly rounded lips

c'   [tʃ'] like English *ch* in *church*, though with a popping sound (glottalization)

d   [t] unaspirated like English *t* in *stop* (not the aspirated *t* in English *top*)

e   generally [ɛ] like English *bet*, except before *y*, where the value becomes [e], as in English or French *sauté*

gʸ   [kʲ] a plain front-velar stop, similar to the unaspirated English *k* in *skin*, with the tongue positioned farther forward in the mouth than with the regular English *k*

ɢ   [ɢ] a back-velar stop, similar to English *g*, though articulated with the tongue farther back in the mouth

i   generally [ɪ] like English *bit*, except before *gʸ, kʸ, ḱʸ* and *y*, where the value becomes [i] like English *machine*; pronounced [u] like English *dune* before *w*

kʸ   [kʲʰ] aspirated like English *k* in *kin*, though with the tongue moved farther forward in the mouth

ḱʸ   [kʲ'] like English *k*, though with the tongue moved farther forward in the mouth and with sharp popping sound (glottalization)

ƛ̓   [tɬ'] a glottalized lateral affricate, like English *kl* in *kleenex*, though with *t* rather than *k*, and with a sharp popping sound (glottalization)

ŋ   [ŋ] like English *ng* in *sing*

o   generally [o] like English *solo*, except when short, where the value is usually [ʊ] like English *oo* in *book*; remains [o] before *h* and *ʔ*, even when the vowel is short; becomes [ɔ] before *y*, like English *o* in *coffee*, as pronounced in New York *q'* [q'] a glottalized back-velar stop, like English *g,* though made with the tongue farther back in the mouth and with a sharp, popping sound (glottalization)

W [ʍ] like English *wh* in *whistle,* when pronounced with considerable breathiness

xʷ [xʷ] like German *ch* in *Bach,* though with tightly rounded lips

ʒ̃ [ts] like English *ds* in *adds,* though without voicing

ǰ̃ [tʃ] like English *j* in *judge,* though without voicing

Many Hupa consonants become slightly breathy at the ends of words. The *d,* *gʸ, ɢ, ʒ̃,* and *ǰ̃* sounds, for instance, receive slight aspiration when positioned at the ends of words; in this environment, Hupa *d* sounds more like the aspirated *t* in English *top* and less like the plain *t* in English *stop.* In a similar way, the *n, l, w,* and *y* sounds often lose their voicing at the end of a Hupa word; in this environment, the Hupa *l* sounds like the voiceless *l* in English *clean.* A raised dot after a vowel symbol (*a·*) indicates a long vowel in Hupa, held for a greater period of time, following Sapir 2001.

YUROK

a a low, unrounded vowel that ranges from [ɒ] as in English *father* to the value [a], where the tongue remains low but is moved slightly toward the front of the mouth

c usually [tʃʰ] like English *ch* in *cheese;* sometimes [tsʰ] like English *ts* in *hats*

c' [tʃ'] like English *ch* in *cheese,* though made with sharp, popping sound, called glottalization; sometimes [ts'] like *ts* in English *hats,* with a popping sound

e ranges from [e] as in English or French *sauté* to [ε] as in English *bet*

g [ɣ] a sound like *g* in English *good,* though with slight friction because the tongue does not make direct contact with the roof of the mouth and the airstream is not stopped

i [i] as in English *machine*

k̓ [k'] like English *k,* though with sharp popping sound (glottalization)

kʷ [kʷ] like English *qu* in *quick*

k̓ʷ [k'ʷ] like English *qu* in *quick,* though with a sharp popping sound (glottalization) o   [ɔ] like English *o* in coffee, as pronounced in New York

p'   [pʼ] like English *pun*, though with a sharp popping sound (glottalization)

r   [ɻ] like English *r* in *run*, though with the tongue curled back more (retroflex)

ɹ   [ɚ] like English *er* in *miller* (double ɹɹ in Yurok indicates greater duration)

u   [u] as in English *dune*

In Yurok, the clusters ʔl, ʔm, ʔn, ʔr, ʔy, and ʔw represent the preglottalized sonorants [ʼl], [ʼm], [ʼn], [ʼr], [ʼy], and [ʼw], articulated with a brief closure of the vocal cords and with a loss of voicing at the ends of words. The Yurok consonants *p, t, c, k,* and *k^w* sometimes sound less breathy than their English counterparts, since they often lose their aspiration in rapid speech. A doubling (*aa*) or tripling (*aaa*) of a vowel symbol represents a long vowel, held for a slightly greater period of time, a convention that follows the current Tribal writing system.

KARUK

a   generally [ɒ] like English *father*, though reduced to [ə] like English *a* in *about* when unaccented and short; becomes [a], where the tongue remains low but is moved slightly toward the front of the mouth, if previous syllable contains *e* or *i*

ch   [tʃ] like English *ch* in *church*, though less breathy (unaspirated)

e   generally [e] as in English or French *sauté*, though lowered to [ɛ] as in English *bet* immediately before an *x*

f   [f] like English *father*

i   [i] as in English *machine*, though the value is [ɪ], as in English *bit*, before *sh* and *ch* when the vowel is short

o   [o] like *o* in English *solo*

r   [ɾ] like English *d* in *ladder;* a single tap sound, in phonetic terms

sh   [ʃ] like English *sh* in *share*

th   [θ] like English *th* in *thin*

v   [β] similar to English *b*, though articulated with audible friction and without fully closing the lips or stopping the airstream

u   ranges from [u] as in English *dune* to [ʊ] like *oo* in English *book*

An acute accent (á) normally represents strong stress and a high level pitch; before a pause, however, a long vowel with an acute accent is usually pronounced with a falling pitch and slight glottal interruption of the vowel (áa > âʔª). In contrast, a circumflex (â) represents falling pitch and strong stress, without glottal interruption. A doubling of a vowel (*aa*) or consonant (*kk*) symbol signals that the sound is held for a greater duration, a convention that follows the current Tribal writing system.

Cultural Contact and Linguistic Relativity
among the Indians of Northwestern California

Introduction

The traditional language and culture of northwestern California has been the subject of continuous scholarly research for over a century now, giving rise to a rich body of literature in the fields of anthropology, linguistics, and Native American studies. One of the primary goals of my early work in this area was to consolidate as much of the previous research as possible, for the purpose of putting forth a broad comparative analysis of the area's many linguistic and cultural traditions. Another long-standing goal of my work has been to apply the linguistic facts obtained by previous scholars to a range of theoretical issues in the fields of anthropology and linguistics. The theoretical issues that have most attracted my attention, as evidenced in the following chapters, are contemporary work on language contact, cognitive linguistics, sociolinguistics, dialogism, ideology, and, especially, linguistic relativity.

HUPA

The first serious work on the Hupa language was carried out by Pliny Earle Goddard, a Quaker missionary–turned-scholar who first arrived in Hoopa Valley during the summer of 1897. Prior to his brief sojourn in this land, several minor vocabulary schedules had been collected by Edward Gibson and others, who obtained limited quantities of data for broad comparative purposes. Quickly becoming a fluent speaker in the context of his religious vocation, Goddard later drew upon his extensive knowledge of Hupa language and culture to produce a doctoral thesis in linguistics at the University of California–Berkeley. After several years of graduate study under the direction of B. I. Wheeler, Goddard completed his classic ethnography of the Hupas, a work entitled *The Life and Culture of the Hupa* (1903). This first book was quickly followed by a collection of myths, tales, and Native ethnographic sketches, dictated by fluent speakers strictly in the Hupa language, many of them recollecting the traditional life as it existed before contact with Europeans in the mid-nineteenth century. This second volume on traditional storytelling was published under the title *Hupa Texts* in 1904.

The following year, Goddard published the first scholarly study of Hupa linguistics in a work entitled *The Morphology of the Hupa Language* (1905), under the tutelage of the famed Indo-Europeanist Benjamin Ide Wheeler, then president of the University of California. A landmark achievement in early Native American linguistics, this book fixed its attention on the elaborate system of the Hupa verb paradigm. As any experienced linguist has discovered, this is one of the most challenging parts of mastering any Athabaskan language, for a single word is often composed of a seemingly endless string of meaningful elements. Despite the depth of Goddard's knowledge (which must have been considerable given that he regularly delivered sermons in the language), the linguistic materials he published were beset by serious technical flaws, both in the representation of the phonology and in the presentation of the grammatical system. Yet the ethnography he presented was of great and lasting value, like the cultural substance of the texts themselves.

Several decades later, Edward Sapir finally set aside time for a trip to Hoopa Valley. Though he had no previous experience with the California Athabaskan languages, he had worked with several related tongues to the north, including Sarcee in Canada and Chasta Costa (or Tututni) in Oregon. Later, in the 1930s, he worked with the Navajos of the American Southwest, for which work he is perhaps best known by nonlinguists. By expanding what was known about the Pacific Coast division of this family, this new work on Hupa was to represent an important aspect of Sapir's total plan of research on the Athabaskan languages. He was especially intent on clearing up the serious technical problems that had long plagued the otherwise valuable materials collected by Goddard several decades before. Yet he also hoped that careful work on Hupa would one day facilitate the reconstruction of the original Proto-Athabaskan mother tongue. In about eight weeks, he managed to collect an impressive body of seventy-seven narrative texts, which he recorded with characteristic accuracy and insightful ethnographic commentary. Yet because of the harried nature of his academic schedule, he was unable to set aside time to complete this new work on Hupa linguistics. So, upon his death in 1939, his notes were eventually transferred to one of Sapir's early students, Harry Hoijer. Toward the end of his own career, Hoijer passed Sapir's materials on to Victor Golla, whose dissertation on Hupa grammar he was supervising during the mid-1960s.

Starting in 1996, I was fortunate enough to collaborate with Golla on the task of preparing Sapir's materials for publication. With the exception of a single article on tattooing (1936a), Sapir was unable to see any of these materials to print during his lifetime. Nearly seventy years after Sapir's trip to northwestern California, the bulk of this material remained unfinished. As a result, years of work were required before the raw field notes could be converted into a polished, edited volume. Not until the summer of 2001 was Sapir's full corpus of work on the Native languages of northwestern California published, as volume 14 of the *Collected Works of Edward Sapir,* under the joint editorship of Golla and myself. While serving as one of the volume editors, I also made substantial contributions to the sections on the linguistic notes and the analytic lexicon.

Following Sapir's fieldwork, the next major event in Hupa linguistics was represented by the completion of Golla's dissertation, *Hupa Grammar,* in 1970. Produced at Berkeley under the direction of Mary Haas and Harry Hoijer, Golla's work on Hupa grammar has in turn exerted a considerable influence on my understanding of this richly polysynthetic tongue. Representing a model in part built on Sapir's earlier work, Golla's dissertation picked up where Sapir had left off. Combining the materials he collected in the early 1960s with those obtained by Sapir a generation before, Golla's efforts led to the first fully modern grammar of the Hupa language, which is also one of the most complete descriptions of an Athabaskan language to date. As with Goddard's earlier work, the bulk of Golla's book focuses on the complex grammatical structure of the Hupa verbal paradigm. Separate sections are also devoted to phonology, syntax, and other word classes. A condensed version of the Sapir-Golla grammar was published in volume 14 of the *Collected Works of Edward Sapir* (2001).

My own work on the Hupa language, which was carried out between 1998 and 2001, focused on the texts originally collected by Goddard at the turn of the twentieth century, which I re-elicited word by word during the course of my stay. I was able to restore most of the volume—which is rich in both ethnographic detail and complexity of linguistic expression—by reading aloud my reconstructed versions to several of the surviving speakers of the language. During the process, I was also able to collect new versions of many of the stories, told in a more modern version of the language, while at the same time collecting newer tales representing the current state of Hupa folklore, mythology, and tribal history. I was also able to translate a number of Yurok and Karuk stories into Hupa, with the aid of Native speakers, so that two or more versions of a tale could be compared, word for word, in each of the languages. All of these materials have been left with the speakers from whom I collected the stories, with the hope that they will one day furnish useful learning material for the tribal language revitalization program.

KARUK

The first serious scholarship on the Karuk language began with the work of John P. Harrington in the 1920s, an effort he continued in fits and starts until nearly the time of his death. There can be little doubt that the Karuk language was a favorite subject for this nearly mythical field linguist, who published two major volumes on Karuk in his lifetime and, as legend has it, once attempted to bribe William Bright to divert his attention away from this language, which he apparently wanted to keep to himself (Hinton 1994:202). Harrington's first volume was published in 1932 under the title *Karuk Indian Myths* and was followed the same year by a detailed study of Native tobacco cultivation practices in his classic *Tobacco among the Karuk Indians*. For years to come, these works stood as the two major printed attestations of the language, both containing exquisite ethnographic detail and both recorded with his characteristic attention to the subtlest phonetic nuances. Yet, despite the depth of his research (the bulk of which remains unpublished), Harrington never put forth a grammatical sketch of this richly polysynthetic language.

During the early 1950s, William Bright was assigned the task of writing a descriptive account of the Karuk language, under the supervision of his mentor, Mary Haas. Rapidly completing this assignment as the topic of his dissertation, he quickly published the results under the title *The Karuk Language: Grammar, Texts, and Lexicon* in 1957. Presenting a detailed description of the language in its structural entirety, this volume has been the primary source for my understanding of the complex grammatical machinery of the Karuk verbal paradigm, in addition to the surrounding phonology and vocabulary of this highly polysynthetic language. The narratives presented in this book also provide a wide sample of the many styles attested in Karuk oral literature, with texts representing the mythic, folkloric, and medicinal genres, together with several Native ethnographic descriptions. This work continues to stand as one of the most complete accounts of a Native American language ever put forth.

During the first half of the twentieth century, Kroeber and his junior colleague Edward Gifford carefully collected an extensive body of Karuk narrative. Yet it was only after Kroeber's death that this work was eventually published under the title *Karok Myths* in 1980, under the editorship of Grace Buzaljko. William Bright supplied a lengthy linguistic index, though reference to the Karuk language is quite sparse throughout the remainder of the volume. In fact, most of the texts were transcribed in English, even when originally dictated in Karuk. The book nevertheless provides a valuable guide to traditional Karuk narrative, containing a broader range of material than available, then as now, in the Karuk language itself. The texts presented in this volume have thoroughly informed my understanding of Karuk oral literature, a tradition that varies in many significant ways from the neighboring Hupa and Yurok traditions. Many of the figures and episodes in Karuk narrative are not to be found elsewhere in the region, while others receive distinctive elaboration within each of the neighboring speech communities.

YUROK

Some of the earliest work on Yurok ethnography was carried out by Alfred Kroeber. Fresh out of graduate school, where he had studied under Franz Boas, Kroeber began collecting material on Yurok ethnography almost as soon as he arrived in California, at the turn of the twentieth century (Kroeber 1976:xix). There can be little doubt that Yurok ethnography continued to be one of Kroeber's favorite subjects over the span of his career, since he returned to the field nearly every time he had a chance and spoke very highly of the Yuroks in many of his scholarly publications. Despite the depth of his research, very little linguistic material was published in its original Yurok form. Nonetheless, the breadth of his work on Yurok narrative is staggering, eventually receiving posthumous publication in 1976 under the title *Yurok Myths*. This massive tome, all of it published in English even when originally transcribed in Yurok,[1] has thoroughly shaped my understanding of traditional Yurok narrative. That anyone will ever again gain access to Yurok oral literature in the same depth is unlikely, as many of these tales have slowly slipped from memory.

Shortly following Kroeber's pioneering work at the turn of the twentieth century, a promising graduate student named T. T. Waterman was sent out to write a descriptive account of this fascinating yet challenging language. Though the linguistic aspect of his project was never completed, Waterman succeeded in writing one of the most detailed studies of Native geographical conceptions ever produced on the North American continent. The study he completed (based on his fieldwork) describes, in exquisite detail, the cultural and mythic status of place among the traditional Yuroks. Meticulously illustrated with maps and thoroughly supplemented with linguistic facts, this work was published under the title "Yurok Geography" in 1920.

During his brief but productive visit to California in the summer of 1927, Sapir was fortunate enough to come into contact with a Hupa speaker who was also fluent in Yurok. This consultant, Mary Marshall, had also worked extensively with Pliny Earle Goddard several decades before, at which time she had supplied many narratives on traditional Hupa medicinal formulas. Representing a long-standing tradition in the region, her mother was born into a Yurok family, though she later married a Hupa man and lived with him in the Hoopa Valley for the remainder of her life. From his work with Mary Marshall, Sapir was able to collect about five Yurok texts, together with a sample of Yurok vocabulary, which would together remain the primary scholarly attestation of the language for years to come.

Before venturing to California to work with the Yuroks firsthand, Sapir had published a brief note on the language in 1913. Here he stated his hypothesis that Yurok and Wiyot, a neighboring language of northwestern California, were both distantly related to the Algonquian tongues spoken in the American Northeast and scattered, in isolated patches, along the plains. Deeply controversial in its day, this assertion on Sapir's part was later demonstrated beyond the shadow of a doubt in 1958, when Mary Haas published her classic paper "Algonkian-Ritwan: The End of a Controversy." Here Mary Haas spelled out the lexical and grammatical affinities between these far-flung languages, all of which now go by the collective name of "Algic."

After a nearly thirty-year hiatus in regular scholarly publications, the first major description of the Yurok language appeared in print in 1958. After several months of fieldwork carried out in the spring of 1951, the British scholar R. H. Robins released his descriptive account of Yurok in 1958, under the title *The Yurok Language: Grammar, Texts, and Lexicon*. Focusing primarily on the inflectional morphology of verb, this book also puts forth a brief sketch of the Yurok classifier system, alongside the tense particles and vocabulary. The selection of texts is, however, quite sparse in Robins's book, consisting of eight short narratives. Unfortunately, Robins's volume remains the primary source on Yurok oral literature, outside of the equally brief set of texts that Sapir was able to collect, if only incidentally, during his short fieldwork stint in the summer of 1927. Perhaps stimulated by the publication of Robins's book, several other scholars quickly moved to fill in the gaps in this work. In the late 1950s and early 1960s, Mary Haas took a series of trips to Yurok country, intent on uncovering the inner workings of the Yurok classifier system, which was only partially explored by Robins during his brief stay. Though she never published all of her data, I have incorporated some of her field notes into my study, furthering the analysis of the materials contained therein.

Several decades later, during the late 1970s and early '80s, Howard Berman, a distinguished linguist from the University of Chicago, journeyed to Yurok country to fill in some of the gaps in the scholarly literature on the vocabulary. While verifying some of the forms obtained by Robins several decades before him, Berman also expanded upon the lexicon by collecting further forms of ethnographic interest. The results of this work were published by Berman in 1982; the substance of his scholarship has contributed greatly to my understanding of traditional Yurok vocabulary.

During roughly the same period, a linguist named Paul Proulx ventured to Yurok country for several short months. A trained Algonquianist who had studied under the famed C. F. Hockett, Proulx sought to uncover the hidden derivational processes still alive in the verb system, however much previous scholars had neglected this phenomenon. The results of his research were impressive, demonstrating that the Yurok verb contained a far more complex system of derivational morphology than had previously been described. Proulx's analysis of Yurok has strongly influenced my understanding of this language, including its complex verbal paradigm. Deeply insightful, his article "Notes on Yurok Derivation," which was published in 1985, is deserving of further attention and follow-up fieldwork.

In recent years, a team of scholars at the University of California–Berkeley has renewed the age-old tradition of Yurok studies at this famed institution. Headed by Andrew Garrett, a study called "The Yurok Language: Description and Revitalization" received support from the National Science Foundation from 2001 to 2004. Focusing on the continuing documentation of this important Algic language, these scholars have aimed to combine older archival materials with fresh fieldwork, some of which has been carried out by graduate students. Garrett is a historical linguist by training and has recently fixed his attention on the reconstruction of the Yurok verb stem, which has also advanced the understanding of the Proto-Algic verb paradigm. The implications for the Algic stock are inspiring, to say the least, and I have taken these findings into consideration wherever possible.

COMPARATIVE STUDIES

For almost a century now, a host of scholars, many of them trained by Sapir or his students, have pointed to the broad theoretical interest suggested by the staggering diversity of languages found in northwestern California. Sapir, for his part, first drew attention to the problem in his classic book *Language* (1921:213–14), in which he pointed to the strong cultural similarities among the Hupas, Yuroks, and Karuks, whose languages are profoundly distinct. Here the area's linguistic diversity brings into question the nature of the relationship between language and culture, shattering the then-popular notion that language is a reflection of "national character," pure and simple. Instead, Sapir suggested that these groups had slowly settled on a similar type of culture over a great span of time, proving that the relationship was not an intrinsic one but instead a product of historical factors and ongoing social processes. Yet Sapir only mentioned the problem in passing and spelled out few of its larger implications, as occurred with so many of the fascinating problems that attracted his attention over the course of his academic career.

Years later, Hoijer suggested that culture areas such as these provide a promising testing ground for theories of linguistic relativity. For, within a culture area such as that of northwestern California, the variable of language, which shifts massively from one group to the next, can be easily isolated from the variable of culture, which holds relatively constant throughout the entire region. In a famous article entitled "The Sapir-Whorf Hypothesis" (1954:103), Hoijer proposed a plan of research that was to focus on the comparative implications for "thinking" within such culture areas, with language serving as the independent variable.[2] Hoijer situated his study in the American Southwest, where strong cultural similarities exist among speakers of many unrelated languages. Yet a similar plan of research could be carried out in northwestern California, where similar factors are at play. No one, however, took Hoijer up on this offer, neither in his generation nor in the one to follow—not in any sustained fashion.

By the mid-1960s, a flurry of articles had begun to appear on the subject. Most of these examined issues of taxonomy in the area's languages, with emphasis on Yurok, Karuk, and Tolowa, and to a lesser extent Hupa. One groundbreaking piece by Jane and William Bright explored the folk taxonomies of the natural world as expressed in several of the area's languages. In their article, entitled "Semantic Structures in Northwestern California and the Sapir-Whorf Hypothesis" (1965), Bright and Bright noted a general paucity of generic terminology in many of the area's languages, more so in Tolowa and Karuk than Yurok. For instance, none of these languages has generic categories for "insects," "plants," or "animals" as general classes of life; instead, there is a profusion of terms for individual species. And while Karuk and Tolowa both lack generic terms for "fish," only Yurok has a general category for these creatures. Similarly, while Tolowa and Yurok distinguish "grasses" from "bushes" with separate generic terms, Karuk collapses both of these into a single category, *pírish,* which translates as "greenery." Following Kroeber (1925:15), Bright and Bright also noted that all of the languages had settled on a common geographical orientation to the spatial world, where mountains and rivers provide the basic frame of reference for establishing spatial relationships in the surrounding world. So, semantically speaking, these languages are far more similar than their surface structures suggest. Yet because these classifications are not identical, just similar, there is also room for a certain type of linguistic relativity here.

In 1967, Mary Haas followed this article with a sharp reply, showing that, on a grammatical basis, the systems of classification are profoundly distinct, especially in Hupa and Yurok, for which classification is especially elaborate. In Hupa, for instance, objects in motion are often classified on the basis of their shape or animacy, while a similar series of categories applies to objects at rest. Similarly, in Yurok, one must state the shape or animacy of an object when counting or attributing features of size, shape, or color to an object. Unfortunately, interest in this perplexing topic evaporated almost as quickly as it surfaced. As a result, other than a few brief articles on the subject (each pointing to the need for further work), little has been said about the comparative linguistics of northwestern California in general. More recently, Lisa Conathan of the University of California–Berkeley has completed a dissertation (2004b) on language contact and linguistic ecology in northwestern California. Her concern, however, is mostly linguistic, less so with culture. My discussion in chapters 10 and 11 includes some of Conathan's results.

My work in this area began in the late 1990s, when I was a graduate student in anthropology at the University of California–Davis. Theoretically speaking, my interests had always revolved around general questions of linguistic and cultural relativism, issues that lay at the heart of the original Boasian vision for the field of anthropology. Whatever one's theoretical orientation, the sheer diversity of cultural institutions found throughout the world's societies is always fruitful ground for social theory, whether in anthropology or in linguistics. Despite the enormous diversity, tantalizing universals always appear to lie just beneath the surface. A case in point is the belief in an afterlife, which has long been regarded as a universal trait present in virtually all religions. Yet on the plane of doctrine, the manifestation of these beliefs is also notoriously diverse. This tension between the appearance of sweeping diversity on the one hand and the implicit presence of underlying universals on the other is certainly one of the great paradoxes of the human sciences. No social theorist, regardless of his or her background, can afford to ignore the role of diversity when contemplating questions about human nature, whether on linguistic or on cultural grounds. Owing to the diversity of languages spoken there, I originally saw northwestern California as a promising testing ground for rethinking many pressing issues in social theory, especially the anthropological literature on language contact and linguistic relativity. Around this time, Leanne Hinton published a survey of general problems in California linguistics in a popular book entitled *Flutes of Fire* (1994). Written in an approachable style, with special attention to matters of social and historical interest, this book profoundly influenced the development of my thinking on this subject.

My dissertation, which was completed in the summer of 2001, focused on the comparative expression of spatial and temporal concepts in the Hupa, Yurok, and Karuk languages. Throughout the work, I devoted special attention to the cultural status of the linguistic categories I examined, as well as to their use in everyday life or religious narrative. So, for instance, when considering the geographical spatial categories found in many of the area's languages, I also considered the role that these concepts play in the area's religious traditions, as speakers call upon these concepts in prayer, spells, and medicinal formulas. Consider spatial concepts, for instance. Linguistically speaking, many of the languages have a special grammatical category for marking motion that heads "upstream." Yet on cultural grounds, the concept of an "upstream" heaven is also a significant one in many of the area's religious traditions, representing an ultimate destination to which souls travel in the afterlife. In daily life, these geographical spatial categories are called upon to construct religious narrative, reflecting a worldview that has been absorbed into the structure of the languages.

Even at the time, I realized that this fine-grained analysis of the conceptual categories of the area's languages held broader implications for many branches of social theory, especially the topics of language contact and linguistic relativity.

For although the speakers of these languages had been in contact for perhaps a thousand years or more, the languages had remained profoundly distinct on a number of fronts. Certainly this fit one model of contact linguistics, in which long-term contact yields conservatism in some spheres and subtle convergence in others. But I also felt that the results of this contact were rife with significance for theories of linguistic relativity, an old tradition in American anthropology that was undergoing revitalization at the time I was writing my dissertation. Yet, surprisingly, these two strands of inquiry—language contact and linguistic relativity—had rarely been connected in any sustained fashion in the previous literature.

A NOTE ON THE LINGUISTIC SOURCES

With minor exceptions, the linguistic examples in this book are presented in the standard citation forms first advanced for the major grammatical sketches of the area's languages. The only major exception is that I have chosen to represent long vowels in Yurok and Karuk with a series of two vowels (*aa*) rather than a vowel followed by a dot (*a·*), as is the practice now in the current tribal orthographies. In addition, in the transcriptions of Karuk employed here, *ch* represents *č*, *sh* represents *š*, and *th* represents *θ*. Otherwise, the Karuk material agrees with the citation forms given in the lexicon of Bright's *Karuk Language* (1957:311–403), the primary source for all Karuk word forms, unless otherwise stated in the text or notes. Similarly, the Hupa forms in this book match the orthography presented in Sapir's *Northwest California Linguistics* (2001), especially the analytic lexicon (pp. 723–812) and the ethnographic lexicon (pp. 873–997). This is the primary source of all the Hupa material, unless otherwise stated in the notes. All Yurok word forms are presented in the standard citation form given in the lexicon of Robins's *Yurok Language* (1958:189–272), unless otherwise noted in the text. These three works represent the default sources for the bulk of the linguistic forms discussed in the present book, and linguistic forms have been standardized to match the orthographies presented in these major references. However, detailed references are given in the notes for all rare forms that were dictated by a particular speaker in the context of storytelling and for those unusual forms that come from other sources, such as the writings of Goddard, Kroeber, Harrington, and other reference materials on the area's languages.

Part I

Language, Culture, and the Principle of Linguistic Relativity

1

Language and Culture in Northwestern California

The Hupa Indians are very typical of the culture area to which they belong. Culturally identical with them are the neighboring Yurok and Karok. . . . It is difficult to say what elements in their combined culture belong in origin to this tribe or that, so much at one are they in communal action, feeling, and thought. But their languages are not merely alien to each other; they belong to three of the major American linguistic groups, each with an immense distribution on the northern continent.

Edward Sapir, Language

As frequent partners in trade and marriage, the neighboring speech communities of the Hupas, Yuroks, and Karuks have long been closely aligned in matters of myth, ritual, and religion, as well as material culture and political organization, despite speaking radically different languages. The traditional homelands of the Hupa, Yurok, and Karuk speakers (see map) converge near the confluence of the Klamath and Trinity rivers, not far from the place that was regarded, in traditional times, as the mythical center of the universe. Several neighboring communities each spoke still other languages.

As Edward Sapir once noted (1921:213–14), the Native languages of northwestern California represent three major linguistic stocks of the North American continent, each with an enormous distribution outside of the immediate culture area. This striking juxtaposition of profound linguistic diversity with relative uniformity in the social sphere has since attracted a great deal of attention in the literature of anthropology and linguistics.[1] Sapir, for his part, drew upon this case in the midst of a larger theoretical treatise in which he sought, for argument's sake, to isolate the variable of linguistic structure from its ultimate social circumstances. While a single thread of culture often weaves across a range of languages within this region, many parallel linguistic features also

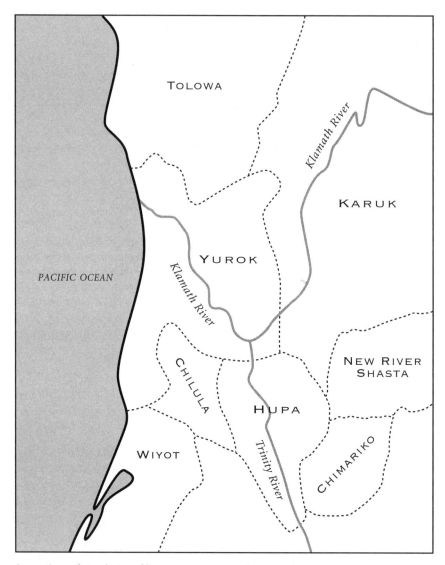

Approximate boundaries of linguistic groups in the area of study

occur alongside otherwise distinctive interpretations of common cultural themes. And even outside of northwestern California, the language families show no particular allegiance to any specific cultural type.

Several years later, Alfred Kroeber echoed Sapir's pronouncement in the introduction to his classic ethnography of the California Indians, *Handbook of the Indians of California* (1925). Somewhat less theoretical in tenor, the point of Kroeber's statement was perhaps merely to cast the long shadow of Yurok civilization onto the ethnographic description of the neighboring groups, which, because of their close similarity to the Yuroks, receive far less attention in his massive treatise on the regional culture: "The Yurok shared this civilization in identical form with their neighbors, the Hupa and Karok. The adjacent Tolowa, Wiyot, and Chilula adhere to the same culture in every essential trait, but begin to evince minor departures in the direction of less intensive specialization" (Kroeber 1925:5). Despite subtle differences in intellectual stance, both Kroeber and Sapir thus strongly asserted the relative homogeneity of the regional social life. Of course, in retrospect, it is possible to argue that both writers overstated the case for rhetorical effect in their zeal to draw out the contrast between the diversity of speech institutions, on the one hand, and the overwhelming similarity of cultural practices, on the other.

A century of ethnographic work has revealed that the traditional culture of northwestern California is surprisingly diverse, in spite of these early claims by such well-known figures as Sapir and Kroeber. That is, neither the language nor the culture of the region holds altogether constant as one passes from one village to the next. Instead, the variables of language and culture achieve a nearly kaleidoscopic variability throughout the area's many speech communities. Taken together, the staggering linguistic diversity and often sweeping cultural variability found throughout this area allow the variables of language, culture, and worldview to be nearly isolated as one passes from one village to another. The sense of worldview, as a distinctive series of beliefs or recurring conceptual motifs, is also heavily localized, yielding a tremendous regional diversity that ultimately rests on differences in both linguistic and cultural patterning.

FUNDAMENTAL ASPECTS OF THE LANGUAGES

The Hupa Language

Spoken inland along the Trinity River, the Hupa language is a member of the Athabaskan family, a group with an enormous distribution along the western half of the continent, stretching in often-isolated patches from the arctic climes of interior Alaska to the arid reaches of the American Southwest. While the Athabaskan languages, as a rule, share a close-knit set of highly distinctive structural traits, the culture areas to which they belong could hardly be more diverse. The Navajos and Apaches have, for example, adapted relatively seamlessly to the highly specialized world of the American Southwest following their southern migration, while the Ahtnas and Gwitch'ins, who remained far to the north, find themselves equally at home in the Native cultural world of interior Alaska.

Yet throughout their vast geographical spread, the Athabaskan languages maintain a core of highly distinctive features, including, first and foremost, a strong predilection toward process orientation.[2] The whole Athabaskan grammatical plan is geared toward the codification of those activities and related temporal sequences, which characterize everything in the surrounding universe—from nouns that portray objects in terms of their most intrinsic acts, to verbs that demand a detailed classification of all events based on the implicit time schedule associated with any unfolding process.

True to the structural blueprint of its source stock, the Hupa language exhibits a characteristic Athabaskan brand of polysynthesis. Here a single word may be composed of a dozen or more distinct structural units whose individual meanings cannot always be clearly isolated; rather, the constituent elements of the word tend to occur in highly idiomatic clusters, wherein the meaning arises through their overall combination. As seen below in examples 1a–c, the elements *di-* and *l-* often occur together in constructions that otherwise refer to collective human action. Yet apart from this general characterization of their combined semantic force, it is difficult, if not impossible, to assign any individual meaning to either of these elements. Together representing the general notion of collective human action, these structural units are represented as "X_1" and "X_2" in the examples below.

(1) Sample Hupa Word Forms

    a. *č'idiwilye?il* '(people) are dancing here and there'
       č'i-di-wi-l-ye?-il-i
       AN.3SG-X_1-prog-X_2-dance-prog-REL

    b. *č'idehłc'e·* '(people) sit or dwell'
       č'i-d(e·)-s-l-c'e·
       AN.3SG-X_1-stative-X_2-stay

    c. *me·ya?diwilwa·W* '(people) began to talk about it'
       m-e·=ya·=č'i-di-win-l-wa·W-i
       INAN.OBJ-about=AN.3SG-X_1-inceptive-X_2-chatter-REL

Time perspective, which is highly refined among the Athabaskan tongues, is a category of analysis that exerts its conceptual presence throughout almost every system within the overall grammatical plan. In 1a, for instance, the notion of "dancing" is twice marked for the progressive aspect, first with the prefix *wi-* and then with the suffix *-il,* both signaling an ongoing stream of action, punctuated, perhaps, with stops and starts over an extended period of time. In 1b, the basic notion of "living" or "dwelling" is, in contrast, placed in the stative aspect, here with the prefix *s-,* indicating that the event produced no discernible movement while extending over a great, and ultimately indefinite, time period. Finally, in 1c, the general notion of "talking" or "chattering" is placed in the inceptive aspect, with the use of the prefix *win-,* here losing its final nasal (*n*) upon its juxtaposition with the following lateral *l-.* Similar temporal concerns surround the representation of directional motion and even the classification of objects according to such seemingly nontemporal features as shape or animacy (see chapter 8). Even common nouns, among the Athabaskan tongues, often carry detailed information regarding the temporal characteristics of the objects they depict (see chapter 6).

The Yurok Language

Spoken from the mouth of the Klamath to its confluence with the Trinity River some thirty miles inland, the Yurok language is a member of the enormous Algic stock and thus represents still another major linguistic group of the North American continent. As a member of this vast group, the Yurok language is distantly related to an entire constellation of Algonquian tongues whose speakers are scattered throughout the central portions of the continent and concentrated in the American Northeast.[3] Though the ancestors of the present-day Yuroks most likely separated from their Algonquian cousins several thousand years ago, the Yurok language still retains many reflexes of its ultimate Algic descent, which can be demonstrated even at the level of ordinary words. Consider for instance the Yurok word *pkenc,* the usual term for "pitch." Ultimately, this noun can be shown to be cognate with the Proto-Algonquian form **pekiwa,* which originally meant something like gum, pitch, or resin before taking on a more specialized meaning as the ancestors of the Yuroks settled into northwestern California.[4] Though not abundant, dozens of other parallels exist at the level of ordinary word forms, all attesting to the common heritage that the Yurok language shares with other members of the Algic stock. Some of the correspondences in sound and meaning are striking. Consider the Proto-Algonquian stem *kemot-, which occurs alongside the related Yurok form kemol- and Wiyot cognate komar, all preserving the core meaning "to steal."[5] On the crucial plane of grammar, Yurok even preserves a reflex of an ancient second-person pronoun, one that survived in Proto-Algonquian as *kiil, while eventually taking the strikingly similar shape keʔl in Yurok.[6] Other correspondences are less far reaching while still pointing to a common heritage. Consider, for instance, the resemblance between the Yurok word knuuu, the ordinary term for the hawk, and the Menominee word keneew, a parallel term for the eagle.[7]

As the examples above clearly illustrate, shared vocabulary often points to descent from a common source stock. Yet one of the most telling hallmarks of Yurok's Algic heritage can be illustrated by its method of composing verbs, which runs parallel to the method still found today among its distant Algonquian cousins.[8] As once described by Leonard Bloomfield in the 1940s, one of the most characteristic traits of the Algonquian stem is its signature tripartite structure.[9] Here the first part in the linear string is known as the *initial,* which is often considered the semantic kernel—or *root*—of the stem because this central unit is always present in every verb form. Initials vary widely in semantic content, ranging from those that convey a fairly traditional verbal meaning (by identifying a type of event or process) to those that convey adjectival properties (such as texture, color, or size) or even an adverbial significance (such as a directional bearing or temporal characteristic). The initial, in turn, is often followed by a suffix known as a *medial,* one that may contribute a fairly concrete meaning based on a physical object, such as a body part, or a fairly abstract meaning, such as a type of event or process. In some cases, the medial is in turn followed by still another suffix known as a *final,* one that sometimes conveys a fairly concrete meaning based on a type of object or event while more often contributing an abstract grammatical significance, identifying, for instance, the number of subjects or objects involved in a scene. Consider, for instance, the Plains Cree stem kanaweeyim-, which loosely translates as "to watch over him."[10] Here the initial kanaw- conveys the concept of "watching," while the medial -eeyi- contributes the sense that this watching is being performed "by mind." At the end of the stem, the final -m signals that this action is specifically directed toward an object, namely, the person or event that the subject of the construction is actively turning one's attention toward. Once the process of stem composition is complete, the resulting stem formation can itself act as the base for further derivation, serving as a new stem-initial unit capable of taking on a medial and final of its own. Consider the related Cree form *kanaweeyim-iskweew-ee-*, which loosely translates as "to watch one's wife." Here the stem *kanaweeyim* 'to watch over (someone)' stands in the initial position, with the medial *-iskweew-* 'woman' signaling that the object of the act is a woman (read as "wife"), while the final *-ee-* contributes an abstract grammatical meaning, namely, by placing the verb in the special "animate intransitives class" where it can no longer accept a separate syntactic object.[11]

Similar derivations are certainly possible in Yurok, sometimes giving rise to complex forms that resemble those found among that language's Algonquian cousins. Consider the verb *menuulowoyek*, which loosely translates as "I'm abducted, enticed away." Here the initial element *men-* indicates that something passes "away from view," while the medial *-uul* conveys the sense that "a load" is being packed. The stem-final suffix *-owoy* then signals that the inflection now marks the object rather than the subject of the event.[12] As a result of this derivation, the first-person marker *-ek* now refers to the entity that is carried away—that is, to the speaker—not to the person who performs the act of carrying this person away.

However reminiscent of full-blown polysynthesis, elaborate derivational processes such as this are fairly rare in Yurok. Ultimately, the relationship to the Algonquian branch of the Algic stock is a distant one, and the Yurok language is far less polysynthetic than many of its Algonquian cousins on the other half of the continent. Instead, the direction of drift is toward a paring down of complex processes of word formation, which are widely attested in the source stock and traceable to its original Algic mother tongue. Where traces of polysynthesis survive in Yurok, it is often in the form of relatively fixed, historically derived stem sets, as can be illustrated with the series of verb forms cited below.

(2) Sample Yurok Word Forms
 a. *naamul* 'to carry a load'
  naam-u(u)l
  away-move.load
 b. *hooluulesek* 'I carry a pack around'
  hool-uul(es)-ek
  around-move.load-1SG
 c. *penuulesek* 'I put down a load'
  pen-uul(es)-ek
  down.to.the.ground-move.load-1SG

All of these stems contain the common medial element *-uul,* which here conveys the concept of "packing a load," though without any specific information about the direction of motion. By combining with different initials, which specify the directional bearing of the event, this medial enters into a series of full-fledged stem forms, all still reflecting the concept of "packing a load." In expressions referring to the act of "packing a load along," the stem-initial directional marker *naam-* combines with this medial to form the stem *naamul,* as illustrated in 2a. Here the resulting verb stem does not permit inflection for subject, keeping this single shape regardless of whether the agent who performs the deed is the speaker, the addressee, or some more-distant third person.[13] In expressions referring to the act of "carrying a load around," the same medial has merged with the stem-initial directional marker *hool-,* as illustrated in the form given in 2b. In contrast, this related expression absolutely requires inflection for subject, here represented by the speaker (*-ek̓*). Upon combining with the stem-initial directional marker *pen-,* the resulting stem, illustrated in example 2c, refers specifically to the act of bringing a pack "down to the ground"; this particular variant also requires inflection for subject, again represented by the speaker (*-ek̓*).

Slowly departing from the hallmark polysynthesis of its Algic source stock, the Yurok language has gradually drifted toward relatively terse constructions at the level of the word. Despite the presence of sometimes-elaborate derivational processes, the language as a whole curiously drifts toward the isolating, or minimally inflective, structural pole, with fewer words carrying a detailed internal analysis. Many Yurok sentences, for instance, are purely isolating in technique,[14] with each word representing a single lexical entry, without derivation or inflection, as seen below in example 3.

(3) Sample Yurok Sentence[15]

šegep	*me*	*k̓ʷeget*	*koohci*	*mɹk̓ʷtikš*
Coyote	PAST	visit	once	Crane

'Coyote once visited Crane.'

This tendency toward morphological minimalism is an anomaly, both within the region and within its source stock, and probably reflects a process set into motion long before the Yuroks arrived in their current geographical setting. In the context of northwestern California, this gradual drift away from polysynthesis is one of the features that sets the Yurok language apart from its closest neighbors, the Hupa and Karuk languages, which are massively poly-synthetic in overall technique.[16]

The Karuk Language

Spoken inland, along the upper arm of the Klamath River,[17] the Karuk lan-guage has no close relatives anywhere on the planet. Yet at a highly submerged level, it shows a number of deep correspondences with the remaining members of the Hokan stock. This linguistic group was, in aboriginal times, widely dis-tributed throughout much of California, Arizona, and northern Mexico, so the fact that Karuk shares a deep historical connection with the other languages long established in the surrounding geographical area is not surprising. Yet the connection between Karuk and the remaining members of the Hokan stock is limited to a handful of words, at the lexical end of the spectrum, and to a strong tendency toward a specific type of polysynthesis at the other, that is, the structural side of things. As is true of other Hokan languages, most word forms in Karuk are massively polysynthetic in structural expression, while the internal analysis is often highly transparent, with each structural unit conveying a relatively discrete element of meaning.[18]

(4) Sample Karuk Word Forms[19]

    a. *kunitfúnnukva* 'they look into an enclosed space, sweathouse'
       kun-it-fú(n)uk-va
       they-look-into.an.enclosed.space-PLURAL.ACTION

    b. *máruk*   *kunithvíripuraa* 'two beings ran a great way uphill'
       máruk   *kun-ithvírip-uraa*
       far.uphill   they-dual.run-hence.uphill

    c. *ishnimvánakach* 'little target shooting down from upriver'
       ishri(m)-va(n)ak-a-ch [bird name = goldfinch]
       shoot.targets-down.from.upriver-NM-DIM

As illustrated in the Karuk examples given above, spatial categories are often highly refined among the northern members of the Hokan stock, with dozens of directional distinctions finding routine expression in the structure of even the most basic word forms, whether nouns or verbs. In 4a, for example, the notion of "looking" occurs with an obligatory marker of directional status, here indicated with the grammatical suffix *-fú(n)uk*, which refers, rather abstractly, to motion that enters into an enclosed space, in this instance a sweathouse. Similarly, in 4b, the notion of "running" also requires a directional marker, here indicated with the grammatical suffix *-uraa,* one that refers, very specifically, to movement that passes "uphill," that is, away from the speaker rather than toward the speaker. Further refining the directional reference, the independent adverb *máruk* indicates that this event continues along this general course for a considerable distance. As seen in 4c, even common nouns in Karuk sometimes include explicit references to directional features, as in the case of the bird that is known as "the little one who shoots down from upriver." Here the directional status of the event is indicated by the grammatical marker *-va(n)ak,* which forms an integral part of this noun form. Like the kindred tongues of the Shasta and Atsugewi, which are also members of the Hokan family, the Karuk language possesses a massive elaboration of spatial categories at the level of regularly differentiated, highly obligatory, grammatical ideas.

CULTURAL SIMILARITIES

As can be seen in the preceding passages, the Hupa, Yurok, and Karuk languages are as profoundly diverse as any three unrelated tongues spoken on this earth—say, Hebrew, Hindi, and Korean, for instance. Given the scale of the linguistic diversity, many observers have been surprised to find that the social institutions of the region are relatively uniform by comparison. As Sapir and Kroeber both observed long ago, deep affinities swept across almost every aspect of the traditional social life, beginning with the basic elements of material existence and moving to the more abstract realms of mythology, folklore, and religious practices.[20]

The traditional material culture of northwestern California belongs, in essence, to the well-known "hunting-and-gathering" type of subsistence, with a heavy emphasis on fishing and acorn consumption.[21] Partaking of the original affluence of an especially lush physical environment, the Native groups of this region enjoyed the material abundance of a near–rain forest ecology. Yet they departed from hunters and gatherers elsewhere by adopting a more sedentary (rather than nomadic) lifestyle and by placing a greater focus on wealth, prestige, and social hierarchy when compared to other groups who eked out a living by gathering plants and hunting the native wildlife. As with many cultures of this type, males principally tended to the pursuit of flesh foods, while women, and sometimes children, largely collected the plant staples and prepared the food for consumption. As occurred in much of California before contact with Europeans, acorns were the principal vegetable crop, and these could be cooked, stored, or transported in baskets of various shapes and sizes. Deer, elk, eel, and, above all, salmon were among the most celebrated of sources of sustenance in the animal kingdom, alongside a host of lesser prey, such as quail, trout, and sturgeon. Even the instruments used to hunt prey animals held relatively constant throughout the region. Larger animals, such as deer and elk, were often hunted with bows and arrows, sometimes after the points had been treated with poison to hasten the kill. Yet, as this process could prove cumbersome in practice, these animals were just as often chased into snares of twine, whether on solid land or in the shallow river waters. Similar snares, on a smaller scale, were also used to trap birds, such as grouse and quail. Fish, another important food source, could be caught in smaller numbers with dip nets or bone hooks or in larger quantities with nets or weirs. Spears were even sometimes used to seize the salmon, one by one, in the crystal-clear waters of late summer and early fall.

Plank dwellings of redwood or cedar[22] were generally set several feet into the ground, where, half beneath the earth, they provided a comfortable home for up to several dozen people year-round. Women, children, and their close female kin occupied the larger dwellings, or "living houses," while fathers and their teenage sons generally passed the nights in the smaller sweathouses nearby.[23]

The primary medium of exchange throughout the region was a type of currency made from the shells of a small saltwater mollusk, known as dentalia.[24] These shells, which as the name suggests resemble teeth, were introduced by way of a vast pre-Columbian trade ring extending nearly a thousand miles down the coast from Puget Sound near present-day Seattle. Naturally occurring in a range of sizes, these shells could be strung together in bands to represent a variety of corresponding monetary values. Uses ranged from daily currency to marriage payments, gambling, or the accumulation of personal wealth. Fines were also assessed for insulting or injuring one's neighbors—mentioning the name of the dead was a particularly serious offence. The most extreme debts were, of course, paid off through the institution of temporary slavery, one of the most dreaded pitfalls of excessive gambling.

Within this village setting, daily social life largely revolved around the leadership of a local "headman," whose authority rarely extended beyond the village where he was born.[25] One important function of the village leader was to arbitrate legal disputes between neighbors, settling on damages that were generally repaid with currency or worked off through debt slavery. Yet the headman also coordinated dances and led his people in times of war, if necessary. Here the possession of symbolic capital played an important role, so that an influential headman usually owned more ceremonial regalia than the heads of other families did. Generally speaking, a headman was a seasoned male elder who gained his authority by amassing enough wealth to influence his subjects with generous gifts. Usually he controlled more property than did others in the village, holding more hunting, fishing, and acorn-harvesting rights than other families. In times of scarcity, a headman was expected to share any surplus food with his neighbors. If successful, this generosity would later be rewarded with loyalty from fellow villagers. Because his authority rested upon his ability to create obligations through various acts of generosity, the headman held no real power to coerce. In the end, a person's fate rested in his or her own hands, and all property belonged to individuals.

A typical village consisted of several households with fifty to a hundred people living together near a river. Beyond the village, however, no larger political units existed; all property belonged to individuals and their families, not to tribes or larger corporate entities.[26]

The traditional religious life revolved around a former race of spirit deities who were thought to have roamed this earth before the coming of humans.[27] Later, as humans began to appear, this original race of spirit beings fled for the heavens, where they continued to watch over humanity from afar. Fortunately, however, some of these spirit beings transformed themselves into many of the sacred animals and plants thought to live quietly in the surrounding countryside even to this day, carrying medicinal properties or serving to protect humanity in various ways. These prehuman spirit deities were said to be somewhat intermediate in appearance between modern-day animals, plants, and humans. From the Native religious outlook, the various forms of life had not yet differentiated at this point in the prehistory of the planet. With the aim of restoring the world to this original pristine condition and guarding it against any evil unleashed by human wrongdoing, a number of taboos were set into place. Among these are avoiding the names of the dead, refraining from the use of coarse language, and striving to remain respectful of one's elders.

In keeping with the precepts set down by these creator beings, the religious person was expected to make a series of prayers throughout the day—when eating, bathing, or preparing for the hunt, for instance. To the same end, a spectacular series of great public dances have long been performed according to a regular annual cycle, with the aim of restoring the world to that original state established by the ancestors long ago, during the prehuman myth times. By atoning for sins and repaying debts that had accumulated over the past year, the ceremony would ensure the return of fair weather and material abundance. Within this deeply religious frame of reference, the orientation to time pointed strongly toward the past, toward that original sacred time when the spirit beings still walked the face of this earth. Yet the era of the ancients was thought to have expired fairly recently, perhaps no more than a handful of generations ago, according to traditional creation lore. In this setting, the names assigned to many things in daily life often reflect their status in ceremony, myth, or regular cultural practices, imbuing almost everything in the surrounding universe with a deep religious meaning.

According to the best of present evidence, the cultural traditions of northwestern California coalesced into something like their present form over the past millennium, with each group arriving in the region along a separate route of migration. Probably the most long-standing residents of the area are the Karuk speakers, whose presumed linguistic brethren, the remaining members of the Hokan stock, are scattered throughout much of California. There is evidence of a rapid wave of settlement beginning perhaps 1,000 years ago along the coast, near the homelands of the Yuroks, Wiyots, and Tolowas (Foster 1996:98). As far as the Hupas are concerned, linguistic evidence has long suggested that their language arrived in its present location over the course of the past 800 to 1,200 years (Hoijer 1956), possibly displacing other languages that may have been spoken in the area before this time.

Storytelling

Storytelling played a crucial role in transmitting the complex mythologies associated with the traditional religious life. Whether recited in evening narratives within the home or celebrated in song on the ceremonial dance grounds, the words and deeds of the ancients were remembered on a nearly daily basis. Early in life, even when learning the names for the flora and fauna of the area, children made their first acquaintance with the central themes in the area's creation stories. Even the names for the most common animals and plants often contained references to related stories from the oral traditions (see chapter 9). Women often knew medicinal formulas for protecting their young, curing common illnesses, or ensuring long life. Traditional healers drew upon their specialized knowledge of local creation stories to contact spirit beings when initiating the process of healing. Knowledge of these tales was a special privilege of religious training, so shamans were inclined to charge a fee for reciting the accompanying story.

Many of these tales run closely parallel throughout the area's speech communities. Consider the many stories surrounding the culture hero known as Across-the-Ocean-Widower. Each group, for instance, sets his birth at the Yurok village of Kenek, where he springs spontaneously into existence and begins to prepare the world for the coming of humans. With him arises the race of prehuman spirit deities, alongside the eternal forces of good and evil. This village, where the era of the transformation begins, is also said to rest at the exact center of the universe. It is here at this symbolically charged location that Across-the-Ocean-Widower begins to embark on those many adventures that come to shape the world as we know it.

Yet, from here, the local oral traditions begin to part ways, as is true of most of the tales that have long circulated in this region. Consider the story of how death enters the world. The Hupas, Yuroks, and Karuks all agree that the original inhabitants of the earth did not know death and that death emerged as the result of some primal misdeed committed long ago in the ancient past. This much is shared fairly uniformly throughout the area's speech communities. For the Hupas and Karuks, Across-the-Ocean-Widower plays a central role in this story; the Yuroks attribute the origin of death to other, more minor characters.

According to one popular Hupa account, death entered the world at the traditional village of Łe·ldiŋ, on the fringe of Hupa-speaking country, as one of Across-the-Ocean-Widower's orphaned sons is mistreated at the hands of strangers.[28] The child is buried alive and nearly dies. Moments before his son's death, Across-the-Ocean-Widower arrives and administers the death as a punishment to all future generations of humans. Here, at this site, the Hupas claim, he also establishes the great religious dances as a means of making reparation for this original wrong. For the Karuks, by contrast, death enters the world at the mouth of the Klamath River (*thúfip*), in Yurok country, as Across-the-Ocean-Widower's father becomes bewildered in his old age and fails to join his sons in the heaven across the ocean downstream.[29] For the Yuroks, Across-the-Ocean-Widower plays no role;[30] instead, the unraveling of life and the emergence of death begins with the first misdeeds of Mole and Jerusalem Cricket in Hupa country, as these beings tamper with important dietary staples and perform nefarious acts beneath the surface of the earth. It is implied that the village of Taʔkʸimiłdiŋ, in Hupa country, may have been the site of their first misadventures.[31] In the end, these miscreants must face up to their acts and make amends on the trails near Weitspus, in the heart of Yurok country, where justice is restored.

Multilingualism and Village Identity

Daily social life afforded members of each group with frequent opportunities to interact with speakers of the neighboring languages. Lucy Thompson, a Yurok woman who wrote a book about her experiences in the early twentieth century, reported that bilingualism was especially common at the religious dances, where neighboring groups often poured in from distant villages speaking utterly different languages: "[T]he upper river or Pech-ic-las [=*pecikla*ʔ, a Yurok name for Karuk speakers] come into the different dances with their valuables as to the line of relationship or old time friendship, and the women put in their wealth and take their places and help to cook and wait on all just the same as the Po-lick-las [=*pulekukla*ʔ, a Yurok name for downriver Yurok speakers], yet they speak a different language but are so closely mixed in marriage and so many of them speak both tongues and the whole meaning of the big dance being just the same to both that there is no mistake between them in any part of the management of the dance" (1916:104–105). Clearly, some of the bilingualism was active as Thompson observed it, since she stated that some of the participants could speak both tongues. Yet it is certainly plausible that some of the bilingualism was passive for others, in the sense that those who were not completely fluent could still understand some of the other languages after years of attending the dances.

As Thompson also noted, intermarriage was common; as a consequence, growing up around speakers of several languages was not unusual. According to genealogical records collected by T. T. Waterman in the Yurok villages of the lower Klamath in 1909, marriages between the Yuroks and their Tolowa-, Karuk-, and Hupa-speaking neighbors were relatively common in places, if not exactly the norm for the entire region. In a classic article on the subject, Waterman and Kroeber (1934) noted a general tendency to marry outside one's natal village: "On the whole, language seems to have been a lesser barrier to intermarriage than distance. The Rekwoi Yurok married almost as often with the Tolowa, and the Weitspus Yurok with their Karuk and Hupa neighbors, as with adjacent Yurok, and more often than with each other or with distant Yurok such as those of the southern coast. It is not contended that language was no barrier; but it evidently was a relatively minor one" (1934:13).

Children, therefore, sometimes grew up in the presence of bilingual parents, whose children were exposed to a range of languages from their earliest days. In the context of an extended family, a person's kinsfolk often encompassed several neighboring linguistic groups, providing frequent opportunities to visit and converse with speakers of many unrelated languages. This is illustrated in the case of Mary Marshall, whose Yurok-speaking mother learned the Hupa language to communicate with her husband's extended family. Thus, Mary Marshall grew up in a bilingual household and remained fluent in both Yurok and Hupa throughout her life, even serving as a bilingual informant for Edward Sapir (Sapir 2001:28).

Trade relations were also strong among the Hupas, Yuroks, and Karuks. Hupa villagers, for example, traded acorns, which were abundant inland, for salt and ocean-dwelling fish, which were abundant among their Yurok neighbors on the coast. The Hupas also needed to trade for redwood for their canoes, since the redwoods grew inland along the coast but not in the Hoopa Valley. In this setting, for very practical reasons, many people were passively familiar with the neighboring dialects and languages, especially those of the smaller groups, such as the Chimarikos.[32] Others were thoroughly multilingual, speaking several languages fluently throughout the course of life, as illustrated in the case of Mary Marshall. Taken together, various factors provide a glimmer of insight into the social circumstances that may have conditioned some of the intergroup influence among the area's languages.

Despite the scale of the linguistic diversity, nearly all of the villages were home to a single dominant language.[33] In this setting, speaking one's native tongue outside its homeland was generally considered improper. On ideological grounds, each village cherished the distinctiveness of its language, regarding it as a primordial bestowal received at the very beginning of time. For instance, according to Hupa storytellers, the neighboring groups were warned not to bother Hupa villagers in times of war, because of the great power this language was said to grant its speakers. This power, it is said, stretched back to the time of creation, when the language was established, alongside the other speech forms in the region.[34] In this sense, each group regarded its language as a source of great religious and ethnic pride.

Geographical considerations also played a major role in shaping the linguistic ecology of northwestern California. Steep mountains, coupled with dangerous rivers, provided a significant barrier to travel, exerting a strong isolating effect on villages that were only twenty miles apart. In traditional times, even a journey of twenty miles was a laborious affair, sometimes taking days to complete by the modes of travel available at the time. On foot, traveling inland from coast could take several days, necessitating that one hike along the rugged trails that traversed the steep mountain terrain.[35] Traveling by canoe was usually feasible only for short stretches, as it generally required frequent portages around the many dangerous areas, where water sweeps over partially submerged boulders to create turbulent "holes" that still drown unwary visitors every year. All of this had an isolating effect on the neighboring village communities and their distinctive languages. Though geography did not prevent trade or intermarriage between the villages, it certainly put a damper on daily exchanges between the groups. Added to this was a strong ideology of localism (see Conathan 2004b: 149–52), as villagers placed a premium on maintaining distinctive local institutions on the planes of both language and culture. In this setting of relative geographical isolation, the fact that the speakers maintained their linguistic differences is less surprising.

CULTURAL CONTACT AND LINGUISTIC DIVERSITY

Though of diverse origins, the Hupa, Yurok, and Karuk Indians of northwestern California eventually settled on a common way of life based on salmon fishing and the acorn harvest. In this sense, the traditional culture of this region can be seen as the product of a long historical exchange among the members of the neighboring village communities, who eventually settled on a common way of life as a by-product of ongoing social contact and intermarriage. Despite this history of intense social contact and widespread multilingualism, the languages of this region have maintained highly distinctive grammars, vocabularies, and even phonologies (O'Neill 2002:87–88).

The staggering social diversity of northwestern California furnishes an exquisite sample of evidence for investigating relationships that obtain between language, culture, and worldview. Although a common series of cultural institutions once swept this region, many sharp linguistic boundaries have long divided the communities. As a consequence, it is possible, at least in principle, to assert a fundamental division between culture, on the one hand (which holds roughly constant throughout the region), and linguistic structure, on the other (which often shifts quite dramatically as one passes from one community to the next). Yet even the common culture of the region was profoundly fragmented by sometimes-significant differences of interpretation at the local level, creating a far more complicated situation not so far beneath the surface. Rather than producing homogeneity or convergence toward a common center, contact between the speakers of the Hupa, Yurok, and Karuk languages has instead provided a powerful ideological motivation for maintaining local linguistic and cultural differences at the village level.

2

Linguistic Relativity and the Puzzle of Northwestern California

Human beings do not live in the objective world alone, nor alone in the world of social activity as ordinarily understood, but are very much at the mercy of the particular language that has become a medium of expression of their society. The fact of the matter is that the "real world" is to a large extent unconsciously built up on the language habits of the group.

Edward Sapir, Selected Writings

Since the introduction of the concept of linguistic relativity by Franz Boas and Edward Sapir, anthropological linguists have long pondered the significance of the enormous conceptual diversity they have encountered in the languages of the world. As any traveler quickly discovers, word meanings and grammatical categories often shift quite dramatically as one passes from one community to the next, so much so that the linguistic habits of one group are often quite unintelligible even to their closest neighbors.[1] In one of its most universal capacities, language plays a central role in facilitating the communication of thought or imagination from person to person, allowing speakers to fashion an almost endless variety of constructions from an otherwise limited stock of words and grammatical ideas.[2]

Given the crucial relationship between language and thought in the context of verbal communication, where language serves as a vehicle for the expression of ideas, these early anthropologists came to ask the following question: Could the regular conceptual patterns of a specific language influence the habitual thought processes of its speakers?[3] If so, the impact on human mental activity would potentially be enormous because of the nearly ubiquitous presence of language in such familiar everyday settings as conversation, storytelling, oratory, prayer, and, very often, even private reflection.

ROOTS OF THE "LINGUISTIC RELATIVITY" PRINCIPLE IN NORTH AMERICA

This stunning proposition, which continues to attract lively scholarly attention throughout the world to this day, largely follows from the view of language that was popular at the time. Early scholars in anthropology and linguistics tended to see languages as fairly rigid structural systems, whose various conceptual elements speakers must internalize in order to communicate effectively. Grammatical categories occupy a particularly important place in the argument, because they are obligatory and are, therefore, pervasively applied to a wide range of speech forms in any given language. Yet vocabulary also plays an important role in the general argument, as the words that speakers know and apply to their experiences often mirror the larger cultural interests that have taken root in their social circle. Without these words, one would neither be able to share one's observations nor be pointed to the observations of those around one. Even sound patterning plays a part, as speakers often import acoustic expectations about the realm of sound onto their perceptions.

To speak a language, according to this familiar line of reasoning, is to enter into an agreement about the meaning assigned to words and about the grammatical rules that must be applied to produce proper forms. Just as words and grammatical categories differ across languages, so too do the concepts that speakers exchange on a regular basis. Yet to communicate effectively, speakers must also conceptualize their own experience in terms of the concepts that are available in their native tongue. So, in a parallel fashion, the concepts that speakers habitually apply to their own experiences also shift as we pass from one language to the next—potentially having a profound impact on one's outlook on life, even if this is all taking place on a relatively unconscious basis. This agreement holds between the speakers of a common language but not necessarily beyond its boundaries, giving rise to a sense of linguistic relativity among the speakers of the world's languages. In this sense, to pass from one language to another is to shift the conceptual lens through which one momentarily views the world, if only for the purpose of communicating with the fellow speakers of a common language. Of course, it is also possible that these linguistic concepts have a more far-reaching influence on the speaker's habitual thought processes, also affecting private reflection and the speaker's routine perceptions of the world.

Significantly, few speakers are ever consciously aware of the daunting structural complexity of their native language. Yet most speakers are highly adept at manipulating the complex grammatical machinery of their native tongue even in early childhood, long before many other, more-advanced cognitive skills have started to develop. So, for most speakers, the structural patterns of one's native language are processed—and produced—on an entirely unconscious basis. Surprisingly, all of this happens relatively perfectly throughout the course of life, and without apparent effort, for most speakers of any given language. Equally important, for the sake of this argument, is the proposition that speakers also unconsciously project the structural patterns of their native language onto their very understanding of the surrounding world. Though this is easily demonstrated in the realm of sound, both Sapir and Whorf suggested that the model also applied to the semantic expectations that speakers unconsciously import into their experiences of the world.

Early in the history of American linguistics, Sapir demonstrated this principle of unconscious projection in the purely formal realm of sound patterning. In an article entitled "The Psychological Reality of Phonemes" (1949 [1933]: 46–60), he sought to show how speakers unconsciously project the structural patterning of their native tongue onto their experience of the surrounding world of sound. That is, he sought to show how these acoustic expectations shape the speakers' rapid-fire perceptions in a nearly gestalt-like fashion.

Though Sapir drew on several Native American languages in his essay, the principle can also be demonstrated in English, a language with which most readers of this book have some personal experience. Consider the set of sounds that English speakers represent with the letter *p*. Nearly all speakers make several distinct sounds here, though each of these sounds serves a similar function in the language, so that few speakers ever notice that the *p* sound in the word *pat* is followed by a sudden puff of air, one that can be verified merely by placing one's hand in front of one's mouth before saying the word. Yet in similar words such as *spat* and *splat,* this sudden puff of air is absent, a fact that can be verified by the same method.

Of course, the variation is predictable. The aspiration, as this sudden puff of air is known, is only present when this *p* sound occurs at the very beginning of a syllable. Yet these two sounds do not signal a difference in meaning in English; if a speaker were to pronounce all of the *p* sounds with aspiration, it would sound odd, but the words would continue to signal the same meaning. For similar reasons, few speakers are aware of the voicelessness of the *l* sound in words such as *clothe* and *clean.* Instead, most speakers assign these voiceless variants to the same functional category as the fully voiced *l* found in the similar words *loathe* and *lean.* Here the environment also conditions the variation, with the voiceless *l* sounds occurring after other sounds that are also voiceless, in effect, making the transition easier on the "voice box," or larynx. Again, the conditions under which these variants occur are completely predicable.

Among linguists, these functional categories are known as *phonemes,* a key concept that Edward Sapir championed in the 1930s when it was, surprisingly, still a controversial new idea. In this framework, both *p* sounds belong to a single category, or phoneme, in English, as do both *l* sounds. As a consequence, English speakers do not habitually distinguish between these fine nuances of sound, simply because doing so is not necessary. That is, because they perform the same functional role in the language, the difference between these *p* sounds or *l* sounds is not significant on the plane of meaning. Nevertheless, the difference is an important one at the unconscious level of speaking with a proper accent!

Yet these phonological processes can hold perceptual implications, which vary according to the speaker's native language. Certainly, most English speakers regard the aspirated and plain variants of *t* as instances of a single type of sound, as found in such words as *till* and *still,* because they are two instances of the same English phoneme, or functional unit of sound. Yet a native speaker of an Athabaskan language would judge these two *t* sounds as utterly distinct because they belong to different functional classes, or phonemes, in this family of languages. Consider the two *t* sounds in the following Hupa words.[4] Without a sudden puff of air, this sound occurs in a word that means "not," which can be phonetically represented as [to·].[5] This is the *t* that occurs in the English word *still.* Yet, when followed by a puff of air, nearly the same sequence produces a word for "water," which can be phonetically represented as [tʰo·].[6] This is the same *t* sound that occurs in the English word *till,* which English speakers do not regularly distinguish from the previous *t* sound. For similar reasons, a native speaker of Welsh would notice the subtle difference between the voiced and voiceless *l* sounds of English. For Welsh speakers, voicing is contrastive with *l* sounds.[7]

The same principle also applies in reverse. What speakers of one language split into two categories, the speakers of another language may regard as a single type of sound. In Japanese, for instance, there is no regular distinction between the sounds that English speakers split into *l* and *r.* On purely perceptual grounds, Japanese speakers often have trouble with the distinction between *l* and *r* in English, because Japanese (like many other languages) does not make this distinction on functional grounds. Yet speakers of English, which lacks a glottalized stop sound (released with a forceful stream of air from the voice box, though without any vocalization from the vocal cords), are preconditioned by experience with English to perceive these sounds as similar to other voiceless sounds, even though, objectively speaking, they are quite distinct.

About a decade later, Whorf took the argument one step further. Echoing a position Sapir had briefly taken in several articles, Whorf suggested that human perception is pervasively shaped by a range of linguistic expectations that speakers regularly bring to their experiences of the world. In other words, Whorf argued that what Sapir had so clearly demonstrated strictly in the realm of sound could also be applied to the spheres of grammar, discourse, and vocabulary.

Much as our perception of the world of sound is conditioned by the familiar acoustic patterns of our native tongue, Whorf argued that our experience of the world in general is influenced by the patterns of meaning we routinely apply to our experiences. Specifically, Whorf referred to the semantic projections that speakers routinely apply to their own experiences of the world.[8] For, certainly, when we are communicating with others, any remark must be reported in terms of the words and grammatical concepts that are available in a particular language, either for the purpose of lending expression to our observations or when receiving observations from others around us.[9] Equally important, of course, is the process of engaging in dialogue with others,[10] whereupon both parties arrive at conclusions that neither would have advanced strictly on their own. Here, again, language also plays a central role in facilitating the negotiation of perspective or worldview.

Yet, more dramatically, Whorf proposed that speakers draw on the same semantic resources when privately reflecting on their own experience in an unvoiced stream of linguistic thought.[11] In advancing this argument, he echoed his teacher, Edward Sapir, expanding on his mentor's ideas with ideas that he had gathered from his own work as a fire insurance inspector:

> We dissect nature along lines laid down by our native languages. The categories and types that we isolate from the world of phenomena we do not find there because they stare every observer in the face; on the contrary, the world is presented in a kaleidoscopic flux of impressions which has to be organized by our minds—and this means largely by the linguistic systems in our minds. We cut nature up, organize it into concepts, and ascribe significances as we do, largely because we are parties to an agreement to organize it in this way—an agreement

that holds throughout our speech community and is codified in the patterns of our language. This agreement is, of course, an implicit and unstated one, BUT ITS TERMS ARE ABSOLUTELY OBLIGATORY; we cannot talk at all except by subscribing to the organization and classification of data which the agreement decrees. (1956:213–14)

In many ways, there is nothing surprising about this proposition. Apart from the strong rhetorical language that Whorf uses to phrase his argument, the whole process of arriving at a shared understanding of the world by using language in creative ways is a rather humdrum, daily occurrence. Most of us have been led to certain observations based on what others have said to us, whether in the form of the written word or spoken language. That is, on an absolutely everyday basis, most of us use language to communicate our perceptions on important matters in the world around us, often drawing attention to details that may have eluded our audience had they not been raised in the course of conversation or monologue. Of course, language also allows our neighbors to influence us, so the whole process is a reciprocal one, in which our observations are constantly shaped by our engaging in dialogue with those around us. In fact, much of what we know about the world, few of us discover completely for ourselves; instead, we learn it from the verbal reports of others. So, in a very significant sense, language plays a critical role in forming an understanding of the world for any normal human. That is, if language has any efficacy at all, speakers use words to draw their audience's attention to certain conclusions or to certain details. Yet this passage by Whorf has stirred a great deal of debate over the years and is still regarded as one of the most controversial propositions in all of linguistics.

Quite dramatically, Whorf went on to propose that one's entire vision of the universe undergoes a parallel kind of shift as one passes from one language to the next. That is, while we often use language actively to share our observations, Whorf suggested that the preexisting concepts of language also have a deeper and more unconscious influence on our general thought processes, even when we are not aware of it. Thus, the habitual concepts of one's language may come, through force of habit, to influence one's personal views in subtle though pervasive ways. More broadly, so might one's vision of life, especially if one had fallen into the habit of regularly seeing things this way. Of course, one's view of the world also hinges on one's personal and cultural expectations, an assumption that Whorf probably took for granted as a Boasian cultural relativist. Indeed, from the start, the architects of American linguistic relativity saw language and culture working in tandem to shape the speaker's perceptions. Infinitely malleable, language and culture were perceived by those such as Whorf as evolving alongside one another. Of course, a person's "vision of the universe" often undergoes radical revision throughout the course of his or her life, but language is usually central to the process of negotiating or promoting certain worldviews or discourses.

A similar point of view is also sometimes attributed to the parallel Saussurean school of linguistics, which rose up in Europe around the time that Boas, Sapir, and Bloomfield were hammering out the details of American structuralism.[12] Based on lecture notes he delivered around the turn of the twentieth century, Ferdinand de Saussure is famous for arguing that the link between sound and meaning is by and large an arbitrary one in all human languages.[13] That is, there is no intrinsic relationship between sound and meaning, apart from the social conventions that have been established in a particular speech community. In other words, the connection is something that speakers adopt through sheer convention, so that the actual sounds associated with the words for common referents such as "tree" and "horse" differ widely throughout the world's languages.

So far, this Saussurean model could be taken to suggest that languages merely have different labels for the same things, or different sounds associated with different referents in the surrounding world. Yet, against this common-sense view of language, Saussure argued that words fundamentally represent concepts, not simply physical referents in the surrounding world. The view was to some extent borrowed from Plato, who argued that words do not simply label "things." If this were literally true, we would have as many words as there are referents in the world! Rather, Plato reasoned, words label categories, or abstract types. As a result, even an apparently simple word such as "dog" represents a fairly abstract category that applies to many referents, whose perceptual similarities are not always obvious, as, for example, in the case of toy poodles and Irish wolfhounds.

Yet Saussure also argued that concepts shift, in structurally significant ways, as we pass from one language to the next. The process is one that he often compared to the game of chess, in which every piece has a place in relation to others. That is, while word meanings differ across languages, so too do their "values" in relation to similar words in the same semantic sphere. His most famous example involves the words *sheep* and *mouton* (*mutton*), the latter being a term that English borrowed from French, introducing a new contrast to the language. While English speakers distinguish between the "animal in the field" and the "meat on the table" with contrasting terms, the French language collapses the two senses into a single category, as represented by the word *mouton*. The meanings of *mutton/mouton* are similar in English and French, but the values are not. That is, in English, there is an added contrast on a lexical basis, with the additional word *sheep*.

The principle of structural contrast also operates within languages, as apparent synonyms often hold different connotative values in relation to one another. To take a fairly stark contrast, consider the expressions "terrorist" and "freedom fighter," which could arguably be applied to the same real-world referent. Yet each expression attributes vastly different features to the same potential actor, namely, a person who fights and injures others for a certain political cause, though without the sanction of a recognized government, as a "soldier" would have.

So, on this basis, Saussure came to argue that both the sound pattern and the associated concept are accepted through sheer convention. Certainly these conceptual agreements are binding within speech communities, where speakers must agree on the concepts associated with words or grammatical ideas. Yet the same concepts do not necessarily extend beyond these social boundaries. It follows that as we pass from one language to another, the labels for the same referents vary almost endlessly, without consistent correlations in either sound or meaning throughout the world's languages. Though based on often-minute differences in meaning or usage, the conceptual implications are far-reaching. That is, as concepts shift from one language to the next, so, too, does the speaker's range of choices for expressing ideas or influencing others with culturally loaded terms.

VOCABULARY AND LINGUISTIC RELATIVITY

Given his broad experience in many Native American societies, Boas urged all serious students of culture to pay close attention to indigenous terminology. In his fieldwork among the Eskimo or Kwakiutl, Boas noticed that word meanings often mirror the cultural interests of a group, providing a window into native categories of thought. So, for instance, speakers often develop concepts that are unique to their culture, such as names for religious figures or social customs not known elsewhere in the world, even among close neighbors. Here translation is often inadequate because close parallels may not exist. Equally often, native terms cast evaluations, or carry connotations, that are easily lost in translation. Animals, for instance, are held in high regard for religious reasons in northwestern California, creating a flattering comparison when a person is granted an animal nickname. Yet here a simple translation into English is misleading, for the same animals may be considered uncouth varmints, as reflected in such expressions as "he *dogged* me all day" or "she tried to *ferret* it out of me." Here the native conception of the referent must also be considered, which in northwestern California includes the sense that the first inhabitants of the earth combined animal and human behavioral characteristics. Just as often, speakers advance unique classifications of phenomena that all humans confront, such as animals, plants, sounds, colors, and natural phenomena. So, for instance, in the introduction to his *Handbook of American Indian Languages,* Boas suggested that native vocabulary provides a record of those implicit classifications that speakers have advanced for the very practical purposes of conveying their everyday thoughts: "Where it is necessary to distinguish a certain phenomenon in many aspects, which in the life of the people play each an entirely independent role, many independent words may develop, while in other cases modifications of a single term may suffice. . . . Thus it happens that each language, from the point of view of another language, may be arbitrary in its classifications" (1966 [1911]:22).

In a nutshell, Boas argued that words reflect spheres of knowledge developed within particular societies.[14] Certainly this principle also holds within languages, where cultural groups invariably develop in-group vocabularies, advancing terms that are often opaque to outsiders. The case of English is instructive here, a language that boasts one of the most massive vocabularies in the world, mostly owing to its long-standing tradition of borrowing from other tongues. The *Oxford English Dictionary,* for instance, identifies over 500,000 words in English, an enormous vocabulary that no speaker ever completely masters in its entirety.[15] Since no one has a complete mastery of the language, the scope of one's vocabulary often reflects the social circles one keeps and the subsequent knowledge one has developed in any given area of learning, from fishing or farming to math or the Internet. At the same time, new words are constantly being advanced to keep up with developments in various spheres of learning, usually beginning in one social circle before spreading to others, as relevant to everyday usage. Ultimately, vocabulary, as much as pronunciation, becomes a badge of group membership, a phenomenon that every actor or lawyer takes advantage of when building a public image.

Merely opening one's mouth sends a loud message about one's social past and depth of learning. The principle applies to every profession or niche, including youth culture and religious sects. In this sense, no two English speakers share exactly the same vocabulary. If the principle holds true *within* languages, why not *between* languages, where the differences are, on average, on a slightly greater order of magnitude?

Exploring the cognitive implications of the problem, Whorf suggested that vocabulary is often closely linked to perception in a range of everyday situations. In an obvious sense, we all use language every day to communicate precise observations about the world around us, based on sharing a common vocabulary and holding common conceptual categories, such as the fine line between "terrorist," "soldier," and "freedom fighter," for instance. That is, there is a necessary connection between vocabulary and perception, one that is absolutely critical to the existence of language, though certainly there is also room for speakers to have widely different ideas about how to interpret a word or phrase.

A strong sense of conceptual relativity can be illustrated even in a single language, as speakers differ in their knowledge of the vocabulary or even in the meanings they assign to the same words. That is, to pass from one "conceptual world" to another, all one has to do is refine one's vocabulary. Or, to approach the process in reverse, as one deepens one's knowledge, a parallel refinement of vocabulary usually follows. For this reason, those at the frontiers of knowledge, such as scientists or philosophers, are constantly coming up with new words to represent the unprecedented concepts they are developing. Yet try entering a new field without learning new concepts and parallel vocabulary. Or try teaching or simply communicating this new knowledge without a specialized vocabulary. Generally speaking, the greater one's knowledge, the greater one's ability to verbalize these concepts with words, facilitating rapid communication among those who share these words and related concepts, yet limiting the ability to communicate with those who do not. Try attending a social event without knowing the requisite language! If this principle holds within languages, it also should be expected to hold between languages, where spheres of knowledge often differ quite massively.[16]

Of course, the absence of a word for something does not block out the perception of this phenomenon. Consider something as tangible as color. Here the lack of a term for a specific color does not prevent the speaker from "seeing" it, at least not in any absolute sense. Yet learning the precise meaning for a word such as *mauve* or *chartreuse* often motivates the speaker to notice it, dwell on it, or perhaps ascribe significance to it, whereas it may have gone unnoticed before. More crucially, having a name for something allows the speaker to communicate very precisely about it, rapidly sharing observations with those who make the same perceptual distinctions on a regular basis. Psycholinguistic studies have demonstrated that having a precise term for something as tangible as color helps speakers notice it and remember it later, because, in the process of naming it, they have learned to habitually attend to it (Lucy and Shweder 1979).

Note that this crucial link between vocabulary and perception operates in several related types of situations. In an active sense, speakers constantly use words to report or share their observations with others, often leading the audience to conclusions that would have otherwise proved elusive. This may be as simple as drawing someone's attention to an object or a patch of color in the room by mentioning its name. Or it could consist of building up an entire world in the imagination through the act of storytelling. In an equally familiar sense, speakers often revise their ideas in public, arriving at conclusions that no one listening would have come to on his or her own. So far, there is nothing controversial about this proposition. Everyone acknowledges that language provides a window into the thought processes of fellow speakers, partly by virtue of its limitless creative capacity to express new ideas.

Whorf went on to suggest that a similar connection between vocabulary and perception operates on a far less conscious basis, where the influence is just as strong. Here he suggests that language also operates in a passive or unconscious mode. In this sense, the very language one speaks influences how one perceives the world, based on how the vocabulary treats a specific phenomenon. Yet here Whorf was not interested in language in the abstract, but in the way language is habitually applied to certain situations in the course of everyday life, which influences how one "sees" this process (if not careful to reconsider this event on one's own terms). Whorf did not dream up this theory in the abstract. Instead, he based the proposition on real-world examples culled from his own experience. In a famous article entitled "The Relation of Habitual Thought and Behavior to Language" (1956:134–59), Whorf shared some of these insights with the general public.

While working as a fire inspector for the Hartford Insurance Company, Whorf noticed that the descriptions provided by witnesses offered a key into how they understood the event. Much as Freud paid close attention to the descriptions his patients offered (taking hedges, substitutions, and slips of the tongue as windows into the unconscious), Whorf used language to reveal how instigators of an accident had analyzed (or *mis*analyzed) the event. What workers, for instance, had come to describe as "scrap-lead" in the everyday vocabulary of the shop was in fact laden with wax, which, as everyone knows, is highly flammable. Here the misleading term "scrap-lead" provides a key into how the misunderstanding arose. That is, we normally think of metal as something that can withstand high heat without igniting, and we all know that wax is flammable. The description was probably based on a misunderstanding that spread within the workplace as the word was repeated, along with the implicit analysis it suggested. Based on the misanalysis suggested by the term, the hapless worker had come to disastrously misinterpret the event, setting the "scrap-lead" next to the fire, where it quickly exploded. Of course, speakers can always appeal to their senses to verify reports received from others in language; language is certainly not all-powerful. And if the workers had been more reflective, they surely could have paid attention to the presence of the wax, even if the misleading term did not help. Yet in the absence of reflection, we often take other people's word for things that we do not thoroughly investigate on our own. If the workers had had a better understanding of the material, they would most likely have chosen different words to describe it. Yet we often accept words at their face value, without a second thought, especially when we do not take the time to verify the analysis with our own experience.

During roughly this same period, the British writer George Orwell (1950) made some similar observations about the power of language in political settings. Though his observations were rooted in a different set of experiences, Orwell shared Whorf's interests in the behavioral implications of everyday language use. During his travels in Africa and India, Orwell had witnessed many grave injustices that were later poorly represented or even glossed over in the popular press. Here the consequences were more far-reaching than in most of the cases discussed by Whorf, though the reports were likewise based on the use of misleading terminology. In the popular press, the expression "pacification" was often applied to situations in which villagers were driven from their homes or showered with machine-gun fire. Here the label "pacification" suggests the opposite of the reality it masks, while suggesting a partial justification for the actual situation it glosses over. If people were shot, burned, or driven from their homes, it was in the interest of "pacification," or so the newspaper reports implied. Of course, it helped that the events were set far from England, so that few of the readers could verify the reports with their own personal experience or hear the other side of the story from the people who were being "pacified" by the troops. With this type of language, Orwell concluded, many grave atrocities could be masked with pleasant-sounding, though highly misleading, language. In the absence of verification through firsthand experience, the public often passively accepts the implicit analysis suggested by the phrase.

So, as Boas, Whorf, and Orwell have all keenly observed, each word suggests a conceptual framework through which to view a phenomenon. Sapir went on to argue that words also hold a symbolic value or aesthetic sense, which must be taken into consideration: "The understanding of a simple poem, for instance, involves not merely an understanding of the single words in their average significance, but a full comprehension of the whole life of the community as it is mirrored in the words, or as it is suggested by their overtones. Even comparatively simple acts of perception are very much more at the mercy of the social patterns called words than we might suppose" (Sapir 1949:162).

Note that this is far from the conventional view, in which words are believed to merely draw attention to preexisting objects of perception already present in the world around us. From this perspective, languages merely have different labels for the same things, nothing more and nothing less. Consequently, linguistic relativity boils down to nothing more than having different names for the same objects, and the whole argument is reduced to a special brand of phonetic relativism, without any conceptual implications. Yet Orwell, Sapir, and Whorf demonstrated that words also routinely shape our perceptions of the referents to which our attention is drawn. As every writer or politician quickly discovers, a word can make all the difference, and the meanings are not the same in the end! "Pacification" and "massacre" do not mean the same thing when applied to the same event, as Orwell showed, though outcry against the latter term can be suppressed by use of the former. Nor, as Whorf showed, do "scrap-lead" and "wax" mean the same or have equally explosive results. Instead, words hold tremendous behavioral implications, as every child learns even on the playground, when the first insults are heard.

GRAMMATICAL CATEGORIES AND LINGUISTIC RELATIVITY

Language is more than just sound patterning and word meanings. At a fundamental level, every language is also based on a core stock of grammatical concepts that ease the flow of speech by expressing often highly abstract ideas in near-shorthand form. Often the categories embedded in the grammatical structure of a language derive from the need to portray fairly common situations, without having to reinvent the wheel every time the speaker opens his or her mouth. Almost universally, these grammatical categories represent the referent's status as the speaker, the addressee, or some more-distant "third person," though with interesting developments in individual languages, such as including the gender of the person in the meaning of the category. Or sometimes these grammatical categories represent the number of referents in a scene, giving rise to fairly common concepts such as singular, dual, or plural, which are found in many languages around the world. Equally common are markers for portraying abstract temporal situations, often giving rise to tense systems, such as the English past tense suffix -ed or the Karuk ancient tense marker =anik.

Here a crucial link between grammatical categories and perception is fairly easy to demonstrate. Like the link between vocabulary and perception, the relationship between grammar and worldview also operates on several related fronts, some of them active and others passive. As Michael Silverstein has pointed out, even pronominal categories such as "us" and "them" are not pre-given but are very much assigned through the act of speech (Silverstein 1976). We all use these concepts every day to include some people in our social group and to exclude others by implication. The consequences for all parties are potentially enormous. In political settings, such as the framing of the U.S. Constitution, the meaning ascribed to a humble grammatical concept such as a common pronoun can make all the difference. For instance, when the Constitution was framed, the pronoun *we* was employed in such a way as to include only the framers and, by extension, other white males. Women, slaves, and Indians were effectively excluded, and in fact these groups had few rights for over a century to come. Of course, most speakers use pronouns such as *us* and *them* on a daily basis, often thereby unconsciously asserting membership in a group or excluding others.

Or consider the distinction between familiar and formal second-person referents, a distinction formalized on a grammatical basis in many Indo-European languages, though, oddly enough, not modern-day English. For speakers of Spanish and French, the speaker must always decide whether to address friends and neighbors as superiors or equals. As everyone learns in even the most rudimentary high school French class, superiors are normally addressed with *vous* forms, while equals are usually addressed with *tu* forms. In English, a vestige of this system survives, though only with various forms of address, such as the first name for equals versus the title and surname for superiors. At one time, however, English speakers addressed equals with *thou, thee,* and *thine,* while reserving *you* and *your* for superiors. Centuries ago, the Quakers, with their strong ideology of equality, protested the sense of hierarchy implicit in the grammar, addressing everyone, including so-called superiors, with the solidarity forms (Bauman 1983). Today, of course, the distinction is no longer an obligatory one on the grammatical plane, and the familiar forms have all but dropped out of the language, except for occasional references to Shakespeare or the King James Bible. Yet to grasp the sense of hierarchy implicit in these grammatical categories, consider how one would address all of one's present friends and neighbors if suddenly forced to revert to this archaic English pronoun system. By addressing a superior as an equal, one risks seriously offending a person with greater power, and by mistakenly addressing an equal as a superior, one potentially admits to holding a lower rank.

Once a grammatical category enters the structure of a language, speakers must consider these concepts nearly every time they open their mouths to talk. Because these concepts enter into so many constructions, their conceptual presence is felt in nearly every phrase or utterance that passes over a speaker's lips. For this reason, grammatical categories play a critical role in the general argument about how the principle of linguistic relativity operates. Of course, with grammatical categories, the options are highly restricted (unlike the parallel situation with vocabulary, for which the choices are many). Here the speaker is forced to choose from a small number of categories that must be habitually applied to experience. It follows that paying attention to these categories of analysis becomes a precondition for speaking the language properly, even if all of this proceeds on a fairly unconscious basis. So, as both Sapir and Whorf came to hypothesize, speakers may also project these grammatical categories onto their experience of the world, as had already been demonstrated with sound patterning and vocabulary. In Whorf's famous words, "the 'linguistic relativity principle' . . . means, in informal terms, that users of markedly different grammars are pointed by the grammars toward different types of observations and different evaluations of externally similar acts of observation, and hence are not equivalent as observers but must arrive at somewhat different views of the world" (Whorf 1956:221). That is, these humble grammatical categories serve a definite functional role in human life, pointing interlocutors to observations of various kinds, though without having to dwell on the often-abstract nature of these distinctions, such as the "in-group" versus "out-group" split that is often unconsciously asserted with pronouns.

Language, in fact, hinges on a crucial link between grammatical categories and perception, without which communication would be difficult if not impossible. Compelling evidence comes from feral children and certain types of aphasiacs, who often do not have normal access to the grammatical features of language. If unexposed to language by the age of thirteen or so, a person rarely acquires grammatical markings such as the English past tense suffix -*ed* or the plural -*s*, which are, for all intents and purposes, off limits, along with sentences over two or three words in length. As a result, communication is severely restricted, and this person is effectively cut off from the world, even though he or she may have acquired a vocabulary of several thousand words or more.[17] In a similar way, an adult who suffers a stroke to Broca's area, a small patch of tissue on the surface of the left side of the brain, typically suffers a severe loss in grammatical ability.[18] In such cases, a speaker may suddenly lose his or her ability to understand the apparently simple tense markers or pronominal forms that most of us take for granted without fully consciously understanding their highly abstract nature. Without these grammatical categories, humans are reduced to using highly ambiguous two- or three-word sentences, with a linguistic ability that is parallel to that of a normal two-and-a-half-year-old. As such, these aphasiacs or feral children are effectively cut off from the outside world, unable to understand others or convey their own thoughts, even though they may posses some vocabulary. Yet most of us take grammatical categories for granted, tapping into abstractions such as the "familiar second person" and "past tense" without a second thought.

Whorf also suggested that grammar operates on an unconscious basis to influence our perceptions in equally pervasive ways. Here he proposed the concept of the "cryptotype," in which speakers apply an abstract conceptual category to a situation, even in the absence of a formal grammatical marker (Whorf 1956:70–71). Many English nouns, for instance, belong to default gender classes, even though gender is not overtly marked in every instance. Membership in the category is established by a number of secondary strategies. Obviously this holds true for personal names, for which names such as "Susan" and "Margaret" are feminine while others such as "Mark" and "John" are masculine, a pattern that can be ascertained just by paying attention to the sex of the referent. Whorf suggested that the distinction is far more pervasive in modern English, with gender marking affecting many of our nouns to this day (1956:90–92). Certainly, on a formal basis, the old Indo-European distinction between masculine, feminine, and neuter is no longer marked on every English noun, as it is in modern Spanish or French. Yet our pronominal system preserves the distinction in the third person, where the gender may be ascertained simply by substituting a noun with the appropriate pronominal form. Here the choices are restricted to "he," "she," and "it." So, for instance, with whales, the default category is feminine, as illustrated in the expression "There *she* blows!" With an insect, the default is neuter, as can be illustrated with the exclamation "Get *it*!" Here Whorf demonstrated that many English nouns continue to belong to a gender category, effectively preserving the vestiges of an old Indo-European pattern that has since been greatly attenuated in modern-day English. In other words, we still do project these ancient categories on an everyday basis, even if the process is unconscious and the marking is not always overt.

NARRATIVE TEXTS, LANGUAGE USE, AND LINGUISTIC RELATIVITY

Vocabulary and grammar also have a setting, one to which language owes its existence. This setting, of course, is the "social life" of language, or the constant exchange or dialogue among its speakers, who use this language to express their innermost thoughts and feelings on a daily basis. It is within this setting, for instance, that children first learn a language—without exposure to a speech community, language never develops normally.[19] And in actual usage within this setting, words and grammatical concepts often take on new meaning as they constantly enter into novel situations. In a very real sense, words and grammatical concepts never enter into the same situation twice, taking on new shades of meaning every time they are uttered.

Realizing the central role that language plays in human life, Boas urged his students to pay close attention to how words and grammatical categories are used in familiar cultural settings, such as storytelling. For his early students, this meant collecting extensive bodies of narrative texts, as native speakers, or "informants," dictated stories about their religious beliefs or social customs to students in the anthropology lab for hours on end. For Boas, language was the primary source document of culture, a position that was not unusual for a scholar of the time, when most educated people studied Latin, Greek, Hebrew, or Sanskrit to shed light on the worldviews, philosophies, or religious beliefs of the ancients. By paying close attention to how speakers phrased their thoughts in their native tongue, Boas hoped that his students would build an accurate record of native social customs from an insider's perspective, though without sacrificing the fine shades of meaning that are so easily lost in translation. Afterwards, the anthropologist could advance a scholarly interpretation of these narratives, but the native voice was central to the work of describing how a culture works.[20]

Boas knew that, through the act of narration, speakers actively construct worldview by drawing on the conceptual resources of their native tongue. The approach is similar to the exegesis of religious documents, in which even the subtlest linguistic nuance can hold profound implications for the interpretation of a text. Here grammatical categories and vocabulary are key to the expression of a cultural perspective or worldview, generally one that must conform to certain guidelines laid down in the surrounding community. That is, through their lexical and grammatical choices, speakers articulate a point of view, typically negotiated within a social setting. Consider the use of the pronoun *we* in the framing of the U.S. Constitution, discussed earlier, by which women, slaves, and Indians were excluded by contextual implication. In this case, a humble grammatical category held profound political implications for over a century. As still another example of this phenomenon, consider the period of history that we know as the "settling of the American West," a formulation that many students passively accept in school, even though everyone knows that Native Americans lived in the West for thousands of years before the cowboys and gold miners arrived. Here the accepted perspective is one that downplays the prior Native American presence to justify mainstream political views. A similar view is encapsulated in the parallel expression "manifest destiny," whereby the suffering of Native Americans is conveniently moved to the background while the Anglo-American dream takes the center stage. Again in this case, a seemingly harmless word choice conveys a powerful political perspective that simultaneously silences other points of view. So, for instance, few history books would contain a formulation such as "the destruction of Indian civilization" as a description of what happened during this era: not because the expression is inaccurate but because it does not resonate with accepted political views.

Speakers, of course, differ in their assessments of the world, something that is also articulated through language. For this reason, Boas encouraged his students to work closely with several key informants, who could furnish contrasting accounts of the same stories or social customs. Some informants are more knowledgeable than others, and most have refined their knowledge in some areas, based on personal interests. Men and women, for instance, often run in different social circles, especially in small-scale societies in which gender roles are generally sharply defined. As a consequence, knowledge of traditional lore often differs substantially across gender lines. In northwestern California, for instance, men were discouraged from practicing some forms of shamanism, so only women had access to certain medicinal texts. Men, in contrast, were often more versed in the details of political leadership. When Sapir traveled to northwestern California in the 1920s, he was careful to work with a number of informants, balancing his exposure to the range of views expressed within the culture, especially among men and women. Drawing from his personal experience in many Native American societies, Sapir came to argue that cultural understanding is not uniform throughout a speech community. Instead, every person often articulates a different position, one that is amenable to narrative analysis in a cultural setting. Language provides categories such as "us" and "them," but speakers decide how to apply the concepts, often in politically charged ways that reveal their own standing within a community.

In many ways, the Boasian approach to language resembles a parallel school of thought advanced by the Bakhtin circle in the 1920s. Like the Boasians, Mikhail Bakhtin and his associates insisted that language must be understood in a social context, within which speakers negotiate meaning in a cultural setting. Like Sapir, Bakhtin argued that speech communities are home to many diverse voices, each representing a different point of view. For Bakhtin, the central reality of language is "dialogue": each party representing a different perspective and arriving at new observations through a process of ongoing cross-pollination. Sapir hinted at a similar process, arguing that languages often undergo subtle revision from one to generation to the next, as a by-product of social interaction among speakers who have their own creative insights: "Language is the most massive and inclusive art we know, a mountainous and anonymous work of unconscious generations" (1921:220). In this sense, languages are made and remade in humble social settings, in which subtle new shades of meaning are constantly assigned to old forms and new forms are added as views change.

RECENT WORK ON LINGUISTIC RELATIVITY

Eventually this line of inquiry crystallized with the formulation of the classic "principle of linguistic relativity," an apt description of an ongoing research program, coined by Sapir but popularized by Whorf. The rest is history; linguistic relativity has been a perennial topic of discussion in anthropological circles ever since and is debated in many college textbooks to this day.[21] Though subject to multiple interpretations, this school of thought essentially holds that language has the potential to wield a pervasive unconscious influence on the mental processes of its speakers, subtly channeling the thoughts that people voice when speaking a particular language, such as one's native tongue.

One important implication is that speakers may come to perceive the world along the lines of those familiar patterns of meaning that are laid down in their native tongue, much as the audience of any gripping literary work or polemical political piece is led to certain observations or conclusions through the careful selection of words and images on the part of the author. Presumably, speakers of diverse languages are led to different observations about the world around them through the constraints of their language, much as cultures have long been thought to condition the perceptions and expectations of those who live within them. And, of course, on the grand historical scale, thought processes may also leave an impression on linguistic structure, as new words are coined or new grammatical categories emerge to lend expression to emerging ideas that need to be voiced on a daily basis.

A recent spate of research on the principle of linguistic relativity, much of it published in the 1990s, has once again lent credibility to this age-old postulate. As a result, there has been a resurgence of interest in this phenomenon, with several new studies now supporting the principle of linguistic relativity on fairly strict scientific grounds. John Lucy, for instance, recently produced two important studies that reexamine the linguistic relativity hypothesis by subjecting it to a number of empirical tests (1992a, 1992b). In these works, linguistic concepts are shown to exert a subtle, though persistent, influence on related thought processes and behavioral patterns, a tendency that is particularly strong with grammatical categories.

In English, for instance, plural marking is generally required when speaking of more than one instantiation of any given type of object. That is, we say "two books," "two cats," or "two lakes," applying the same plural marker -s to animate and inanimate objects alike. This pattern is far from universal, though. In Yucatec Maya, for instance, plural marking is available only for the class of living beings, yet even there it is not a strict grammatical requirement, only an optional consideration.

On the basis of these contrasting patterns of grammatical marking, Lucy hypothesized that English speakers would be more attentive to the number of animate and inanimate objects than speakers of Yucatec Maya would be, for grammatical considerations in Yucatec Maya do not "point" these speakers to such observations. When shown pictures containing various types of objects,

English speakers were consistently attentive to the number of animate and inanimate bodies, mirroring exactly those features that are marked in the grammar. In contrast, speakers of Yucatec Maya were far less sensitive to the number of objects than these English speakers were, while paying slightly more attention to the animate objects than the inanimate ones. These observations follow the pattern of grammatical marking in Yucatec Maya, in which plurality is not required but is nevertheless an option for animate bodies. Here Lucy was also careful to test the subjects' performance on nonverbal tasks, such as sorting the pictures for perceived resemblances, demonstrating that grammatical marking molds general behavioral predispositions, even outside the formal linguistic realm.

Lucy has dubbed this phenomenon the "Whorfian effect," after one of its most popular early proponents, showing that language indeed exerts an unconscious influence on human mental operations, most measurably in terms of perception.[22] Yet by breathing new life into the postulate, Lucy's work has once again opened the field to new studies exploring the various cognitive effects and behavioral implications of linguistic categories. Stephen Levinson and his associates at the Max Planck Institute for Psycholinguistics have recently demonstrated parallel "Whorfian effects" in many other cognitive domains, most dramatically in the realm of spatial cognition (see chapter 3). In this setting, my own study is the first to investigate the cognitive implications of linguistic diversity within a single culture area, a classic but unresolved problem that Lucy points out in his study (1992a:85–88).

THE RELATION OF LANGUAGE TO CULTURE:
AN APPARENT WHORFIAN PARADOX

The same figures who transplanted the legacy of linguistic relativity from Europe to North America (namely, Boas, Sapir, and Whorf) also strongly advocated for the parallel principle of cultural relativism. Representing one of the fundamental postulates of the anthropological tradition, they argued that one's entire sense of reality shifts as one passes from one community to the next—something most travelers experience firsthand in the form of "culture shock." In this sense, cultures are regarded as shapers of ideas, laying out those core attitudes and beliefs—or institutions and rites—that every member of a community must come to terms with. While the principle of cultural relativism was taken for granted in these circles, the parallel principle of linguistic relativity probably followed along quietly in its wake, almost without being given a second thought. In fact, the principle of linguistic relativity was probably suggested as something of a corollary to the nearly axiomatic principle of cultural relativism among the early Boasians. Whether or not every member of a group is ever completely in step with the habits and ways of their peers, each participant in the collective social life must ultimately grapple with the considerable intellectual currents that hold sway in their community, a formidable challenge in many parts of the world, wherein each speaker must master an impressive body of oral literature comparable, in many respects, to the Old Testament or the classical mythology of the ancient Greeks.

Here we have stumbled onto a great philosophical quandary that has never been fully resolved, or even adequately addressed, in the now-extensive litera-ture on linguistic and cultural relativism. Simply put, if language truly exerts a pervasive influence on human thought, by lending palpable expression to the images and ideas that regularly pass through the mind, then one would expect languages to fall into close conceptual alignment with those cultural universes that their speakers inhabit.

Yet if language may be said to encapsulate worldview and reflect its cultural subject matter—as the principle of linguistic relativity suggests—then the sharp linguistic diversity of Native northwestern California presents something of a paradox, at least on the surface. Whereas the area's languages are profoundly distinct on structural and semantic grounds, each of the linguistic groups has long shared in a common series of daily social institutions. On the surface, at least, no single, all-encompassing correlation appears to connect the baffling diversity of linguistic and cultural practices that once spread throughout this region. By all appearances, the linguistic and cultural universes are profoundly out of sync with one another.

Several partial solutions apply to the overall problem of this apparent "Whorfian paradox" when the various implications are considered. Suffice it to say that the area's languages may be more closely aligned on the conceptual plane than their surface structures suggest, potentially representing what William Bright has recently called an *ethnolinguistic area* (2005). Yet the potential cognitive implications of these sharp linguistic differences need not be dismissed out of hand. Several types of relationships may develop between languages and their cultures.

The Supposed "Autonomy" of Language and Culture

When the vast distribution of linguistic and cultural traits is surveyed across a range of societies, the most obvious conclusion is that language and culture, as structural systems, are capable of varying independently of one another—at least at the greatest levels of abstraction from the actual circumstances of communication. This is roughly the conclusion reached by Sapir in his most detailed statement on the subject (in his 1921 book, *Language*), where he draws upon the case of the Hupas, Yuroks, and Karuks to illustrate the point that language and culture are "not intrinsically associated" (1921:213–14).[23] Following this traditional line of reasoning, laid down by Sapir almost a century ago, many contemporary linguists see no particular reason to pursue relationships between language and culture.

Just as it is possible for a range of languages to share a common culture or way of life, so, too, is it common for a single language, or family of languages, to spread across a number of otherwise distinctive cultural worlds. Consider the case of the Indo-European family, which, before the time of Christ, had stretched from Ireland to India, at the outer fringes of its total geographical spread, reaching across an enormous range of distinctive culture areas in the intervening territory. Similar patterns, of course, are found on every continent— where a single language family may reach across a number of culture areas or where a single culture area may contain a diversity of languages.

The structural relationships between language, culture, and worldview, as envisioned under this hypothetical model of autonomy, are diagrammed in figure 2.1. Over the generations, speakers of three unrelated languages (L_1–L_3) have adopted many common cultural traits (C_0) as a by-product of long-term social contact and intermarriage. Over time, the speakers of these languages have settled on a common material culture, based on fishing and the acorn harvest, and a common religious orientation, based on a race of prehuman spirit deities said to have established many of the dances still practiced in the region today. As a result, speakers of these three unrelated languages have come to share a similar way of life, without any strict connection between linguistic structure and cultural outlook throughout the region as a whole.

In the form originally suggested by Sapir, the position of autonomy reflects the fact that the variables of language and culture appear to vary fairly independently of one another, when considered on comparative grounds. Yet on a smaller scale, the position does not eliminate the possibility that a separate

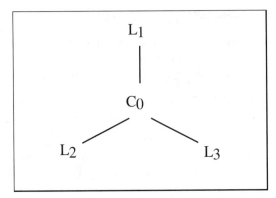

Figure 2.1. Autonomy

relationship may eventually develop in each speech community, as each group develops its own solution to the problem of representing daily cultural concerns in regular habits of speaking. In a practical sense, the minute one opens one's mouth to speak, a perspective must be expressed. If the communication is to be effective, this point of view must resonate with the background assumptions shared by other participants in the exchange, so that one's efforts are not in vain and one's words do not fall on deaf ears. Though not intrinsically associated, language and culture regularly come into alignment in actual exchanges, whereby speakers articulate common assumptions, outlooks, ideologies, or worldviews. Though worldview may not be intrinsic to language in a primordial sense, speakers actively construct worldview in interpersonal terms, or language conveys nothing at all.

Over time, language and culture often come into close alignment with one another, as speakers find new ways to express ideas that are of mutual concern to the participants involved in an exchange. Even a fairly short time span will suffice, as is demonstrated again and again when speakers adopt a new religious outlook, which must be translated into native linguistic concepts, or when new subcultures rise up almost overnight, with radically new perspectives on the common culture. A case in point is the Anglo-Saxon conversion to Christianity during the fifth century C.E., when such key concepts as "altar," "candle," and "creed" were first introduced from Latin and Greek. During the same era, native words took on new meaning, so that *bless* no longer means "to consecrate with blood" and *heaven* no longer means "tent" or "canopy" (Barfield 1985:51). Today, both *bless* and *heaven* have been thoroughly Christianized, even for non-

Christian English speakers, who speak a language profoundly influenced by a Judeo-Christian worldview, regardless of their own personal beliefs. Here the relationship between the English language and Judeo-Christian ideas about life is not an intrinsic one, though eventually the language rose to the occasion.

From this perspective, any language should be capable of representing any worldview, more or less without limit, as seen every day when English is used to convey the competing worldviews of opposing segments of society, such as democrats and republicans or monotheists and atheists. Since the inception of the modern linguistic theory, in the hands of such scholars as Wilhelm von Humboldt and, much later, Noam Chomsky, linguists and philosophers have stressed the creative side of language. Humboldt is famous for arguing that language opens up unlimited expressive horizons to the speaker, regardless of the language being spoken, a point Chomsky later echoed, to great critical acclaim, in the mid-twentieth century. That is, from a limited stock of words and grammatical ideas, the speaker can fashion an almost limitless number of potential sentences, frequently allowing speakers to voice thoughts that may have never been expressed before. Echoing Humboldt, Sapir also argued that language is "nothing short of a finished form of expression for all communicable experience" (1921:220), suggesting that any thought process that occurs to the speaker can ultimately be expressed in any language, in some fashion. Sapir's formulation of this idea became famous: "To put the matter of the formal completeness of speech in somewhat different words, we may say that a language is so constructed that no matter what any speaker of it may desire to communicate, no matter how original or bizarre his idea or his fancy, the language is prepared to do his work. He will never need to create new forms or to force upon his language a new formal orientation—unless, poor man, he is haunted by the form-feeling of another language and is subtly driven to the unconscious distortion of the one speech-system on the analogy of the other" (Sapir 1949:153).

Sapir's stance on the creative potential of language suggests that he never believed that language places any outright limitation on thought, as critics of the Sapir-Whorf hypothesis have suggested as a sort of straw man position (based on little or nothing he actually said). Rather, the speaker works within a creative tradition, wherein one expresses ever-new ideas, provided that certain basic conditions are met. Here Sapir argued that language reserves the potential to guide the speaker's thoughts in certain ways, as the underlying experiences are shaped to meet the conceptual demands of a given tongue, such as grammatical categories that must be expressed in one or another form. To take one familiar example, consider the masculine, feminine, and neuter options that the English language provides, where the referent must be fit into just one of these categories when using a third-person pronoun. Yet because language is creative at heart, every language is free to establish any number of expressive ties with the cultural world of its speakers, much as any event can be captured in an infinite number of potential poems, even in a single language. In this sense, thought processes are free to enter into a range of creative outlets upon finding expression in a given tongue, whether in the novel use of individual speakers or in those regular habits of speaking that typically rise up in surrounding speech communities. Given this creative leeway, there is evidence that each speech community in northwestern California has settled on a unique strategy for representing the daily cultural concerns that have long swept the region.

Linguistic Relativity: The Influence of Language on Culture

As one of the central hallmarks of our species, speech plays a critical role in human life in all societies, where everything from neighborhood gossip to epic storytelling hinges on the existence of a common language that facilitates communication between the members of this group. Here speakers must express their thoughts in terms of the pre-given categories present in the language they choose to speak, whether in terms of its words or grammatical categories. Because these words and grammatical concepts have been provided by past generations, it is difficult for speakers to change the language, rapidly, in synchronic terms. Though speakers are granted considerable creative leeway, they cannot reinvent the language in a single generation. In this way, the conceptual patterns of the language necessarily exert an influence on the form and content of any related cultural expression, however subtle or far-reaching.

Stronger forms of linguistic relativity hold that languages pervasively channel the mental habits of their speakers, wielding an influence over such psychological processes as thought, perception, memory, and even flow of ideas in the process of "silent thinking." As discussed earlier in this chapter, recent experimental studies have confirmed some of these long-standing suspicions about the influence of language on cognition. By contrast, the alternative model of linguistic relativity entertained in this section merely proposes that the regular conceptual patterns of language may exert a far-reaching influence on those surrounding cultural ideas, including storytelling traditions, that are regularly voiced in daily habits of speaking. For hypothetical purposes in the following discussion, the influence of language on cultural expression prevails over any related influences of culture on language. Of course, if this proposition holds true at the level of whole languages, it should also hold true of styles, registers, and dialects within languages, where substantial differences in conceptual patterning are also common.

On linguistic grounds alone, the Native peoples of northwestern California certainly occupied somewhat different conceptual worlds. That is, many of the neighboring village communities spoke utterly different languages, with substantial differences in vocabulary, grammar, and oral literature. Given the scale of this conceptual diversity, it is possible that each language promoted a slightly different sense of the parallel cultural traditions that have long spread throughout the region. In other words, differences in linguistic habit may have actually conditioned some of the surrounding cultural variation that is so widely attested throughout the area's speech communities, whether these differences were present from the outset or emerged within the context of northwestern California. From this perspective, no two languages are ever fully commensurable, detail-to-detail, and translation is always an approximation.

The structural relationships between language and culture as envisioned under this model of linguistic relativity are diagrammed in figure 2.2. Here the conceptual patterns of a given language exert a pervasive influence on the surrounding processes of thought, perception, and any resulting cultural understanding. Though many parallel cultural traditions (C_0) spread throughout this region during traditional times, a distinctive or local sense of worldview eventually takes root in each of the neighboring communities. Here the local sense of worldview rests, in part, on regular differences in linguistic structure (L_1–L_3) and cultural patterning (C_1–C_3). As the local language and culture continue to interact over a great span of time, a distinctive outlook on life eventually emerges among each of the neighboring linguistic groups, all of them representing a separate instantiation of the general culture or worldview otherwise shared by all. In sum, the area was home, during traditional times, to three very different languages (L_1–L_3) and three highly distinctive senses of common culture or worldview (C_1–C_3).

This particular model of linguistic relativity raises the intriguing possibility that subtle traces of former ancestral perspectives may be loosely retained in each of the neighboring languages. The force of linguistic habit is strong, often preserving core structural traits or characteristic semantic tendencies for enormous stretches of time, even for many thousands of years.[24] In this sense,

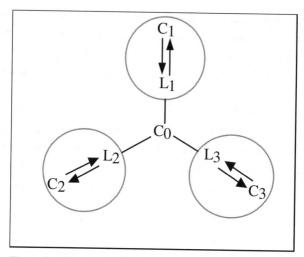

Figure 2.2. Linguistic relativity

each group may have lingering traces of an ancient ancestral outlook, inherited from each of the respective source stocks. Some of these traits may have undergone intensification in northwestern California through a process of linguistic purism, in which speakers strive to maintain separate identities by asserting their differences on the plane of language. Yet other tendencies may represent vestiges of former ancestral perspectives carried over from the outside source stocks.

Action focus, for instance, reaches a great height in the Hupa language, in which many nouns have been replaced, over the generations, with complex nouns of action that assign "names" to things based on related activities.[25] However commonplace within its Athabaskan source stock, this characteristic trait has been carried to an unusual extreme among the Hupas. Consider, for instance, the old Athabaskan word for "rain," which can be reconstructed in the form of the original root *k^yan. In Hupa today, the sole surviving reflex of this root occurs in the expression for a "thunderstorm," $k^yaŋ$-kyoh, in which the augmentative marker -kyoh contributes the sense that the reference was once to a "big rain" (Sapir 1949:80–81). Over time, this root has been replaced with the form na·nyay in modern Hupa, an explicit noun of action that refers to the force of nature "that comes down (from above)." Spatial orientation, in contrast, reaches a great height among Karuk speakers, for whom dozens of directional concepts are differentiated with regular grammatical categories and many common nouns portray spatial features of the objects they designate.

Yurok speakers participate less than their neighbors in either of these competing semantic trends. In Yurok, water-based directional concepts are highly refined in the semantic structures of the verb paradigm, perhaps in part reflecting the Yuroks' deep ancestral ties with the world of fishing and water-related activities (see Proulx 1985b).

Cultural Relativism: The Influence of Culture on Linguistic Practice

Speech is everywhere guided by cultural conventions, which are often as strict as the grammatical rules provided in language. That is, as speech habits take root under the guiding influence of culture, the attitudes and beliefs shared within this community often become crystallized in the group's regular habits of speaking. The prevailing conceptual concerns, regularly voiced within a community, often exert a pervasive influence on the form and content of the language. Over time, every language necessarily absorbs some of cultural concepts held by its speakers, who draw upon the resources of this language to voice their thoughts on a daily basis. From this perspective, many differences in linguistic habit can be traced back to those cultural rifts that typically rise up among speech communities. These cultural premises may eventually become embedded on a number of levels, including the realms of vocabulary, grammatical categories, and narrative texts.

The Hupas and Karuks, for instance, both attribute a similar episode to a bird known in English as the dipper or water ouzel. Both agree that this animal was a terrible father long ago in the ancient past. And both agree that this bird was to receive an eternity of punishment for these actions (not unlike the plight of Sisyphus in Greek mythology). Where the groups begin to depart is in the punch line of the story: according to the Hupas, he is condemned to having sex with stones, while the Karuks maintain that he will have to suck moss from the floors of rivers for all eternity. This minor cultural difference, which occurs primarily on the plane of oral literature, is, in turn, reflected in the structure of the area's vocabularies: in Hupa, the name for the dipper is glossed as 'the-one-who-copulates-with-stones'; in Karuk, the same bird is given a different name, glossed as 'the-little-one-who-eats-river-moss'. Both stories are succinctly encapsulated in vocabulary, creating a linguistic difference that reflects a larger cultural rift or split. As I elaborate in coming chapters, the common culture of this region is often profoundly fragmented on the local level, with subtle schisms spreading across almost every area of social patterning, ultimately encompassing everything from myth to folklore and cosmology.

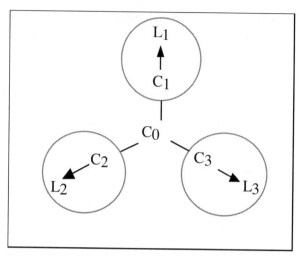

Figure 2.3. Cultural relativism

The structural relationships between language, culture, and worldview, as envisioned under this contrasting model of cultural relativism, are diagrammed in figure 2.3. Common elements of the regional cultural traditions (C_0) receive separate elaboration in each of the neighboring speech communities. As a consequence, distinctive elements of the local cultural life (C_1–C_3) are secondarily absorbed by each of the neighboring linguistic traditions (L_1–L_3). Over time, each language becomes a repository for those distinctive conceptual concerns that rise up in each of the neighboring speech communities. Eventually, these subtle differences in worldview are integrated into the semantic structure of the languages, including word meanings, grammatical categories, storytelling traditions, and even folkloric expressions, such as sayings or aphorisms.

Many of the subtle differences in linguistic habit found throughout northwestern California indeed have roots in divergent readings of shared cultural motifs. That is, some linguistic differences can ultimately be traced to nonlinguistic sources that are only secondarily reflected in language. However widespread, many of the common episodes in the folklore and mythology of this region shift in detail and arrangement as one passes from one community to the next. Sometimes the gender of a character switches from male to female as the story passes from village to village. In other cases, the religious status of an actor undergoes an inversion from sacred to profane. These minor cultural differences, or consistent choices of interpretation espoused by neighboring speech communities, are then secondarily reflected in the oral literature and vocabulary of the various linguistic traditions.

THE CONTINUING DEBATE ON LINGUISTIC RELATIVITY

The place of language in the mental life of our species has long been debated, especially among those who take the scope of human diversity as their primary theoretical concern, including anthropologists, linguists, and philosophers. Centuries of scholarship on the subject have produced many extreme and often contrary positions, leaving much of the problem unresolved to this day. Indeed, the concept of linguistic relativity remains one of the most hotly debated topics in all of anthropology, with many active and rabid rivalries on both sides of the debate. Despite the range of theoretical positions,[26] nearly all who have commented on this perplexing topic have acknowledged that there are indeed differences, some profound and others minute, in linguistic structure, cultural outlook, and psychological orientation among the human societies attested in the anthropological record.

Some have proposed that language plays a pivotal role in the very functioning of the human mind, hinging to some extent on the regular conceptual patterning of specific linguistic systems. Here the reference is to the tradition of linguistic relativity, first introduced by Humboldt during the 1830s. Sapir, who certainly read Humboldt as a student, is famous for speculating that language exerts a subtle influence on the process of thinking, as words and images pass through the mind, even when silently contemplating (1921:14–17). Humboldt, for his part, regarded language as an organ of thought, reasoning that the structure and semantics of one's native tongue may exert an influence on perception and imagination, even as he maintained a keen interest in universals that he considered true for all languages (1988 [1836]). Other philosophers before Humboldt, such as Herder, argued that language is an inherited stream of words and images passed down over the generations, like a massive poem, composed by whole speech communities through an ongoing creative process. Each year, new evidence in support of linguistic relativity continues to pour in from scholars all around the world. Lucy's work (1992a, 1992b) has demonstrated that grammatical categories exert an unconscious influence on mental processes. Gumperz and Levinson (1996) have offered a nuanced reassessment of linguistic relativity especially sensitive to universals, as suggested in Humboldt's original plan of research. For a more recent survey of original research on the topic, see Gentner and Goldin-Meadow 2003.

Others have contended that speech is merely an epiphenomenon appearing on the surface of a generalized psychology whose features hold relatively constant for all people. Here the reference is to the contemporaneous tradition of "universal grammar," which was also introduced by Humboldt in the nineteenth century, with roots in the Port Royal Grammar, the rationalist philosophy of Leibniz, and even Platonic idealism.[27] What this downplays is the staggering diversity of the world's languages, which are far from mutually intelligible and surprisingly diverse in conceptual content and grammatical structure, as the following pages attest. Interestingly, Whorf did not see universals as a challenge to relativism; indeed, he suggested many universals in his writing. As is the case with Einstein's theory of physical relativity, theories of linguistic and cultural relativism only refine our sense of the accompanying "constants" in the universe of human experience. Of course, in Humboldt's original conception, these universals merely allow us to calibrate the differences, as separate instantiations of widespread tendencies in human thought, culture, or grammar.

Part II

The Spatial World

3

Geographical Spatial Orientation

[P]robably the apprehension of space is given in substantially the same form by experience irrespective of language. The experiments of the Gestalt psychologists with visual perception seem to establish this fact. But the concept of space will vary somewhat with language, because, as an intellectual tool, it is so closely linked with the concomitant employment of other intellectual tools, of the order of "time" and "matter," which are linguistically conditioned.

Benjamin Lee Whorf, Language, Thought, and Reality

As Whorf hints in the above epigraph, many early speculations regarding the presumably universal foundations of human spatial cognition took an egocentric frame of reference largely for granted. From this familiar framework, the subject adjusts to the space by projecting the spatial categories of his or her body outward into the surrounding world, as may be illustrated, for instance, with the common English terms *left, right, front,* and *back*. Perhaps because these categories of thought are found in many European tongues, even Whorf appears to assume that this bodily based frame of reference is shared by all of humanity. Yet the anthropological record suggests otherwise. Far from representing a universal psychological orientation, some constant in human experience, this bodily sense of space instead represents just one of several available systems for thinking about the surrounding spatial world, as recent research in anthropological linguistics has revealed. Indeed, even in English, several alternative frames of reference are available.

COMMON SYSTEM OF SPATIAL COORDINATES

The Yurok, and with them their neighbors, know no cardinal directions, but think in terms of the flow of water. . . . If a Yurok says "east" he regards this as an English word for upstream, or whatever may be the run of the water where he is.

A. L. Kroeber, Handbook of the Indians of California

As Kroeber noted in the early twentieth century, many of the Native languages of northwestern California subscribe to a pervasively geographical sense of the surrounding spatial world.[1] From this contrasting frame of reference, most concepts based on the spatial geometry of the human figure hold little place in everyday vocabulary or communicative practice, a pattern that continues today, even following the shift to English.[2] Instead, mountains and rivers act as the primary points of reference for establishing spatial relationships in the surrounding world of everyday experience, rooting spatial thought, in a pervasive way, in these prominent and unmistakable features of the local geography.

The geography of northwestern California is fraught with countless mountainous peaks, rising, often dramatically, from the floors of an almost endless succession of river-bearing valleys below. Flat expanses, by contrast, are not common, and even where present for the briefest of stretches, any small plot of level earth is usually divided by rivers and utterly surrounded by mountains. Owing to the invariably dry conditions found in the high mountain country, traditional villages were virtually never found anywhere near their steep slopes. Yet people did sometimes journey to their peaks to receive specialized religious training or travel along their faces, via trails, to get to distant villages located on the other side. In popular folklore, terrible giants are sometimes said to inhabit this remote mountain country.

From any given point along the slope of a mountain, two opposing directional paths are routinely distinguished in the area's languages. While one faces "up" this slope and "away" from the river, the other category points "down" this incline "toward" the riverbed below. Generally speaking, these contrasting concepts can be faithfully translated as "uphill" versus "downhill." Yet, in a sense, these slope-based categories also partially refer to the rivers, so that a path that leads "uphill" also travels "away from the river," while a path that heads "downhill" also leads "toward the river." These slope-based categories can be projected from either side of a river, to the steep mountain inclines that typically rise up on both sides (see figure 3.1). That is, from one side of a river, one trajectory points "uphill" to the mountain above that bank; from the other side of the river, still another trajectory points to the mountain "uphill" from this opposite shore. These two "uphill" trajectories are about 180 degrees apart, each one referring to a different slope above one of the two opposing riverbanks.

Similarly, at the base of every mountain are a number of streams, creeks, and springs of various capacities. During traditional times, human life utterly revolved around these watercourses, which explains the near-total absence of any regular human presence beyond walking distance from the rivers. Animals, too, regularly flock to these rivers, whether to drink, swim, or feed on the abundance of life-forms that thrive there. As a consequence, few of the major villages, or even the minor ones, for that matter, are found along the slopes of the mountains; instead, nearly all of them have traditionally been located along the area's many rivers. In this sense, the Native peoples of northwestern California can be described as profoundly riparian in their general orientation to life, a fact that is duly reflected in the semantic content of all of the area's languages.

From any given point along a river, still another series of directional possibilities can be identified in the area's languages. While one of these opposing directions faces "downward" into the flow of water, the other faces "upward" against the current. Generally speaking, these concepts can be faithfully translated as "upriver" versus "downriver," as they derive their sense, fairly transparently, from the directional flow of river currents. Note that this pair of paths is almost perfectly perpendicular to the complementary set of courses projected from the mountains nearby. In other words, "upstream" and "downstream" are almost exactly 90 degrees apart from "uphill" and "downhill," as illustrated in figure 3.1. Relative to this set of current-based categories, still another trajectory can be established, one that faces "across the stream" and perpendicular to the water flow, whether projected from the river's center or from the shoreline nearby.

As a system of interlocking categories, these geographical spatial concepts take the shape of a rotating grid of interrelated directional coordinates. A small circle in the center of the diagram represents a crucial "point of origin," which can be momentarily fixed anywhere along the flow of a river. As a consequence, these geographical directional concepts are all highly general in meaning, without referring to any particular river, mountain, or fixed directional region.

Depending on where the speaker fixes the "floating" point of origin, this system of interlocking directional coordinates can be situated almost anywhere in the surrounding territory. So, for instance, "upstream" may loosely correspond to the compass point southeast at one point along the course of the

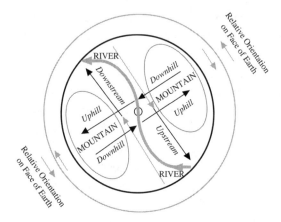

Figure 3.1. Common system of spatial orientation reflected in the Hupa, Yurok, and Karuk languages

river, whereas at the next bend, "upstream" may suddenly correspond to south. Of course, depending on where one is standing, "upstream" could also briefly correspond to nearly any other point on the compass.

STATUS OF NONGEOGRAPHICAL SPATIAL CONCEPTS

The degree to which the Native speech is affected by this manner of thought is remarkable. A house has a door not at its "western" but its "downstream" corner. A man is told to pick up a thing that lies upstream from him, not on his "left."

A. L. Kroeber, Handbook of the Indians of California

Yurok speakers strongly favor spatial concepts that have their roots in the surrounding geography. That is, speakers generally prefer geographical concepts to nearly all other systems of directional reference. An object, for instance, is often situated either "upriver" or "downriver" from an established position in the immediate environment, though rarely in relation to the speaker's "right" or "left." From this pervasively geographical perspective, the speaker is forced to adjust to his or her place within the immediate environment, noting the location of objects as they are positioned with respect to the local mountains and rivers.

Most competing systems of spatial reference, including those based on the fixed points of the compass or spatial geometry of the human figure, hold little place in the Native languages of northwestern California. Indeed, even when present, most of these nongeographical concepts are relegated to a place of little use and rarely characterize the position of objects in the surrounding world.

The Spatial Geometry of the Human Body

Certainly, terms for the sides of the body can be easily identified in each of the area's languages. Yet these concepts are primarily used to distinguish between the hands or, by extension, the "right" and "left" sides of the body. Beyond the scope of human frame, the concepts of "left" and "right" are rarely extended any farther into the surrounding world. That is, unlike their geographical counterparts, which are applied to a wide range of situations, the terms for the "left" and "right" hands are usually restricted either to the body itself, or to the immediate environment alongside it. Even the body is sometimes conceptualized in terms of geographical concepts, with the area around the waist, for instance, sometimes separating an "uphill" region from another one "downhill."[3]

Among the Hupas and Yuroks, the names for the hands are cast in evaluative terms, with expressions that literally refer to the "good" and the "bad" sides of the body. Here the reference, at least in an etymological sense, is simply to the unequal dexterity of the hands. Among Hupa speakers, for instance, the right side of the body is known simply as "the good side," or *niWon-č'iŋʔ*, an expression that is based on the stem *-Woˑn*,[4] which, together with the prefix *ni-* before it, forms a verb of condition referring to the ongoing condition of being "good" or "pleasing." The directional marker *-č'iŋʔ*, at the end of the form, signals that the reference is to a region that lies "toward such a place." As a unit, the expression refers to that side of the body that is "good," "pleasing," or in this case, more "dexterous." According to this formula, the right hand is known as "the hand on one's good side," or *niWon-č'iŋʔ-xolaʔ*, as Hupa speakers call it. Here the noun form *xolaʔ* refers to "someone's hand," while the directional phrase *niWon-ʔ-č'iŋʔ* indicates that it is the one "(on) the good side."[5]

By the same token, the "left" hand is situated on the "poor side" of the body, as reflected in the Hupa expression *nič*ʷ*inʔ-č'iŋʔ*. This descriptive term is based on the verb stem *-č*ʷ*inʔ*, which, together with the prefix *ni-* before it, forms a verb of condition that refers to the state of being "bad," "displeasing," or "ugly." Here the directional marker *-č'iŋʔ* then adds the meaning "toward such a place," while the expression as a whole refers to the side of the body that is "bad," "poor," or in this case, simply less "dexterous." In this setting, the left hand is known as "the hand on one's bad side," or *nič*ʷ*in-č'iŋʔ-xolaʔ*, as Hupa speakers usually put it. Here the noun form *xolaʔ* refers to "one's hand," while the directional phrase *nič*ʷ*inʔ-č'iŋʔ* indicates that it is the one "(on) the bad side."

In practice, speakers use these phrases to refer either to the hands or, by extension, to an entire side of the body. When speaking of the right side of a person's body, one might say, *niWon-č'iŋʔ* '(on) one's right side' *xok*ʸ*aŋʔay* '(of) one's body' *č'itiłiw* '(someone) smeared (paint) along'. Here the reference is to the smearing of paint alongside the right side of the recipient's body in a ceremonial context. Note that the spatial reference does not extend beyond the scope of the subject's body.

The equivalent terms in Yurok are *-nekomewet* and *-kesomewet*, two inalienable nouns that refer to "good side" and "bad side" of the body, respectively. Etymologically speaking, the term for the "right" side is based on the element *nekom-*, an initial that occurs in many forms referring to the skillful performance of an act, as reflected in the related verb stem *nekomeweks-*, which means "to be clever," or the stem *nekomur-*, which means "to swim well." In the related noun stem *nekomuy*, the reference is to "ability." In a similar fashion, the term for the "left" side of the body is based on the element *kesom-*, a stem-initial that generally occurs in forms that refer to "bad" or "poor" states of existence, as reflected in the related verb stem *kesomeweł-*, which means "to be homesick," or in the stem *kesomewep-*, which means "to be lonely." In the case of the related noun *kesomuy*, the reference is either to the "state of death" or the "corpse" that accompanies it. Both terms also contain the medial *-etew*, an element that is generally associated with the action of the hands, occurring, for instance, in the verb *mewoletew-* 'to wipe one's hands' or in the noun *ceyketew* 'little finger'.

Karuk speakers also assign separate labels to the two hands, with the term *kútukuk* corresponding to the "left hand" and *yáastiik* to the "right hand." There is no evidence that these terms are projected outward into the surrounding spatial world. Instead, their use is restricted to the body. Yet, to reverse the picture, the body is sometimes conceptualized in geographical terms. A case in point is the Karuk directional term *sáruk*, which generally translates as "some distance downhill." However, in a secondary and somewhat metaphorical sense, this term is also capable of referring to the lower reaches of the human body (see Bright 1957:377).

Terms for the "front" and "back" of the body are, however, projected slightly farther into the surrounding world, where they provide an alternative frame of reference rooted not in the landscape but in the geometry of the human figure.

These terms are generally used to highlight the presence of an animal or person in the environment, though not as a default strategy for establishing spatial relationships in general. Beyond the area around this creature, spatial concepts stemming from the landscape are preferred.

Some of these concepts derive their sense from actual body parts, representing direct spatial projections from the body out into the surrounding world. A case in point is the Karuk term *ʔáavkam,* which refers to the space in front of something. Etymologically, this expression is based on the noun root *ʔáav,* which refers to the "face." By combining with the spatial modifier *-kam,* which suggests just one "side" of a more complex object, the reference is to the region that extends out from "the face side" of an animal or person. Over time, the expression has taken on a more abstract meaning. That is, though the concept derives its sense from the "face side" of an animal or person, eventually its spatial sense has been extended outward for a distance into the surrounding environment, to encompass the creature's entire field of vision.

For comparison, consider the similar Hupa expression *xoǯeˑʔ-xʷ,* which also refers to the space in front of a living being, usually an animal or a person. This expression is based on the inalienable noun *-ǯeˑʔ,* here occurring with the third-person possessive marker *xo-* to form an expression that refers to "something's breast." With the locative marker *-xʷ,* the reference is extended to the general area that surrounds this being. Literally, the expression refers to the general region around the "breast" of an animal or person, though, over time, the meaning has become more abstract. Today, the expression refers to the entire region that reaches out from "the breast" into the surrounding environment.

In a similar fashion, several Hupa expressions for the area "in front of something" derive their sense from a root that refers to the "eye." A case in point is the expression *xonaˑɬ,* which loosely translates as "in one's presence." At the core of the expression is the noun root *naˑ,* which refers to the "eyes." The expression also contains the spatial marker *-ɬ,* which refers to the close proximity of two things: the "eye" and the region enclosed by its implicit field of vision. The third-person possessive marker *xo-* establishes this "field of vision" relative to a specific living being. Or consider the related form *naˑceh,* which generally translates as "ahead of others." In addition to the noun stem *naˑ* 'eye', this compound form contains the root *ceˑ,* which designates the "head." When the two elements combine, the reference is to the region that stretches out "in front of" a living being, reaching from its "head" outward into its entire field of vision, as suggested by the presence of the root for "eye."

Certainly some nongeographical concepts are present in each of the area's languages. Yet because of the strong preference for geographical concepts, the body rarely serves as a general frame of reference for assessing spatial relationships in the surrounding world. As shown in the preceding examples, spatial concepts rooted in the geometry of the human figure are normally restricted to the immediate environment alongside the body, without receiving any widespread extension into the surrounding spatial world.

Fixed Compass Points

In the Native languages of northwestern California, the cardinal points of the compass also hold little place in the conceptual flow of everyday speech. Through sheer coincidence, however, these geographical directional concepts sometimes briefly correspond to the north, south, east, or west of the compass. Yet because the underlying geographical concepts are not fixed, the next bend in the river or shift in the surrounding mountain terrain quickly obliterates this purely accidental correspondence.

Among the Hupas, for instance, the points of the compass are sometimes approximated through reference to purely geographical concepts. Hupa speakers introduce a series of paths exactly halfway between the categories based on mountains and rivers, which, as seen in figure 3.2, occur at natural right angles. The resulting series of subcategories is highly refined. So, for instance, because "uphill" and "downstream" are 90 degrees apart, the halfway point, created by combining the terms, adds still another trajectory to the total set of directional possibilities. From the four primary spatial concepts, a total of eight interlocking directional categories can be derived, each of them 45 degrees apart.

Each directional category is calculated by fixing the reference at a specific site along the eastern bank of the Trinity River as it flows, on a roughly northwesterly course, through the upper end of Hoopa Valley. This point of origin is established with the phrase *de-noho*, an expression that translates as "here with us." From this well-known point of origin, the directional path that is midway between "downstream" and "uphill," which here corresponds to the compass point north, is referred to by the phrase *yide?i-yidaɢ*. In a similar fashion, the phrase *yinaɢi-yice?n* refers to a directional course midway between "upstream" and "downhill," here loosely corresponding to the compass point south. From the same location, east is reckoned as a path midway between "upstream" and "uphill," as reflected in the phrase *yinaɢi-yidaɢ*. Finally, west can be calculated

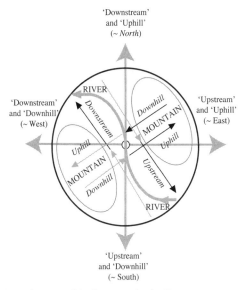

Figure 3.2. Projection of geographical categories in Hupa

as a directional path midway between "downstream" and "downhill," as reflected in the phrase *yideʔi-yiceʔn*.

From another point of view, the concepts of "east" and "west" can be derived from reference to the "rising" or "setting" of the sun over the neighboring mountains. In the Karuk language, the east is known as *várupravakam*, "the side through which (the sun) comes (up)." Based on the general verb of going *va-*, this expression also contains the directional modifier *-rúpra(v)*, which usually refers to motion through solids, such as the sprouting of a shoot through the soil. The following suffix *-a* then creates an abstract noun referring to the act of "going through a solid," while the spatial marker *-kam* transforms the entire expression into an elaborate spatial adverb by contributing the sense that this event is located "at such a side." The original reference, implicit in etymology, is probably to the rising of the sun through the "solid mass" of mountainside to the east.

In a similar fashion, west is known among the Karuks as *vákurihakam*, "the side where (the sun) goes into the water." This parallel expression features the contrasting directional modifier *-kúrih*, which generally refers to the process of sinking into a body of water. Here the allusion is probably to the sun "sinking" into the ocean. As I discuss in chapter 5, the ocean was thought to be similar to a river in many respects, swirling constantly around the edges of the earth.

Among the Hupas, concepts of "east" and "west" similarly derive their sense from the motion of the sun over the neighboring mountains. In Hupa, the east is known as *xaʼsinahW-diŋ*, "the place where (the sun) goes uphill." Based on the third-person form of the singular verb of motion (*-naʼW*), the reference here is restricted by the directional marker *xaʼ=s(i)-* to motion that "rises up to the top of a slope." Meanwhile, the locative marker *-diŋ* converts the entire expression into a noun phrase that refers to a region where such an event occurs, namely, in the land of the "east." Similarly, the west is known as "the place where (the sun) goes downhill," based on the expression *xodaʼnahW-diŋ*. Here the directional modifier *xo-daʼ=* signals motion that travels "downhill."

The concepts of "east" and "west" do not hold any great conceptual significance in Hupa or Karuk, for they are derived through circumlocution. Instead, these notions are secondary concepts that rarely enter into everyday directional use.

For the Yuroks, in contrast, some of the neighboring mountains and rivers do correspond to actual compass points, at least within the coastal portion of their homeland. A case in point is the initial element *wohp-*, which enters into a series of directional adverbs, including *wohpekʷ*, *wohpew*, and *wohpewk*, all loosely translating "across the sea." Though the primary reference is to the water, these terms through sheer coincidence also correspond to the compass point west.

Similarly, the initial *pur-*, which refers to spatial paths bearing down along the coast toward the mouth of the Klamath river, also yields a series of directional adverbs, including *pur* and *pureyow*, as well as their demonstrative counterparts *hipur* and *hipureyow*. All of these loosely translate as "north." Yet the primary reference is to the flow of water along the coast toward the mouth of the Klamath, not to an abstract directional path that holds constant throughout the region. (Here it is also important to note that the ocean was conceived of as a river flowing clockwise around a disc-shaped earth, with north corresponding to a downstream flow along this stretch of the coast.) In a similar sense, a related set of directional terms, whose reference is to the "south," probably derive their sense from the opposing path, the one heading upstream along the coast, away from the mouth of the Klamath. This series includes the near equivalents *pɹwɹh*, *pɹwɹw*, *pɹwɹy*, and *pɹwɹʔkuk*, all of them loosely translating as "south."[6]

Though "east" is not a primary term in Yurok, it can be derived, secondarily, through a process of circumlocution. Consider the phrase *ku ho kyegah*, which refers to that direction "where the sun continually rises." This expression is composed of three elements. The first, *ku,* is an article referring, by implication, to a specific directional region. The second, *ho,* is a preposition meaning "to" or "toward," here with reference to the following element, which signals "the sun." The final element, *kyegah,* is the intensive form of the verb *kyah,* which is formed by introducing the infix *-eg-,* shifting the form to *kyegah.* Though the verb normally means "to rise," the intensive infix shifts the meaning to "repeatedly rising."

GEOGRAPHICAL ORIENTATION AND
ITS COGNITIVE IMPLICATIONS

Given the rugged nature of the local geography, it is not surprising that mountains and rivers figure so prominently in the conceptual geometry of spatial reference. In fact, in this type of steep mountain terrain, geographical orientation provides a fairly sensible means of coping with a potentially confusing physical environment. To some extent, the speakers of the Hupa, Yurok, and Karuk languages have adjusted, fairly pragmatically, to an especially rugged physical world, where mountains and rivers provide the most salient markers of spatial relations. Speakers of these three languages take their cues from the most salient directional landmarks in the area, the local mountains and rivers, which shift course every couple hundred yards, potentially conflicting with any attempt to stay on a fixed course, such as north or south. Even if one were to head east toward the morning sun or west toward the sunset, no particular landmark would keep the traveler on a fixed course for the rest of the day as the sun begins to change its position in the sky. For this reason, following a river or well-known trail, however sinuous its course, is easier. Fortunately, as the myth figures often note in creation stories, the river flows only one way! In a similar way, the traveler always knows exactly where a trail leads, even if it twists and turns along a fairly unpredictably course.

Of course, similar systems of geographical reference occur elsewhere in the world, though they do not always take on exactly the same sense they have acquired in northwestern California. In less-rugged terrain, categories such as "uphill" and "downstream" often take on constant meaning, rather than the shifting sense found among the Native peoples of northwestern California. In these constant directional systems, geographical concepts such as "upstream" and "downstream" refer to a single set of paths whose bearings hold fairly constant throughout the territory, following the general lay of the land. In a similar fashion, concepts such as "uphill" and "downhill" do not shift their bearing as one passes from one site to the next but hold roughly constant throughout the territory, like the mountain slopes themselves. Penelope Brown and Stephen Levinson (1993) describe one such system among the Tenejapa Tzeltal speakers of southern Mexico, in which "uphill" roughly corresponds to the southeast and "downhill" to the northwest, following the nature of the geography. The mountains of northwestern California are far too numerous and too variable in directional status to allow any such constant system of spatial reckoning.[7]

However, even under similar conditions, other types of directional systems are sometimes equally effective, showing that geographical orientation is not always a simple response to the local environment. Consider, for instance, the cardinal points of the compass, which also provide a sensible means of coping with unpredictable landscape, as long as the speaker can maintain a constant sense of the absolute directional bearing. A case in point is the Guugu Yimidhirr language of northern Queensland, Australia, where speakers regularly confront a highly varied terrain that includes bogs, swamps, sand dunes, rivers, and even some mountains.[8] Rather than basing their directional system on prominent landmarks, such as mountains and rivers, the speakers of the Guugu Yimidhirr language eventually settled on a system of fixed directional points that roughly correspond to English "north," "south," "east," and "west." According to Levinson, every directional path in the language is expressed in cardinal terms, so every-thing from a rock on the ground to a trip across the swamp must be stated strictly in terms of the compass points. For the Guugu Yimidhirr, relative ego-centric terms, such as "left" and "right," are not normally used when speaking the language. Nor do Guugu Yimidhirr speakers take their cue from prominent landmarks in the surrounding countryside, having settled on a more abstract system of constant directional concepts.

Each type of directional system holds far-reaching implications for non-linguistic thought, potentially affecting the speaker's performance far outside the realm of verbal communication. Recently, Levinson (1992) has shown that speakers import these general categories to a range of nonlinguistic situations, such as remembering the orientation of objects in relation to a particular frame of reference, either absolute or relative. Dutch speakers, for instance, tend to orient objects relative to their own bodies, following, in turn, the dominant directional categories of the language. Thus, when asked to remember the orientation of, say, two objects on a table, Dutch speakers tend to remember the orientation relative to their own bodies, not in relation to absolute compass points. If the same table is then rotated 180 degrees and the speaker faces it from the same side as before, the subject would recognize it as the same set, relative to one's body. For Guugu Yimidhirr speakers, by contrast, the configuration has changed as the table is turned, because the object that once faced "east" now faces "west," even if it is in the same place relative to the subject's body, such as the speaker's "right." In these studies, which were conducted by the Max Planck Institute for Psycholinguistics in the 1990s, 100 percent of the Dutch speakers oriented the objects along a left–right axis, while 90 percent of the Guugu Yimidhirr subjects remembered the absolute orientation according to the compass points. The studies suggest that the force of linguistic habit is strong, conditioning performance even on explicitly nonlinguistic tasks.

Though of diverse origins, the Native languages of northwestern California have settled on a common geographical orientation to the world, wherein mountains and rivers provide the primary points of reference for identifying spatial relationships in the surrounding universe. In this setting, concepts such as "upriver" versus "downriver" and "uphill" versus "downhill" provide the primary framework for adjusting to space, an orientation that is pervasively reflected in the vocabularies and grammatical structures of the Hupa, Yurok, and Karuk languages. Yet, contrary to early models of human spatial cognition, most concepts stemming from the geometry of the human figure among speakers of these northwestern California languages are relegated to a place of little use, all but eliminating concepts such as "left" versus "right" and "front" versus "back" as general directional categories. To a considerable extent, this shared geographical orientation reflects a fairly pragmatic adjustment to the rugged nature of the local landscape. As I discuss in coming chapters, this shared orientation to the spatial world holds broad implications for religious life as well.

4

Linguistic Systems of Spatial Reference

To the English speaker, one of the most amazing aspects of the grammar of most California languages is how much can be said in a single word. Verbs, especially through processes of affixation, are incredibly rich in meaning. Directional affixes are part of this complex verb structure in many languages. . . . Directional prefixes or directional suffixes take up pages of description in grammars of California languages.

Leanne Hinton, Flutes of Fire

Though the speakers of the Hupa, Yurok, and Karuk languages have settled on a common geographical orientation in referring to the surrounding spatial world, this orientation is reflected in a slightly different fashion in each of the neighboring linguistic traditions. The core geographical concepts, which derive their sense from the mountains and rivers of the surrounding countryside, are most exquisitely reflected in the regular structure of Karuk grammar, in which the directional coordinates are carved into the widest range of subcategories and extended in practice to the widest range of situations. Though possible by means of circumlocution elsewhere in the region, this refinement of spatial reference is less systematic in the other speech communities.[1]

VERBAL PARADIGMS

The Karuk Verb: Symmetry and Precision of Reference

In the semantic structure of the Karuk language, each geographical region is carved into two opposing frames, one heading toward this region as a *goal* and another returning from the region as a *source*. The complementary nature of these opposing paths can be illustrated, from the perspective of a single uphill region, with contrasting phrases such as "heading uphill" versus "coming from uphill." In Karuk grammar, each directional path is marked with a separate suffix, representing a shift in perspective that the speaker must make in order to communicate effectively and, of course, grammatically. A similar distinction applies to river flows, with contrasting suffixes that distinguish paths that "head upstream" from those "come from upstream." However elaborate in Karuk speech, such refinement of reference is not routinely expressed in the neighboring traditions of the Hupa and Yurok languages.[2] Nor do these fine-grained distinctions achieve the same kind of frequency in the oral literature or daily communicative practices among the Hupa and Yurok speech communities. Yet among the Karuks, these subtle geographical distinctions are not only commonplace but also obligatory. Moreover, these subtle directional distinctions also spill over into the specialized terminology of religious language and oral literature among Karuk speakers.

From any given point of reference along a mountain slope or river current, the Karuk speaker must consider four potential spatial paths, in accordance with the basic directional categories presupposed in the structure of the verb. One set derives its sense from the "upper" side of a mountain slope or river current, where the opposing frames "heading into" or "returning from" this region are distinguished. Another set derives its sense from the "lower" side of the slope or flow, where another pair of paths "heading into" and "coming from" this opposite region are differentiated. The full set of categories is illustrated in figure 4.1 (see also Bright 1957:95).

From any given point along the slope of a mountain, the Karuk speaker must distinguish two pairs of potential paths, one pair "above" this reference point and another pair "below" it. Where an object is moving "up" a slope,[3] the speaker must state whether it is "approaching" a point of reference "from downhill" or whether it is moving "away" from this reference point and, therefore, heading still farther "uphill."

Consider a scene in which an animal or person is traveling uphill. Where someone is running uphill and away from an arbitrary point of reference along the slope, a speaker might say *máruk ʔukvíripuraa,* an expression that loosely translates as "one being ran some distance uphill from here." This construction is based on the singular verb of going *ikvirip-,* here occurring with the third-person subject marker *ʔu-* and the directional suffix *-uraa,* which contributes

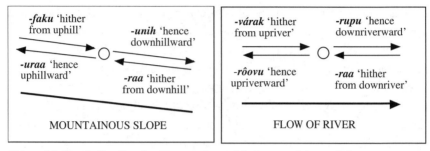

Figure 4.1. Karuk directional suffixes as they relate to mountains and rivers

the meaning "(heading off) someplace uphill from here." The freestanding adverb *máruk* then refines the directional status of the event, indicating that the motion continues for a considerable distance along this uphill course. In the case of people moving uphill "toward" this point of reference rather than "away from" it, the speaker must distinguish this from the previous situation by saying *máruk kunithvíripraa,* which loosely translates as "they ran a great way uphill from someplace downhill." This contrasting expression is based on the dual verb of motion *ithvírip-* and contains the directional suffix *-raa,* which signals that the motion "comes from someplace downhill." Again, the freestanding directional adverb *máruk* indicates that the motion continues along this "uphill" course for a "considerable distance."

Now consider the reverse scenario, in which the motion bears downhill. Again the Karuk speaker is obliged to state whether an object is approaching the point of reference "from" uphill or moving "away" from it and thus heading farther downhill from this arbitrary point. Where a group is running downhill, away from the point of reference established by the speaker, the speaker could say *sáruk kunithvíripunih,* which translates as "they ran a great way downhill from here." This expression is built around the verb of dual motion *ithvírip-,* here with the third-person plural subject marker *kun-* and the directional suffix *-unih,* which contributes the sense that the event "heads someplace downhill from here." The independent directional adverb *sáruk* then refines the directional status of the event, indicating that the motion continues for "a great distance downhill." If, however, a person is moving "downhill" toward the point of reference from someplace uphill, the whole event must be rephrased. Here the speaker could say *sáruk ʔuʔárihfaku,* which translates as "one being ran some way downhill toward here from somewhere uphill."[4] This construction is built around another singular verb of motion, *ʔárih-,* here occurring with the third-person subject marker *ʔu-* and the directional suffix *-faku* '(coming here) from someplace uphill'. Again, the independent directional adverb *sáruk* 'some way downhill' clarifies the overall spatial status of the event, stating that the motion continues along this course for a considerable distance.

From any given point along the river, Karuk grammar distinguishes a similar series of directional paths, one pair "above" this reference point and another "below" it. So, for instance, if an object is traveling up the river, the Karuk speaker must state whether the object is approaching the point of reference "from downstream" or moving away from the reference point and thus heading "farther upstream" beyond the reference.

Consider a situation in which an animal or person is traveling upriver. Where a person is moving upstream, "away" from the arbitrary point of reference established by the speaker, one might say *ʔuʔárihroov,* which loosely translates as "one being went upriver from here." This construction is built up around the third-person form of the singular verb of going, *ʔárih-,* here occurring with the directional suffix *-rôov(u),* translating "(heading) toward someplace upriver." Yet where people are traveling upstream "toward" the point of reference from someplace downstream, one must reconsider the whole situation. Using the proper directional categories, here one says *kunípviitraa,* which translates as "they paddled back here from someplace downriver (heading upriver)." This expression is built around the general verb of conveyance by canoe, *vit,* here with the iterative prefix *íp-,* which adds the meaning "back again." The directional suffix *-raa* then contributes the sense that the event "(comes) from someplace downriver," while the plural marker *kun-* indicates the subject.

Now, consider the reverse scenario, in which the motion bears downstream. Here the Karuk speaker must consider two types of situations, one in which people are "approaching" the point of reference from somewhere upstream and one in which they are "moving away" from it and thus heading farther downstream. When a person is moving "downstream," away from the point of reference, one says *ʔukvíriprup,* which loosely translates as "one being ran downriver from here." This expression is based on the singular verb of going *ikvirip-,* here with the third-person subject marker *ʔu-* and the directional suffix *-rupu,* which contributes the sense that the event "(heads) toward someplace downriver from here." Yet if the body is moving downstream "toward" the point of reference "from someplace upstream," the speaker says *ʔuʔárihvarak,* which loosely translates as

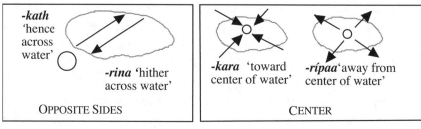

Figure 4.2. Other water-based directional suffixes in Karuk

"one being ran downriver toward here from someplace upriver." This contrasting expression contains the directional suffix *-várak,* which contributes the sense that the event here "(comes) from someplace upriver."

Karuk grammar also distinguishes another series of directional paths when facing out across a body of water toward the opposite shore: one points "toward" the opposite side, while the other heads "away" from the opposite side toward the shore of origin. Here the concepts apply not just to rivers, which have a current, but also to lakes, in which the water is stationary. The first perspective is designated by the suffix *-kath,* translating as "(facing) across the water from a position on this side," while the latter perspective is represented by the opposing suffix *-rina,* translating as "toward a position on this shore from (the distant shore) across the water." Fixing on a point in the middle of the water, two similar frames are regularly differentiated, the first represented by the suffix *-rípaa* 'away from the center of body of water (on a horizontal plane)' and the second by the suffix *-kara* 'toward the center of the water (horizontally)'. The two sets of directional frames that establish spatial relationships relative to bodies of water are illustrated in figure 4.2 (see also Bright 1957:97–101).[5]

As illustrated in the preceding passages, the Karuk language carves the spatial world into an elaborate series of fine-grained directional categories. Here the core geographical concepts that are found throughout the area's speech communities are represented with great symmetry and precision on a regular grammatical basis. To speak the language properly, the Karuk speaker must always state whether a body is "approaching" or "moving away" from any point of reference the speaker might wish to establish along a mountainside or river current. As we shall see in a moment, this is not the case for all of the area's languages. Such refinement of expression, though possible through circumlocution, is not a strict grammatical requirement in many of the area's remaining linguistic traditions.

The Hupa Verb: Lesser Emphasis on Geographical Concepts

In sharp contrast to the situation in the neighboring Karuk language, geographical directional concepts such as "upstream" and "downstream" are only partially woven into the regular semantic structure of the Hupa verb paradigm. As a consequence, the Hupa speaker is not obliged to observe many of the subtle spatial distinctions required of Karuk speakers on an obligatory grammatical basis. For instance, the distinction between the source and goal of motion is not crucial to the construction of well-formed verbs in Hupa, as it is in Karuk— though, through a process of circumlocution, such distinctions are certainly available to Hupa speakers on a nonobligatory basis. Nor is the Hupa speaker required to observe the distinction between motion that travels upstream and motion that travels downstream when forming regular verbs in the language. In sharp contrast to the situation in Karuk, many of these distinctions are not critical to the construction of well-formed verbs in Hupa.

Several prefixes in the Hupa verb system are devoted to motion that travels along the slopes of mountains or, by extension, other types of inclines. Where a living being is headed up a slope, the Hupa speaker might say *xa·ʔasyay*, which loosely translates as "one being has gone to the top of an incline." Here the directional marker *xa·=* signals that the event, as a whole, travels "up" along the face of a slope toward its peak. Depending on the situation, the same form could also apply to any similar type of ascent, whether up a hill, a mountain, or a riverbank. In religious narrative, the same form could also be used to refer to a journey into one of the heavens beyond the horizons. If a person were headed in the opposite direction, however, down toward the base of a slope, the Hupa speaker could say *xohč̓iwinyay*, a variant form of the same paradigm of motion that loosely translates as "one being came down off a ridge" or "one being went down the bank of the river." Here the directional modifier *xoh=* indicates that the event, as a whole, bears in the opposite direction, in this case "down" the slope toward its base. Both of these forms are based on the same paradigm of motion, here signaled in the third person with the special verb stem *-yay*, which contributes the meaning "one thing has gone." The perfective shape of this stem (*-yay*) indicates that the reference is to a single, complete instantiation of the event. Each verb also contains a marker that specifies the time frame from which the event is to be viewed, a requirement that applies to all directional markers upon entering the perfective mode, where the reference is to a single complete occurrence of the event.[6] Consider the form *xa·ʔasyay*, which translates as "one being went up to the top of a slope." This verb features the oblig-atory temporal prefix *s-*, a marker generally associated with forms that portray scenes that continue over an extended period of time. In contrast, consider the previously mentioned *xoh č'iwinyay,* which features the prefix *win-*, usually found in forms that depict events with a rapid or sudden onset. The fact that the "ascent" is associated with the stative time frame may, in part, reflect the difficult nature of the climb, against the force of gravity, whereas the "descent" may be linked with the inceptive time frame because of the relative ease of heading off downhill, with the force of gravity on one's side.

River-based directional concepts, in contrast, are only partially woven into the semantic structure of the Hupa verb paradigm. For instance, in the Hupa language, no special prefix specifies motion that heads "upstream." As a conse-quence, this directional course is not critical to the construction of well-formed verbs in Hupa. On an optional (nonobligatory) basis, however, the Hupa speaker can still refer to motion that bears "upstream" by using a freestanding adverb that specifies the direction of motion outside the verb paradigm (as discussed in the next section, on adverbial systems).

As far as river currents are concerned, only the so-called transverse axis, the one that heads out "across the stream," has entered into the regular fabric of the verb paradigm. When speaking of a living being who is crossing a river, one might say *yima·n na'ninyay,* which translates as "one being went across a river (or flow of water)." Here the directional marker *na·=n(i)-* signals that the event bears out across a stream on a fairly linear course, at a right angle in relation to the river current. This form is built up around the verb stem *-yay,* the perfective form of the singular verb of motion, while the independent adverb *yima·n* clarifies the direction of motion, restating the path "across the river" outside the verb paradigm.

Another directional prefix refers to motion that bears down an incline of some kind, effectively collapsing "downhill" and "downstream" into a single category. Consider the form *xoda'winyay,* which loosely translates as "one being went down an incline." Here the directional modifier *xo-da=* potentially refers to the act of heading down a mountain slope or floating down a river, with the current. In creation stories or prayer, the same form could also refer to trails that one walks while making the descent to the underworld. Again, this form is based on the regular singular verb of motion, here occurring in its perfective configuration, as signaled by the stem *-yay,* alongside a reduced form of the animate third-person prefix *č'i-*, which indicates that a living being (animal or human) occupies the role of subject. This particular directional modifier always occurs with the temporal marker *win-* in perfective forms, a prefix that is usually associated with events that have a rapid or sudden onset.

The Yurok Verb: Minimal Grammaticization of Geographical Elements

The situation is still more extreme in Yurok, for which only a handful of verb stems specify directional motion along mountains and rivers. For Yurok speakers, stating the directional bearing of an event is rarely an obligatory matter, in sharp contrast to the situation in the neighboring Karuk tradition, in which speakers often must state a definite directional path in relation to the surrounding mountains and rivers. Instead, most of the Yurok stems that express geographical directional distinctions occur in relatively fixed, historically derived combinations, rarely entering into the construction of new forms.

Several initial elements signal motion along the slopes of mountains. Consider the initial *sloy-,* which often signals motion that bears "downhill," though in a primary sense the reference is to the act of "sliding along a surface." Another stem internal element, the initial *hoon-,* applies to motion that travels up an incline toward its peak and, secondarily, to paths that bear "upstream." Consider a scene where the speaker is walking down a slope. Here one might say *sloyecoǩ,* a form that loosely translates as "I go downhill." In this construction, the final *-ec* signals the process of going, here occurring in the first-person singular with the inflectional marker *-(o)ǩ.* Or consider a scene where a speaker is carrying a pack down an incline. In this type of situation, one might say *sloyuuleseǩ,* which loosely translates as "I take a load down the hill." Here the medial element *-uul* signals the act of "packing a load," while the inflectional marker *-(e)ǩ* signals that the subject is in the first person. Or consider a situation where a person climbs uphill. Here one could say *hoonecoǩ,* which loosely translates as "I climb, walk uphill."[7] (In another context, the same form could also refer to the act of wading upstream, where it is clear that the reference is to a river.) For mysterious reasons, the initial *hoon-* is far less productive than its downhill counterpart, occurring in relatively fewer forms.

In Yurok, in contrast with the neighboring languages discussed above, only one marker refers exclusively to motion along rivers, namely, the initial *wohp-,* which signals the transverse axis, bearing "across the stream." By far the most common geographical directional element in the stem system, this initial most often enters into scenes of conveyance by canoe. Consider the form *wohpecoǩ,* which loosely translates as "I cross a stream by boat." Here the initial *wohp-* signals the direction of motion, combining with the final *-ec* 'to go', again with the first-person singular inflectional marker (*-eǩ*). The initial *wohp-* also enters into verb stems that refer to the act of traveling by foot. Consider, for example, the form *wohpeyoʔrepeǩ,* which loosely translates as "I wade across the stream."[8] Here the initial *wohp-* combines with the medial *-oʔr,* which here signals the act of "running." Of course, the "upstream" directional course can also be derived from the marker that refers, in its primary sense, to paths that lead "uphill." Where it is obvious that the reference is to a river, not to a mountain, one might say *hoonecek̆,* which means "I go upstream by boat."[9] Here the initial *hoon-* combines with the stem final element *-ec,* again in the first-person singular (*-eǩ*). The one category absent from the Yurok verb paradigm is the "downstream" directional course (rather than the "upstream" trajectory, as is the case in the neighboring Hupa language).

ADVERBIAL SYSTEMS

On a less obligatory basis, freestanding adverbs also allow speakers to state the directional bearing of events, sometimes narrowing the scope of the reference by explicitly signaling an element of relative distance. For Karuk speakers, these adverbs largely complement the spatial concepts marked on the verb by clarifying the relative distance of the directional path, which often goes underspecified by the verb. For Hupa speakers, in contrast, these adverbs allow the speaker to make optional distinctions between the source and goal of motion, with separate categories for events that, for example, "head" toward some region versus those that "come from" some region. However, the element of relative distance, which is fundamental to the structure of the Karuk adverbial system, is not routinely expressed in the Hupa language. For Yurok speakers, however, directional adverbs provide the primary means of marking the geographical bearing of events, since the verb stems only minimally facilitate the expression of concepts such as "upstream" and "downstream." In contrast to the situation in Karuk, the relative distance of a spatial path is not systematically expressed in Yurok, nor is there any regular division into source and goal of motion, as is common in the neighboring Hupa and Karuk languages.

Karuk Directional Adverbs

As discussed earlier in this chapter, many permutations of directional motion can be freely expressed in the Karuk language through the use of verbal

Table 4.1. Karuk geographical adverbs

	Root	Short distance	Long distance
Uphill	*maʔ*	*mâakam*	*máruk*
Downhill	*saʔ-*	*sâakam*	*sáruk*
Upriver	*kaʔ-*	*kâakam*	*káruk*
Downriver	*yuʔ-*	*yûukam*	*yúruk*

suffixes. Within the semantic structure of the Karuk verb, separate grammatical markers are devoted to each of the basic directional regions in the surrounding countryside, even going so far as to allow a regular distinction between the source and goal of motion. The system of independent adverbs subdivides each of the major geographical regions into a series of trajectories that head either "a short" or "a long" way along any particular directional trajectory.

Three degrees of relative distance are regularly expressed in Karuk grammar. Consider the "uphill" directional course, for instance, in which the most general member of the set consists of the adverbial root *maʔ*, which refers to a path that heads "uphill" and, therefore, "away from the river." Though the root is ambiguous as to the distance it expresses, the adverbs *mâakam* and *mâam* signal paths that extend just "a little way" up the slope, while the adverb *máruk* specifies a geographical course that heads "a great distance" uphill. The full system of geographical adverbs is outlined in table 4.1 (see also Bright 1957:83–84).

In practice, Karuk verbs are often accompanied by adverbs that state the relative distance of the directional path. Karuk speakers, as a consequence, are often very precise about the extent of directional motion. Consider, for instance, the word form *ʔukvíripuraa*, which loosely translates as "one being ran uphill." Though ambiguous as to the distance it signals, this construction can always be modified with an independent adverb to state the extent of motion. Where the motion continues over a short distance, one might say *mâam ʔukvíripuraa*, where the adverb *mâam* specifies that the event continues only "a short way up the hill." The construction, as a unit, loosely translates as "one being ran a little way uphill." Yet where the same type of event continues over a greater extent, one might say *máruk ʔukvíripuraa*, which loosely translates as "one being went a great way up the mountainside." Here the adverb *máruk* signals an uphill journey that continues for a "considerable distance."

Similar possibilities exist for each of the remaining directional courses. A case in point is the "upstream" directional course, in which the root *kaʔ-* simply indicates a path that points "upstream." Here the derived form *káruk* specifies that this course continues "a great way" in this direction, whereas the related form *kâakam* signals a path that reaches just "a little way upstream." An indefinite verb form such as *ʔuʔárihroov*, which translates as "one went some way upstream," can be modified with one of several independent adverbs to indicate the relative extent of the journey. Where the event continues for a great distance, one says *káruk ʔuʔárihroov*, which loosely translates as "one went a great way upstream." Yet where the event continues for a shorter stretch, one might say *kâakam ʔuʔárihroov*, which means "one went a little way upstream." To speak of an even longer journey, the special adverb *yiiv* can be used; this indicates a particularly great distance, though without carrying any special geographical significance. When speaking of a distant voyage in the mountains, therefore, one might say *yíiv máruk ʔukvíripuraa*, meaning "one ran an especially great way uphill from here." To apply this type of construction to a trek into the upstream country, one might say *yíiv káruk ʔuʔárihroov*, which means "one went a great way upriver."

Two highly specialized Karuk adverbs refer to imaginary diagonal paths that rest exactly halfway between the neighboring mountains and rivers. Both derive their primary sense from the directional flow of rivers, and both signal an imaginary diagonal course that lies exactly halfway between the two geographical landmarks. Pointing into the flow of the river and turning 45 degrees uphill toward the mountains above produces an imaginary path that rests halfway between "downstream" and "uphill." The Karuk term for this course is *yúrukam*, an adverb based on the directional root *yuʔ*, which signals a region "downstream," here occurring with the suffix *-kam*, which suggests a path that turns "sideways" from this flow toward the mountains above. Facing up against the current and turning 45 degrees uphill toward the mountains above produces still another imaginary path that rests halfway between "upstream" and "uphill." The contrasting term for this path is *károokam*, which signals the imaginary directional course that is both "uphill" and "upriver." This particular form is often contracted as *károom*, which suggests a great frequency of usage.

Hupa Directional Adverbs

In Hupa speech, geographical directional concepts reach their expressive high point in the system of independent adverbs, in which a separate adverbial form is devoted to each of the basic spatial regions in the surrounding countryside. From any given point along a mountain slope, two opposing directional paths can be differentiated, one facing up toward the slope and another down toward the base. Here the adverb *yidaɢ* signals an "uphill" course, while the contrasting adverbial form *yiceʔn* signals paths that lead "downhill." Similarly, from any point along a river, another pair of directional paths can be established, one facing down into the current and another pointing up against the flow of the water. Here the adverb *yinaɢ* signals the "upstream" directional course, while the contrasting form *yideʔ* specifies motion that travels "downstream." The so-called transverse axis is signaled by the adverb *yima·n,* which refers to motion that heads out "across the stream."

Often an adverb alone indicates the directional bearing of an event. Consider a basic verb of motion such as *čitehsyay,* which loosely translates as "one being goes along," without specifying an exact directional path. Though the basic verb is ambiguous as to the path, a series of adverbs can always be added to form a phrase that specifies a definite directional course. Consider the phrase *yideʔ čitehsyay,* in which the adverb *yideʔ* signals that the event, as a whole, travels toward some destination downriver. This construction, as a unit, loosely translates as "one being went downstream." To reverse the scenario, one could say *yinaɢa čitehsyay,* which translates as "one being traveled along upstream." Here the adverb *yinaɢ* indicates that this event, as a whole, travels "upstream." In both cases, the general motion verb *čitehsyay* refers to an event that takes a fairly linear course, while the adverb specifies a precise directional path within the surrounding countryside.

Each geographical region can also be considered from two opposing points of view within the semantic structure of the adverbial system. While one heads toward the region in question as the goal, the other returns from this place as a source. Though the distinction is critical to the construction of well-formed verbs in the Karuk language, the division into source and goal is not obligatory in Hupa. Nor do Hupa speakers exploit the possibility with great regularly—in sharp contrast to Karuk speakers, whose grammar absolutely requires them to make this distinction.

Consider, for instance, the general verb of motion *čitehsyay,* which simply signals an event that takes a roughly linear course, without stating anything further about the directional path. By adding a geographical adverb to the phrase, a number of directional paths can be distinguished. Take, for example, the basic adverb *yinaɢ,* which gives rise to the combining form *yinah.* By combining with an additional directional modifier, two additional phrases can be formed: *yinah-čiŋʔ,* which means "heading toward upstream (as a goal)," and *yinah-čiŋ,* which means "coming from upstream (as a source)."[10] Where a living being heads downstream, one might say *yide?* *č'itehsyay,* a phrase that loosely translates as "one being went along downstream." Yet where the same actor heads downstream from a similar point of reference upstream, a speaker might say *yinah-č'in č'itehsyay,* a contrasting phrase that translates as "one came (downstream) from upstream."

Like their Karuk neighbors, Hupa speakers also recognize a series of diagonal courses that rest halfway between any two geographical landmarks. Because mountains and rivers are situated at natural right angles to each other, the combination of the concepts produces a series of diagonal courses midway between these geographical landmarks. Here the Hupa language offers up a precise fourfold division (in contrast to the situation in Karuk, in which only two such paths are distinguished). Facing "downstream" into the flow of the river while turning 45 degrees "uphill" toward the mountains above produces an imaginary trajectory halfway between these two landmarks. Called *yide?i-yidaG* in Hupa speech, this term refers to a diagonal course that rests halfway between "downstream" and "uphill." In the Hoopa Valley, this is a particular trajectory briefly corresponding to the compass point north at one point at the upper end of the valley, where the river flows on a roughly northeasterly course. Here the "uphill" component of the compound corrects the path by 45 degrees to the west, producing a bearing that heads exactly north. However, the categories of "uphill" and "downhill" are not fixed concepts in Hupa speech, so the combination of these two terms can potentially refer to any point on the compass, depending on where the point of origin is established.

Three additional compound directional concepts are present in Hupa speech. By facing "downstream" into the flow of the river and turning 45 degrees "downhill" away from the river, another imaginary diagonal course can be produced, one that rests halfway between these two landmarks. The Hupas know this diagonal course as *yide?i-yice?n,* a phrase that translates as "downstream and downhill." At the upper end of the Hoopa Valley, this particular trajectory briefly corresponds to the compass point west. Similarly, facing up against the current and veering 45 degrees uphill away from the river produces another imaginary diagonal path that rests halfway between "upstream" and "uphill." The Hupas know this diagonal course as *yinaGi-yidaG,* which translates as "upstream and uphill" and briefly corresponds to the compass point east in the Hoopa Valley. By facing up against the current and turning 45 degrees "downhill" away from the stream, one can produce another diagonal course, which rests halfway between "upstream" and "downhill." The Hupas know this diagonal course as *yinaGi-yice?n,* which translates as "upstream and downhill." At the upper end of the Hoopa Valley, this trajectory briefly corresponds to the compass point south (see figure 3.2).

Though diagonal concepts receive a great emphasis in Hupa speech, it is rare for Hupa speakers to state the relative distance of the directional course. Of course, when pressed, a Hupa speaker can state the relative distance, though for mysterious reasons the distinction is rarely made in actual practice. In particular, two demonstrative elements are available for the purpose of expressing two degrees of relative distance, one referring to a "nearby" region and another to a "far away" place. The terms are *yo·w* and *ye·w,* which translate as "near" and "far," respectively. When speaking of a voyage into the downstream country, one could say *yo·wi yide? čitehsyay,* which translates as "one being went a little way downriver." To indicate a longer journey, one could instead say *ye·wi yide? čitehsyay,* which means "one being went a long way downriver." Though the distinction can be made in the Hupa language, in practice few speakers actually state the relative distance of a directional path. Yet, as can be seen in the previous section, the distinction is a common one in Karuk speech.

Yurok Directional Adverbs

In Yurok speech, as with the Hupa language, geographical concepts reach their expressive high point in the system of independent adverbs, in which each directional region in the surrounding countryside is represented by a series of related adverbs that convey roughly the same meaning. Though Yurok verb stems rarely signal geographical concepts such as "upstream" and "downstream," similar distinctions can be made outside the verb paradigm through the use of freestanding adverbs. Yet the distinction between the source and goal of motion is rarely overtly stated in Yurok, however common in Hupa speech and however central to Karuk grammar.

In the semantic structure of the Yurok adverbial system, a separate root is devoted to each of the primary geographical regions. Most of these roots enter into several related forms of loose functional equivalence. The root *pec,* for instance, enters into the forms *pecik, pecku, pecow, pecu(s),* and *hipec,* all conveying approximately the same meaning, namely, "upstream." Some occur with the element *-k,* giving rise to such variants as *pulik* and *pulek^w(s),* both loosely translating as "down at the mouth of the stream." Historically, this set may derive from the locative suffix *-k,* perhaps originally meaning "going all the way in a given direction to the end." Other directional adverbs occur with the rounded element *-ew, -u,* or *-ow.* Consider the adverb *hełku,* which loosely translates as "on land or ashore," in which the final element, -*u,* contributes the sense that the region lies "toward" the edge of the land, without reaching far into the interior. Compare this with the related adverb *hełkik,* which loosely translates as "inland" or even "in the mountains." Here the final element, -*k,* contributes the sense that this directional region is actually situated "in" the mountains, not merely "toward" this land, as indicated in the previously discussed form. (In historical terms, the word *hełku* may have once signaled the concept of the shoreline by literally referring to a region that is "toward the solid land or the mountains.") Other adverbs feature the initial element *hi-,* whose semantic effect is subtle though probably demonstrative. The forms *pec* and *hipec,* for instance, are usually glossed 'downstream'. Waterman, who spent many years working among the Yurok in the early twentieth century, once suggested that the element *hi-* conveys the sense of relative "proximity," or perhaps even "visibility," though none of the subsequent investigators confirmed this important insight (see Waterman 1920:194).

DOUBLE DIRECTIONAL EXPRESSIONS

Often it is possible to state the direction of motion twice within a single construction. Here any given scene can be surveyed from two contrasting points of view, once from the perspective of the source and once again from the perspective of the goal. This particular possibility reaches a great height among Karuk speakers, for directional marking is especially elaborate throughout the structure of the language. In Karuk speech, it is not unusual to hear directional constructions that translate as "Coyote was heading a long way *upriver* from someplace *downriver."* Shifting perspective, it is equally common to hear Karuk constructions that translate as "Coyote was going a great distance *uphill* from someplace *downhill."* Parallel constructions, stating both source and goal of motion, are almost completely absent in Yurok, in which geographical elements are primarily expressed by adverbs and rarely marked by elements internal to the structure of the stem. Hupa speakers make only sparing use of this possibility.

Karuk Double Directional Expressions

In Karuk speech, an inflected verb is often accompanied by a freestanding adverb that refines the scope of the reference by stating the relative distance of a directional path. Sometimes the goal of the activity is stated twice over, once by a verb suffix and again by a freestanding adverbial element. Equally often, an adverb states the goal of the activity, while a suffix specifies the original source region. Yet when the directional bearing of an event is marked by two grammatical systems at the same time, Karuk speakers often state both the source and goal of the event at once, indicating, for instance, that an object is "moving from an uphill source toward a goal downhill" or that a body is "heading toward a goal downstream away from the reference position here." Though common in Karuk speech, such constructions are rare elsewhere in the region.

Often the verb signals the source while an adverb specifies the goal. Here a single scene is effectively surveyed from two contrasting points of view at once. The phrase *sáruk ʔuʔárihfaku,* for instance, loosely translates as "one being came a long way downhill from someplace uphill." In this case, the suffix *-faku* signals that the event emanates from an uphill source, while the adverb *sáruk* specifies that this activity bears a considerable distance "downhill" toward its ultimate goal. From the opposing perspective, one might say *máruk ʔúkfuukraa,* a phrase that loosely translates as "one being climbed a great way uphill from someplace downhill." Here the suffix *-raa* indicates that the event emanates from a downhill source, from the perspective of some arbitrary reference region above it, while the adverb *máruk* indicates that this activity, as a whole, bears a considerable distance "uphill" toward its ultimate goal.

Occasionally, directional concepts based on two entirely different geographical regions are simultaneously present in a single construction. Consider the phrase *sáruk ʔuvuunváraktih,* for instance, which loosely translates as "(the river) flows a great way *downhill* from *upstream.*" Here the suffix *-varak* indicates that the event starts from an upriver source, while the adverb *sáruk* signals that this activity, as a whole, bears a long way "downhill" toward its goal.

Sometimes a single directional path is stated twice over, once by a prefix and once more by a freestanding adverb, which specifies the relative distance. The phrase *sáruk kunithvíripunih,* for instance, loosely translates as "they ran a great way downhill from here." In this case, the directional suffix *-unih* and the adverb *sáruk* both indicate that the event bears down a slope toward a destination "downhill." Here the directional suffix signals that the event moves away from an established point of reference toward a goal "downhill," while the adverb contributes the sense that this event continues on for a great distance.

Hupa Directional Expressions

Stating both the source and goal of motion is exceedingly rare in the neighboring Hupa language. If the direction of motion is signaled by two grammatical systems at once, usually the goal of the event is stated twice in Hupa speech. Hupa speakers rarely survey an event from two directional frames at the same time, stating both the source and goal in a single construction, as is common in the neighboring Karuk language. The reason for this is unclear.

Generally speaking, the directional bearing of an event is stated only once in Hupa speech. Usually an adverb or an affix (rarely both at once) performs this work. When speaking of an event that bears downstream, for instance, one could say *yide? čitehsyay*, where only the adverb *yide?* signals the "downriver" directional course. This phrase, as a unit, translates as "one being goes along downstream." Here all of the directional work is carried out by the adverb, while the verb *čitehsyay* ("one being goes along") merely signals an event that takes a fairly linear course. In the same situation, the speaker also has the option of saying *xoda?wila·d*, an expression that loosely translates as "one group floated down (river)." Here the directional marker *xo-da·=* specifies the directional bearing of the event. Because the bearing of the event is succinctly expressed through the process of affixation, this type of construction requires no further adverbial modification for directional bearing.

Where an adverb signals the direction of motion, Hupa speakers usually specify the source or goal of the event, though not both at once. To state the goal alone, one could say *yide? čitehsyay*, in which the adverb *yide?* signals the "downhill" goal toward which the event heads, while the verb *čitehsyay* merely indicates an event that takes a linear path. To state the source alone, one could say *yinah-čin čitehsyay*, a similar phrase that translates as "one came along from someplace upstream." Here the adverbial phrase *yinah-čin* signals the "upstream" source from which the event emanates.

Sometimes Hupa speakers do state the direction twice in a single construction. However, in this case the second grammatical form merely restates the goal toward which the motion heads. Consider the phrase *yidac xa·?isyay*, for instance, in which the adverb *yidac* signals that the motion bears "uphill," while the prefix *xa·=s-* reinforces the directional status of the event, specifying that the movement heads "uphill toward the top." This construction, as a unit, loosely translates as "one went uphill." Here both the adverb and the prefix signal the uphill goal toward which the motion heads.

Though Hupa speakers rarely exploit the possibility, one can state both the source and the goal of an event in a single phrase in the Hupa language. Consider the phrase *hayi yinah-čin xoda·nče·*, where the adverb *yinah-čin* indicates that the motion emanates from an upstream source, while the verbal modifier *xo-da·=*

signals that the event, as a whole, heads "down an incline" toward a place at a lower elevation. This expression, as a unit, loosely translates as "the wind that blows down from upriver." This unusual double-directional construction is not an everyday form but occurs in the specialized language of prayer.[11]

DIRECTIONAL VERSUS NONDIRECTIONAL VERBS

Each language also places certain restrictions on the types of verbs that can be modified to express directional paths. Directional marking is extended to the widest range of events in the Karuk language, whether in terms of grammatical possibilities or through related items of vocabulary. Yet directional marking is severely restricted in Hupa, in which most verbs fall into discrete grammatical classes, with only a small fraction of these permitting modification for spatial paths. Though the Yurok language appears, on the surface, to extend directional modification to a wide range of events, few of the categories marked on the verb are geographical in nature. Instead, most of these categories convey more-abstract spatial possibilities.

Karuk Directional Marking: Broad Flexibility

The Karuk language extends directional possibilities to an enormous range of events. Many Karuk verbs require a grammatical marker that specifies the directional bearing on an obligatory basis. A case in point is the verb root *ʔárih-,* a form that usually depicts fast-paced activities such as "running" and "jumping." This particular verb always requires a marker that specifies the directional bearing of the event. As such, it combines freely with many geographical markers. Consider the form *ʔuʔárihroov,* for instance, which translates as "one being went upriver." Here the directional suffix *-rôov(u)* specifies a path that heads "upriver." Or consider the related form *ʔuʔárihvarak,* which translates as "one came down from upriver." Here the contrasting directional suffix *-várak* indicates a geographical path that comes down from upriver. Ultimately the verb accepts modification for any directional path. Consider the form *ʔuʔárihfak(u),* for instance, which translates as "one went downhill." Here the directional marker *-faku* signals a path that heads "downhill" toward a point of reference established by the speaker. Yet this verb stem is not capable of occurring without a marker indicating the direction of motion; leaving the directional bearing unspecified would yield an unacceptable construction, producing purely ungrammatical results.

Other verbs accept directional marking on an optional basis, even those that portray events similar to those represented by the inherently directional forms. A case in point is the root *ikvip*, another motion verb, which can occur in such unmarked forms as *ʔúkvip* 'one being runs', here without a marker of its directional path. Yet the same underlying root is also capable of entering into such inherently directional forms as *yúruk ʔukvíriprup(u)*, which loosely translates as "one being ran some distance downriver." In this instance, the direction of motion is overtly stated with the marker *-rupu*, which contributes the meaning "(heading) downriver," while the stem is modified to the shape *ikvirip*. In a similar fashion, the root *vit*, which depicts scenes of conveyance by canoe, usually occurs in forms marked for a particular directional course. A typical formation is *kunvítvarakva*, a construction that loosely translates as "they paddled downstream from someplace upstream," where the verbal marker *-várak* signals the "downriver" course. Yet sometimes the directional course can be omitted. Here consider the form *kunípvit*, which simply translates as "they paddled repeatedly." Or consider the root *ʔih*, which usually depicts the directionless act of "dancing" around in one place. Yet in some cases, this root does accept marking for a specific geographical path, signaling that an entire troop of dancers moves, as a collective mass, from one place to another. The form *kunʔíihvarak*, for instance, loosely translates as "they dance toward here from someplace upriver." Here the suffix *-várak* signals an event that bears "down from someplace upriver," while the grammatical marker *kun-* signals a plural third-person subject. Consider the parallel construction *kunʔíihruputih*, which loosely translates as "they continue dancing downstream from here." Here the downriver course is specified by the directional suffix *-rupu*, which contributes the sense that the activity passes "downriver (from someplace here)." Though acceptable in Karuk speech, many of these constructions are illicit in Hupa grammar.

Directional marking is also extended to many events that only loosely involve motion through actual physical space. Fire, for instance, is often said to "burn along" a particular course, perhaps, in a sense, consuming objects that come into its path. Consider the form *ʔuʔiinaa*, which loosely translates as "fire burns toward uphill from someplace here." This expression is built around the verb stem *ʔiin-*, which refers to the act of burning along in a particular direction, here combining with the suffix *-raa*, which indicates that the activity heads uphill from someplace downhill. Somewhat poetically, the northern lights are said to "burn down" across the sky from a source somewhere "upriver" from Karuk country. The corresponding expression is *ʔiinvárak,* which translates as "to burn down from upriver." This expression, the usual Karuk name for the northern lights, is derived from the verb *ʔiin,* which refers to the act of "burning along" on a particular directional route, here combining with the directional marker *-várak* '(coming) down from upriver'.

Even rays of light are sometimes said to take a particular geographical route while traveling through space. The form *ʔimshírihraavish,* for instance, loosely translates as "you will shine upriver quickly."[12] This formulaic phrase used in prayer is directed at salmon, whose annual return heralds the coming of spring, as first signaled by the glistening bodies of these fish as they swim upriver from the ocean downriver. This expression based on the verb *imshírih-,* which portrays the act of "shining" along a directional way, here occurring in second-person form, with the directional marker *-raa* 'coming upstream from someplace downstream.' The tense marker *=(a)vish* at the end of this construction places the event in the future.

In a similar fashion, drowning is known, somewhat euphemistically, as the act of "dying into the water." The relevant expression is *ʔíimkara,* a form that is derived from the otherwise nondirectional root *ʔiv* (also *ʔim*), which denotes the process of "dying," here combining with the directional marker *-kara* to signal a course that leads "into a body of water, such as a river."

Metaphorically, shuffling hands or sticks in gambling is known as the act of "moving things into the water (away from view)." Here the expression is *ʔeéthkaanva.* This form is based on the verb root *ʔeeth* 'to carry', here occurring with the directional marker *-kara* (*-kaan*) 'into the river' and the plural action suffix *-va,* suggesting the continuous motion of several sticks as they are "submerged" in succession. In this expression, moving a physical object beneath the cloudy surface of the river is implicitly compared with shuffling gambling sticks beyond view.

Even the act of "looking" requires a marker that specifies the path of the gaze. Here the verb root is *it-,* a form that always requires a directional marker, which is often stated in geographical terms. The form *yúruk ʔutrûuputih,* for instance, loosely translates as "one looked a long way downriver." Here the marker *-rupu* indicates the directional course of the gaze in geographical terms, namely, '(heading) downriver'. To reverse the scenario, one could say *káruk kunítroovutih,* which loosely translates as "one looked a long way upriver." Here the marker *-rôovu* signals the opposite directional trajectory, namely, one that "(heads) upriver." Both forms otherwise feature the animate third-person subject marker *ʔu-* and the durative temporal marker *-tih,* indicating that this activity continues on for some time.

In many Karuk expressions, directional marking is extended to activities that involve no actual movement through space. In one idiom, one can even speak of "telling stories" while facing a particular direction, as reflected in the expression *pikvahrúpukva,* which literally translates as "to tell stories while facing outdoors." Here the cultural reference is to the act of preparing for the hunt by singing songs, an act that is usually performed while facing down toward the river below, the direction in which the door to a traditional living house generally points. This expression is derived from the verb stem *pikvah,* which refers to the act of "telling stories," here occurring with the directional marker *-rúpuk* '(facing) outdoors'[13] and the plural suffix *-va,* indicating that several stories might be told, or songs performed, on these occasions.

Even where an object rests motionless in one position, its geographical status is often significant on a grammatical basis. That is, for some verbs of position, a marker indicating the geographical directional status is obligatory. A case in point is the verb *(ʔi)ku-,* which refers to the act of "lying motionless" while facing a particular direction. This single root gives rise to a number of related forms that specify a geographical course. Consider the construction *ʔúkuroovutih,* which loosely translates as "one lies motionless, pointing upstream." Here the directional marker *-rôovu* contributes the sense that the object "faces upriver." Or consider the related form *ʔukúripaahitih,*[14] which translates as "it came to lie pointing motionless across the stream." Here the directional marker *-rípaa* contributes the sense that this motionless event points "across the river." Otherwise, both forms feature the third-person subject marker *ʔu-* and the durative marker *-tih,* indicating that the activity continued for some time. Switching stems, one could also say *ʔuxvâahiroovu,* an expression that loosely translates as "one lies pointing upriver." This construction is based on the noun root *axvâah* 'head', which becomes a directional verbal base with the addition of the derivational suffix *-hi.* Here the directional marker *-rôovu* indicates that this event as a whole faces upriver, yet this verb base also accepts other directional markers, such as *-rupu,* indicating, for example, a geographical bearing heading downriver.

Hupa Directional Marking: Strong Grammatical Restrictions

In Hupa speech, directional marking is extended to fewer types of events than is possible in Karuk. Most Hupa verbs fall into discrete grammatical classes, which often restrict the possibilities for directional bearing. Some of these verbs absolutely require a grammatical marker to specify the directional bearing of the event, as is sometimes the case in Karuk. Others, however, are classified as invariant with respect to direction, never accepting a geographical marking under any condition—in sharp contrast to Karuk, in which spatial marking is extended to a far wider range of events.

Verbs of motion generally fall into three discrete grammatical classes in Hupa. Typically, these verbs portray scenes where a conscious subject moves through space of its own volition. Although one of these classes requires directional specification, the others remain indefinite as to directional status. Where an actor is engaged in the act of traveling along over a relatively brief time span, this type of event can potentially be portrayed from several contrasting points of view. While some of these depictions require a definite directional component, others lack it.

One part of this motion paradigm, known as the *momentaneous,* always requires the specification of a directional path. These verbs, as a class, usually portray activities that are relatively brief in nature, while taking a clear-cut directional course over this span of time. Consider the verb stem -*na·W,* a third-person form of the general motion paradigm, which, as a member of the momentaneous class, always requires a marker of its directional path. At an abstract level, this stem simply refers to the act of "heading somewhere" over a relatively short stretch of time, leaving the directional modifier to signal one of its many potential spatial courses. Consider the form *xoda·ʔana·W,* which translates as "one goes downhill." Here the marker *xo-da·*= signals that this particular instantiation of the event specifically heads "down an incline." To see the event in still another light, consider the contrasting form *tahč'ina·W,* which translates as "one being comes out of the water." Here the marker *tah*= signals that this instantiation of the event emerges from "out of the water." From still another point of view, one might say *č'eʔina·W,* which translates as "one goes outdoors." Here the directional marker *č'e·*= signals that the event emerges from "out of an enclosure." Each form also takes one of the two variants of the third-person subject prefix, either *č'i*- or *ʔ*-, depending on phonological environment.

Another part of the motion paradigm, known as the *continuative,* allows the speaker to be less explicit about the path the event takes. These verbs, as a formal grammatical class, generally apply to events with a more open-ended time frame than the momentaneous series. Typically, these events continue for a considerable span of time, without following any particular spatial route. Consider the related form *na·ʔaya·,* which loosely translates as "one goes around," with nothing specific expressed about the directional path. Here the grammatical marker *na·=,* at the beginning of the construction, indicates that the event takes no particular directional course, while moving here and there within a fairly broad radius.

Still another part of the motion paradigm, known as the *progressive,* applies to events of even greater duration. Here the directional path remains open-ended, though a roughly linear course is often implied. Where the event continues on for a greater period of time, one might say *čiɢa·l,* which loosely translates as "one goes along." Here the stem-shape *-ɢa·l* signals the shift to the progressive aspect, while the grammatical marker *či-* indicates a third-person subject. This form signals an event that is ongoing and likely to continue along a fairly indefinite, though often goal-oriented, course over a considerable span of time.

The same pattern of marking also applies to situations in which the object is propelled through space by an outside force. Again, only one part of this paradigm explicitly requires an obligatory marker of directional bearing. Consider the stem *-ʔa·W,* a form that is specifically concerned with the motion of round objects. As a member of the momentaneous class, this stem always requires a special grammatical modifier indicating the specific directional path. At an abstract level, the stem refers to the act of moving a "round object" somewhere, while an obligatory directional modifier specifies one of many potential spatial paths. If the object is raised into the air, one might say *ya·ʔaʔaW,* which translates as "one raises up a round object." Here the directional marker *ya·=* signals motion that reaches upward toward the heavens. If the object is taken from a body of water, one might say *tahč'aʔaW,* which translates as "one removes a round object from the water." Here the directional marker *tah=* designates motion that passes "out of the water." If the object is lowered to the ground, one might say *no·ʔaʔaW,* which loosely translates as "one lowers a round object to the ground." Here the directional marker *no·=* designates a movement that culminates in a state of rest, usually through a process of sinking down to the ground. Each form also features the third-person subject prefix in one of its manifestations, either *či-* or *ʔ-,* depending on the phonological environment.

When the same type of event continues for a considerable time span, assuming a number of directional paths on the way, one might say *na·ʔaʔa·,* which means "one being carried a round object around." Here the shift to the continuative time frame is signaled by the special stem-shape *ʔa·,* which refers to the process of "moving a round object around somewhere" over an extended period of time. Here the grammatical marker *na·=* indicates that the event follows no particular path, traveling around "to and fro" within a fairly broad radius.

When the event continues for an even greater span of time, one might say *č'iwa?al,* which loosely translates as "one carries a round object along." The last part of this paradigm is marked with the special progressive stem *-?al* and the progressive prefix *wi-.* Together, these grammatical markers signal an ongoing stream of action, punctuated, perhaps, with momentary stops and starts along the way. Again, for ongoing events such as this, the speaker is not required to state a particular directional course.

Directional marking applies, fairly uniformly, to events that stretch through space along a fairly continuous course. Consider the verb stem *-lin,* which generally occurs in forms that depict the act of flowing along on a consistent path. When speaking of the mouth of a river, one might say *č'e·wilin,* meaning "(the waters) flow out." In this form, the directional marker *č'e·=* signals a course that reaches out of an enclosure (here, by implication, the mouth of a river). The presence of the inceptive marker *wi(n)-* in this construction places focus on the initial phases of this process of emergence. When speaking of an eddy, one might say *xahslin,* which means "(the water) flows upward." In this form, the directional marker *xa·=s-* signals a course that reaches up to the top, here a current that swirls upward (in circles) toward the surface. The presence of the stative temporal marker *s-* in this form places focus on the middle stages of the ongoing process. When speaking of a headwater, one might say *no·wilin,* which means "(the water) flows to a limit." Here the directional marker *no·=wi(n)-* signals a course that reaches toward a boundary or limit of some kind. The presence of the inceptive marker *wi(n)-* in this form again places focus on the initial phases of this process of reaching a limit, fixing on the moment before the current actually stops flowing. Yet the directional course is often far less explicit. One could, for instance, say *ninlin,* which translates as "(the water) flows somewhere." Here the directional marker *ni-(wi)n-* contributes the sense that the event arrives someplace, though in an indefinite way. When speaking of wind, one could say *xoda·nč'e·,* which means "(the wind) blows downstream." This form places a definite directional spin on the situation with the marker *xo-da·=(wi)n-,* which signals motion that bears either downstream or downhill. One could also say *tehsč'e·,* which translates as "it blows along." This contrasting form merely refers to a linear path, without indicating anything further about the geographical bearing.

Similarly, the act of "looking on" or "gazing" is also classified as an event that extends across space in an inherently directional way. The related expression permits only one directional path, while never admitting other spatial markers, certainly not geographical ones. In this setting, one could say *č'itehsʔeʔn,* "one being looked along." This expression is derived from the verb stem *-ʔinʔ* or *-ʔeʔn,* which refers to the act of "looking" somewhere. When specifying a directional path, this stem combines with the marker *t(e)-,* which indicates a linear course, though nothing explicit about the geographical surroundings. Reversing the scene, one could say *naʔtehsʔeʔn,* which loosely translates as "one looked back along." Here the reversative marker *na·=* conveys the sense that the gaze travels "back again." Both forms feature the temporal marker *s-,* fixing on the middle stages of the process and indicating that the event continued for a period of time. In rare instances, speakers indicate a geographical bearing with a freestanding adverb. The phrase *yideʔ č'ite·ŋʔeʔn,* for instance, translates as "one being looked downstream." Here, the verb indicates only the linear course taken by the event, as marked with the otherwise ambiguous spatial prefix *t(e)-,* while the freestanding adverbial element *yideʔ* 'downstream' clears up the matter of the path. Directional marking is far more circumscribed for most other classes of events—apart from these verbs of "going," "handling," and "extension." In addition, stating a specific directional path is not obligatory in Hupa, as it is in Karuk.

Many Hupa verbs permit only a few minor directional variants, including some events with an intrinsic spatial element. Consider the specialized verb paradigm that refers to the act of "scraping." One could, for instance, say *tiWsow,* which means "I scrape them together." Here the directional modifier *t-(i)-* signals that the objects of the act are brought into contact with one another or are simply drawn close together. Similarly, one could also say *xahWsow,* meaning "I scoop them up from beneath the ground." Here the directional modifier *xa·=* signals that the objects of the act are dug out from beneath the surface of the earth. Both forms are based on the stem *-sow,* which signals the act of "scraping," here occurring with the first-person subject marker *W-.* Apart from these two directional markers, few other paths are possible for this verb paradigm. No one, in my experience, ever spoke of scraping something while pointing "upriver" or "downriver," with respect to the surrounding countryside.

For many types of events, directional marking is strictly forbidden on a grammatical basis. Consider the expressions for "shooting" and "holding a religious dance," both of which accept directional modification in the Karuk language, though not among Hupa speakers. A case in point is the act of "dancing," which is depicted as a process that lacks an inherent directional component, as reflected in the Hupa expression for holding a world renewal ceremony. When speaking of a religious dance, one might say *č'idilye·*, which loosely translates as "a community engages in religious dance." Though this form does not accept directional marking in the Hupa language, the parallel expression in Karuk does (see previous section).

Or consider the act of "shooting," which in Hupa is always directed toward an object, one that the speaker must specify for purely grammatical reasons. Other than stating the goal toward which the motion heads, the speaker is not required to state anything further about the directional path taken by the event. In particular, one need not state anything about its geographical bearing within the surrounding countryside. The expression *kʸoWʔiʒ*, for instance, translates as "I shoot at something." In this construction, the geographical bearing of the event is omitted on the linguistic plane. Instead, the verb states only that this act is directed toward some specific "thing" in the environment, one that is designated by the indefinite object prefix *kʸi-*, which here suggests a "target" or "mark" of some kind. This form is built up around the verb stem *-ʔiʒ*, which designates the act of "shooting." Here the spatial marker *o·-* indicates that the event is directed at some outside object without necessarily reaching this goal, while the prefix *W-* indicates that the agent is in the first person.

Other verbs occasionally accept directional modification, even when normally treated as nondirectional for purely grammatical reasons. Hupa speakers, for instance, usually refer to the act of urinating in a fairly nondirectional way. The form *č'iliʒ*, for instance, simply translates as "one being urinates." This expression is, in turn, based on the verb stem *-liʒ*, which refers to the act of "urinating," without any indication of direction. Yet in some cases, the speaker can say *deʔdiliʒ*, which loosely translates as "one being urinates into the fire." Here the directional modifier *de·=di-* refers to motion that "enters into a fire," occurring with a contracted form of the third-person subject marker, a mere glottal stop (-ʔ-), sandwiched between its two elements. While there is no record of anyone saying "I urinated upstream (or downstream)" in Hupa, such an expression is conceivable if directional marking is, in a restricted sense, permitted.

In contrast to the situation in Karuk, directional bearing in the Hupa language is rarely extended to activities that involve no actual motion: a motionless event receives no directional marking. Generally the act of "looking," for instance, requires no particular attention to directional bearing. Instead, one marks the object toward which one's gaze is directed. One could, for example, say *č'iWinił'e·n,* which loosely translates as "one being is looking at me," where the marker *W-* indicates a first-person object. Or one could say *č'ixonił'e·n,* which loosely translates as "one being is looking at someone," where the marker *xo-* indicates a third-person object. With respect to the surrounding countryside, the directional path receives no attention in either construction. Here the stem *-'e·n* 'to look' occurs with the element *ni-,* which is often found in forms that portray activities that lead to a goal. The classifier element *ł-* is usually found in forms with a definite object. Both forms feature the third-person subject marker *č'i-.*

Among Hupa speakers, the acts of "singing," "speaking," and "dying" are generally treated as motionless events, with no inherent spatial component. While Karuk speakers sometimes extend directional possibilities to similar events, Hupa grammar usually does not permit directional modification for these acts. Generally, for example, one says *č'ixine·W,* which means "one speaks," in reference to a person who is talking. This expression requires no attention to the directional status of the speaker within the surrounding countryside. When speaking of a person who is singing, one says *na'k'ʸa'aw,* which means "one sings." This form likewise requires no particular attention to the performer's directional status. To speak bluntly of death, one could say *č'ič'id,* which simply means "one being dies." Again, this form does not permit any type of directional marking. That is, in the Hupa language, the direction one faces while singing, dying, or telling stories is rarely significant, however critical to the formation of many equivalent verbs in the Karuk language. Of course, on historical grounds, speakers could have introduced these types of expressions to the Hupa language, so that they would eventually be deemed acceptable by Hupa speakers today, as they are in the speech of the neighboring Karuks. For mysterious reasons, however, Hupa speakers consider these constructions highly ungrammatical in their sense of the language.

Where an object rests motionless in one place, Hupa grammar rarely requires directional marking.[15] That is, in contrast to the situation in Karuk, in which the distinction is often optional and sometimes obligatory, Hupa speakers rarely state the directional bearing of an object that rests in one place without moving. In fact, for most verbs that depict motionless states, directional marking is strictly barred in Hupa grammar. When speaking of a stick resting somewhere, one might say *sita·n,* which loosely translates as "a long object rests motionless in one place." Similarly, when speaking of a stone lying on the ground, one might say *sa'a·n,* which loosely translates as "a round object lies motionless."

Here neither form gives any information about the potential directional bearing of the object. Yet directional marking is required for the same objects when motion is involved. So when lifting a stick, one might say *yaʔwinta·n,* which loosely translates as "one raised up a sticklike object." Or when raising a stone, one might say *yaʔwiŋʔa·n,* which means "one raised up a round object."

In contrast, forms that mark the transition into the state of motionlessness do sometimes include an optional adverbial modifier that specifies the directional status. Yet, in general, the reference is only to the place where this object came to lay at rest. The form *saʔa·n,* for instance, means "a round object lies there motionless," though this form does not usually occur with a marker of its directional bearing within the surrounding territory. However, the related form *wiŋʔaʔ,* which means "a round object lies there motionless," sometimes features a freestanding adverb that indicates the place where the object came to rest. Consider the related phrase *yiceʔni-wiŋʔaʔ,* for instance, which loosely translates as "a round object came to rest motionless (somewhere) downhill (from here)." Even this more elaborate construction does not clear up the question of which way the object faces. Instead, this form merely states the direction it lies in relation to another point of reference, such as the location where the speaker and audience stand.

Yurok Directional Marking

For Yurok speakers, directional marking is rarely obligatory. That is, relatively few verb stems explicitly mark the geographical bearing of an event, though directional marking can be extended to a wide range of situations on an optional basis. Few of the directional categories are geographical in nature, so the Karuk language still holds the majority of the forms that specify the geographical bearing of events.

Though rarely an obligatory matter in Yurok speech, directional modification can be applied to many Yurok verbs on an optional basis. A case in point is the productive final *-ec,* which occurs in many stems that portray scenes of conveyance by canoe. Sometimes this final enters into forms that are inherently directional, such as *slekʷecoḱ,* which means "I paddle backward by boat." Here the initial *slekʷ-* indicates motion that heads "backward" relative to the subject. To further illustrate the point, consider the related form *hoonecek̓,* which means "I go upstream by boat."[16] Here the initial *hoon-* indicates motion that bears upstream (or, in some cases, uphill). However, the final *-ec* is also capable of entering into indefinite forms, such as *recoḱ,* which means "I paddle (somewhere)," where no there is no indication of a directional path. This form features the indefinite initial element *r-*, which is found in stems that remain unmarked for a directional path. In each case, it is the stem-initial element that signals the shift in directional status, while the underlying concept represented by the final holds roughly constant. Each form also includes the regular first-person subject marker *-(e)k̓*.

To further illustrate the point, consider the productive medial *–oyk̓*, which occurs in stems that depict the process of liquid flowing. Often this medial enters into directional stems such as *sɹɹnoyk̓*, which loosely translates as "(the river) winds along." Here the initial *sɹɹn-* indicates that the event weaves along in a serpentine fashion. Or consider the related form *pk̓ʷɹyk̓*, in which the initial *pk̓ʷ-* specifies that the motion flows out of an enclosure, such as the mouth of a stream.[17] This contrasting form loosely translates as "it flows out." The same root also occurs with the indefinite form *royk̓*, which loosely translates as "it flows (somewhere)," without indicating a specific directional course. This form features the nondirectional element *r-*, which usually occurs with verb stems that remain unmarked for a particular spatial route.[18]

Some stems, however, take a general directional marker, which accepts refinement in the form of a freestanding adverb. A case in point is the productive medial *-ol*, which is found in stems that portray scenes of "flying" or "hovering about" in the air. Often this element enters into inherently directional constructions such as *laayoʔł*, which means "it flies along." In contrast is the indefinite form *loʔł*, which simply means "it flies," without specifying anything further about the direction. However, the same productive medial also accepts the stem-initial element *soon-*, which highlights the presence of a general spatial path, usually one that must be stated with a freestanding directional adverb. Consider, for instance, the form *soonoʔł*, which translates as "it flies (somewhere)." This construction can be modified with the geographical adverb *wohpeku* to signal that the event heads "across a body of water," as illustrated by the phrase *wohpeku soonoʔł*, which loosely translates as "it flies across (the water)."[19]

A further illustration of this point is the productive medial *-ełk*, which often occurs in stems that portray scenes of "crawling" along the face of the earth. Sometimes this element enters into inherently directional forms, such as *hewełkepek̓*, which translates as "I get up." Here the stem-initial element *hew-* suggests the motion of awakening from the state of sleep, as the subject passes from a resting to a standing position. Similarly, consider the indefinite form *leṭkeloypeḱ,* which translates as "I crawl," without indicating anything about the direction of motion.[20] The same productive medial accepts the initial element *soon-,* which highlights the presence of a general spatial path. Consider the related form *sooneṭkepeḱ,* which also translates as "I crawl." This construction can be modified with the adverb *wonew* to signal that the event passes "above, toward the heavens," as in *wonew sooneṭkepeḱ,* "I crawl up."[21]

OVERLAP WITH TEMPORAL MARKING

In each of the languages, the spatial and temporal characteristics of an event can be isolated into separate layers of analysis for grammatical purposes, with special linguistic markers for signaling relationships in space and time. Each language also places certain restrictions on the possibilities for combining these two layers of analysis. In Hupa, spatial and temporal marking are closely intertwined, with strict rules that govern the co-occurrence of these elements on the grammatical plane. In the neighboring Yurok and Karuk languages, however, space and time are treated fairly independently, without any binding links between these two layers of grammatical analysis.

Time and Direction in Karuk: Separate Analytic Categories

In the Karuk language, the spatial and temporal characteristics of an event are split into two fairly independent layers of grammatical analysis.[22] As a consequence, many events can be considered from whatever temporal perspective the speaker wishes to state, regardless of the directional course the activity takes. Karuk grammar does not place any particular restrictions on the possibilities for combining spatial and temporal marking within a single construction.

From a single directional frame, several contrasting temporal perspectives can be differentiated. Without overt marking for time perspective, the verb is ambiguous as to the phase of motion. Consider the temporally unmarked form *ʔuʔárihroov,* for instance, which loosely translates as "one being goes upriver." This construction is formally neutral with respect to the expression of time perspective, so that the motion could be in its initial, middle, or final stages. When the verb is placed in the perfective mode, with the addition of the grammatical marker *t(a)=,* the reference is restricted to a single, internally complete occurrence of the event, often with an implicit focus on the culminating stages of the total flow of motion, as can be represented by the related form *tuʔárihroov,* which means "one being went upriver." In the durative mode, which is marked with the suffix -*tih,* the middle stages of the event come to the fore, though without explicit allusion to the early or concluding phase of the activity, illustrated here with the form *ʔuʔárihroovutih,* which translates as "one being is going upriver." From the perspective of the iterative mode, which is marked with the prefix *ip-,* a repetition of the entire act can be invoked, without explicit emphasis on any specific phase within the total flow of motion. A case in point is the iterative form *ʔuppárihroov,* which simply translates as "one went on upriver (once more)."[23] In the Karuk language, a single scene can usually be considered from whatever temporal perspective the speaker wishes to designate, regardless of the directional course the activity takes.

Marking Space and Time in Hupa Grammar

In Hupa grammar, however, directional marking is highly sensitive to the temporal schedule on which an event unfolds. In contrast to the situation in the Karuk language, in which spatial and temporal perspective are largely independent layers of analysis, each directional modifier in Hupa carries certain restrictions regarding the temporal markers that can combine with it. In contrast to Karuk, elements of spatial and temporal analysis are closely intertwined in Hupa grammar.

Verbs of motion or position fall into four major classes, based on the spatial and temporal dynamics of the surrounding scene. Significantly, only one of these classes requires the specification of a particular directional path, while the remainder of the classes strictly bar directional marking on a grammatical basis.

The briefest phase of motion is represented by a special *momentaneous* paradigm. As a grammatical class, these momentaneous forms always require a marker that specifies the directional bearing the event takes. In terms of translation, these forms generally refer to the act of "traveling along a path" but not to "traveling" in a more general way. Every verb in this class gives rise to an enormous series of contrasting directional forms, depending on the bearing of the event. When speaking of the motion of a single actor, one might say *yehčʼiwinyay,* which translates as "one being went inside." Here the directional marker *yeh=* indicates motion that passes, fairly swiftly, into an enclosure. From another point of view, one might say *čʼitehsyay,* a contrasting expression that loosely translates as "one being went along." Here the directional marker *teˑ-* signals motion that bears along a relatively linear course over a somewhat more open-ended time period. From still another point of view, one could say *č'e'ninyay,* which loosely translates as "one being went outside." Here the directional marker *č'e·=* refers to an activity that emerges, fairly rapidly, out of an enclosure, ultimately arriving somewhere outside of this area of safety. Otherwise, each form features the third-person prefix *č'i-,* which is reduced to *ʔ-* in the final construction (*č'e'ninyay*), where it closes a syllable.

A special *continuative* paradigm marks events of greater duration. As a formal grammatical class, these continuative forms do not accept marking for direction. Generally, continuative forms refer to the act of "going around" for an extended, though indefinite, period of time. Another part of the singular paradigm for "going" can be represented by the form *na·ʔasyaʔ,* which translates as "one being went around." Here the reference is to an event that continues on for a time, without following any particular spatial route. This form features the prefix *na·=,* which generally occurs in forms that depict a nonlinear, or vaguely circular, activity.

Events of greater duration are marked with a special *progressive* paradigm. Although these progressive forms do not require any explicit directional marking, a linear course is implied, one that continues on indefinitely from the moment of inception, without any sense of an end point. Here the third-person form of the general paradigm for singular motion can be illustrated with the construction *č'iɢa·l,* which loosely translates as "one being is going along."

In situations where motion is absent, however, directional marking is strictly prohibited in Hupa grammar. When speaking of a person at rest, one might say *č'iste·n,* which loosely translates as "one living being lies motionless somewhere." When speaking of a person who is lying very still, one might say *č'ista·n,* which loosely translates as "one being lies motionless in the fashion of a stick." Both of these constructions feature the stative prefix *s-,* which suggests a continuous state without a definite onset or conclusion. Neither form can be modified with a directional marker to indicate its positional status within the surrounding environment.

The Initial Phases of Motion. Every directional marker in the Hupa language falls into one of three grammatical classes, each one holding certain temporal ramifications. Many directional markers, for instance, combine exclusively with the inceptive prefix *wi(n)-* when entering the perfective mode, in which the reference is to a situation that is loosely bounded in temporal scope. This series, as a formal grammatical class, focuses semantically on the initial phase within any given flow of motion, often fixing on rapid-fire activities with an instantaneous or sudden onset.

Some of the directional modifiers in the inceptive class place explicit focus on the onset of an act. A case in point is the form *č'idiwila·d,* which translates as "one being floated off." Here the directional marker *di-* signals the onset of an event based metaphorically on the more concrete concept of physical protrusion. Or consider the expression *dah č'idiwiłła·d,* which translates as "one being drew away fast, took off running." Here the two-part directional modifier *dah=di* indicates movement that draws away stealthily from its starting point. Otherwise, both of these forms also feature the third-person animate subject marker *č'i-* and the inceptive temporal prefix *win-,* whose final consonant, *n,* assimilates to an *l* before an *l* sound.

Other directional modifiers in the inceptive class signal the process of entrance, marking a rapid transition from one location to another. A case in point is the verb *yeh č'iwinyay,* which translates as "one being went inside." Here the directional marker *yeh=* signals entrance into an enclosure. For further illustration, consider the related form *teh č'iwinyay,* which translates as "one went into the water." Here the directional marker *teh=* signals entrance into a state of immersion beneath the surface of the water. To take another example, consider the form *de'diwiŋ'a·n,* which translates as "one being put a round object into the fire." Here the two-part directional modifier *de·=di-* signals motion that reaches into the heart of a fire, usually for the purpose of cooking. Again, each form features the inceptive prefix *win-,* though Hupa grammar does not permit the use of any other temporal marker with this particular set of directional modifiers. By a similar logic, the process of sudden emergence also involves a rapid transfer between two points. A case in point is the form *xa'wiŋ'a·n,* which loosely translates as "one being dug it up." Here the prefix *win-* conveys a sense of rapid emergence, while the directional marker *xa·=* signals motion that reaches upward from beneath the ground.

At the other end of the spectrum, several directional modifiers in the inceptive class designate events that start off toward a goal, without necessarily reaching it. A case in point is the verb form *ya'wiŋ'a·n,* which translates as "one raised it up." Here the directional marker *ya·=* indicates motion that reaches upward toward the heavens. Consider, for further illustration, the related form *xoda'winyay,* which translates as "one headed off downstream." Here the marker *xo-da·=* indicates motion that reaches down toward the base of a mountain or the mouth of a stream. Again, each form features the inceptive prefix *win-*; the grammar does not permit the use of any other temporal marker with this particular set of directional modifiers.[24]

Sometimes the reference is to rapid-fire events, especially those that are suddenly engaged and quickly withdrawn. Consider the form *ǰeʔwiłtʼiW,* which, for instance, translates as "one being splits it apart." Here the directional marker *ǰeˑ=* designates a pair of trajectories that start from a common center before quickly splitting apart from one another or forking. Or consider the form *xeʔeʔwinyay,* which translates as "one disappeared." Here the directional marker *xeʔeˑ=* signals a trajectory that rapidly extends beyond view, a point past which the observer gathers no further knowledge, discovering nothing of its eventual conclusion. Again, both forms take the inceptive prefix *win-*; Hupa grammar does not permit other temporal markers with this set of directional modifiers.

Elsewhere in the language, the inceptive prefix *win-* is associated with forms that mark the point of entrance into an ongoing state or condition. Consider, for example, the form *niWoˑn,* which translates as "it is good." This special verb of state gives rise to the related transitional variant *niwiŋWoʔn,* which translates as "it became good." Both forms are based on the verb stem *-Woˑn,* which in its ordinary sense means to be "good" or "pleasing," with the special transitional variant *-Woʔn* where the reference is to the related process of "becoming good or pretty." Here the special transitional form takes the inceptive prefix *win-,* marking the onset of the condition. Even without a directional association, the temporal marker *win-* still signals the condition of onset.

The Middle Phases of Motion. Other directional markers combine exclusively with the prefix *s-* when entering into the perfective mode. This series, as a grammatical class, focuses on the middle phases of any total flow of motion. In a secondary way, the reference also sometimes encompasses the early phases or final phases of motion that either follow or precede these middle stages. Some of these directional modifiers refer to situations of continuous contact. Consider, for instance, the form *mehsƛoˑn,* which translates as "it is tied to (something)." This expression makes no reference to the process that initiated the ongoing association between the objects or to that final event that may one day end it. Here the directional marker *eˑ=* signals motion that pushes toward something else, the object of which is marked with the prefix *m-,* indicating something inanimate, perhaps a skirt. While the verb stem *-ƛoˑn* conveys the concept of "tying" or "weaving," the subject remains unmarked, because the form is passive. This form could refer to a skirt that is tied around a person continuously, without a definite onset or endpoint.

Other markers in this class signal events that continue on in one place, without reference to either the onset or the conclusion of the total process. For instance, consider the form *niŋʔisdeˣ,* which loosely translates as "they danced up and down in one spot." Here the directional marker *nin=* signals motion that rises and falls relative to the solid ground, while the stem *-deˣ* refers to the motion of two or more beings, here the dancers. Again the third-person subject *čʼi-* is sandwiched between these prefixes in its reduced form, as a glottal stop. Other markers signal entrance into an ongoing process, with focus on the continued nature of the motion. The previously discussed form *čʼitehsyay,* for instance, loosely translates as "one started off, heading continuously along." Here the directional marker *te·-* signals motion that follows a fairly linear path over an extended period. At the other end of the spectrum, several of the directional markers in this class signal the culmination of an ongoing process, up to and including the approach of completion. The form *tahsyay,* for instance, translates as "they emerged from the water," or "they gradually came out of the dance." Here the directional marker *tah=* signals motion that gradually emerges from the water over an extended period. Similarly, the directional prefix *e·=,* which indicates motion that heads toward some object, occurs with the marker *s-* in forms referring to the ongoing, and not always successful, approach of a goal. Consider, for instance, the form *me·ʔisyay,* which loosely translates as "one climbs up along something, without necessarily reaching its top." Here the object toward which this event leads is marked with the prefix *m-,* indicating an inanimate entity (usually a mountain), while the subject who makes this ascent is marked with the reduced form of the third-person prefix *čʼi-.* The directional marker *xa·=s-,* which refers to motion that heads up along the face of a mountain, also belongs to this class, referring as much to the ongoing process of ascent as to the approach of the goal. Consider, for instance, the form *xa·ʔasyay,* which loosely translates as "one climbs up." Here the directional marker *xa·=* signals motion that heads "upward," while the temporal prefix *s-* indicates the potentially lengthy process of reaching this goal.

Elsewhere in the language, the stative prefix *s-* is associated with ongoing processes that lack a definite onset or conclusion. Consider, for instance, the form *sita·n,* which loosely translates as "a sticklike object lies motionless." This form is based on the verb stem *-ta·n;* with the *s(i)-* before it, the reference is to the static position of a sticklike or "long" object.

The Final Phases of Motion. Another series of directional modifiers combines exclusively with the prefix *nin-* when entering into the perfective mode. As a class, these modifiers focus semantically on the final phases of a process. One marker in this class signals the arrival at a destination. Consider, for instance, the form *č'ininyay,* which translates as "one being arrived (or came here)." In this example, the directional marker *ni-* indicates an event that heads toward a point of reference understood by context, usually an existential or deictic "here." Another directional modifier in this class signals the culmination of a process, usually involving a termination of motion. A case in point is the form *noʔninyay,* which translates as "one stops going, comes to a halt." Here the directional marker *noˑ=* indicates a spatial path that reaches a point of termination while running along the face of the earth. Or consider the form *noʔniŋʔaˑn,* which translates as "one put in down." This marker indicates a similar termination, here a descent to the ground below. The final member of the series signals the act of exiting. Consider the form *č'eʔninyay,* which translates as "one came out of the house." Here the directional marker *č'e=* signals motion that leads out of an enclosure, the subject ultimately arriving outside of it; emergence, in this sense, represents the final phase of enclosure.

The semantic structures of these contrasting grammatical classes are illustrated in figure 4.3, in idealized form. Circles represent consecutive phases of an unfolding process, while the arrows indicate both the passage of time and the directional flow of motion. Larger circles highlight the specific time frames: the inceptive frame focuses on the initial phases of motion; the stative frame on the middle phases; and the conclusive frame on the final stages.

The match is not always perfect. Instead, each class acts as a prototype, with most of the members sharing the core features, while allowing for a number of minor departures. Inceptive forms, which usually refer to events with a rapid or sudden onset (such as the striking of a target after the sudden release of an arrow), sometimes embrace the endpoint as well. Stative forms, which usually place focus on the middle stages of an event, sometimes embrace the onset or conclusions of an act, though usually with emphasis on the ongoing process as a whole. Yet conclusive forms fairly uniformly signal events that rapidly reach an inevitable endpoint.

Spatial and Temporal Marking in Yurok Grammar

Though Yurok stems often express spatial and temporal distinctions, these two categories of analysis rarely interact on the semantic plane. Most medials that

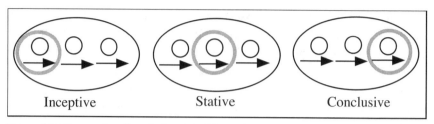

Figure 4.3. Phases of motion distinguished in perfective temporal subframes in Hupa

accept directional modification also accept marking for shifts in time perspective. Yet in the semantic structure of the language, few verbs accept both temporal and directional marking at the same time, however much this is a requirement when speaking Hupa. Consider the productive medial -o?r, which occurs in many stems that depict scenes of "running." Often a directional marker specifies a particular spatial path, as illustrated in the form hooro?repek̓, which loosely translates as "I run around." Here the stem-initial marker hoor- signals indefinite motion that winds around within a fairly wide area. If the directional marker is shifted to noow-, reference can be made to the arrival at a specific goal, as illustrated in the contrasting form noowo?repek̓, which loosely translates as "I arrive here running." In lieu of directional marking, this medial also accepts marking for time perspective, as illustrated by the form himo?repek̓, which translates as "I run fast." In this instance, the prefix himo- signals that the event is carried out at a fairly rapid pace. Otherwise, all of these forms feature the first-person marker -(e)k̓ as well as the suffix -epe, which is often associated with self-oriented activity. Each form is marked either for directional bearing or for temporal features but not for both at once.

The same pattern applies to many other stems in the Yurok language. Consider, for example, the productive final -(e)c, which often occurs in stems that depict scenes of "going" or traveling on foot. In some forms, this final occurs with an initial that marks the directional bearing of the event, as in sloycok̓, which translates as "I descend, head downhill." Here the initial sloy- specifies a spatial path that descends down an incline, here a mountainside. To consider the same type of event from a specific temporal perspective, one might say woycok̓, which translates as "I am gone overnight." Here the temporal marker woy(k)- signals that this event continues over a period of one night but lacks any specific information about the directional frame.

Even where the reference is to inanimate objects, spatial and temporal per-spectives are not normally combined in any single stem construction. Consider the medial *-ekoyoʔ*, for example, which generally occurs in stems that depict the fluid motion of water currents. In some cases, this root can be modified to express a spatial path, entering into such forms as *hoolekoyoʔ*, which translates as "water flows around." Here the directional marker *hool-* specifies motion that circles around in one place. To indicate a temporal perspective, one might say *tʔekoyoʔ*, "the water is placid, stops flowing."[25] Here the temporal marker *tʔ-* signals that the flow of motion has come to a halt.[26]

CONCEPTUAL IMPLICATIONS OF SPATIAL REFERENCE

As I discuss in the previous chapter, the Hupas, Yuroks, and Karuks have all settled upon a pervasively geographical sense of the surrounding spatial world. Despite the gross similarities in the languages, the conceptual implications of spatial reference often shift quite dramatically as one passes from one community to the next. Far from holding constant, these geographical directional categories take on a range of symbolic overtones in the grammar, vocabulary, and oral litera-ture of the three neighboring groups. Indeed, many objects of experience have long been "named" for their familiar associations with particular geographical regions, including everything from animals and plants to people, ceremonial events, and even the corners of the living house (see chapter 9).

Expressive High Point in Karuk Grammar

Geographical directional concepts reach their expressive high point in the structure of the Karuk language. In Karuk speech, directional categories such as "uphill" and "downhill" are pervasive in both vocabulary and grammatical struc-ture. Structurally speaking, Karuk directional markers occur in complementary pairs, with separate suffixes that routinely differentiate such perspectives as "coming here from upriver" from the opposing viewpoint "heading toward some-place upriver from here." For Karuk speakers, such shifts in directional status are consistently marked with separate verb forms, so that making these subtle directional distinctions has become a precondition for speaking the language. In a similar way, adverbs in the Karuk language routinely distinguish the relative distance of geographical reference points; separate terms, for instance, distinguish "a long way downriver" from "a short way downriver." Among storytellers, a single scene is often surveyed from two opposing viewpoints at once, creating a kind of double directional perspective. In this setting, one might say, "Coyote was coming a long way downriver from someplace upriver." Significantly, such statements, which are common in Karuk, explicitly identify both the ultimate upriver source and the eventual downriver goal of the stated event. In Karuk vocabulary, these fine-grained geographical distinctions are extended to a sweeping range of phenomena, allowing such idiomatic formulations as "to lie with one's head pointing downriver," "to die into the river," and "to burn down from upriver."

Hupa and Yurok Reflections

To a lesser extent, similar geographical conceptions also enter into the regular structure of the neighboring Hupa and Yurok languages. Yet neither the Hupas nor the Yuroks are obliged to state the relative distance of any given point along a watercourse or mountain slope, as one must when speaking Karuk. At the same time, neither the Hupas nor the Yuroks are obliged to state both the source and the goal of an event when reporting its basic directional bearing, as is often the case for Karuk speakers. The overall conceptual implications also differ widely across the neighboring linguistic traditions.

For Hupa speakers, time perspective is closely linked to spatial marking. In fact, every directional prefix in the language is consistently associated with a single obligatory temporal marker. To take a spatial perspective in the Hupa language, the speaker must also specify a corresponding temporal perspective. Yet this is not a requirement for speakers of the Yurok and Karuk languages. So, for instance, when reporting that an event is bearing either downhill or downstream, the Hupa speaker is obliged to mention that the situation is in its initial stages, purely on the basis of the temporal perspective preselected by the grammatical structure of the language. When crossing a body of water, one is obliged to mention that the event is decisively heading toward an inevitable conclusion.

In contrast, spatial and temporal marking are entirely separate matters in Yurok grammar. One states either the directional bearing of an event or its temporal status. The speaker is not required to state both at once, as the Hupa speaker must.

Ultimately, to speak a particular language in the Native world of northwestern California is to participate in a world of spatial associations, cast from the conceptual ground of any of the area's linguistic systems outward into the classification of everyday experience.

5

Geography and Cosmology

The Yurok imagines himself to be living on a flat extent of landscape, which is roughly circular and surrounded by ocean. By going far enough up the river, it is believed that "you come to salt water again." In other words, the Klamath river is considered, in a sense, to bisect the world. This whole earth-mass, with its forests and mountains, its rivers and sea cliffs, is regarded as slowly rising and falling, with gigantic but imperceptive rhythm, on the heaving primeval flood.

T. T. Waterman, "Yurok Geography"

As can be seen in previous chapters, the Native peoples of northwestern California subscribe to a pervasively geographical sense of the spatial world. Though rooted in observable features of the surrounding environment, this system of geographical reference is also extended outward into the very conception of the universe. Here even the contours of the cosmos are conceptualized in terms of these humble, if ubiquitous, geographical notions. Each geographical region takes on a number of symbolic associations in the folklore and mythology of the region, in which nearly every direction is linked with a particular spirit realm or heaven. Within this religious framework, even the concepts of "up" and "down" take on a strong cosmological symbolism; the reference begins with the "ground below" and "sky above," and these concepts have also come to occupy a place of considerable importance in the realms of folklore and mythology.

TRADITIONAL CONCEPTION OF THE UNIVERSE

In the traditional conception of the universe, the earth was conceived of as a disc-shaped expanse with a radius of perhaps a hundred miles.[1] Around the perimeter of this islandlike earth, an enormous "river" was thought to circle in

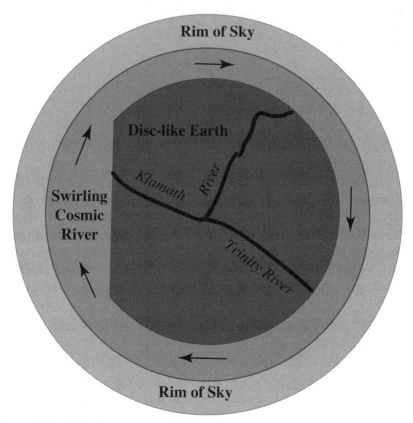

Figure 5.1. Traditional conception of the cosmos

a clockwise fashion around the shoreline. Of course, this motelike river, which was thought to reach from the rocky shores of the earth to the fringes of the heavens, corresponds to what we call the "ocean" in English. Though obviously larger, saltier, and more treacherous, this swirling body of water was said to be very similar to the area's inland rivers. Like a river, it was thought to flow along in a continuous fashion, ultimately forming a huge ring that would take travelers back to their original starting point once the circular voyage around the earth was complete (figure 5.1).[2]

Enclosing this quaking mass of solid earth at the center of the universe was an equally solid, dome-shaped sky. Beyond the sky lay a series of heavens, representing the eternal home of the spirit deities and the destination to which departed souls travel after death.

Yet this basic conception of the universe was splintered into a welter of less-than-fully-reconcilable reflections throughout the area's speech communities. Consider the terms for the "world," "universe," or "cosmos," for instance. In the Yurok language, a single expression encompasses everything in the universe, taking its primary sense from the realm of the "sky above" but also referring secondarily to the "earth below" and all the waters that flow upon it. This expression is *ki ʔwesʔonah,* which translates as "earth," "world," or "universe." The phrase takes its primary meaning from the noun *ʔwesʔonah,* which usually refers to the "sky above," and nothing more, while the first element, *ki,* an article, makes the reference a little more definite, referring in this context to the entire "realm of the sky" and the entire world below that it encloses (Waterman 1920:191).

In Hupa, however, the most general term for the "world" is *ninisʔaˑn,* an expression that derives its sense from the "solid ground" that lies below. Generally speaking, this term refers exclusively to all that would be described in English as the "earth," "country," "landscape," or "mountains." Yet in some cases, this form can also refer to the heavens beyond the horizon, where solid land was thought to lay. On structural grounds, the term is based on the verb stem *-ʔaˑn,* which, with the prefix *s-* before it, forms an expression referring to the motionless position taken by a round object. The first element, *nini,* refers etymologically to the "dirt," "earth," or "ground," which, in this instance, following the semantics of the preceding verbal unit, has come to rest in one place without perceptible movement. The expression, as a whole, literally refers to "the solid earth that rests there motionless," taking its primary sense from the land that lies beneath us. Another expression is required to speak of the heavens, namely, *deˑnohqʼid,* which translates as "here above us." Thus, in contrast to Yurok, the Hupa language has no single term that encompasses everything in the entire universe—the earth, the skies, the waters, and the heavens, all at once.

Karuk, like Hupa, has a similar term that refers, in essence, to the solid earth that lies around us. Yet in Karuk this expression is usually not extended to the heavens, for which there are other terms. The Karuk term for the surrounding countryside is *ithívthaaneen,* an expression built up around the root *thiv,* which refers, like its Hupa counterpart, to the condition of "resting motionless in one place." This element, in turn, is fused with the adverbial element *thaneên,* which indicates a wide and even distribution in the surrounding spatial world, often conveying a meaning that is similar to the English preposition "around." As a unit, the Karuk expression for the "world" literally refers to that relatively stationary tract of land "that lies around us."

MYTHICAL REALMS UPSTREAM

By going far enough along any of the area's rivers, the traveler eventually comes to the edge of the water, as the universe was once conceived by the Native peoples of northwestern California. The traveler then arrives at one of several mythical lands thought to rest at the upstream fringes of the universe. One such realm is said to lie beyond the horizon, at the upstream limit of the swirling cosmic river thought to circle around the coastline. Others are said to rest at the headwaters of several of the area's "inland" rivers, where the land was said to come to an abrupt halt before slipping off into the cosmic waters thought to circle the perimeter of the disclike earth. In this sense, the concept of a mythical land "upstream" is a common one throughout the region. Yet each group ascribes a different set of episodes to these heavily fabled sectors of the cosmos.

The Spirit Heaven Upstream

Starting at the mouth of the Klamath River and traveling from there upstream against the current of the swirling cosmic river thought to circle the earth, the traveler eventually comes to the "upstream" spirit heaven. Before arriving at any such destination, one must pass beyond the rim of the solid dome-shaped sky. Then, by slipping beneath a passageway at the rim of the sky, the traveler arrives at this mythical "upstream heaven" beyond the horizon.

In the Yurok conception, this is the land to which the central figure in the creation pantheon (Across-the-Ocean-Widower) fled after abandoning the world he had originally prepared for the coming of humans (see Waterman 1920:191). Here in the upstream spirit heaven, he leads the other spirit deities in a nightly performance of the White Deerskin Dance. According to the Yuroks, Across-the-Ocean-Widower established this tradition during the transformation, when he and the other myth figures first took refuge here. In the Yurok language, this realm is known as ʔɹ-kɹgɹʔ,[3] a specialized term that possibly means "where he lives."[4] Like the Hupas, the Yuroks believe that the souls of the dead travel to the heaven where their favorite dance is performed. For the Yuroks, this means that those who follow the White Deerskin Dance ultimately travel to the "upstream spirit heaven" upon their death.

The Hupas, in contrast, attribute nearly opposite features to this heaven. For instance, in the Hupa conception, it is the Jump Dance rather than the White Deerskin Dance that is performed in the upstream heaven.[5] As far as the

Hupas are concerned, the Jump Dance has been performed in the upstream heaven every night since the time of the great transformation, when the spirit deities first took refuge there. Like the Yuroks, the Hupas also believe that the souls of the dead travel to the spirit heaven where their favorite dance is always performed every night.[6] Yet the two groups hold different views about where the dances are held. The Hupas call this land De·-noho⅃-yima·ni-yinaɢ, meaning "(the spirit heaven) here with us across the waters upstream." The first part of the construction, *de·-noho⅃,* which translates as "here with us," fixes this point of reference at the ceremonially significant village of Taʔkʸimi⅃diŋ, where the Trinity River passes through the Hoopa Valley on a northwesterly course. The directional adverb *yinaɢ* then situates this spirit heaven somewhere "upstream" from this point of origin, which here corresponds to the compass point southeast. The second directional adverb *yima·n* signals a path that heads out "across the water"—here, implicitly, across the cosmic river that was thought to circle around the earth, toward the heavens at its fringes. In the Hupa conception, Eel was born in the upstream heaven before traveling downstream to the mouth of the Klamath, where this animal would later embark on its annual travels throughout the world's inland waters.[7]

Karuk storytellers, for their part, sometimes speak of an upstream heaven where great dances are performed.[8] These dances are so furious, it is said, that Coyote sometimes soils himself in the frenzy, after he has made his long and treacherous journey to one of these distant mythical heavens.[9] In the Karuk tradition, this realm is known as "the world's upstream limit," or Káruk Ithívthaaneen-ʔíppan, a place perhaps more closely connected with the upstream boundary of the universe, located near the headwaters of the Klamath. Apart from these few references, the Karuks do not appear to have participated in this aspect of the cosmology as thoroughly as their neighbors, the Hupas and Yuroks.

Before arriving in this heaven upstream, according to the Yuroks, one comes to the place where First Salmon fled after being freed from his primordial captors, long ago, during the ancient myth times.[10] From that moment on, First Salmon continued to lead the other salmon here, each year, on their annual migration. Starting in the area's inland rivers, all the salmon travel down to the mouth of the Klamath before entering the cosmic river at the edge of the earth. Then, by traveling against the current and toward the solid sky at the horizon, they arrive at the solid land that is thought to rest across the cosmic waters, beyond the rim of the sky. Every year the voyage is repeated.

The Upstream Edge of the Earth

Beginning one's journey along an "inland" river and traveling from there up against the current to its farthest extent, one eventually reaches another upstream limit. Several such regions are distinguished in the area's religious traditions.

In the Hupa conception, this upstream edge of the land corresponds to the farthest reaches of the Trinity River, the familiar watercourse that passes through the Hupas' homeland (Sapir 2001:995). Located near its headwaters to the "southeast" (to fall back on familiar English concepts), the inland waters of the Trinity River were here thought to slip off into those vast, swirling cosmic waters thought to circle the fringes of the solid land. The Hupas know this heaven by the expression YinaGi-ninisʔaˑn-noˑŋʔaˑ-diŋ, which means "the world's upstream limit." This particular phrase is based on the verb form noˑŋʔaˑ, which refers to a point beyond which "(something) reaches no farther." In this case, the reference is to the "boundary" or "limit" of the earth, as denoted by the noun ninisʔaˑn, which generally translates as "world," "earth," or "country." While the adverb yinaG signals a directional region "upstream," the locative marker -diŋ converts the entire phrase into an elaborate noun that refers to the mythical land where the "world comes to its upstream limit." It was at this spot, the Hupas maintain, that First Salmon was held captive before being freed from his primordial captors, thereafter venturing to the upstream limits of the universe to make his new home until the end of time. According to Hupa tradition, this is also the land where the wind settles in the spring, blowing gently for a time, while causing relatively little harm.[11]

In the Yurok and Karuk conceptions, the upstream limit of the world corresponds to the farthest reaches of the Klamath River, the primary watercourse along which both groups have made their homes. Among the Yuroks, this land is called Peckuk (see Waterman 1920:192), based on the adverb pecku, which points to a directional region someplace "(toward) upstream." The locative suffix -k, at the end of the form, situates this land "at" a site upstream. The resulting form loosely translates as "(the place) at the farthest upstream extent (of the universe)." According to Yurok and Karuk storytellers, this is said to be the place where First Salmon was held captive before eventually being freed. Little more is attributed to this region among the Yuroks, for whom this realm, far outside their homeland, would remain shrouded in mystery.

For the Karuks, in contrast, the upstream spirit realm is closely associated with Money's Home, where lives a figure who is often said to have settled near the Klamath Lakes, at the farthest upstream limit of the local Klamath River.[12] It is to this realm, as well, that First Eel continually strives to make its annual return, having been born at the downstream end of the world but knowing that its mother was from the upstream end of the universe, where it would hope, one day, to be reunited with its family. Among the Karuks, this realm is called Káruk Ithívthaaneen-ʔíppan, which loosely translates as "the world's upstream limit." This construction is based on the noun *ithívthaaneen,* which refers to the "earth" or solid land that lies around us. The directional adverb *káruk* places this land someplace "upstream," while the spatial modifier *-ʔípan* specifies that it lies at the world's "end or limit."

MYTHICAL REALMS DOWNSTREAM

Beginning one's journey at the mouth of the Klamath and traveling from there "down" into the current of that vast, swirling cosmic river thought to circle the earth, the traveler eventually arrives a "downstream" spirit realm. Before arriving at this destination, one first must pass under the rim of the sky and emerge on the other side to enter the mythical "downstream" heaven. Though the Native peoples of this region agree that such a place exists, little consensus surrounds this particular spirit heaven.

In the Hupa conception, this is the land to which Across-the-Ocean-Widower fled after abandoning the world that he had originally prepared for humans. For this reason, the Hupas link the downstream heaven with the White Deer-skin Dance, which Across-the-Ocean-Widower is said to have instituted long ago as a ritual for repairing the wrongs that accumulate in this world as a result of human misconduct (see Sapir 2001:897). (As I discuss in the previous section, the Yuroks attribute similar features to the opposite heaven upstream.) The Hupas know this land as Deˑ-nohoł-yimaˑni-yideʔ, an expression that refers to the spirit heaven "here with us across the water downstream." Again, the familiar phrase *deˑnohoł,* which loosely translates as "here with us," fixes the point of reference in the Hoopa Valley, pointing from there out across the universe to the heavens at its fringes, while the adverb *yimaˑn* signals a directional bearing that reaches out "across the water," by implication the cosmic waters that circle the earth. The second directional adverb, *yideʔ,* indicates that the speaker is referring to the particular spirit heaven found at the "downstream" end of this water flow—as projected from the Trinity River, which flows on a roughly northwesterly course through the Hoopa Valley, thought to be roughly where this spirit heaven rests relative to the Hupa homeland. It is toward this land, the Hupas maintain, that First Salmon fled after being freed from his primordial captors.

The Yuroks share few of these views with their Hupa neighbors. Instead, the Yuroks hold that the "downstream" heaven is a slightly less sacred land, one associated with the birth of gambling and several of the more humble religious figures, whose primary role is to rid of the world of such loathsome pests as snakes and monsters. In the Yurok language, this realm is known simply as Pulekuk (see Waterman 1920:191), a term that is identical with the directional adverb *pulekuk,* merely indicating a "downstream" path. Yet in this context the term specifically represents the cosmological limit at the farthest downstream extent. Nearby is the home of Money, whose resting place the Yuroks place farther downstream than do their Hupa neighbors, who instead associate Money's Home with the upstream heaven.

In the Karuk conception, in contrast, the downstream realm is associated with the mythical land where Eel was born.[13] Among the Karuks, this land is called Yúruk Ithívthaaneen-ʔifuth-kam, which literally refers to "the world's down-stream behind side." The expression is based on the noun form *ithívthaaneen,* which generally refers to the solid "earth" that lies around us. The spatial marker *ʔifuth* situates this site "behind" the land visible from Karuk country, while the directional adverb *yúruk* signals that this place lies "a great way downstream." At the end of the form, the spatial marker *-kam* specifies that this land is on another "side" of the world.

Heading slightly farther into the current of this vast, swirling cosmic river, one eventually reaches the farthest downstream limit of the universe, into which all of the world's inland waters flow. The Hupas call this realm Yideʔ-ninisʔaˑn-noˑŋʔaˑ-diŋ (see Sapir 2001:993), which translates as "the world's downstream limit." This expression is based on the verb of linear extension *noˑŋʔaˑ,* which refers to a point past which something reaches no farther. Here reference is made to the "boundary" or "limit" of the earth, as denoted by the noun *ninisʔaˑn,* which generally translates as "world," "earth," or "country." While the adverb *yideʔ* signals a directional region "downstream (from the speaker)" the locative marker *-diŋ* converts the entire phrase into an elaborate noun that refers to the mythical land where the "world comes to its downstream limit." In the Hupa conception, this is the land where the wind was born, blowing most furiously from this direction during the winter months. Later in the season, the wind would travel to the opposite upstream edge of the world, where it would cause no further sickness during this brief but happy spell.[14]

The Karuks call this realm Yúruk Ithívthaaneen-ʔíppan, meaning "the world's downstream limit." This parallel expression is based on the noun *ithívthaaneen,* which refers to the solid earth that lies around us. The directional adverb *yúruk* situates this mythical land somewhere "far downstream" from the heart of Karuk country, while the spatial maker *-ʔípan* at the end of the form places this site at the world's "end" or "limit." As with the downstream limit of the universe, the Karuks also attribute great dances to this opposite land on the other side of the cosmos. Again, these dances are so furious that Coyote sometimes soils himself in the frenzy. Spirits are also said to pass tassels between the "upstream" and "downstream" ends of the universe, while Dog, who is considered one of the most sacred animals in creation, fetches them each time.[15]

Farther downriver, according to the Hupas, lies still another heaven, one known by the expression Deˑ-nohoł-yideʔi-yidaɢ, which literally refers to the spirit realm that rests "here with us downstream and uphill." The directional bearing is projected from the village of Taʔkʸimił-diŋ, reaching from there out across the universe to the heavens at its fringes. At this location, "downstream" briefly corresponds to the compass point northwest, while "uphill" loosely corresponds to northeast. In the middle of these two paths lies a land roughly to the north; relative to the swirling cosmic river thought to circle the earth, this land is located a little way "downriver" from the mouth of the Klamath. For the Hupas, this mythical land is associated with the powers of doctoring, representing a realm from which shamans draw their powers.[16]

Because all of the area's inland rivers eventually flow downstream into the mouth of the Klamath, each realm represents one or another of the possible destinations one might reach in heading far enough "downstream," regardless of where one originally starts out.

THE HEAVENLY REALM BEYOND THE SKY

Reaching out beyond this earth in every direction, as far as the eye can see, is said to rest an equally solid, dome-shaped sky. The rim or base of this sky is said to dip into the cosmic waters thought to circle constantly around its perimeter. Beyond the boundaries of this fixed ceiling lies another world, with features similar to those found on earth, though inhabited not by mortals but by spirits. Here the souls of the dead live together with the spirit deities, who fled for the heavens long ago, during the time of the transformation, when the world was being prepared for humans.

Though mortals did not regularly journey to these lands, one could gain access to the heavens by climbing an invisible ladder near the center of the universe, beneath the apex of the sky, only a short distance downstream from the village of Kenek (Waterman 1920:190). The other way of entering this mythical land beyond the sky is far more treacherous, requiring that one pierce the solid surface of the sky with an arrow before climbing up to the heavens on a rope attached to the arrow. Coyote is said to have tried this once, falling for ten years before returning to the earth, only to be crushed to death.

Both the Hupas and the Karuks refer to this realm as "the world above us"; among the Yuroks, in contrast, the expression for the heavens also secondarily applies to all that lies beneath the heavens, both the earth and its waters included. In Hupa this realm is called De·-nohq'id, which translates as "(the world) here above us." This expression is based on the spatial element -q'id, which conveys the sense of both "above" and "on top of," while the first-person plural marker noh- specifically situates this land above "us," or the realm of humans. At the beginning of the form, the demonstrative element de· contributes the sense that this land is directly above one's place of standing. The Karuks, in contrast, call this land Páy Nanuʔávahkam, which means "the side or face (of the cosmos) that is above us." This construction is based on the root -ʔávah-, which refers to a region "above" something, here in relation to a group of people, as denoted by the possessive first-person plural prefix nanu- 'us'. At the end of the form, the suffix -kam signals that the reference is to the "side" that is above us—by implication, the realm of the sky. The article pay then makes the reference more definite, indicating that specific realm, known by all, to rest in the heavens above us since the beginning of time. Among the Yuroks, this realm is called Ki (ʔ)Wesʔonah, a construction that literally refers to the sky, while encompassing everything that rests beneath the heavens, including the earth and waters below.

THE LAND OF THE DEAD

Far from the land of ordinary human experience is said to rest a hell or purgatory of almost unspeakable agony. For fear of stirring the dangerous spirits said to dwell there, most avoid the subject, along with other unspeakable evils.

In the traditional Yurok conception, this fear-inspiring "land of the dead" is said to rest directly beneath this world, where a series of trails along the coast lead down into the belly of the earth (Waterman 1920:192). Before entering this hellish realm, the traveler must cross a lake that marks the threshold between the land of the living and the land of the dead. The Hupas, in contrast, place this land of the dead out along the horizon, near the land of the setting sun, where a similar trail leads to this heavily fabled sector of the cosmos. The Hupas locate this land not directly below ground but farther outward along the horizon, at the fringes of the universe.[17] The Karuks place the land of the dead above us, near the heavens, though without attributing to it those fearsome qualities that the Hupas and Yuroks ascribe.[18] Like the Hupas and Yuroks, however, the Karuks also hold that trails lead to this land. Like their neighbors, the Karuks likewise hold that one must cross a great lake before passing the threshold to the realm on the other side.

THE MIDDLE OF THE WORLD

Roughly at the center of this disc-shaped earth rests a region known as the "middle of the world." The exact center of the universe is usually said to rest at the Yurok village of Kenek. More generally, the "middle of the world" also encompasses much of the surrounding territory, within a fairly broad radius. Throughout the region, major episodes of the creation myth are usually set in the "middle of the world," together with many of the events that followed during the time of the transformation. It was here, for instance, that the central myth figure of the region, Across-the-Ocean-Widower, first sprang into existence, initiating the creation of the world and embarking on those great adventures that eventually shaped the world as we know it today. With him arose an entire race of prehuman spirit deities, alongside thereafter-eternal forces of good and evil.

More generally, the concept of a "middle" or "center" occupies a place of intense symbolic concern in the traditional Native cultures of northwestern California. According to the common cosmological framework shared throughout the area's speech communities, the earth was said to rest roughly at the "center" of the universe. Yet each group situates the precise "middle" of the world somewhere near its own homeland. Continuing in this vein, the era of the transformation has always been the dominant concern in the local folklore and mythology, representing a period that lies "midway" between the most ancient times and the present epoch. Significantly, it was during this crucial turning point in the prehistory of the planet that the world as we know it first began to take shape. During the final phases of the transformation, the spirit deities realized that the human era was about to begin only when they saw smoke hanging "halfway" down the neighboring mountains, "midway" between the peak and base. In ceremonial settings, singers and ceremonial leaders often perform at the "middle" of the group. Similarly, these specialists often bear names that reflect their spatial position at the "center" of the dance. Sometimes a transformation from ordinary to sacred occurs at some symbolically charged "middle ground." Sometimes a blessing is also conferred at a region in the "center," portending a movement from the mundane to the sacred. According to one popular tale,[19] a boy was once instantaneously transformed into a spirit deity as he leapt headlong into the "center" of a boat, his eyebrows miraculously turning feather-red to mark his newfound status as a member of the spirit world. In other cases, it is evil that lurks at some place in the middle, here perhaps marking a reverse transition from safety to danger. Girls were warned, for example, of the perils they might encounter when heading out to the "middle" of a field by themselves. And when confronting a monster became necessary, it was important to travel "halfway" into the territory surrounding its home yet never completely into its path.

CULTURAL CONVERGENCE AND
ACCENTUATING LOCAL DIFFERENCES

The Native peoples of northwestern California have settled on a common cosmological framework in which the earth is a disc-shaped mass of quaking land that rests at the center of the universe. Beyond the swirling "cosmic river" that surrounds the human world is the rim of a solid, dome-shaped sky. By passing under the rim of the sky, one enters into one of the heavens at the fringes of the universe, where the souls of the dead join the spirit deities who have made their eternal home there. Each heaven is associated with a different type of dance, and those who are devoted to a particular dance travel to the corresponding heaven at death.

Despite these many points of agreement, striking differences persist at the local level, with each group holding a very different vision of the universe. Some of the differences may represent vestiges of former ancestral conceptions, predating the contact between the groups in northwestern California. A case in point is the Yurok concept of an ocean of pitch, a concept that is not found anywhere else in the region and bears a striking affinity to Algonquian creation stories (Waterman 1920:191). Even where the groups have settled on a common element of belief, there is often substantial evidence of inversion. Though the Hupas, for instance, situate the White Deerskin Dance in the downstream spirit heaven, the Yuroks place it in the opposite heaven, at the upstream edge of the universe. Similarly, while the Yuroks place the land of the dead directly beneath the human-occupied world, the Hupas situate this underworld out along the horizon, near the land of the setting sun. Despite the many surface similarities, each community maintains its own distinctive sense of worldview, often in sharp opposition to the beliefs of its closest neighbors.

Part III

The Realm of Time

6

The Linguistic Classifications
of Time

*I find it gratuitous to assume that a Hopi who knows only the Hopi language
and the cultural ideas of his own society has the same notions, often supposed to be intuitions, of time and space that we have, and that are generally
assumed to be universal.*

Benjamin Lee Whorf, Language, Thought, and Reality

Centuries of scholarship in the field of linguistics have demonstrated that
all languages provide formal mechanisms for signaling shifts in time perspective, a category of analysis that probably has its basis in panhuman psychological considerations.[1] Often these shifts in perspective are facilitated by
specialized grammatical categories, which signal abstract temporal relations in
an abbreviated and regularized fashion.

A case in point is the category of *tense,* which, for instance, makes its
appearance in many of the world's languages, even if tense marking is not,
strictly speaking, absolutely universal. Some of these categories establish a
"past" or "future" in relation to an implicit "present." The concept of a "past
tense" rests, in large part, on the common human capacity to recall one's former
experiences and to extrapolate from these memories to the past experiences of
others, even historical personages. By the same token, all human societies
share a strong concern with the past, which is typically recounted in storytelling in preliterate societies or documented in literature where writing is
present. In a similar fashion, the concept of a "future tense" has roots in the
common human tendency to forecast possible scenarios in the imagination,
often based on expectations gained in the past. Because the concept is deeply
rooted in the human psyche, nearly all societies show some concern for "the
future," often based on religious prophecy, cosmological conceptions, or political

rhetoric. Yet as conceptions of the past and future differ profoundly even in our own society, frequently according to scientific doctrine or to religious belief, so also can we expect other societies to construct a different sense of time according to local cultural expectation. So, for instance, a staunch creationist and a modern-day physicist may map very different conceptions on their understanding of the past, present, and future of the universe, all of which can be conveyed in English to various degrees.

Or consider the related distinction between "complete events" and those that are still in the process of unfolding. Similar conceptual splits make their appearance in many of the world's languages, often with uncanny semantic regularity, even among languages that are in no way related through common ancestry or regional contact. Formally known as *aspectual markers,* these grammatical categories often specify the relative duration, completion, or repetition of a process without necessarily placing it in the past, present, or future. Here the reference is to the internal time schedule on which a process unfolds, not its status relative to an implicit present. For, in a very significant way, an event can be complete, ongoing, or repeated at any point in time, and whether it is in the past, present, or future is immaterial to this sense of the internal time schedule of the process itself.

As Whorf hints in the famous passage that is this chapter's epigraph, temporal categories often differ substantially in detail and arrangement across the range of human languages. Consider, for instance, the Native languages of northwestern California. In each of the languages, tense-based categories such as "past" and "future" are universally available to speakers, though with substantial differences in meaning throughout the area's speech communities. For some, such as Karuk speakers, the past can be succinctly tied to the era of creation, with a single suffix that can be attached to any verb in the language to place the scene in question in these most sacred times. For others, such as Hupa speakers, explicit reference to the past often involves a sense that these historical events have been decisively severed from the era of the living present, a unusual conceptual implication not found in the neighboring linguistic traditions.

It is one thing to compare categories in the abstract, as has been popular in linguistics for over a century now, starting with the early structuralism of Ferdinand de Saussure and continuing today with the "scientific framework" of modern linguistics. It is another to put oneself into the shoes of the speakers when these categories refer to actual experiences or entire cultural universes. That is, in actual use, linguistic categories always refer to the flesh-and-blood experiences of real people, however apparently abstract the concepts found in all human languages. In practice, for instance, the "present" is not always set at the exact moment the speaker opens his or her mouth. Instead, the present is often placed at some imaginary point in the fabric of a story line. Here the "fictive present" is often set long ago, in the "ancient past." By the same token, in creation lore, the "distant future" of the story line may actually refer to the present moment of narrative, as this time is projected from the past.

In the end, every language imposes a different set of categories onto the realm of time, encompassing everyday activities as well as those distant historical events reported in narrative and preserved through storytelling. Many of the categories found in northwestern California run loosely parallel throughout the region. Consider, for instance, the case of the future tense, within which many of the languages have developed a special grammatical distinction between the "near" and the "distant" future. Other categories are restricted in distribution to a particular linguistic tradition and are not to be found elsewhere in the region. Consider, for example, the concept of the "distal future," carried out at another location, one that finds grammatical expression in only a small handful of languages, including the Yurok language of northwestern California. Or consider the special progressive aspect of the Hupa language, which can be applied to any verb in the language to indicate that the activity in question is repeated, in stops and starts, over a great span of time, while the subject moves along a fairly linear course. To speak a given language is thus to participate in a particular scheme of classification, one that is projected from the conceptual framework of one's native language outward into the world of everyday experience.

GENERAL SEMANTICS OF TIME IN KARUK

The Karuk verb in its basic form is fairly timeless in scope unless specifically marked for temporal features, which is not always required. As such, the Karuk verb is often capable of referring to activities that are just starting out or to those that are still in the process of reaching completion. In addition, the Karuk verb in its unmarked form is equally capable of referring to events that are situated deep in the mythical past and to those that may one day come to pass, perhaps sometime in the distant future.

Though many Karuk verbs remain unmarked for time perspective, imposing a definite time frame onto any event reported in speech is always possible. By modifying the verb with one of several grammatical markers, the speaker can state that an event is habitual in nature or has been carried out continuously over an indefinite period. With other markers, the speaker can specify that the event took place deep in the mythical past or that an action is merely being contemplated for the future.

For the Karuk speaker, such temporal distinctions are largely optional, however, representing a possibility that is not always exploited with great regularity, especially in oral literature. Instead, the verb often remains unrestricted in temporal scope, with a sparing use overall of those temporal markers that are available in the language. In oral literature, for instance, most verbs remain unmarked for time perspective, with only the occasional tense markers that place these otherwise timeless scenes at a specific point in time—such as in the "ancient past" or the "distant future." Yet in everyday life one must always state a time frame, indicating, for instance, that an event is either complete or ongoing. When the reference is to a complete event, one says, for instance, *papihnêefich káan tuʔuʔáhoo,* which translates as "the coyote went there (just now)." Here the perfective particle *t(a)* at the beginning of the verb signals that the reference is to a single complete instantiation of this event. When the reference is to an ongoing activity, one says *papihnêefich káan ʔuʔáhooti,* which translates as "the coyote is (in the process of) going there." Here the durative suffix *-ti(h)* at the end of the verb signals that the event continues for some time. Interestingly, this pattern does not apply to narrative, in which most forms remain "tenseless" or unbounded in potential temporal scope. So, in a creation story, one could say *pihnêefich káan ʔuʔáhoo,* which loosely translates as "Coyote went/goes there," leaving the time frame completely unspecified.[2]

Karuk Aspect

Without explicit marking for time perspective, the Karuk verb is essentially unbounded in scope, indicating a general process but not the duration of the process or its status in relation to an implicit present. Yet any verb can be modified to express a number of permutations of the process depicted in its general or unmarked form.

To start with a relatively "timeless" construction, one that carries no specific information about the temporal qualities of the event, consider the expression *ʔuʔárihroov,* which loosely translates as "one being goes upstream." This construction is based on the verb stem *ʔárih-,* which refers to the act of "going," often at a rather hurried pace, here occurring with the directional suffix *-rôovu* 'heading upriver from here' and the third-person prefix *ʔu-,* which signals that either an animal or a person is in the role of subject. In this form, the verb is unrestricted in temporal scope, referring only to the process in a very general way, without placing any specific limitation on the time frame from which this event is to be viewed. Signaling only a general instantiation of the process of "going upstream," this form remains ambiguous as to whether the event is starting out, entering its middle phases, or approaching completion. And as no limitations have yet been placed on the scope of the activity, this form could be set in the past, the present, or the future, with equal validity.

With the addition of the durative marker *-tih,* any event can be stretched out over a considerable span of time. Simply by attaching this affix to a verb, the general process can be considered over a substantial period, with focus on the middle stages of the unfolding process. Consider, for instance, the unmarked form *ʔuʔárihroov,* which conveys nothing about the scope of the event, simply translating as "one being goes upriver." The durative form is *ʔuʔárihroovutih,* which translates as "one being is engaged in the process of going upriver." Minimally distinct from the general, or unmarked, form of the verb, the durative form extends only the time frame with the addition of the suffix *-tih.*

In creation stories, durative forms often highlight episodes that the narrator wishes to stretch out for a time in the fabric of the story line. The durative form also functions to draw attention to a scene that may have been carried out for a longer span than the narrator is able to dwell on. Sometimes a durative form highlights a characteristic act that later comes to define a figure for all time thereafter, as when Coyote declares that he is eating his own excrement, saying *ʔaaf* 'excrement' *paʔniʔáamtih* 'it is that I am eating'.[3] Though certainly true at the time when the story was set, this declaration on Coyote's part continues to hold validity today, representing a familiar scene that can still be seen in the world around one. In a sense, the activity stretches continuously from the era of creation into the living present. Here the durative marker stretches out the scene in the imagination of the audience, whether only for a moment or, by implication, for all eternity.

A verb can also be modified to signal the recurrence of an event over a considerable span of time. For this purpose, a special marker known as the iterative prefix specifies that an event takes place repeatedly. Again, consider the unmarked form *ʔuʔárihroov,* which translates as "one being goes upriver." Here the iterative variant is *ʔuppárihroov,* which explicitly expresses the meaning that this being goes upriver "once more." Taking the shape of the prefix *(i)p-,* the presence of the iterative marker in the second construction signals that the reference is now to a repetition of the entire event, namely, that of heading off someplace upriver, after having done it once before. In verbs that lack an element of motion, iterative marking lends itself to a more subtle reading, generally referring to the persistence of a condition over a considerable time span, one that is often punctuated by fluctuations in perceived intensity. Consider the form ʔupíkrii, which loosely translates as "one stays there again and again," based on the unmarked form ʔúkrii, which simply means "one stays there." Here the iterative marking signals that the subject inhabited a particular site continuously over a fairly open-ended yet extensive period.

In creation stories, iterative forms often draw attention to activities mentioned earlier in the tale, signaling the return of this event. Often these iterative forms highlight the repetition of a significant episode. For example, when Coyote is heading upriver, iterative forms placed sporadically throughout the tale remind the audience that it is toward the upriver world that Coyote is still heading, even though he may have stopped along the way. In the timeline of the tale, he may have been distracted over the course of his journey, often to engage in some kind of mischief. Sometimes the reference is to a troublesome event that repeats itself for a time, until it can be resolved. When a tick lodges itself in Across-the-Ocean-Widower's penis, for instance, this troublesome pest remains there in a recurring and perhaps painful way until this creation figure is able to remove the intruder.

The verb can also be modified to indicate that an event has been repeated for a spell, as a matter of custom or habit. Known as the habitual prefix, this marker signals that the activity portrayed by the verb in its general form is here performed repeatedly—as a matter of custom or habit—over a considerable span of time. To start with an unmarked form, one that carries no explicit information about the scope of the scene, consider the relatively "timeless" construction ʔuvâaram, which loosely translates as "one being goes off." Based on the verb stem vâaramu, which refers to the act of "going off," this construction occurs in the third person with the subject marker ʔu-, referring, again, to either an animal or a human in the role of subject. With the habitual marker -oo, together with the durative suffix -tih, the form becomes ʔuvaaramôotih,[4] while the meaning shifts to "one being always goes off." As illustrated in this example, the habitual and durative markers often occur together, suggesting an activity that is repeated habitually over a considerable time span. In creation stories, habitual forms often highlight important episodes whose repetition holds lasting significance for the scenes to follow. Though established in the past, these activities are often still performed to this day. In oral literature, Bear, for instance, is always going off in the evening, a characteristic act that is still ascribed to this figure even today.

Any Karuk verb can also be modified to refer to a single, complete instantiation of the general event portrayed in its unmarked form. This shift in perspective is marked with the perfective particle *t(a),* which occurs immediately before the verb. Consider again the unmarked form *ʔuʔárihroov,* "one being goes upriver." Here the contrasting perfective form is *tuʔárihroov,* which translates as "one being went upriver just once having completed the act." With the addition of the perfective marker, the scope of the event is no longer open-ended; instead, the reference is to a specific occurrence, which took place only once and is therefore complete for all intents and purposes. In this particular case, the perfective particle, which elsewhere occurs as *ta,* is loosely bound to the verb, a situation that occurs in many cases where the verb form begins with a glottal stop that is immediately followed by a vowel. In creation stories, perfective forms are frequently invoked to mark the completion, or culmination, of an action that has already begun, representing a "mission accomplished." Coyote, for example, finally arrives upriver, a destination he is always striving to reach.

Karuk Tense

The Karuk verb can always be modified to situate an event squarely in either the past or the future. Yet these tense-based categories are only sparingly applied in oral literature, in which most verbs remain unrestricted in scope. The past is more heavily subdivided than the future in Karuk, as is the case in most of the neighboring languages. For the distant future is a realm of far less cultural interest, except when it is projected from the ancient past. No special category exists in Karuk to mark the present. Yet any verb that lacks an overt tense marker can be interpreted as carrying a present tense reading, depending, of course, on context. The fundamental tense categories of the Karuk language are outlined in figure 6.1.

The past is split into three divisions in the Karuk language, each one concerned with the relative distance between an implicit present and the episode that precedes it. The most remote category is the "ancient past," which is signaled by the marker *=anik.* Here the reference is generally to events that took place before recent memory. Most of the time, the reference is to the mythical era of creation, which is set before the arrival of modern humans. Yet in some cases, this marker

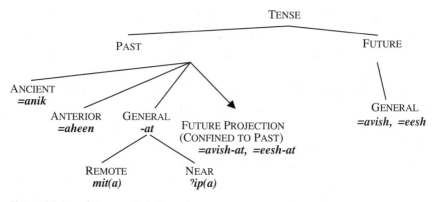

Figure 6.1. Karuk tense categories

can also refer to the period following the transformation, namely, to the prehistoric times when people first began to walk the earth.

One mention of this category anywhere in the story line is enough to set an entire string of surrounding scenes in this most sacred period, placing the whole plot of the story before the era that anyone can remember from personal experience. Sometimes this marker of the ancient past is applied early in the narration, even in the first few lines, letting the audience know that the entire succession of scenes to follow all took place long ago, in the ancient past. Yet in the majority of cases, this marker is reserved for that most pivotal scene that brings the story to a point of culmination, often for an ancient act that sets the present world into motion. Occasionally, the marker of the ancient past is liberally applied throughout an entire story line, setting every act, in a very definite way, deep in the past. Yet few speakers exploit this option when telling creation stories.

The marker of the "general past," in contrast, simply refers to events that come before the basic temporal ground, or implicit present, established by the speaker. Consisting of the suffix -at, the general past enters in two primary configurations, one occurring with a separate word or particle marking the "near past" and another with a particle marking the "remote past."

The "near past," which is marked with the particle ʔip(a), signals an event of some immediacy, having just taken place in the evolving context of the story line. For example, when Coyote seals up his anus to prevent food from spilling out, he announces this proud accomplishment with a form marked for the near past, saying, *ta* 'complete event' *ʔíp* 'near past' *nishivshápat* 'I've sealed up'.[5] In the not-so-distant future that follows, his rear end catches fire, for he foolishly plugged it with highly flammable sap.

The "remote past," in contrast, refers to events that are greatly removed from the living present, having taken place some time ago, though their effects may still be lingering. It is marked with the particle *mit(a),* provided that the verb has already been situated in the general past with the suffix *-at.* When, for instance, after many sustained efforts on their parts, all the animals are unable to stop fire in its path, this is announced with the words *yukún* 'so it is' *púxay* 'not' *vúra* 'indeed!' *mít* 'remote past' *ʔisháxxishrihmathat* '(they) stopped (fire)'.[6] Here the use of the remote past stresses that a great span of time has elapsed since the animals came to this ancient realization that they would not be able to stop the fire.

A separate anterior tense signals a time more distant than the general past but not quite as remote as the ancient times. In another sense, the anterior tense also refers to scenes that fix the temporal ground for the events to follow, with the highlighted anterior episode coming before those in its aftermath. The concept is signaled with the marker *=aheen,* which can be attached to any verb to place the event in the anterior tense. When, for instance, Grizzly Bear scratches out the land containing a pond, eventually freeing the way for a future waterfall, this deed is set in the anterior tense with the word *ʔuʔakxáraprupaheen* '(Grizzly Bear) scratched (the falls) toward downriver'. In the next line it is revealed that a barrier once blocked the way, a former condition that is set in the ancient past with the word *ʔuttássunihtihanik* 'a barrier (existed) in ancient times'.[7] Here Grizzly Bear's former act is not quite as distant as the ancient past, merely anterior to the state of affairs that came to follow this world-transforming event. Soon afterward, for instance, Duck Hawk expressed concern about what would happen to the pond she once enjoyed, whose sounds had now ceased.

The future, in contrast, is split into just two categories in the Karuk language, one of them deriving from the other. The rationale may be partially cultural, representing a general trend that is also reflected in the neighboring languages. Simply put, the future is of far less cultural concern than the past in the Native religious traditions, for which the bulk of the material is set in the past, to various degrees.

The most general category of the future tense is signaled by the marker *=avish* (also *=eesh*), an element that can be attached to any verb to place the scene in question after the basic temporal ground already established by the speaker. Often storytellers use the "general future" to frame the wishes or desires of the myth figures, as when Coyote plots, with wildcat and spider, to make a trip to the heavens to pursue an elusive deer that has taken refuge there. These intentions are stated in the general future, with the collective pronouncement, on the part of all the animals, *nukuníhuraavish* 'we can shoot (the twine) up'.[8] Based on the verb *kuníh,* which refers to the act of "shooting," this form also contains the directional marker -*uraa,* which signals that the movement extends up into the heavens.[9] Here the general future marker is =*avish,* while the grammatical marker *nu-* signals that the subject is in the first-person plural. In oral literature, the "distant future" of the present era is often projected from deep in the ancient past, straight from the lips of the myth figures, who use the general future to talk about present times that have not yet arrived.

Where future expectations are made and later realized in the past, another tense marker comes into play. This special marker combines the general future with the general past to yield the form =*avish-at* (also =*eesh-at*). Generally signaling past pronouncements eventually realized in the past, this marker is also capable of referring to expectations that were merely anticipated at one time, even if these prognostications are never realized. When Coyote, for instance, plots to twine string so that he can gather money on it and one day become rich, this former wish is stated in the "near future," as the narrator announces *ʔuvúppareeshat pamúspuk* 'he was going to string beads'.[10] Originally stated in the past, this intention is also fulfilled in the past. Here the implication is that the deed will be performed right away.

GENERAL SEMANTICS OF TIME IN HUPA

The Hupa language, in contrast to Karuk, projects an elaborate series of temporal categories onto all events reported in speech. That is, every verb in the Hupa language conveys detailed information about the temporal dynamics of the scene, a pattern that also applies to all words derived secondarily from verbs. Often these temporal categories are highly subtle. Some indicate that an event is starting out, others that an event is approaching completion. Still other categories indicate that an event is of an ongoing nature or is performed intermittently as a matter of custom or habit. From the frame of reference presupposed by Hupa grammar, attention to the time schedule on which events unfold is highly obligatory. Indeed, attention to this aspect of reality is a precondition for speaking the language properly. Yet the status of an event with respect to some other point in time, such the "past" or "future," is a matter of far less concern in Hupa grammar.

Aspectual Categories of the Hupa Language

Every verb in the language belongs to one of two major temporal categories, one known as the *perfective* and the other the *imperfective*. The imperfective category is reserved for events of a general and ongoing nature, with an essentially unbounded temporal scope. Here no particular focus is placed on any particular phase in the process, whether its onset, middle stages, or conclusion. The perfective is the polar opposite. In contrast, it refers to an event whose scope is inherently bounded in some way, usually with an explicit focus on either the early, middle, or final stages of the total process. Each category, in turn, is divided into a number of subcategories. And each category can be comfortably placed in the past, present, or future, as both categories are concerned with the internal time schedule on which the event unfolds rather than with the status of an event relative to the present.

Every verb in the language also occurs in another pair of configurations, known as the "light" and "heavy" shapes of the stem. This distinction applies to both perfective and imperfective stems, creating a two-way contrast within each of these categories. Both hold loose temporal implications. The "light" form refers to an event in a general, temporally indefinite fashion, while the contrasting "heavy" form signals a particular instantiation of the activity portrayed by the verb. On one hand, the "heavy," or more definite, forms generally enter into constructions that are placed in the past—situations, significantly, over which the speaker has great certainty. On the other hand, the "light," and less definite, forms often occur with constructions that are placed in the future, encompassing a general range of events over which the speaker holds a lesser degree of certainty.

Most Hupa verbs alternate between both of these forms, one perfective and therefore bounded in potential reference, and the other imperfective and therefore more open-ended in scope. Yet a few verbs are frozen in a single time frame, without allowing a shift in perspective on a grammatical basis.

Hupa Verbs of Action

Most Hupa verbs of action alternate between perfective and imperfective stem shapes, while only a small number of minor temporal subclasses are distinguished. As a group, these verbs of action primarily depict scenes in which a subject engages in an activity that follows a relatively fixed, or somewhat restricted, series of directional courses. The system of categories surrounding scenes of action in Hupa is illustrated in figure 6.2.

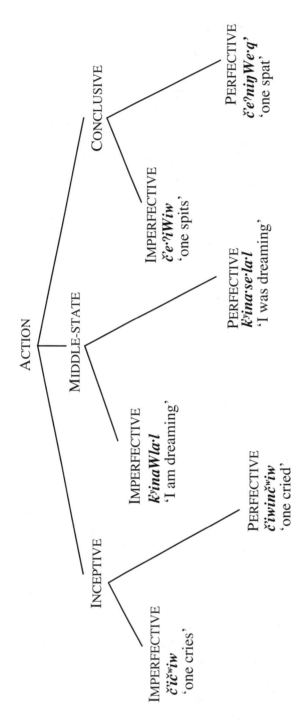

Figure 6.2. Time frames associated with scenes of action in Hupa

One series enters the perfective mode with the inceptive prefix *win-*. As a class, these verbs typically refer to activities that are characterized by a rapid or sudden onset. Consider the stem -*čʷiw,* for instance, which enters into two contrasting configurations, both of them referring to the act of "crying" or "weeping," yet from different temporal perspectives. To start, the general imperfective form *čičʷiw* simply translates as "one being cries." Compare this with the perfective variant *čiwinčʷiw,* which focuses on a single, complete instantiation of the event. This form, in contrast, loosely translates as "one being (just) cried." Elsewhere in the language, the prefix *win-* distinguishes verbs of onset or transition from those that ordinarily depict ongoing states. Consider, for example, the form *niwiŋWoʔn,* which translates as "it became good," a transitional form based on the verb *niWoŋ,* which simply means "it is good."

Another series enters into the perfective mode with the stative prefix *s-*. These verbs, as a class, refer to activities whose middle stages are drawn out, with a possible, secondary focus on the onset or conclusion of the event. Consider the verb stem -*la·l,* which enters into two contrasting configurations, both of them referring to the act of "dreaming," but from different temporal perspectives. To begin, consider the general imperfective form *kʸinaWla·l,* which loosely translates as "I am dreaming." Compare this with the perfective variant *kʸina·se·la·l,* which loosely translates as "I was dreaming (for a time)." Here, even the first-person singular subject marker is sensitive to the shift in time perspective, occurring first as *W-* in the imperfective variant and then as *e·-* in the contrasting perfective alternative. The directional marker *na·=* that occurs in both forms conveys the sense of motion that weaves around in circular fashion. The indefinite object marker *kʸi-* probably refers, historically, to the dream itself, with the implication that the subject experiences oneself circling around in the process of dreaming. Elsewhere in the language, the prefix *s-* is associated with stative verbs that designate ongoing states, crucially lacking a particular onset or conclusion, though with a potentially infinite, or unlimited, duration.

Another series enters the perfective mode strictly with the conclusive prefix *nin-*. These verbs, as a class, refer to activities that reach a definite endpoint, conclusion, or period of culmination. The verb, for instance, that represents the act of "spitting something out" also admits a similar shift in time perspective. To begin, consider the imperfective form *čeʔiWiw,* which loosely translates as "one being spits it out." Compare this with the perfective alternative *čeʔniŋWeʔqʼ,* which means "one being spat it out." Here the shape of the stem also plays a role. The stem -*Wiw* signals the imperfective mode, while the perfective is marked with the contrasting stem shape *-We·q'*. Otherwise, both forms feature the directional marker *če·=*, which indicates motion that exits an enclosure. The third-person subject marker occurs in its reduced form *-ʔ-* in the middle of the word. Similar pairs of stems, signaling shifts in time perspective, are widely attested in the Hupa language, historically emerging from suffixes that no longer generate new stem shapes in Hupa. Though long extinct in modern-day Hupa, these former suffixes have left behind residual alternating stem shapes that are still functional in many of the verb paradigms.

The verb paradigm for "sleeping" also signals the shift between the imperfective and perfective modes with contrasting stem shapes. Consider the imperfective form *xokʸiwa·n*, which loosely translates as "one being sleeps." In this instance, the perfective variant is *xokʸiwiɲwaʔn*, which means "one being entered a state of sleep." Here the shift to the perfective mode is signaled by the special stem *-waʔn*, which features a shortened vowel and a glottal element (*ʔ*) that is absent from the imperfective form *-wa·n*. Both forms occur in the third person, which is ordinarily indicated by the prefix *či-*, though here this marker has been replaced with the possesive prefix *xo-* since the verb literally refers to "owning" or "having" sleep.

Hupa Verbs of Spatial Extension

Some Hupa verbs do not normally permit the distinction between the perfective and imperfective modes. Instead, some verbs are restricted to one mode or the other, not allowing this shift in perspective. Most verbs that portray extension through space, for instance, hold their primary existence in the perfective mode. As a formal grammatical class, these verbs typically refer to processes that pass through space in a fixed fashion. Examples include the steady course of the blowing wind or the inherently directional flow of streams, which are marked with verbs that are frozen in the perfective mode. Like action verbs, verbs of extension also occur in several temporal subclasses, which are sensitive to the directional bearing of the event. The basic system of temporal categories surrounding scenes of extension is illustrated in figure 6.3.

Consider, for example, the special paradigm for referring to the continuous projection of a single object through a single dimension of space. Every verb in this paradigm must occur with a perfective marker that places focus on either the initial, middle, or final stages of the activity. Based on the stem *-ʔa·*, the paradigm takes the perfective marker *win-* in all forms that depict extension along vertical paths that reach upward toward the sky. Consider the form *yaʔwiɲʔa·*,

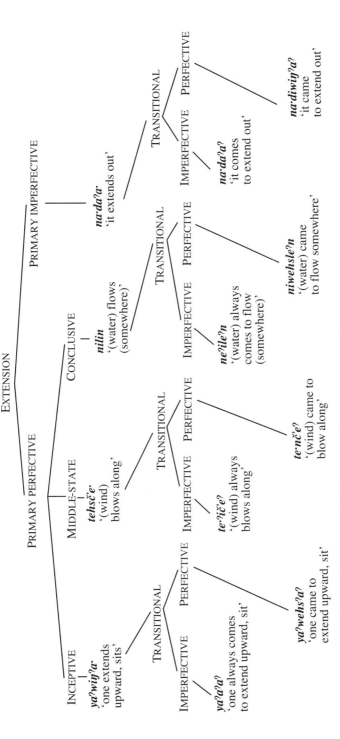

Figure 6.3. Temporal categories associated with scenes of linear extension in Hupa

which loosely translates as "one being extends upward (or sits upright)." Here the directional marker *ya·*= signals the upward path that the process takes in traveling through space, while the third-person singular marker *ʔ-* indicates that the subject is a living being, an animal or a human.

A similar paradigm depicts the activity of the blowing wind. Like the previous form, the paradigm is usually restricted to the perfective mode. Here the speaker must place focus on the early, middle, or final phases of motion. Based on the stem *-č'e·*, this paradigm always takes the perfective prefix *s-* in forms portraying a continuous stream of motion that reaches no definite end. Consider the form *tehsč'e·*, which loosely translates as "(wind) blows along." Here the directional marker *te·-* signals the continuous, linear path taken by the wind, though without specifying anything more definite about this course, such as whether it is through a river valley or along a mountainside.

Or consider the paradigm for the extension of a river along a particular directional route. Like the previous forms, this verb paradigm also occurs primarily in the perfective mode, always with explicit focus on a particular phase in the flow of motion. Based on the stem *-lin*, the related verb paradigm occurs with the prefix *ni-* in forms that specifically refer to the current's arrival at a particular destination, such as the mouth of the river. Consider, for example, the form *nilin*, which translates as "water flows (somewhere)." Here the directional prefix *ni-* indicates motion that reaches toward a goal, a marker that usually occurs with the temporal prefix *nin-* in the perfective mode, with a regular loss of the nasal before a stem beginning with *l-*.

Every extension verb gives rise to a secondary transitional form, which signals the entrance into the condition of extending across space. The resulting paradigm exhibits a regular contrast between perfective and imperfective configurations, allowing both bounded and unbounded interpretations of the situation.[11] Consider the verb stem *ʔa·*, for instance, which abstractly represents the spatial projection of a single object. In all transitional forms, the shape shifts to *-ʔaʔ*, here referring to the point of entrance into a condition of continuous spatial extension. The derived transitional construction, in the imperfective configuration, is *yaʔaʔaʔ*, which loosely translates as "one always comes to extend upward." In this case, the customary marker *ʔ(a)-*, itself a subcategory of the unbounded imperfective mode, indicates that this activity is repeated as a matter of custom or habit. This transitional stem also freely enters into perfective constructions, as may be illustrated with the form *yaʔwehsʔaʔ*, which translates as "one came to extend upward." Here the special prefix *we·s-* signals a relatively

rapid entry into this ongoing state of linear extension, a marker based, historically, on the combination of the inceptive marker *wi(n)*- and the stative marker
s-, semantically marking the entry into an ongoing state or condition.

Similarly, the stem -*č'e·*, which signals the blowing of the wind, gives rise to
the transitional variant -*č'eʔ*, which refers, in this derived shape, to the point of
entrance into blowing along a particular spatial path. Entering into the imperfective configuration yields the form *te·ʔič'eʔ*, which loosely translates as "(the
wind) always blows along." Here the customary marker *ʔ(i)*-, a subcategory of the
imperfective, again indicates an ongoing process that has been repeated with
great regularity over an otherwise indefinite span of time. Entering into the
perfective configuration yields the form *te·nč'eʔ*, which translates as "(the wind)
came to blow along." Here the inceptive marker *(wi)n*- occurs in its reduced
form (*n*), a regular process following the long vowel of the preceding prefix (*te·*-).

A similar process applies to the stem -*lin*, which yields the transitional
variant -*leʔn*, referring to the entrance into a process of flowing along a particular directional course. Entering into the imperfective mode yields the form
neʔileʔn, which translates as "(water) starts to flow (somewhere)." Again, the
customary marker *ʔi*- signals that this ongoing process is repeated as a matter
of custom or habit. Entering into the perfective configuration yields the form
niwehsleʔn, which translates as "(water) started to flow somewhere." Here the
temporal marker *we·s*- signals entrance into a condition of linear extension,
with an explicit focus on the initial stages of the process.

Occasionally a verb of extension is frozen in the imperfective mode instead
of the perfective mode. In this case, a secondary transitional stem allows the shift
between imperfective and perfective time frames. Consider the stem -*ʔa·*, which
refers to the extension of a single physical body, holding its primary existence in
the imperfective mode when referring to scenes of spatial protrusion marked
with the directional prefix *d(i)*-. For most of the remaining directional frames,
however, this verb paradigm is frozen in the perfective mode. The imperfective
form is *na·daʔa·*, which loosely translates as "it extends out (again)." In this
form, the iterative prefix *na·*= signals that the process has been repeated at least
once, while the absence of a perfective prefix indicates that the event is viewed
from a relatively open-ended time frame, without focus on the early, middle, or
final phases of the projection through space. In this configuration, this construction could refer to someone tilting his or her head or, more abstractly,
offering attention when listening, for instance, to a conversation. Shifting to
the transitional stem places focus on the point of entrance into this ongoing

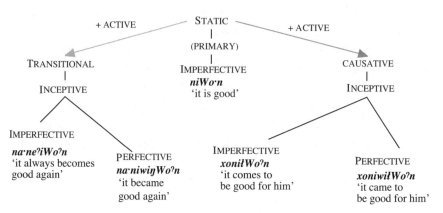

Figure 6.4. Time frames associated with states and conditions in Hupa

state. Consider the imperfective form *na·da²a²*, for instance, which translates as "(a single object) comes to extend outward." Or consider the perfective variant *na·diwiŋ²a²*, which translates as "(a single object) came to extend outward." Here the second form, which carries the inceptive marker *win-*, represents the perfective variant. Either of these forms could refer to an arrow coming to lodge somewhere, perhaps in the ground or in someone's chest.

Hupa Verbs of State or Condition

Most verbs that depict states or conditions, however, hold their membership in the imperfective mode. Most of these verbs refer to fairly permanent physical characteristics, such as the possession of a particular shape, size, or color, with a small handful that refer to tactile features. The full system of temporal categories surrounding ongoing states and conditions in the Hupa language is illustrated in figure 6.4.

Consider, for example, the verb stem *-Wo·n*, which signals a state of being "good" or "pleasant." This form holds its primary existence in the imperfective mode, without a perfective alternative. A case in point is the form *niWo·n*, which translates as "it is good." (This can be compared to the related form *čiŋWo·n*, which means "one being is good or pretty.") Here the prefix *ni-* indicates inherent characteristics, generally occurring in verbs portraying specific shapes, sizes, tactile, properties, or weights.

Yet it is always possible to form a verb of transition that signals the point of entrance into such an ongoing condition. Here the transition variant is signaled with the alternative shape *-Woʔn,* referring, in this derived form, to entrance into the general state of being "good" or "pleasant." Placing the stem in the imperfective mode yields the derived form *naˑneʔiWoʔn,* which loosely translates as "it always becomes good again." Here the customary marker *ʔ(i)-,* a subclass of the imperfective, indicates that this ongoing condition has been repeated over an indefinite interval. The iterative prefix *naˑ=* reinforces the notion that it happened again, having most likely slipped out of this fortuitous state for a period. The same stem also enters into perfective constructions, as may be illustrated with the form *naˑniwiŋWoʔn,* which translates as "it became good again." Here the inceptive marker *win-* places focus on the onset of this condition, while the iterative marker *naˑ=* signals that this state was entered and dropped at least once beforehand.

Hupa Verbs of Motion and Position

Verbs of motion and position, in contrast, enter into a complex series of interrelated temporal subcategories. Verbs in this series are devoted to scenes of "going," "handling," and "resting motionless," where the reference is to a particular class of objects, most of them based on features such as shape, animacy, substance, or number. When one is handling an object or describing a similar object at rest, the division into the perfective or imperfective mode is still critical. Each category is further divided into a number of internal subcategories. Figure 6.5 illustrates the full set of temporal classes concerned with the motion and position of various classes of objects.

One part of this paradigm refers to events of relatively brief duration. Verbs in this class always require an obligatory marker that specifies the directional bearing of an event. Here the selection of the perfective prefix hinges on the spatial route the event takes. This part of the paradigm is marked by a set of *momentaneous* stem shapes, with separate perfective and imperfective variants. Where the motion enters into the water, as signaled by the directional marker *taˑ=,* the verb takes the inceptive prefix *win-* when entering the perfective mode. Consider, for example, the perfective form *taʔwintaˑn,* which means "one took a long object into the water." Compare this with the contrasting imperfective complement *taˑʔatiW,* which translates as "one takes a long object into the water." Here the imperfective form is set apart by the stem shape and by the

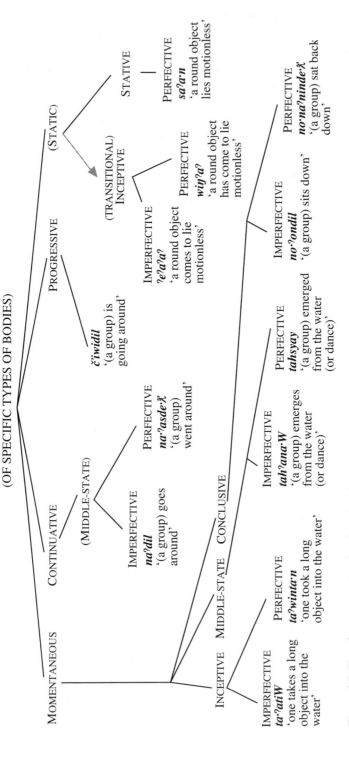

Figure 6.5. Time frames associated with verbs of motion and position in Hupa

absence of the inceptive marker *win-*. This pair selects the class of long objects, referring, perhaps, to a stick, a canoe, or even a person holding very still while being handled by someone else. Here the perfective stem shape is *-taˑn,* while the imperfective shape is *-tiW.*

Where motion emerges from the water, as signaled by the directional marker *tah=,* the verb takes the stative prefix *s-* when entering the perfective mode. Consider, for example, the form *tahsyay,* which means "(something) emerged from the water." Here the imperfective complement *tahʔanaˑW* translates as "(something) emerges from the water," a form that is distinguished by the shift in stem shape and by the absence of the stative marker *s-.* This pair refers to the motion of a single perceptual unit, such as an animal, a person, or a mass of objects. Here the imperfective stem shape is *-naˑW,* while the perfective shape is *-yay.*

Where the movement sinks rapidly toward the earth, as signaled by the directional marker *noˑ=,* the verb takes the conclusive prefix *nin-* in the perfective mode. Consider the form *noˑnaʔnindeˑx̣,* which means "they sat back down." Here the imperfective complement is *noˑʔondil,* which translates as "they sit down," a form that is distinguished by the shift in the shape of the stem and by the absence of the conclusive marker *nin-.* This pair refers to the movement of two or more bodies, usually several people, though occasionally animals or inanimate objects. Here the perfective stem is *-deˑx̣,* which shifts to *-dil* in the imperfective mode. In this case, the iterative prefix *naˑ=* occurs with the perfective form, which indicates a repetition of the act, here suggesting that the entire group had once been seated before.

Another part of the motion paradigm always occurs with the marker *naˑ=,* indicating that a given event follows no particular spatial route. Generally referring to events of greater duration than momentaneous verbs, these forms enter into the perfective mode with the stative prefix *s-.* This part of the paradigm is marked by a distinctive set of *continuative* stem shapes, again with separate perfective and imperfective forms. Where the reference is to the class of long objects, the imperfective form is *naˑʔatin,* which loosely translates as "one carries a long object around." The contrasting perfective form is represented by the verb *naˑʔasteʔn,* which means "one carried a long object around." Here the stem shapes signal the shift to the continuative perspective, with the imperfective shape *-tin* versus the perfective shape *-teʔn,* each one referring to the same class of "long objects" discussed above in the momentaneous paradigm. Here the reference could be to an arrow, stick, cane, quiver, plank, empty basket, or, again, a person lying very still. When speaking of two or more actors, another continuative paradigm comes into play. Consider, for example, the imperfective form *naʔdil,* which means "two or more go around." In this instance, the perfective complement is *na·ʔasde·x̌,* which loosely translates as "two or more went around." Here the shift to the continuative paradigm is marked by the use of the nondirectional prefix *na·=* and the stative prefix *s-.* Otherwise, the stem shapes are identical to the momentaneous forms cited earlier for the same class of events, namely, the class of "two or more objects."

Another part of the motion paradigm always occurs with the progressive prefix *wi-,* while admitting no perfective, or temporally bounded, variant. This part of the paradigm is usually marked with a distinctive *progressive* stem shape, itself a subclass of the temporally unbounded imperfective class, though here occurring without a perfective complement. If one is again speaking of the class of long objects, the progressive form in the third person would be *č'iwitil,* which means "one is carrying a sticklike object around." Here the reference is to a continuous process, often of considerable duration, which involves an explicit element of motion every step of the way. The prefix *wi-* and the stem shape *-til,* together, signal the shift to the progressive paradigm. Similarly, if one is again referring to the movement of two or more actors, the progressive form in the third person would be *č'iwidil,* which loosely translates as "two or more objects (or beings) are going around." Here it is principally the progressive prefix *wi-* that signals the shift to the progressive time frame, though the stem shape *-dil* is identical to the imperfective stems of the momentaneous and continuative paradigms.

The final part of this paradigm is reserved for scenes where motion is either absent or withdrawn. As a class, these forms take the stative prefix *s-* and a verb stem that is generally identical to the perfective form of the momentaneous paradigm. Formally, stative verbs are linked to the perfective mode, as reflected by the use of the perfective prefix *s-* and the perfective shape of the stem. Semantically, stative forms refer to motionless scenes of potentially great duration, though without a definite onset or conclusion.

When speaking of the class of long objects, the stative form of the paradigm is *sita·n,* which loosely translates as "a sticklike object lies motionless." Here the reference is to a scene where the element of motion is absent for a considerable span of time. A stative form does not exist for the class of "two or more actors," because the stative paradigm generally applies only to things that are generally "handled" or "carried," such as objects, though not to bodies that serve in the role of subject elsewhere in the motion system.

Most stative forms can be placed in the transitional time frame, where the reference is to the point of entrance into a motionless state. In this case, the resulting transitional paradigm exhibits a regular contrast between perfective and imperfective temporal perspectives. Consider, for example, the stative form *saʔaˑn,* which refers to a situation where a round object rests motionless in one position. As the time frame shifts to the transitional perspective, the shape of the stem undergoes a change from *-ʔaˑn* to *-ʔaʔ.* In the perfective configuration, the transitional form *wiŋʔaʔ* refers to a situation where "a round object has come to lie motionless." In the imperfective configuration, the derived transitional form *ʔeʔeʔaʔ* refers to a more open-ended condition where "a round object always comes to lie motionless." In this particular imperfective form, the customary marker *ʔ(e)-* contributes the sense that the activity is repeated, for a time, on a habitual basis.

Hupa Subcategories of the Imperfective

Most verbs in the Hupa language can be modified to express several permutations of the general, unbounded process portrayed by the verb in its unmarked, imperfective form. Each of these derivative categories represents an expansion of the general imperfective process, so that all of the resulting subcategories are similarly unbounded in temporal scope.

Most imperfective forms can, for instance, be placed in a special "customary" time frame, which signals the repetition of the event as a matter of habit. Consider, for example, the imperfective form *čič̓ʷiw,* which means "one cries." With the addition of the customary prefix *ʔi-,* this form can be modified to yield the contrasting form *čeʔič̓ʷiw,* meaning "one always cries." Here the customary derivation indicates that this activity has been performed again and again by one known to weep habitually. Or consider the imperfective form *deʔditiW,* a verb of action that means "one puts a long object into the fire." The same grammatical machinery transforms this expression into its customary variant *deʔdeʔitiW,* which loosely translates as "one always puts a long object into the fire." Here direction is indicated by the marker *de·=di-,* which signals that the object passes "into the fire," while the third-person subject prefix *či-* is sandwiched, in reduced form, between the two halves of this compound marker.

Many imperfective forms can also be placed in a special *progressive* time frame, which signals a steady stream of action punctuated with stops and starts for a considerable span of time. Consider the imperfective form *čič̓ʷiw,* "one cries." Progressive derivation yields the contrasting form *na·č̓iwič̓ʷeˑl,* which means "one cries along going backward." Here the reference is to an ongoing stream of crying, as the subject walks along a path he or she once took before. The shift to the progressive time frame is signaled by the progressive prefix *wi-* together with the progressive suffix *-l*. The iterative marker *na·=,* here taking a reversative reading, indicates that the event takes a path that repeats, in reverse, a sequence of steps it took once before. Or consider the expression *deʔditiW,* "one throws a long object into the fire." The same grammatical machinery transforms this expression into the progressive variant *deʔdiwitiWil,* which, in contrast, translates as "one threw long objects into fires, here and there, while moving along."

Hupa Tense

Surprisingly, the status of an event relative to a fixed point in time, such as the "present," is often a matter of secondary importance in the Hupa language, despite the intensive focus on the internal dynamics of temporal processes. Granted, one is required to specify the inner time schedule on which an event unfolds when speaking Hupa, but not necessarily in relation to an implicit "present."

Although categories of "past" and "future" can be specified on an optional basis, in practice many forms remain "tenseless" in oral literature and everyday life. Structurally speaking, Hupa tense markers occur as enclitic elements only loosely bound to the verbs they modify. Many of the tense markers appear to have entered the language fairly recently, through the process of grammaticalization, perhaps, in part, under pressure to express salient concepts significant in the local culture, where tense plays a major role in oral literature. The basic categories are illustrated in figure 6.6.

Hupa grammar splits the realm of the past into two discrete categories. Both markers of the past tense generally occur strictly with heavy stem shapes, marking definite instantiations of events over which the speaker holds a fair amount of certainty, perhaps simply because of the fact that events in the past have already taken place.

One of these markers, known as the "locative past," sets the scene relative to another event whose time frame has already been established. Loosely translating as "when such an event occurred," this marker requires familiarity, on the part of the audience, with the defining moment that the speaker uses to establish the time frame. Structurally speaking, this marker takes the form of the enclitic *-daŋ?,* which immediately follows the verb that establishes the basic temporal ground. The moment of reference could be a certain period in a

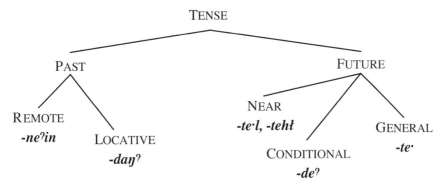

Figure 6.6. Hupa tense categories

person's lifetime: childhood, for instance, when this person was small. Here one could say *simiWɢiyˀ-daŋˀ*, which translates as "when I was small." With this phrase, an entire story line could be sent within this period of the narrator's life. Alternatively, an entire text can be set in the era of creation with the words *čʼixolčʷeˑ-daŋˀ*, an expression that translates as "when the world was being created."

Another category, known as the "remote past," refers to events that have ceased to exist or no longer maintain an active connection to the living present. When applied to nouns, this marker often signals a deceased relation or bond of support that has since expired. Consider the form *Wičʷoˑ-neˀin*, which means "my former grandmother." Or consider the related form *Waˀad-neˀin*, meaning "my former wife." Sometimes the reference is to a status that has since been supplanted, as illustrated by the form *tʼehxiჳ-neˀin*, which means "once a girl." When applied to an inanimate object, the reference is often to something that has since been destroyed. For example, consider the form *kʸimaˑw-neˀin*, which means "old-time medicine," referring to a cure that has since lost its efficacy or is no longer practiced. In prayer, the reference is often to states or conditions that the speaker hopes to place squarely in the past, severing them, once and for all, from the present. A case in point is the form *ˀah-neˀin*, which means "clouds that once were." Or consider the form *kʸičʼind-neˀin*, which translates as "sickness that once was." With words such as these, a priest might convey his wish to put clouds and sickness into the far-off past, where they would bother humans no more. With customary forms, the reference is often to a former habit that has since been broken. Consider the form *kʸimaˑw ˀeˀiłčʷeˑ-neˀin*, which translates as "I always used to make medicine." Here it is implied that the speaker has since abandoned the practice. Because the myth times maintain a strong connection to the living present, speakers rarely apply this marker to narratives set in the era of creation. This point receives further attention in chapter 7, where reference to the mythic past is discussed in greater detail.

The future is split into three categories in Hupa. Two of these reflect the relative distance between the projected future and an implicit present. The other takes the relative reality of the situation into consideration. In contrast to markers of the past tense, future forms generally occur only with light stem shapes, marking situations over which the speaker perhaps holds a lesser degree of certainty.

One of these markers, known as the "general future," conveys statements of expectation, whether this projected state of affairs is to arise through wishing, planning, or inevitability. By implication, any statement cast in the "general future" is more distant than the same pronouncement when stated with the marker of the "near future." Yet the general future is not heavily constrained in scope, if only for the reason that an event in the future has yet to reach its manifestation. When stated in the first person, the reference is often to a wish or intention. A case in point is the form *nise·sehłwin-te·*, which means "I will kill you." Or consider the similar form *niWcis-te·*, which means "I'll see you (sometime)." When phrased impersonally, the reference is often to a hope or expectation, sometimes one that is willed upon the world in prayer. A case in point is the form *na·ysxan-te·*, which means "(someday) it will dawn again," a common wish expressed before a dance. The future is also sometimes projected from the past, as when myth figures speculate about the human world that will one day emerge. When Dog, for instance, pledges to watch over humans when they enter the world, he says *kʸiwinyaʔnya·n* 'people' *me·na·yliW-te·* 'I will watch over'.

Another category, known as the "near future," is reserved for events that are on the cusp of reaching fulfillment. A case in point is the phrase *xoŋʔ-na·ʔasweʔ-tehł*, which translates as "they will have a brush dance." Or consider the related form *kʸiłčixa·ʔinahW-tehł*, which translates as "there is going to be a fight." In narrative texts set in the ancient past, the "near future" is often used to forecast the imminent arrival of humanity, as when the spirit deities say *kʸiwinyaʔn-ya·n* 'humans' *na·na·ndeʔX̌-tehł* 'will soon come into existence'.

Still another category, known as the "conditional future," is available for the purpose of referring to situations that may potentially arise, provided that certain conditions are met. When Across-the-Ocean-Widower announces that people will be safe from rattlesnakes if they can only remember to carry his protective cane, he makes his proclamation in the conditional future, with the words *Witic'eʔ* 'my cane' *č'itehstan-deʔ* 'if he carries along' *do·-xoliŋ-č'iɫcis* 'one will not see' *miɫcah-xosin* 'rattlesnakes'.[12] Sometimes the myth figures say that a wind will one day blow down gently if people continue to place incense root in their ceremonial fires. This sentiment is usually expressed in the conditional future, with the expression *deʔdiwaʔaWiɫ-deʔ,* meaning "if one keeps putting (roots) in the fire."

Aspectual Marking on Hupa Nouns

In the Hupa language, even common nouns often carry detailed information about the time schedule on which a related process unfolds. Generally, any verb, however elaborate, can be transformed into a derived noun of action with the relativizing marker *-i,* which is added to the end of the construction. By signaling that the reference is to a recurring process, one that is associated with a definite class of actors, this marker contributes the sense that the activity in question is characteristically performed by the referent at hand. In practice, this relativizing marker rarely occurs on the surface, though in an underlying sense it is responsible for the regular alternation between "light" and "heavy" shapes of the stem. Where a light stem form refers to a process in a general sense, the related heavy stem construction signals that the reference is to a recurring instantiation of the phenomenon, one associated with a particular type of actor. For this reason, nouns of action virtually always occur with heavy stems.

Many Hupa nouns are set in the imperfective aspect when the reference is to a general, ongoing process regularly associated with the referent. Consider, for instance, the noun *yehč'itaɫ,* the usual word for the traditional buckskin moccasin or modern-day shoe. Literally, this construction refers to the object that "one steps into" on a regular basis. Here the heavy stem *-tal* signals a general instantiation of the recurring process of "stepping into something," one that is linked with a specific type of referent, here the moccasin. Otherwise, the modifier *yeh=* specifies that this event reaches "into an enclosure," while the subject marker *č'i-* indicates a general, third-person agent. Compare this with the contrasting light stem variant *yehč'itaɫ,* which simply means "one steps into something." This construction, in contrast, is typically used to refer to the process as it is happening now, or in the future, but not to the entire class of objects that "one steps into" in a regular way. Like many other nouns of action, the word for moccasin is set in the imperfective mode, indicating that it refers to the general process in a fairly open-ended way. Compare the word for moccasin with the related perfective construction *yehč'iwinta·x̂,* which loosely translates as "one stepped into it." This form refers to a single, complete instantiation of this event rather than to the class of objects, as a whole, associated with this act.

Occasionally, a noun is set in the customary aspect, as when the reference is to a recurring process that is associated with the referent through the force of habit. Consider, for example, the noun *miq'id-kʸiŋ-kʸeʔitwal,* the word for the traditional drum that accompanies a guessing-game played with sticks. Literally, this form refers to "the instrument one always pounds with a stick" when playing a guessing-game. This elaborate construction is based on the verb *kʸeʔitwal,* which means "one pounds something." Here the adverbial modifier *e·=* specifies that the act approaches an object of some kind, while the indefinite object marker *kʸ(i)-* signals that this object is defined by context, implicitly, the surface of the drum that one hits with the stick. Immediately before the stem, the valence prefix *t-* indicates that this form assumes the existence of both an agent and a patient, here the person and the stick one strikes against the drum. In the middle of the construction, the subject marker *-ʔ-* signals that the instigator of the act is a general third-person agent. So far, this construction is in the imperfective mode, though the derived noun is in the customary aspect. Shifting to the customary time frame, the form becomes *kʸeʔitwal,* which, in contrast, translates as "one always pounds something." Here only the vowel *e·* has been reduced. Yet at an underlying level, the customary prefix *ʔi-* has been added; this joins with the subject marker *ʔ-* to create the cluster *ʔ-ʔi-.* The resulting geminate consonant has the effect of shortening the long vowel *e·-* in the customary form, cited above, where this extra prefix is present.[13] Finally, the presence of the heavy stem *-wal* in the derived noun of action indicates that the expression refers to a general instantiation of this surrounding process, one that is specifically associated with a particular object, namely, the drum. The noun also features two other elements, which specify the instrument and the location of the related process. While the locative marker *miq'id* specifies that the pounding is performed "on top of something" (here the drum), the noun *kʸiŋ* designates the "stick" that is used to perform this act.

Other nouns are set in the progressive time frame, as when the reference is to a process that is carried out continuously over a considerable span. A case in point is the word *yidaɢa-dahwintał,* one of several Hupa names for the "blue jay." This particular construction is based on the progressive form of the stem *-ta·d,* which, with the prefix *l-* or *n-* immediately before it, refers to the act of passing through space at a rapid pace. Here the time frame is signaled by the progressive prefix *wi-* and special progressive stem *-taʟ,* while the directional marker *dah=* suggests an activity that hovers about effortlessly in the air. This noun remains in its light stem form, referring to an activity in general, not necessarily to any particular instantiation. At the beginning of the form, the adverb *yidaɢ* specifies motion that generally points "uphill," which, in this case, suggests that the bird flies up along a tree, a detail must be inferred by context, however obvious it may be to anyone who has seen this bird in flight. Literally, the derived noun refers to a familiar actor that is always engaged in the process of hovering toward the mountains above. The construction as a whole refers to the act of hovering upward while engaging in bursts of fairly rapid-fire activity that implicitly refer to the bird's habit of flapping its wings in flight.

Other derived nouns of action emerge from the special motion paradigm, most of them belonging to the momentaneous, continuative, progressive, or stative time frame. Consider, for example, the noun *nandil,* the usual Hupa name for "snow." Set in the momentaneous paradigm, this construction focuses on a brief event that follows a specific directional path. Here the heavy stem *-dil* refers to a general instantiation of the process of "traveling together," one that can be associated with a specific real-world phenomenon, namely, snowflakes coming down from the sky in groups. Compare this with the light stem form *nandiɬ,* which means "several things are coming down," though without referring to the entire class of objects that performs this act on a regular basis. The related noun of action, in contrast, literally refers to the class of referents that "drop down multiply" in a familiar way. Here the marker *naˑ=* signals that the event passes down on a vertical path from a condition of suspension, with focus on the process of the descent, not the eventual contact with the ground below. The element *n-* before the stem *-dil* is a normal part of the momentaneous paradigm for the motion of two or more subjects.

Other motion-based forms are set in the continuative time frame, for which the reference is to the process of traveling around from place to place without following a particular route. Consider, for example, the word *ḱʸiɬ-naˑdil,* the ordinary Hupa name for the wolf, one that literally translates as "the ones who go around with something." Compare this construction with its light stem counterpart *naˑdiɬ,* which simply means "two or more go around." Here the heavy stem *-dil* signals that the reference is to a particular instantiation of this event, one associated with this particular class of beings. The initial element $\hat{k}^yi$-ł refers to an object that these beings go around with, bones or prey, perhaps, which they carry or pursue.

Some motion-based forms are set in the progressive time frame, as when the focus is on a continuous stream of action, one that often follows a linear or goal-oriented route. Consider, for example, the noun *ma·-č'iɢa·ł*, the traditional Hupa word for a ceremonial leader; the descriptive content of this word loosely translates as "the one who goes along for the sake of the dance." Compare this construction with its light stem counterpart *č'iɢahł*, which simply means "one is going along." With the heavy stem *-ɢa·ł*, the reference is to a general instantiation of the phenomenon, one connected with a specific ceremonial actor. At the beginning of the construction, the adverbial modifier *ma·* signals that this act is carried out "for some purpose," here meaning that the leader walks along on behalf of others, namely, the followers whom the ceremonial leader guides through the procession.

Other motion-based nouns are set in the stative time frame. A case in point is the noun *ninis'a·n*, the ordinary Hupa word for the earth, world, or universe. Literally, this construction refers to "the solid ground that rests there motionless." Here the verb base is minimally distinct from its light stem variant *sa'aŋ*, which means "a round thing lies motionless somewhere." The heavy stem *-'a·n* signals that the reference is to an instantiation of the process, one that is associated with the world itself. The element *nin(i)* at the beginning of the word suggests the "ground" that rests beneath us, namely, the earth itself, which lies there without perceptible motion.

A few derived nouns are set in the perfective time frame, indicating that the reference is to an event that is specifically bounded in scope. Here the resulting construction places explicit focus on either the early, middle, or final stages of a total flow of motion. The name of the figure who fled this world for the heavens at the fringes of the universe, is, for instance, set in the inceptive mode; the reference is to the moment he left this world, never to be seen again. The Hupa describe this figure as *yima·n-tiw'winyay*, "the one who went astray across the waters." (Compare this construction with its light stem counterpart *tiw'winya·*, which simply translates as "one being became lost among the trails.") The presence of the heavy stem *-yay* signals that the reference is to an instantiation of this process, one specifically associated with the actor Across-the-Ocean-Widower. The directional marker *tin=* signals motion that is directed outward among the trails, where the subject eventually becomes lost.

This directional modifier enters into the perfective configuration with the inceptive prefix *win-*, indicating that the focus is on the initial phases of the total process. Sandwiched between the directional marker *tin=* and inceptive prefix *win-* is a form of the third-person prefix *ʔ-*. On the surface, these prefixes combine to form the regular cluster *tiwʔwin-*. The directional adverb *yimaˑn* specifies that this activity reached out across the waters, eventually leading toward the heavens at the fringes of the universe.

The name for the wind, in contrast, is set in the stative aspect; the reference is to a process that passes through space continuously, without specifically considering the source where it originated or the goal it may one day reach. The Hupa refer to the wind using the word *tehsčʼeˑ*, a term whose descriptive content literally translates as "what blows along." Here the heavy stem *-čʼeˑ* signals a particular instantiation of this process, one associated with the wind itself, while the directional marker *teˑ-* specifies an event that extends along a relatively linear path. The stative prefix *s-* places focus on the middle stages of the process, without necessarily taking the source or goal of the activity into consideration.

As yet another example, the name for a sacred village where a culture hero was once said to have been dug up from the ground is specifically set in the conclusive time frame, with the focus on the moment he emerged, once and for all, from beneath the earth. The Hupas describe this village with the term *čʼeˑʔindiɢoʔ-diŋ*, which literally refers to "the place where one wriggled out." This construction is based on the verb stem *-ɢoˑtʼ*, which, when preceded by the element *di-*, refers to the act of "creeping about" on hands and knees. Here the directional marker *čʼe=* signals that this motion passes out of an enclosure, here the earth, from which this figure was said to have emerged during the creation times; the subject marker *-ʔ-* specifies a third-person agent. In the middle of the form, the conclusive prefix *n(in)-* places explicit focus on the final stages of this process, namely, the moment of emergence from beneath the surface of the earth. At the end of the construction, the element *-diŋ* transforms the entire phrase into an expression referring to a place where this event once happened, while also triggering the contraction of the stem (from *ɢoˑtʼ* to *-ɢoʔ*).

THE SEMANTICS OF TIME IN YUROK

Generally speaking, the Yurok verb is almost completely timeless in scope. In fact, not one affix exists for the purpose of marking tense in Yurok, while only a handful of stem-initial elements explicitly mark the internal temporal dynamics of events. As a consequence, the Yurok verb is often capable of referring to events of nearly any duration occurring at almost any particular moment in time. Yet outside the system of the verb paradigm, time perspective can be richly expressed on a syntactic basis. That is, in the Yurok language, tense and aspect are marked by a series of independent words that only loosely surround the verbs they modify.

Yurok Tense

In this sense, Yurok possesses by far the most elaborate tense system in the region. Many of these tense categories also convey aspectual features. As a consequence, it is often possible to situate a scene at a particular moment in time while providing detailed information about the inner temporal features of the scene. So, for instance, one can often succinctly state that an activity is either ongoing or approaching some definite conclusion within a particular period of time. The system of freestanding particles divides the "past," "present," and "future" into an enormous range of categories, which are diagrammed in figure 6.7.

The Yurok language splits the realm of the past into many discrete categories, most of them concerned with the proximity between a given event and the implicit present established by the speaker. One category, the *general past,* typically refers to conditions that may have once existed but have not been carried forth into the living present. Often the reference is to fairly recent times, though occasionally it is also extended back into the mythical past. When speaking of a woman, now deceased, who had a grandson, one might say *woʔoot* 'she' *ho* 'past' *ʔokʷs* 'existed' *ʔuk̓ep'ew* 'her grandson'. This phrase, as a unit, translates as "once her grandson existed, stayed with her there."[14] In this instance, the tense particle *ho* indicates a former condition that no longer continues to exist today, referring, ultimately, to a period before recent memory, though not as far removed from the present as the era of the myth times.

When the reference is to an event that took place at a particular site, another marker, known as the *locative past,* comes into play. This marker situates an event at a given place whose time frame is already understood by the audience. Here the proximity to the present is variable, ranging from a moment deep in the mythical past to a recent event held at a well-known site. In creation stories, the narrator often announces, even in the first few lines, that the events to follow once took place here in this world, though very long ago. Consider, for example, the expression *ʔela* 'there (on earth) in the past' *hooleʔmoni* 'they were dwelling', for which the reference is to a time when all the world's creatures once lived

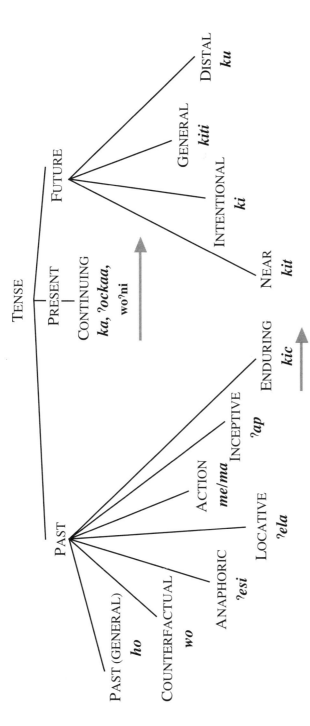

Figure 6.7. Yurok tense categories

together, whiling away their time with gambling.[15] In this case, another marker, *hikon,* which appears earlier in the sentence, places the entire scene in the mythical past, as an adverb, not a tense particle.

When the speaker wishes to focus on an activity that took place in the past, a marker labeled *past action* can be used. This marker is generally used when an element of motion is involved. In creation stories, the past action marker often highlights an event of great significance. When, for instance, Coyote goes to visit Crane, this event (ripe with meaning for all the scenes to follow) is announced with the marker of past action, with the words *šegep* 'coyote' *me* 'past action' *kʷeget* 'visits' *koohci* 'once' *mɹkʷtikš* 'crane'.[16] This bold act on Coyote's part would, in turn, precipitate an entire string of events, resulting in Coyote's tricking Crane out of his wives, then releasing them back to Crane, with whom they fly for the rest of eternity along the coastal waters that circle the earth.

Other temporal markers provide information about the time schedule on which an event unfolds. One category, known as the *past inceptive,* places focus on the earliest phases of activity for an event that is otherwise situated in the past. When Dove, for instance, learns that his grandfather has died, this unsettling realization is cast as having just entered its earliest stages, as reflected in a construction recorded in the first text of Robins's *Yurok Language*: *ʔap* 'inceptive past' *newok* 'I see' *kic* 'enduring past' *ʔumerkewecek* 'he die(d)'.[17]

Sometimes a past event exerts a lasting effect on the sequence of events to follow, as when its effect or influence is felt for some time to come. Consider, for example, the particle that marks the concept of the *enduring past,* which refers to events that hold lasting implications for the sequence of scenes to follow or, in some cases, for all eternity. When Dove, for instance, announces that he will gamble once more, despite the fact that his grandfather is on the verge of dying, the narrator is quick to note, with the marker of the enduring past, that Dove was winning at this moment. In Yurok narrative, this scene is expressed as *kic* 'enduring past' *rewpeʔn* 'he wins'.[18] Of course, the fact that Dove was winning at this point shapes all of the scenes to follow. For having failed to pay his final respects to his dying grandfather, Dove would pledge to mourn this loss for all eternity, if only to alleviate his guilt.

Often a hypothetical event has no actual basis in fact. Here the Yurok language provides a special grammatical category known as the *counterfactual past,* which refers specifically to past events that never in fact existed. Often speakers use this marker to couch past scenes in negative or subjunctive terms.

When a young man attempts to win a girl in marriage from a far-away land, something strictly forbidden in Native law, his proposal is flatly rejected, an event that is reported with the marker of the counterfactual or negative past as *nimi* 'not' *wo* 'counterfactual past' *ṭiʔ* 'it is accepted'.[19] Subjunctive readings are also possible, though this form, *wo*, is never used to refer to scenes that are known, as a matter of fact, to have actually existed.

Sometimes a time period is already known to an audience, having been mentioned earlier in the process of storytelling or conversation. Here the Yurok language provides a special grammatical category known as the *anaphoric past*, which situates one event relative to some other event that preceded it, however near or far either episode is to the implicit present. The entire series of ceremonial rites that lead up to the eating of First Salmon would, in this sense, serve as the antecedent to the eventual act of actually feasting upon the flesh of this sacred fish. In one construction, reported in Robins's *Yurok Language,* the narrator situates the eating of the salmon after its antecedent, the ritual preparations, as reflected in the following construction: *wiʔiit* 'this' *hewoni* 'first' *sonkiʔ* 'it is done', *ʔesi* 'anaphoric past' *nepuʔ* 'you eat' *ki* 'the' *nepuy* 'salmon'.[20] The phrase, as a unit, translates as "this is done before you eat the salmon."

Several preverbal particles refer specifically to the present, an unparalleled state of affairs in the area's remaining languages, among which the temporal ground of the current moment (whether fictive or real) tends to remain unmarked. Both particles refer to ongoing activities that continue indefinitely into the immediate future to follow. One of these markers often foregrounds a scene in the fictive "present" of the imaginary story line. Syntactically, the expression of this category is discontinuous, stretching across a phrase in two divisible parts. When, for instance, Coyote journeys to the heavens to kill the Sun, upon his arrival he was said to have heard the Sun People eating there in the house one evening, an event that the narrator sets in the "living present" of the imaginary story line. In the words of Mary Marshall, who dictated this tale to Sapir in the summer of 1927, this scene was formulated as follows: *koʔmoʔy* 'he hears' *ʔoc* 'ongoing present' *koʔl* 'something' *ka* 'ongoing present' *nepeʔm* 'they eat' *cmeyonen* 'evening'.[21] Here the discontinuous marker *ʔoc-ka(a)* signals an ongoing moment that continues forward from the "imaginary present" of the story line.

The other marker of the present tense is generally restricted to the moment of the utterance. That is, unlike the remainder of the tense markers, this one does not normally enter into the "imaginary present" of a story line;

such an extension of this marker is not attested in the Yurok narratives currently available. An example of the usage of this reference to the present is the phrase *nek* 'I' *woʔni* 'continuing present' *koʔl* 'something' *nepek̓* 'I eat'. This sentence, as a unit, loosely translates as "Now I am having something to eat" (Robins 1958:101).

The future is also split into several categories in the Yurok language. Some of these are concerned with the evidential basis of the speaker's projection, while others reflect the relative distance from some implicit present. One marker, known as the "general future," is associated primarily with statements of expectation. Often this marker is used when the reference is to an impersonal sequence of anticipated events, of nearly any time depth, though more often close at hand than distant. When Coon, who had long been beleaguered by Fox, declares that he will soon lose his fishing place, he announces this sad realization in the general future, as reflected in the phrase *kiti* 'general future' *too̓melek̓* 'I will lose' *ku* 'the' *ʔnek^wol* 'my fishing place'.[22] Here there is no suggestion of intention, merely a general statement of expectation, a course of events that to Coon seems all but inevitable at this sad pass.

Other markers convey an explicit element of intentionality. One of these, here labeled the "intentional future," is generally used to signal pronouncements of volition, especially those of wish, desire, or future resolve. In most cases, these refer to situations in which the speaker performs the deed in question, often with the sense that the act will be carried out fairly soon. When, for instance, Dove announces that he will have another fateful gamble before going to visit his dying grandfather, he makes this pronouncement in the intentional future, saying *ki* 'intentional future' *kem* 'again' *ko* 'at that time' *gook^wcek̓^w* 'I gamble'.[23]

Often a wish is deferred until circumstances permit its fulfillment. For this purpose, the Yurok language provides a special category for the "distal future," which specifies that the activity will be carried out later. Often this deed is carried out at another location, after undergoing a period of postponement. When Crane announces to Coyote that he will go fetch his wives so that they can be turned over to Coyote, this statement is couched in the distal future, as reflected in the expression *ku* 'distal future' *niiʔnowoš̓oʔ* 'I look for them'.[24] The suggestion is that the event will be carried out later at another location, where these women are dwelling, off in the distance.

Another category, here labeled the "near future," is primarily concerned with events that are close at hand. Yet in another sense, the reference is sometimes to a state of affairs that already exists and is expected to continue for a short time to follow. When a messenger arrives to tell Dove that his grandfather will soon die, this pronouncement is cast in the near future, as reflected in the phrase *kit* 'near future' *merkewec'* 'he dies', a line that translates as "he will soon die."[25] Here the use of the near future marker grants the news great immediacy and the scene great urgency. As another example, when Crane sees Coyote approaching after Coyote has tricked him out of a spear, Coyote's imminent arrival is cast in the near future, as reflected in the phrase *šegep* 'coyote' *kit* 'near future' *neš* 'come', loosely translating as "Coyote is (fast) approaching, about to make his arrival."[26]

Yurok Verbal Marking

Generally speaking, the Yurok verb is neutral with respect to time perspective, relying instead on the many precise distinctions available outside the verb paradigm, in the separate system of tense particles. By itself, the Yurok verb is often capable of referring to events of nearly any duration, occurring at almost any point in time. Yet a few markers are capable of refining the scope of an event within the confines of the verb paradigm. Only one of these markers, however, enters into a wide range of forms, while the others are mostly restricted to a number of derived stems. As a class, most of these aspectual markers are unproductive, and few of them enter freely into all of the stems in the language.

By far the most productive aspectual marker is the intensive infix *-eg-*, which signals a range of related meanings, most of them revolving around the repetition of the event.[27] When applied to an action that is carried out by a living being, the reference is often to the habitual performance of this deed over a certain period. Consider, for instance, the basic form *meykʷeleʔweyk̓*, which simply means "I mourn." With the addition of the intensive infix *-eg-*, this form can be modified to produce the variant *megeykʷeleʔweyk̓*, which loosely translates as "I always mourn."[28] Here the intensive infix *-eg-* signals a repetition of the action over an extended period of time. In other settings, the intensive infix signals repetition within a more restricted time frame, often an activity that is performed repeatedly until it comes to some implicit end. Consider, for example, the basic form *niiʔnowok̓*, which simply means "I look for it." Compare this with the intensive variant *negiiʔnowok̓*, which translates as "I look for it over and over again."[29] In this instance, the intensive infix *-eg-* suggests that the activity is repeated, perhaps desperately, until its implicit goal is eventually realized. Where there is no motion, the intensive infix often signals the continuation of the activity over an extended period. Consider the form *cyuukʷiʔn*, which means "one being sits," while the intensive variant *cyeguuk̉ʷiʔn* loosely translates as "one being always sits."[30] With descriptive verbs, the intensive infix often suggests intensification of this state. Take the form *teytkoʔł*, which by itself means "it is steep." With intensive derivation, the form becomes *tegeytkoʔł*, while the meaning shifts to "it is quite steep."[31]

For some stems, the concept of repetition, usually over a relatively short span of time, can be signaled through a grammatical process of *reduplication*. Here a portion of the stem, usually the first syllable, is repeated to create a new extended form of the stem.[32] Consider the stem *pegon-*, for instance, which normally means "to split." By simply repeating the first syllable of this stem, the related form *pegpegon-* can be created, meaning "to split in several places." Similarly, when the stem *pɹk̉ʷɹh(s)-* is modified to form the repetitive variant *pɹk̉ʷpɹkwɹh(s)-*, the meaning shifts from "knocking or pecking" to "knocking or pecking repeatedly." Other stems take on more-idiomatic meanings when modified through reduplication. Take the stem *ckem-*, for instance, which normally refers to the act of "counting." When modified through reduplication, the form changes to *ckemckem-*, while the reference is now to a very specific type of counting, one that is involved in the process of "making small tattoo marks."[33]

The remaining stem-internal temporal modifiers are more restricted in occurrence, finding expression in only a handful of verb stems. One pair is concerned with the pace at which an activity is carried out, mostly applying to verbs of motion. Here one stem-initial element indicates a rapid or hurried pace, and another a comparatively leisurely or relaxed tempo. Consider, for example, the final *-ec,* which often occurs in stems portraying scenes of motion. In the form *himecok̉,* the initial *him-* signals a rapid pace, while the construction as a whole loosely translates as "I hurry along." In the related form *k̉ʷoycok̉,* which means "I go slowly," the initial *k̉ʷoy-* indicates a more relaxed tempo. Neither initial element is widely attested, only occasionally entering into stems that signal motion. A case in point is the form *himɹcɹwɹk̉,* which means "I weave quickly." Another example is the form *k̉ʷoyekik̉,* which means "water flows slowly."[34]

Another set specifies duration. Here one stem-initial element indicates a great span of time, while the other signals a period of just one night. Consider, for example, the final *-ec,* which refers to the act of "going" or "moving." In the form *cpaanecok̉,* the stem-initial element *cpaan-* signals a period of considerable duration, while the construction, as a unit, loosely translates as "I go away (for a) long time." Or consider the related form *woycok̉,* for which the contrasting stem-initial element *woy(k)-* signals a stay of "just one night" while the construction as a whole translates as "I stay overnight." Elsewhere in the language, the root *cpaan(i)* occurs as an independent adverb, signaling "a considerable stretch of time." Similarly, the root *woy(k)* also occurs in several freestanding word forms. For instance, the noun *wook* means "morning," while the related adverb *ʔowook* means "tomorrow." The fact that these initials also occur as separate words suggests that the Yurok verb stem is still in the process of absorbing new elements from other word classes. Neither element is widely attested, however, only occasionally entering into other verb stems. A case in point is the related form *woyekiĸ*, which means "water flows overnight." For a comparison, consider the form *cpaaninepeĸ*, which translates as "I feel the time drag."

Another pair of stem-initial elements mark either the onset or the conclusion of an event. While one designates a relatively instantaneous flight into action, the other signals a sudden halt in activity. Both elements are fairly rare in speech. Consider the form *nohsoʔt*, in which the marker *nohs-* signals that the event has a rapid onset, while the form as a whole means "it flies away." Or consider the form *tʔoʔronepeĸ*, in which the marker *tʔ-* signals that the event comes to a sudden halt, whereupon all activity ceases. This expression, as a unit, loosely translates as "I stop running." Other common instantiations include *nohsuuleseĸ* 'I pick up a pack' and *tʔekiĸ* 'water stops flowing'. Yet because these temporal markers are applied to only a handful of forms, many of them historically derived, the vast majority of the verbs in Yurok remain relatively timeless in scope, unless modified by a freestanding tense particle.

LANGUAGE AND SCHEMES OF CLASSIFICATION

To speak a given language in the Native world of northwestern California is to participate in a particular scheme of classification, one that is projected from the conceptual ground of this language outward into the reported events conjured in the mind through the evocative use of words. Some of the categories, such as the general notion of a future tense, run loosely parallel throughout the region. In this sense, many of the languages have developed a grammatical distinction between the "near" and "distant" futures. Other categories are restricted to a particular tradition, such as the complex aspectual system of the Hupa language and the distal future of Yurok grammar. In the end, each language imposes a different system of categories onto the realm of time, encompassing both everyday activities and those distant historical events reported in narrative and preserved in storytelling.

The Karuk verb, in its basic form, is fairly timeless in scope unless specifically marked for temporal features, which is not always required. As such, the verb is often capable of referring to activities that are just starting out or to those that are still in the process of reaching completion. In its unmarked form, the verb is equally capable of referring to events that are situated deep in the mythical past and those that may one day come to pass, perhaps sometime in the distant future. Yet it is always possible to impose a definite time frame onto any event reported in speech. By modifying the verb with one of several grammatical markers, the speaker can, for example, state that an event is habitual or has been carried out continuously over an indefinite period. Several tense-based distinctions are also available in the Karuk language, allowing the speaker to place a scene in either the past or the future, for instance. Yet storytellers generally make sparing use of these categories, leaving the bulk of the forms unrestricted in temporal scope. As is the case in most of the neighboring languages, the past is more heavily subdivided than the future. In the Karuk language, the past is split into three divisions, each one concerned with the relative distance between an implicit present and the episode that precedes it. The most remote is the so-called ancient past, for which the reference is generally to events that took place before recent memory. The future is split into just two categories in the Karuk language, one of them deriving from the other. Often, storytellers use the "general future" to frame the wishes or desires of the myth figures. However, such distinctions are largely optional for the Karuk speaker, representing a possibility that is not exploited with great regularity. In oral literature, for instance, most verbs remain unmarked for time perspective, with only the occasional tense markers that place these otherwise timeless scenes at a specific point in time, such as in the "ancient past" or the "near future." (Yet in everyday life, one must state a time frame, indicating, for instance, that an event is either complete or ongoing.)

The Hupa language, in contrast, projects an elaborate series of temporal categories onto all events reported in speech. Every verb in the language belongs to one of two major temporal categories, one known as the "perfective" and the other the "imperfective." While the imperfective category is reserved for ongoing events, with an essentially unbounded temporal scope, the perfective is the polar opposite, referring to an event whose scope is inherently bounded in some way, usually with an explicit focus on either the early, middle, or final stages of the total process. Every verb also occurs in another pair of configurations, known as the "light" and "heavy" stem shapes. This distinction applies to both perfective and imperfective stems, creating a two-way contrast within each of these categories. While the "light" forms refer to events in a general or indefinite fashion, the contrasting "heavy" forms signal a particular instantiation of the activity portrayed by the verb. In sharp contrast to the situation in Karuk, in which many forms remain unmarked for time perspective, every verb in the Hupa language conveys detailed information about the temporal dynamics of the scene, a pattern that also applies to all nouns derived from verbs. In Hupa, even common nouns often carry detailed information about the time schedule on which a process unfolds. Surprisingly, the status of an event relative to a fixed point in time, such as the "present," is often a matter of secondary importance in the Hupa language, despite the intensive focus on the internal dynamics of temporal processes. Certainly, one is required to specify the inner time schedule on which an event unfolds when speaking Hupa. Yet the status of this event in relation to an implicit present usually receives far less attention in this language.

By itself, the Yurok verb is often almost completely timeless in scope. In fact, not one affix exists for the purpose of marking tense in the Yurok language, while only a few markers are concerned with the internal temporal dynamics of events. Instead, time perspective is richly expressed on a syntactic basis outside the verb paradigm with a series of preverbal particles. That is, in the Yurok language, tense is marked by a series of independent words that only loosely surround the verbs they modify. In this sense, Yurok possesses by far the most elaborate tense system in the region. Many of these tense categories also convey aspectual features. As a consequence, it is often possible to situate a scene at a particular moment in time, while providing detailed information about the inner temporal features of the scene. So, for instance, one can often succinctly state that an activity is either ongoing or approaching some definite conclusion within a particular period of time. Generally speaking, the Yurok verb is neutral with respect to time perspective, relying on the many fine-grained distinctions available outside the verb paradigm, in the system of tense particles. Yet some markers are capable of refining the scope of an event within the confines of the verb paradigm, specifying aspects such as repetition of the event, the pace at which an activity is carried out, duration, and the onset or the conclusion of an event. Most of these aspectual markers are unproductive, and few enter freely into all of the verb stems in the language. Instead, the Yurok verb by itself is often capable of referring to events of nearly any duration, occurring at almost any moment in time.

7

The Linguistic Construction of Time in Narrative

In aboriginal thought there was no conception of a human history, but rather all culture was believed to have been inherited from these miraculous beings, who had occupied the territory just a few generations before. The early Indians believed that they lived where the wo'gey had lived, fished where they had fished, and spoke prayers and sang just as the wo'gey had done. Indeed the prayers and songs Indians used were gifts from the wo'gey, who felt sorry for humans and wanted them to have medicine.

Richard Keeling, Cry for Luck

Though the Native peoples of northwestern California have settled on a common sense of the mythic past, the linguistic traditions of the region could hardly be more diverse in their representations of these parallel episodes in the history of the world. Ultimately, each language is capable of evoking the same periods in the common folklore and mythology of the region. Yet a certain amount of conceptual triangulation is necessary to capture these parallel moments in the shared understanding of the universe. And in the end, the meaning is not always the same, for each language ultimately puts forth a slightly different sense of many otherwise-identical events.

THE ANCIENT ERA OF CREATION

By common assent, the era of creation is set deep in the past, far beyond the experience of any living person. Yet the events that took place during this critical turning point in the prehistory of the planet had a lasting impact on the world, as we know it today, having once upon a time shaped its most essential characteristics. On the one hand, the living present is separated from the mythical past by the unbridgeable chasm of the transformation. Yet on the other, the era of creation is just around the corner, having taken place right here in the world around us perhaps only a handful of generations ago.

According to local oral literature, many of the familiar scenes in myth and folklore are said to have set the present world into motion. The impact of these events can still be felt here today in the world around us. Even the spirit deities, who are said to have fled for the heavens long ago, during myth times, are said to watch over us from their homes at the fringes of the universe, so that they are not completely set apart from us, just very distant. Of course, other figures remained in this world, some of them transforming themselves into the many sacred species of plants and animals that continue to benefit humanity in the aftermath of the creation times, while others became frightful monsters, tormenting humanity or wreaking havoc on those who violate the principles of the Native religions.

While the mythic past is remote and distant in one sense, it is also curiously close and immediate in still another respect, because it laid the foundations for the present world and continues to animate every twitch and turn in the world around us. This tension between the "complete" and "ongoing," or the "distant" and "close at hand," creates a fundamental ambiguity in the oral traditions of the region. Yet this opposition is reflected in a slightly different fashion in each of the neighboring speech communities.

The Karuk Ancient Tense

In the Karuk language, the era of creation can be invoked with a single verbal suffix, one that may potentially be applied to almost any form within the fabric of a story line. While this marker is always available to the speaker, most narrators choose to leave the bulk of the verbs fairly unrestricted in scope. Many of these verbs potentially refer to events occurring long ago, in the ancient past, or to those that are still happening today, in the living present. Significantly, many of the episodes portrayed in creation stories do in fact hold a certain timeless validity. Having first taken place in the ancient past, many of these mythic acts continue on indefinitely into the future, for all time to follow, a general state of affairs that is captured in the prevailingly "timeless" phrasing of Karuk oral literature.[1]

Often the narrator reserves the special marker of the ancient past for a scene that brings the entire plot to a point of culmination. Only after this crucial turning point has passed does the narrator announce that the story is set in the myth times. All the episodes that precede it and those that follow remain fairly unrestricted in potential temporal scope, without a special marker to place these other scenes in any particular time period. Each one, in a sense, holds a certain timeless validity.

One of the most common ways of situating a scene in the ancient past is with the terse, if efficient, construction ʔukúphaanik, which loosely translates as "this one did so anciently." Highly general in meaning, this form often applies, backwards in the story line, to the whole sequence of scenes that precedes it. For example, after all of Coyote's deeds have been portrayed in a succession of scenes that bear no particular time frame, all of his acts are suddenly situated in the ancient past, with a single, well-placed form often at the high point of his adventures. Yet in the aftermath of the creation times, many of these ancient acts became a regular part of the world, where many of these mythical deeds can still be witnessed today.

Perhaps Coyote has gone out in search of money and women, only to get lost and thirsty; on arriving at death's door, he loses sight of his mission. Or maybe his body has withered away for lack of sustenance, only to rise again when the yellow jackets pierce the loins of his rotting corpse. Perhaps he has tricked a woman into having sex with him by pretending to be a doctor. Or maybe he has just sampled his own excrement only to find it rather tasty, feasting upon it, here and there, for all time thereafter, as all canines do. Then, after recounting all of these episodes—which, by virtue of their "timeless" phrasing, could just as well be taking place right now—the narrator says ʔukúphaanik, which loosely translates as "he did so anciently." In many cases, this is the only form in the entire story to bear an overt tense marker, placing this particular act squarely within the realm of the ancient past. As much as these episodes were a part of the ancient past, certainly some can still be witnessed, or in part projected, even today.

Less often, the narrator announces (even in the first several lines) that the entire sequence of events that follow should be placed in the era of the ancient past. Even in these stories, however, the majority of the forms usually remain unrestricted in potential temporal scope, with the remainder of the episodes implicitly holding a certain timeless validity. When fire, for instance, declares that nothing can put him out, this proclamation is situated squarely in the ancient past, with the word ʔúppaanik 'he said anciently'.[2] Yet when fire is eventually extinguished, this former state of affairs is overturned, along with its provisional validity. These other episodes remain essentially timeless in scope, including rain's success in stamping fire out and the failure of all the other animals in this pursuit. Here each form that is stated in this "tenseless" fashion also holds a certain timeless validity, while the one statement that is situated in the ancient past—that absolutely nothing, once upon a time, could put fire out—was later reversed. Fortunately, rain can still stamp fire out!

Sometimes the narrator reserves the marker of the ancient past for the most pivotal scene in the story line, with all of the other events in the story also holding a certain timeless validity. When Coyote crashes down from the heavens to land at Burrill Peak, for example, this deadly fall is squarely placed in the ancient past, as the narrator says *poopikyívishrihanik* 'it was there that he (Coyote) anciently landed (from the heavens)'.[3] The monument, indeed, still stands there today, in the form of a stone that is eternally associated with this ancient and comical fall from grace. Or when Towhee's eyes turn red from looking too long into the intense blaze of the fire, this event is also situated in the ancient past, with the telltale word, announced only in the closing lines, *poomchaaxrípaanik* 'from the heat's coming out anciently'.[4] Certainly this one particular event (the permanent alteration of Towhee's eyes) is unique, having occurred only once during the ancient era of creation, with lasting implications for the future of the world. Yet the results of this singular event, Towhee's blazing red eyes, nevertheless retain a certain timeless or eternal validity.

In Karuk creation stories, most forms remain relatively timeless in scope, with bounded forms only occasionally cropping up to place selected scenes—not the entire story line—squarely in the ancient past. Where tense markers are used, they are generally only sparingly applied, while most forms remain timeless or at least unbounded. This tendency, which reaches its high point in Karuk, in part reflects the sense in which the mythic era is not entirely closed off but in many ways continues to shape the living present.

The Ancient Past in Hupa Narrative

The Hupa storyteller has no such recourse to a special marker of the ancient past. Yet this same period in the prehistory of the planet can be invoked by falling back on several alternative strategies, often involving either circumlocution or broad implication. As in Karuk creation stories, most forms in Hupa narrative also remain tenseless. Yet in Hupa, many forms are explicitly bounded in temporal scope, as the shift between the perfective and imperfective time frames is intrinsic to the structure of the verbal paradigm.

Among Hupa storytellers, the era of creation is usually invoked by mentioning the deeds that took place during this time, though without any explicit reference to the past, either through tense marking or circumlocution. Because the audience is aware of the status of the event in the fabric of mythic time, the surrounding sequence of events can be safely placed in the realm of the past, through a general process of inference. For this reason, there is rarely any need on the narrator's part to spell out the time frame explicitly. Like the time periods, even the names of the myth figures are rarely stated directly. Instead, the audience must infer their identities through familiarity with their deeds, exactly as a period in myth must be surmised through familiarity with the episodes that took place during those times.

Consider, for instance, the central story in Hupa lore, which begins with the simple words, "This one grew up at creation place." From this simple statement, which is rife with implication, the audience must infer both the time frame and the identity of the protagonist. In the words of Emma Frank, who dictated this story to Goddard in 1901, *čixolč"e·-diŋ* 'at creation place' *ʔe·na·ŋʔ* 'it was' *naʔtehłdič"e·n* 'he grew (back) up'.[5] Here neither the time period nor the myth figure is mentioned by name. Yet to anyone versed in the creation lore, the reference to Across-the-Ocean-Widower is unmistakable. As most learned early in life in traditional times, this is the figure who sprang into existence at precisely this site. Here he initiated the very creation for which the village of 'creation place' (*čixolč"e·-diŋ*) is named.

This is far from an isolated case, as most creation stories adhere to this pattern; indeed, many contain references that are more oblique than this one, though rarely with any explicit reference to the actual time frame. In a similar fashion, few characters are explicitly mentioned by name, even when they are human rather than prehuman figures. Representing still another reflection of the pan-Athabaskan predilection for process orientation, both the myth figures and the time periods are largely understood according to the actions that define them.

Though no special suffix exists for the purposes of situating events in the ancient past, the narrator can sometimes evoke this period with a special phrase that refers directly to this entire era. Adhering to a familiar pattern in Hupa oral literature, this expression defines the era in relation to its most pivotal event, namely, the act of creation itself. Hence, the Hupas know the myth times by the phrase *čixolč"e·-daŋʔ*, a descriptive expression that loosely translates as "(the era) when (the world) was created." The expression is based on the verb stem -*č"e·*, which, together with the element *l-* before it, refers to the act of "creation." Normally, the element immediately before the stem is *ł-*, as can be illustrated with the active form *čixolč*ᵂ*e·*, which translates as "one being makes something." The shift to *l-* generates an abstract noun that refers to the general action of "creation." The prefix *xo-* in the middle of the form refers to the place that was created as a result of this act, here the earth or world by implication, while the prefix *či-* signals that the actor who performed this deed was animate. Here the reference is to the myth figure Across-the-Ocean-Widower, though the reference must be teased out through inference. At the end of the form, the locative marker *-daŋʔ* converts the form into a temporal phrase that refers to the era when this deed was carried out, namely, during the era of creation.

In actual practice, speakers rarely use this expression to set a story in the ancient past. More often, the phrase is invoked in daily life, giving the speaker a precise way of referring to the creation times. One might, for instance, draw upon the expression when stating the origins of a ceremony, saying *hay* '(in) the' *čixolč*ᵂ*e·-daŋʔ* 'myth times' *ʔa·čilaw* 'he did so'. The sentence as a whole loosely translates as "one (established the dances) during the ancient myth times."[6] More often, the plot alone sets a tale in the myth times, effectively eliminating the need to refer to the era of creation in a more specific way.

In sharp contrast to the speakers of the neighboring languages, the Hupas rarely invoke the past tense when situating a scene in the ancient era of creation, for in Hupa, the most general marker of the past tense refers to conditions that have ceased to exist, signaling that the event in question is entirely closed off from the temporal ground of the living present. Yet most of the scenes portrayed in oral literature continue to exert a lasting influence on the present world.

Where the remote past marker enters creation lore, it generally refers to conditions that once held true before the transformation, though which have ceased to exist in their former state. For instance, according to traditional religious beliefs, the spirit deities once inhabited this world, abandoning it shortly before the time when humans began to arrive. In creation stories, there are occasional references to the former presence of these sacred beings in this world, whose severance from ordinary human experience (if not the fabric of the universe) is now considered a permanent state of affairs. In referring to their former presence in this world, speakers sometimes say *kʸixinay-neʔin,* which loosely translates as "the spirit deities of a bygone age." Otherwise, the word *kʸixinay,* the Hupa name for the spirit deities, rarely occurs in the past tense. For according to the traditional religious beliefs, these spirit beings have not ceased to exist; they have merely fled the world of ordinary human experience. In fact, the Hupa word for these sacred beings literally refers to the beings "who survive." Of course, it is said that after abandoning this world, the spirit deities made their homes in the heavens at the fringes of the universe, where they still live today. There they still watch over humanity.

Or consider the popular story of a Hupa Indian who was once transformed into a spirit deity by supernatural means. When speaking of his former status as an ordinary human, speakers report this past state of affairs in the ancient times, as reflected in the construction *kʸiwinyaʔnyaˑn-neʔin*, which loosely translates as "the one who was once an Indian." Though many scenes in creation lore hold a timeless validity, this particular state of affairs ceased to hold true once this character was transformed, once and for all, into a spirit deity. That is, after becoming a spirit deity, this figure was no longer considered an ordinary human.

Though tense marking is rare in Hupa narrative, most of the episodes reported in stories are loosely bounded in potential temporal scope. For unknown reasons, Hupa storytellers rely almost exclusively on heavy stem constructions when reporting events set in the creation times. Consider the heavy stem *-čʷiw*, which occurs in the construction *čičʷiw*, where it means "one being cries." In relation to tense marking, heavy stem constructions, which are common in creation stories, cannot generally be placed in the future, only in the past. Consider the form *čičʷiw-neʔin*, where the tense marker *-neʔin* signals that a being specifically cries "in the past." Compare this with the light stem *-čʷeh*, which occurs in the contrasting form *čičʷeh*, where it means "one being is crying (now)." This light stem construction, in contrast with a similar heavy stem construction, can be situated in the present or the future but usually not in the past. Consider the form *čičʷeh-teˑ*, for instance, where the tense marker *-teˑ* signals that this act will take place "at some future time." Whereas light stem constructions cannot be placed in the past, heavy stem constructions, which are common in narrative, cannot usually be placed in the future.

Outside of creation stories, these heavy stem constructions are associated with situations over which the speaker holds a fair amount of certainty. Consider derived nouns of action, for instance, for which the reference is to a process regularly associated with a specific actor. One example is the derived noun *xonsiɬ-čʷiw*, which means "the one who cries in the summertime." Here the reference is to the mourning dove. The contrasting light stem form *xonsiɬ-čʷeh* simply means "one cries in the summertime," with reference to an ongoing act, not a particular class of actors. With nouns of action, the heavy stem contributes the sense that the activity is linked for all time with a specific actor, as a defining characteristic. Likewise, the episodes reported in creation stories are connected with specific figures that are also identified by their characteristic acts, which often hold equal validity in the past, present, and future. Outside of creation stories, these heavy stem constructions are also closely associated with customary forms. Here the reference is to a process that is repeated, with regularity, over a considerable span of time. Consider the customary form *č'e'ič"iw,* which translates as "one always cries." Here the reference is to a specific actor who regularly cries as a matter of custom or habit. Likewise, the episodes reported in creation stories are also linked to specific actors, known by all, who carry them out repeatedly over a great span of time. Or consider past tense constructions, in which the reference is to an instance of an event over which the speaker holds a reasonable amount of certainty. These constructions also invariably feature heavy stems. Consider the form *č'ič"iw-ne'in,* which loosely translates as "one being used to cry." Here the reference is to a specific actor known to have performed this act for a time in the past. Like past tense constructions, the episodes reported in creation stories are associated with specific classes of actors over which the speaker holds a reasonable degree of certainty.

This tendency to extend a measure of specificity to events carried out in the ancient past, through the use of heavy stem verb constructions, exists in stark contrast to the storytelling traditions of the neighboring groups. Instead, for the Yuroks and Karuks, most verbs remain far less restricted in scope. In a similar vein, perfective forms are common in Hupa creation stories, in which a definite onset, duration, or conclusion is often specifically granted to an act. This tendency is rare elsewhere in the region. As discussed in chapter 6, for example, Across-the-Ocean-Widower's flight from the ordinary human world is cast in the inceptive time frame, while the emergence of another mythic figure from beneath the earth is cast in the conclusive time frame, as reflected in the village name *Č'e·'indiɢo'diŋ,* meaning "the place where he wriggled out." In contrast, a character's thought is often cast in the stative time frame, with emphasis on the continued nature of the process, as reflected in the expression *'a·č'ondehsne'* 'one thought (so)', a form that features the stative marker *s-.*

The Ancient Past in Yurok

The Yurok language, in contrast to its neighbors, possesses a special grammatical marker that refers to the ancient times preceding recent memory. Though similar to the Karuk marker of the "ancient past," the parallel Yurok category is only occasionally applied to creation stories. Instead, in Yurok oral literature, the time frame is often implied by the story line, mirroring the same trend in Hupa narrative, though on a lesser scale. As is the case in the neighboring Karuk language, many verbs in Yurok creation lore remain unrestricted in temporal scope. Yet some constructions in Yurok narrative are specifically marked to suggest events that continue to exert a lasting effect on the living present.

Often the time frame is briefly established in the first few lines, as the narrator announces that all of the scenes that follow took place long ago, either in the time of creation or in the distant human past, well before recent memory set in. From there, the audience is able to infer the precise era through familiarity with the following scenes. For example, in the opening lines of a creation story, the narrator often declares that the full cast of characters lived together "long ago." In Yurok, this notion can be expressed as follows: *hikon⁷* 'once upon a time' *ku* 'the' *ʔela* 'there on earth' *hooleʔmoni* 'they were dwelling'.[8] Here the temporal reference is somewhat ambiguous. While the tense marker *hikon* signals the broad period preceding recent memory, the particle *ʔela* establishes the scene "here on earth" in the past. The rest of the scene clearly places the story in the era of creation, as the narrator introduces Dove and the remaining cast of characters. For during this period, the animals established many of the features of the present world, including Dove's penchant for weeping in the summertime to grieve the loss of his grandfather during these ancient times.

More often, a pivotal event is reported with a special marker that accentuates the lasting effects of this past episode. As Dove, for instance, made the fateful decision to forgo his grandfather's funeral, he was, just at that moment, winning a game of gambling. Here the whole scene is cast in the enduring past with the words *kic* 'enduring past' *rewpeʔn* 'he was winning'.[9] If Dove had not been winning at this point, the world might be different today. That is, Dove would be neither guilty nor perpetually mournful. As it came to pass, the fact that Dove was winning at this point irreversibly altered the entire sequence of events to follow, so that he had to pledge to mourn every summer thereafter, until the end of time. Or consider the episode in which Across-the-Ocean-Widower opens the door for salmon, freeing them, once and for all, from their primordial captors early in the creation times. Again, this critical event is announced with the marker of the enduring past, with the words *kic* 'enduring past' *ʔo* 'there' *gunkek* 'he opened the way'.[10] Similarly, when Crane's wives return after having been stolen by Coyote, the reunited flock flies across the ocean together once more. Again, this sequence of events is announced with the marker of the enduring past, with the words *ʔo* 'there' *piškaał* 'at the ocean' *kic* 'enduring past' *leʔm* 'they go'.[11] Though completed in the past, this event holds lasting implications for the present. For Crane and his wives, the ducks, may still be seen flying together today.

RECURRING EPISODES IN MYTH OR FOLKLORE

Sometimes a key episode recounted in oral literature represents a crucial turning point in the history of life on earth. Often this event establishes a legacy, the lasting effects of which may still be apparent for all to see in the world today. Here the deed performed by this figure long ago, during the ancient past, becomes its hallmark trait or defining characteristic for all time thereafter. In other cases, the figure leaves behind a monument attesting to its former presence in this world, sometimes in the form of a place that comes to be associated with its former beneficence or mischief. Other figures continue to live in this world following the creation times, after being transformed into some sacred species, such as an animal or plant.

Karuk Durative and Iterative Forms

In the Karuk language, a scene of great significance can be drawn out or accentuated with one of several markers, each of them expanding the scope of the event portrayed by the verb in its usual form. Although each of these markers extends the scene in the fabric of the story line, sometimes the reference is also to an event that reaches from the ancient past into the living present, whether continuously or in stops and starts.

Often Karuk storytellers use durative markers to extend a scene over a considerable span of time, usually for a well-defined period within the fabric of the story line. Coyote, for instance, always finds himself desperately thirsty when venturing out on one of his ill-fated missions to find money and women. When Coyote finally arrives at a spring and hears the tantalizing sound of water flowing, the narrator often announces this scene with a durative form, saying *paʔíshshaha* 'the water' *ʔúxxaaktih* 'was sounding'.[12] Much to Coyote's chagrin, the water usually vaporizes the minute he sets foot near it. Similarly, when Coyote chokes down some grasshoppers to stave off his hunger, they only continue falling out his rear, until he finally settles on the unfortunate solution of plugging up his rear with sap. Later in the story, his rear end catches fire!

The extended nature of this unsettling scene is reflected in his declaration *napávyiihrishuktih* 'they're coming out my rear',[13] a construction again containing the durative marker *-tih*. In a similar fashion, Coyote's penchant for singing as he travels along is often portrayed with durative forms, as reflected in the word *?upakuriihvutih*, which loosely translates as "he was singing here and there while going along."

In other cases, the activity continues, by implication, to reach outside the story line, stretching from the ancient past into the living present, where the activity in question can still be witnessed in the world around us today. When Coyote, for instance, eats his own excrement, this familiar scene is set in the durative time frame, as he exclaims *?aaf* 'excrement' *pani?áamtih* 'it is that I am eating'.[14] When Coyote proclaims that the rivers ought to flow downstream, this incipient state of affairs continues to hold true for some time to follow, eventually becoming a condition that remains equally true today. And it is with a durative form that Coyote wills this state of affairs onto the world, saying *yúruk* 'downstream' *kámvuunupahitih* 'let it continue flowing down'.[15] Before Coyote brought about this unfortunate transformation, the rivers flowed both ways, making conveyance by canoe an essentially effortless matter, until this happy state of affairs was irreversibly upset through Coyote's characteristic mischief.

Similarly, when Coyote frees the salmon from their primordial captors by smashing them out from behind the walls of the house where they are trapped, a great stream of water comes gushing out. This unexpected flood initiates the downward flow of the rivers and upstream migration of the salmon. Significantly, both events are marked with durative forms, with the words *?áama* 'salmon' *?ukvíripraatih* 'run upriver continuously' and the narrator's earlier statement *?ussaamnúputih*,[16] meaning "(water) flows downriver continually." Though established in the past, both conditions continue to hold true today.

Sometimes storytellers use iterative marking to highlight the recurrence of an episode in the fabric of the story line. When a tick, for instance, lodges itself in Across-the-Ocean-Widower's penis, the general form of the verb is not used; instead, the iterative variant is used, suggesting that this event was continuously, and perhaps painfully, repeated over and over again during this time. Indeed, the narrator announces this painful intrusion with the iterative form *?upíkrii*, which translates as "one stays there again and again."[17] Compare this with the unmarked form *?úkrii*, which simply translates as "one stays there," based on the verb stem *ikriv*, here occurring in third-person form, with the subject marker *?u-*. Incidentally, this episode is only resolved when Across-the-Ocean-Widower cuts off the diseased portion of his member and releases it into the river, where-upon it is transformed into the Eel.

Hupa Customary Forms

Hupa storytellers tend to mark similar episodes with customary forms. Here the reference is to the recurrence of an event over a period of great, though essentially unrestricted, scope—often as an episode that was repeated habitually for a time within the fabric of the story line. Yet in many cases, speakers refer to actions that continue to recur, in spells and patches, beginning in the ancient times, while reaching into the living present.

Often Hupa storytellers use customary forms to highlight episodes that recur for a time before coming to a definite end of some kind. Consider, for instance, the story of the young man who used to watch his father throw him-self with an arrow, often flying a considerable distance before landing on solid land. Eventually, when the young man mastered the trick for himself, he no longer needed to observe his father. Yet when the storytellers announce that this young man used to observe his father, this former practice is often set in the customary aspect. Here the narrator usually says *naʔxodeʔilʔeʔn,* which loosely translates as "this one always watched (his father)." Here the customary variant contrasts with the unmarked form *naʔxodileʔn,* which simply trans-lates as "this one watches him." Of course, the character stopped observing his father once he mastered the trick for himself. To capture the repeated nature of the activity, the narrator specifically selects the customary aspect to speak about this past habit, even though it has now been discontinued.

Or consider the former travels of Across-the-Ocean-Widower. Before leaving this world for the heavens at the fringes of the universe, he traveled widely throughout the region, where he established many of the dances and medicines that are still practiced there today. When speaking of his former travels, Hupa storytellers tend to rely on customary forms, with the focus placed on the repeated nature of his treks, saying *ninisʔa·n* 'the world' *me·qʼ* 'inside' *čiteʔina·W* 'one being always went along'. Compare this construction with the contrasting imperfective form *čitina·W,* which simply means "one goes along," without marking for the customary aspect. Because Across-the-Ocean-Widower no longer travels in this world during modern times, the customary nature of this former practice applies strictly to the time before the era of the transformation.

Yet sometimes a customary act established during the creation era eventu-ally gains a certain timeless validity, as it continues to recur, according to a regular cycle, for all time to follow. A case in point is the story of the lunar eclipse, which is considered to be the result of rebellion on the part of the Moon's pets, who occasionally rise up against him and devour his flesh. Just as the Moon is almost gone, his wife, Frog, comes along to fend off these disobedient pets, which allows for the return of the Moon and the end of the eclipse. This entire episode, which repeats itself every now and then (ever since the creation times), is usually reported with customary constructions to highlight the recurring nature of the process. When the Moon ventures out on this night from beneath the horizon, this act is portrayed as happening not once but regularly, with the form *čiteʔina·W*, which loosely translates as "one being (the Moon) always goes along." This construction features the customary form of the imperfective verb *čitina·W*, which simply translates as "one goes along." Of course, the use of the customary form stresses the recurring nature of the sporadic event. Similarly, when the Moon's pets rise to eat him, this episode is also portrayed with customary forms, as the narrator says *yixoʔiyaʔn* 'they always devour him'. Here the contrasting imperfective form *yixoʔiya·n* translates as "they eat him (once)." When, at the end of the cycle, his wife nurses him back to health, this scene, too, is marked for a habitual reoccurrence, with the expression *naʔneʔiWoŋʔ*, which means "(the Moon) always gets well again."[18]

Oftentimes Hupa storytellers use customary forms to refer to events that were first established in the past, only to be carried forth into the modern era. A case in point is the expression *čeʔicid*, which loosely translates as "one always pounds up (medicine root)." Typically this form refers to the priest at the Jump Dance, whose role is to crush incense root to dust before throwing it into the fire, to consecrate the sacred dance grounds. Though established in the ancient past, this sacred act continues to play an important role in the living present.

Similarly, a mythic adolescent who remains forever on the verge of womanhood is said to have once led warriors into battle. Though she later journeys to the heavens, where she continues to watch over humanity from afar, all of the rites she once established, during the ancient era of creation, still remain a part of the world today. To highlight the continuous and recurring nature of these rites throughout the ages, all of the activities surrounding this figure are generally reported with customary forms. When a party of warriors attacks her, the enemy rises not just once but habitually, as the narrator announces with the word *xʷeydeʔiliw* 'they always attack'. She, in turn, always defeats the enemy, as the narrator reports: *čiseʔiɬweʔ* 'she always kills them'. Because her followers strive to duplicate her proven success in battle, their ceremonial actions are generally reported with customary forms as well. In hopes of repeating her legendary success, her followers are instructed to bundle sticks together before battle, following the example she set on many occasions in the past. When speaking of this habitual practice, one says *łeʔiloyʔ* '(the practitioner) always ties them together'.[19]

Occasionally, Hupa storytellers use iterative forms to mark the repetition of an act that holds great significance in religious life, such as the institution of a medicinal practice or the emergence of an important myth figure. When a figure establishes a medicinal formula, for instance, this ancient act is usually said to have occurred not just once but repeatedly, as reflected in the expression *ʔaˑnaˑčʼidiyaw*, which literally translates as "one did so again." Though generally translated into English as "one established (a medicine)," this form literally refers to the repetition of this ancient and sacred act. Compare the verb in this idiom with the contrasting form *ʔaˑčʼidiyaw*, which means "one did so," where the reference is to a single instantiation of the act of accomplishing something. With the addition of the iterative marker *naˑ=*, the reference is to the recurrence of the practice. In a sense, the deed is reenacted every time the medicine is performed today or every time the story is recounted. Both acts invoke a certain repetition of the ancient deed in the fabric of time. Similarly, when a myth figure grows up, this character is said to have emerged not once but repeatedly, as reflected in the expression *naʔtehłdičʷeˑn*, which translates as "one grew back up again." Compare the verb in this idiom to the unmarked form *čʼitehłčʷeˑn*, which simply translates as "one grew up." Here the iterative markers *naˑ=* and *di-* explicitly signal the repetition of this otherwise singular event, which is invoked again and again in the fabric of narrative each time the story is recounted.

Yurok Intensive Forms

Yurok storytellers report similar episodes using intensive forms, which stress the repeated nature of an act that is carried forth, in stops and starts, from the ancient times forward. Often the lasting effects of this ancient act continue to echo across all time. When Dove, for instance, pledges to mourn the loss of his grandfather, whose funeral he missed on account of his excessive gambling, this intention is reported, in Dove's words, with the form *megeykʷeleʔweyk̓* 'I (will) mourn repeatedly'. Compare this intensive form, marked with the infix *-eg-*, with the otherwise timeless variant *meykʷeleʔweyk̓* 'I mourn (generally)'.[20] In a similar sense, Fox once charged Raccoon with stealing fish along the log where Fox liked to scamper. This accusation on the part of Fox is stated with an intensive form, *kegemoleʔm* 'you are always stealing (fish)', suggesting a characteristic act carried forward from the most ancient times and remaining equally true of this little one's behavior today.[21]

Or consider the story of First Salmon, who began the annual migration along the area's rivers long ago during the ancient creation times. After First Salmon is released from his primordial captors at the head of the river, all the salmon continue to remain homesick for their birthplace, returning to this destination each year after swimming back downriver to the sea. In this setting, the annual return and constant homesick state of the salmon are reported with intensive forms. A case in point is the form *kʷegmteʔm,* which translates as "they return repeatedly." Or consider the expression *kegesomewtet,* which translates as "they always become homesick."[22] Both forms refer to an annual cycle that has been repeated since the very beginning of time.

Similarly, Owl was condemned to hoot in the canyons for all eternity in punishment for the fact that he was a poor father in the past. From that moment on, he would never again break into song, though sometimes he continues to alert people to the presence of evil. In general, Yurok storytellers report this characteristic act with the intensive verb *ʔeʔgoloyew,* which refers to the practice of "hooting repeatedly."[23] Compare this intensive form with the unmarked variant *ʔoloyew-,* which simply refers to the act of "hooting," though not on more than one occasion.

PROJECTING THE FUTURE FROM THE ANCIENT PAST

During the ancient era of creation, the myth figures frequently speculated about the human world that was soon to emerge in the not-so-distant future. The ancients, for instance, often announced that those who knew their secrets would be blessed in the times that lay ahead. Many of the actions these figures contemplated, such as medicines or religious practices, would one day be continued for all time thereafter. Though first set down in the creation times, these acts were intended by the ancients to be carried forth into the indefinite future.

Karuk: Durative Future

In Karuk creation stories, predictions about the "distant future" of the present era are often reported with future forms that also feature the durative marker *-tih.* Here the reference is to a continuous stream of activity stretching from the ancient times forward, without a break in the action. When Water Ouzel's wife, for instance, finds that he has been hiding food from his family and keeping it to himself, she condemns him to an eternity of eating nothing but the mud from the floors of creeks, saying *ʔaratváraf* 'mud' *kích* 'only' *ʔiʔáamtiheesh* 'you will be continuously eating'.[24] Here the fate of Water Ouzel is announced with a construction that contains both the durative marker *-tih* and the future marker *=eesh*. Otherwise, the curse is cast with the root *ʔa(a)(m)*, which refers to the act of "eating," while the second-person subject marker *ʔi-* extends this fate to Water Ouzel's husband, the addressee in the story line. Here the curse refers to what eventually became a continuous stream of action, one that began with this ancient proclamation, only to ring across all time.

Similarly, when the spirit deities first establish the World Renewal Cere-monies, during the myth times, they announce that human beings will one day carry these rites into the future, saying *pakunkupítiheesh* 'they (also) will be doing like that'.[25] In the hopes that these rites would be repeated each year until the end of time, to purify the world and free it of illness, the spirit deities state their prediction in a form that again indicates both the futurity of the action (*=eesh*) and the continuous nature of its performance (*-tih*). Similarly, just before the arrival of humans, Tan Oak once proclaimed that she would one day be the most important food source: *kích* 'only' *kanáʔaamtiheesh* 'me they will be eating'.[26] Expecting that people would always be eating her, from the moment of their arrival until the end of time, she makes her proclamation with a form that is again marked both for a general futurity (*=eesh*) and for a continuous enactment (*-tih*). The fusional prefix *kána-* signals both a third-person subject and a first-person object.

Hupa: General, Near, and Progressive Future

The Hupa language splits the future into several categories. Two of these reflect the span of time between the moment of utterance and the realization of the prediction. Another category asserts a sense of continuity between the ancient past and the distant future.

Sometimes Hupa storytellers cast past pronouncements in the "near future," granting a certain immediacy to the predictions made by the characters in the story. From another perspective, these past pronouncements imply that the mythic past is not far removed from the present world, the eventual realiza-tion of which the spirit deities once regarded as imminent. When, for instance, the spirit deities talk about the coming of humans, they often announce this heavily anticipated time as if it is very close at hand, saying *kʸiwinyaˀnyaˑn* 'people' *naˑnaˑndeˀx̌-tehł* 'are about to come into existence'. Here the tense marker *-tehł* stresses the immediacy of this event. Similarly, when a spirit deity pledges to establish a medicine, this past intention is often situated in the near future, as the character announces, *noˑnaˑkʸinaˑˀan-tehł* 'I'm going to leave something (medicine)'. Again, the marker *-tehł* indicates that the myth figure regards the world of humans as being very close at hand.

More often, the "general future" is used to frame these ancient pronouncements without necessarily hinting at the immanency of their realization, though often with the implication that a far greater distance separates the ancient past and living present. Dog, for instance, pledges to remain in this world following the transformation, so that he can watch over humanity by barking in the presence of danger. All of his pronouncements about his future duties are cast strictly in the general future, suggesting that a considerable stretch of time may separate his past life from the one he plans to lead, from that moment, until the end of time. At one point, Dog proclaims *naˑyyaˀ-te·* 'I will go around'. Later he announces *meˑnaˑyliW-te·* 'I will watch (people)'. Significantly, both pronouncements refer to a distant future far removed from his life in the mythic times, during which, among other things, he could still speak. Similarly, when Across-the-Ocean-Widower created a medicine that allows people to walk among rattlesnakes without being bitten, he announces that in the distant future, he and all those who know his medicine will whip ahead of themselves with a cane, scaring away the rattlers. In this setting, he proclaims *ˀaˑdinaˑce·* 'ahead of myself' *kʸiteˑsehłcahs-te·* 'I will whip', suggesting that in the distant times to come, this method would still prove valid.

Other pronouncements are stated with progressive forms. Sometimes these are placed in the general future, suggesting a continuous stream of activity that is maintained from the most ancient times onward. When a Hupa Indian is transformed into a spirit deity, by virtue of his great merit at the religious dances, he states all of his plans in the progressive future, indicating the deeds that he will thereafter carry out, each year, for all time. He announces, for example, that every year, at the time of the Jump Dance, fog will always be descending on the valley: *noywiłkʸilił-te·* 'fog will (always) be reaching down'. This construction, in turn, represents the progressive variant of the basic imperfective form *noyniłkʸid*, which by itself translates as "fog or smoke descends downward." Later, the same character informs all those living in the valley that he always will be looking on, each year, into all eternity, as they perform their annual rites, a sentiment that he again expresses in the progressive future: *na·tehWʔiŋʔiɬ-te·* 'I will be looking back (upon the dance)'. Finally, he announces that there will always be a dance at this site of his birth, one that will always be associated with him into perpetuity, saying *čidiwilye·liɬ-te·* 'they will always be dancing'. Again, the verb in this construction is the progressive variant of the form *čidilye·* 'they dance', while the marker *-te·* suggests that this ongoing activity will be carried out continuously and indefinitely, into the distant future.

The Yurok Intensive Future

In Yurok creation stories, ancient events with lasting implications are generally stated with intensive constructions also marked for future reoccurrence. This combination of categories suggests an act that began in the past that will continue, in spells and patches, into the distant future, reaching from the myth times into the living present.

When Dove, for instance, pledges to mourn his grandfather's loss, he states this future intention with an intensive form situated in the future, with the words *ki* 'future wish' *nooɬ* 'then' *megeykʷeleʔweyk̓* 'I (will) mourn repeatedly'.[27] When First Salmon's captors state that their former victims shall always return to home, this pronouncement is again stated with an intensive form marked for a continuous recurrence, with the words *k̓i* 'the' *nepuy* 'salmon' *ki* 'future hope' *kʷegmɬeʔm* 'return continuously'.[28] Similarly, when Owl's wife condemns him to an eternity of hooting without the mercy of song or melody, she casts her curse in an intensive form also placed in the intentional future: *ki* 'future (wish)' *cpi* 'only' *ni* 'there (in the canyons)' *ʔeʔgoloyew* 'hoot repeatedly'.[29]

TEMPORAL STRUCTURE IN ORAL NARRATIVES

To speak a particular language in the Native universe of northwestern California is to share in a world of associations cast from the conceptual ground of a given linguistic system outward, into the classification of the events portrayed in everyday life or storytelling. For speakers of Yurok and Karuk, the verb in its basic form is relatively timeless in scope, referring equally to activities occurring now, in the ancient past, or in the distant future, with only a small number of categories conferring definite limits onto the overall reference. This general orientation is echoed in oral literature, where most forms remain relatively timeless in significance. The Hupa verb, in contrast, imposes an elaborate series of obligatory temporal categories onto all events reported in speech, often conferring a definite onset, duration, or conclusion onto any given scene in creation lore. In Hupa, even nouns are not exempt from this all-pervasive focus on the internal temporal characteristics of events, for many convey a precise temporal classification of the phenomenon at hand. The relative timelessness of many Yurok and Karuk verb forms also resonates with the sense of timelessness conveyed in the local creation lore, in which many characteristic activities first established during the ancient times would be continued there-after, for all eternity. For Hupa speakers, however, the scenes portrayed in creation lore are often granted definite onsets or conclusions, while most forms in Hupa narrative feature the so-called heavy stem formations, which refer to specific instantiations of an event, linked eternally with a particular actor. This alternative orientation reflects the sense in which the myth times are partially closed off from the living present, as a distinct era whose episodes are now complete, however much these ancient acts came to shape the present world.

When tense marking comes into play, Karuk alone possesses a special marker that refers specifically to the ancient past, though in general this category is only sparingly applied in creation lore. Generally this marker is applied only to scenes that are confined to the past, though not to the remainder of the events that retain a certain timeless validity within the fabric of the story line. Yurok, how-ever, does possess a special tense marker that refers to activities whose lasting effects continue to influence the course of events to follow. The primary "past tense" marker in Hupa refers specifically to scenes whose connection to the living present had been decisively severed at some point. While the Yurok marker of the "enduring past" is frequently applied to creation stories, where it refers to scenes whose lingering effects continue to echo across all time, the Hupa marker of the "remote past" (or the "no longer existing") is used to refer to states and conditions that have ceased to exist since the time of the transformation, such as the former presence of the spirit deities within the human world. Otherwise, the Hupas make sparing use of tense, leaving the audience to infer the era from the deeds that took place within the fabric of the story line.

Where the reference is to eternal events, whose validity stretches from the ancient past into the living present, the Karuks principally use durative forms, sometimes with reference to an activity that reaches continuously, across all time, in an essentially unbroken chain. The Hupas and Yuroks, in contrast, usually use iterative forms to mark similar events, with emphasis on scenes that will be repeated, in stops and starts, for all time. For the Hupas, this is realized in the form of customary verbs, suggesting repetition as a matter of habit, while for the Yuroks, a similar effect is achieved with the use of intensive verbs, suggesting an intrinsic repetition that reaches outward into infinity.

When the future is forecast from the ancient past, each language marks the parallel conception of a continuous futurity in its own distinctive fashion. While Karuk speakers combine the general future with the durative marker, suggesting a continuous stream of action reaching from the ancient past into the ever-after, the Yuroks use the intentional future with a marker of intensification, which suggests an event that reaches, in stops and starts, from the mythic past onward. For the Hupas, the usual practice is to combine the general future with progressive forms, suggesting a continuous stream of action reaching from the ancient past across all eternity. Yet in the context of forecasting the future condition of the universe following the transformation, the Hupas alone make ample use of the near future, suggesting the imminent arrival of humanity and, by implication, the relative proximity of the ancient past to the living present.

Part IV

Classification and Cultural Meaning

8

Classifying Experience through Language

Thus one must learn as part of learning Navaho that "sorrow" belongs to the "round" class. . . . Likewise with the various covert categories of exotic languages: where they have been thought to be recognitions of objective differences, it may rather be that they are grammatical categories that merely accord up to a certain point with objective experience. They may represent experience, it is true, but experience seen in terms of a definite linguistic scheme, not experience that is the same for all observers.

Benjamin Whorf, Language, Thought, and Reality

The capacity to assign an enormous range of experiences to a highly restricted series of conceptual categories, learned and shared among the members of one's social group, is probably a basic condition for communication in all speech communities. In an ideal sense, the purpose of speaking is to draw attention to those concepts that the speaker wishes to designate, whether present in the immediate environment as actual physical referents or conjured in the imagination through the evocative use of words. In this sense, the meaning of even the most ordinary word necessarily isolates one set of concepts, or potential referents, from all others even remotely related to it.

Consider the language of color, for instance, in which many potential referents are collapsed into a highly restricted series of preestablished categories. Unless the speaker suffers from an impairment of some kind, the average person can detect many thousands of shades of color. Yet every language collapses the full spectrum into no more than eleven basic categories, as Brent Berlin and Paul Kay demonstrated in their groundbreaking study *Basic Color Terms,* published in 1969. Whatever the language, however, the set of basic terms always covers the full range of colors visible to the eye. For although everyone is capable of "seeing" the same colors, languages carve up the spectrum into different categories. Of course, there is often a gap between the potential capacity to see something and falling into the actual habit of noticing it.

In some languages, such as Dani of New Guinea, the entire color spectrum is collapsed into just two predominant categories, one denoting all "light" colors and another those that are "dark." Any color visible to the human eye can be placed into one of these contrasting categories. So, for instance, the color labeled *green* in English is placed with "dark" and *yellow* with "light." Of course, among English speakers the categories of "light" and "dark" are further divided into a series of subclasses, giving us eleven basic classificatory terms for color: *black, white, red, yellow, green, blue, brown, purple, pink, orange,* and *gray.* Though Dani speakers are capable of "seeing" these colors at a perceptual level, all of them are collapsed into just two categories for linguistic purposes. So, in regular communicative practice, Dani speakers do not always distinguish many of the fine shades of color that are familiar to English speakers, at least within the context of regular discourse. By the same token, English speakers do not always notice the fine shades of color that are routinely collapsed into categories, such as "red" and "blue," which can be almost infinitely subdivided into minor subclasses as the need arises. Artists, for instance, are far more precise than the remainder of the English-speaking public and often break these categories into subsets not regularly employed by the masses, such as "magenta," "chartreuse," and "taupe."

Not to be taken for granted, this ability to classify lies at the very heart of the human capacity for language, serving as the bedrock for the formation of vocabulary and grammatical categories. Recognizing the conceptual basis of language, the ancient Greek philosopher Plato once remarked that words do not simply label referents in the external world. Instead, he argued, words establish general cognitive categories, capable of lumping many potential referents into a single conceptual class. For if words simply labeled things, every potential referent would require its own unique label, to take this position to its logical extreme. Instead, Plato argued that linguistic concepts designate conceptual categories, or Platonic essences, which, as Aristotle later pointed out, frequently lend themselves to metaphorical extensions.[1]

Yet the ability to intuit the meaning of a conceptual category is no simple feat, even for something as tangible as a basic color term or a common noun. As recent work in cognitive linguistics has demonstrated, even a word such as *bird* carries an enormous conceptual load, potentially encompassing a range of animals that do not necessarily share a great deal on the perceptual level. Psycholinguistic studies suggest that children often learn these categories through a process of trial and error, so that some overextend the category to apply to, say, all winged animals, such as insects and flying fish, while others underextend the category to apply to nothing more than the family parakeet.[2] Once the average English meaning of the category is acquired, everything from finches to penguins and ostriches can be subsumed under a single class, without sharing much common ground on a perceptual basis. Yet any attempt to identify common features shared uniformly by all of the members of this group, such as a general physical appearance or a common suite of behavioral characteristics, is quickly thwarted by countless exceptions, such as the flightless ostrich and the swimming penguin.

Though categories are rarely uniform as manifested by each individual member, many categories are based on a common prototype, or most central member, that serves as the "best example" of the entire conceptual class. For many English speakers, for instance, the sparrow or robin stands as the most central member of the class of birds, as Eleanor Rosch demonstrated (1975) in a series of experimental studies carried out during the 1970s. Anchored in this best example, most of the remaining members of the conceptual category share at least a few of the features that typify the sparrow, such as the capacity for flight, the ability to lay eggs or a penchant for nesting, and a relatively small stature. Here every member of the class is linked to a common prototype at the center, though without strong similarities among the less-central members, such as chickadees and penguins, which share some features with the sparrow, though little with each other. Like sparrows and robins, both lay eggs and have feathers, though, while the chickadee is quite small, the ostrich is both large and flightless. In this sense, even the most peripheral members are linked to the common prototype, however little they share with each other. The process can be likened to a series of spokes radiating from the hub of a wheel, with each member of the category pointing off in a different direction from the prototype at center. For this reason, the linguist George Lakoff (1987:91–114) once suggested that many conceptual classes in fact represent "radial categories," for which the individual members share very little except a prototype at the center of the entire class, which binds everything together.

Similar processes are at work with color terms, for which human perception is strongly guided by certain universal physiological biases that act as prototypes. In English, for instance, a category such as "red" applies to an enormous range of potential referents on a perceptual basis, with many thousands of real world examples, each one subtly different from the others. Yet most speakers regard a particular variety, known as "fire engine red," as the best example of this category. Even where a basic category such as "red" enters into the vocabulary of other languages, the same shade tends to stand out as the most central member of this category, based on our common physiology, which predisposes us to notice this variety above all others. The same holds true for focal yellow, blue, and green, which our common physiology predisposes us to see more readily than the countless other shades, which, because of common physiological biases, are not as salient. After working for years with the Dani two-term color system, Eleanor Rosch demonstrated the relative ease of introducing new words for focal colors such as "green," for speakers learn and apply these words fairly naturally, owing to our common human physiology.[3] Furthermore, these focal colors are fairly stable across languages because they stand out to all people on a perceptual basis. Yet speakers are not always in perfect agreement about where the boundaries between opposing categories lie. So, for instance, within a single language such as English, there is far from a complete consensus about where the boundaries between, say, "red" and "orange" lie.

In some instances, however, the prototype is not clear, allowing speakers to settle on several potential members at the center of the category. Because the Dani, for instance, collapse so many colors into just a few categories, speakers are not in complete agreement when it comes to specifying where the most central members lie. So, for instance, some speakers regard green as the most central member of the "dark" category, while others regard black as the best example. Of course, English speakers face a similar problem when using general terms such as *red* and *blue,* which potentially signal a range of shades to the listener, without necessarily corresponding to the concept in the speaker's mind. This ambiguity decreases as more terms are introduced—as every artist learns when acquiring a more nuanced color vocabulary, as required in this profession.[4]

Because color categories are relatively tangible, color terminology has always been a popular arena for testing relationships between language and perception, including theories of linguistic relativity. Certainly the ability to direct the listener to a specific color, whether present in the environment or conjured in the imagination, rests on a certain refinement of color vocabulary, a process that can be easily demonstrated on addressees who are not familiar with the precise meaning of obscure color terms such as *chartreuse, magenta,* and *taupe.* This principle, in addition to operating in a single language for which speakers differ in their knowledge of the vocabulary, should also apply between languages even though the categories themselves differ. As John Lucy and Richard Schweder have demonstrated in a series of experimental studies, the ability to label a specific color has subtle consequences for a range of related cognitive processes, especially once the universal bias toward focal colors is taken into consideration (1979). For the focal colors themselves are fairly easy to notice and remember, due to physiological considerations alone. In contrast, the finer shades are more language-dependent, as far as codeability and recall are concerned. Here one's command of color vocabulary affects related mental operations, such as noticing a fine shade in the first place and remembering a particular color after viewing it briefly.

As the work on color clearly demonstrates, powerful universals exist alongside the potential for many diverse classifications. Despite strong physiological biases toward a small set of focal colors, the number of basic terms ranges from two to eleven, giving rise to a wide range of attested classifications for the world of color. Yet artists, whose way of life demands precision in the visual world, often vastly refine their nonbasic terminology for the purpose of conveying more precise distinctions. Of course, English speakers vary considerably in their knowledge of color vocabulary beyond the eleven basic terms known to all. In this sense, there is room for linguistic relativity even in a single language, such as English, based on the speakers' refinement of knowledge in the sphere of color, with practical implications for communication, habitual perception, and long-term recall.[5]

GRAMMATICAL SYSTEMS OF CLASSIFICATION

So far, in the realm of vocabulary, the speaker is relatively free to choose from a range of available concepts, with the possibility of occasionally augmenting these choices with new word forms, every now and then, as the speakers of the language see fit. Speakers, for instance, are constantly expanding their color terminologies as the need to distinguish new shades arises. The same holds true in nearly every sphere of learning, as speakers create new words to match the new concepts that emerge on almost an everyday basis.

Outside the realm of vocabulary, most languages also incorporate a similar series of categories into their regular grammatical inventories. Here the speaker must always choose between a finite set of preestablished concepts in certain types of situations. In this sense, English speakers must state the gender of the referent when using a singular third-person pronoun, necessarily choosing between those categories that the language has provided. When speaking of a single third-person referent, the word chosen must be either the masculine *he,* the feminine *she,* or the neuter *it,* nothing more and nothing less.[6] Like lexical categories, grammatical categories often adhere to a common prototype. So, although a human female may rest at the center of the feminine category "she," the concept is sometimes extended to other referents, such as cats, as a default category, based on perceived similarities to women, such as gracefulness. By a similar logic, dogs are often placed in the masculine category, by default, based on perceived similarities to human males, such as gruffness.

Though gender marking is restricted to third-person referents in English, some languages require grammatical classification in a wide variety of situations. Consider the Dyirbal language of Australia, for instance, in which all nouns must be placed in one of four grammatical classes, regardless of the type of statement the speaker wishes to make (Dixon 1972). When speaking of human males, rainbows, or the moon, for instance, the noun must be preceded by the word *bayi,* which acts as a classifier by announcing to the audience the referent's grammatical class. When speaking of women, stars, or the sun, one must use the contrasting classifier *balan* immediately before any of these nouns. When speaking of non-flesh food, such as edible fruit, tubers, or cake, one must use the classifier *balam* to set these referents apart from the other categories. The special classifier *bala* is reserved for any referent that does not obviously fit into one of the previous categories, including body parts, bees, meat, and the wind.

Though the Dyirbal system of classification may appear arbitrary at first, the linguist George Lakoff once demonstrated that the categories themselves are motivated by a series of common prototypes (1987:92–104). At the center of the first category, for instance, are human males. Rainbows also belong in this category because they, like the moon, are said to be mythical men in creation stories. Several distinct prototypes lie at the center of the second category, including women, fire, and dangerous things. Here the stars are included because they are linked with fire in the same domain of experience, while the sun is added for mythical reasons, because it is said to be the wife of the moon. Some of the connections are even more extended, giving rise to a process Lakoff calls "chaining," because a peripheral member is often several links away from the common prototype at the center. A case in point is the hairy mary grub, which is placed in the second class, with women. Because it inflicts a painful sting, this insect can be placed in the same domain of experience as a sunburn, which can, in turn, be linked to the sun. And the sun, of course, is considered a woman in creation stories. Clearly, these connections are powerfully motivated by cultural factors, so that the categories are not a simple reflection of nature or innate mental concepts shared by all humans, as is the case with color.

GRAMMATICAL CLASSIFICATION IN NORTHWESTERN CALIFORNIA

Specialized systems of grammatical classification are especially elaborate in many of the Native languages of northwestern California, as the linguist Mary Haas once noted in a classic article on classification and linguistic relativity among the Hupas, Yuroks, and Karuks (1967).[7] To expand on her point, I would note that objects in motion are often classified on the basis of their shape or animacy among Hupa speakers, while a similar series of categories applies to objects at rest. Similarly, in Yurok, one must state the shape or animacy of an object when counting or attributing features of size, shape, or color to an object (though no special attention is paid to the relative state of motion, as is the case in the neighboring Hupa language). Like the languages, which descend from three of the major North American stocks, the classificatory systems of the Hupa, Yurok, and Karuk languages are remarkably diverse in structural expression.[8] Because these classificatory systems enter into very different areas of regular grammatical patterning, speakers of each language apply the categories to different types of situations in everyday life. Despite centuries of contact and multilingualism, the language-specific systems of classification remain highly distinctive on the planes of both grammar and semantic structure.

As Haas (a former classmate of Benjamin Lee Whorf at Yale in the 1930s) certainly understood, the concept of grammatical classification was central to the original Whorfian project, in which, according to one popular interpretation, the principle of linguistic relativity rests heavily on grammatical differences among languages. The logic of this argument is fairly straightforward. Because grammatical categories are central to the structure of any given language, the concepts associated with these grammatical ideas often become highly obligatory in those situations where speakers must apply the categories in everyday life. Though the argument is a general one—capable of referring to everything from Hopi tense categories to gender marking on English pronouns—Whorf was particularly fascinated with classificatory semantics, as reflected in the epigraph at the start of this chapter.

Thus, the shape of the referent is also significant in many of the world's languages. In Hupa, for instance, the speaker must consider the shape of the referent when picking something up, placing it, for instance, in the special category for "long objects" or for "round things," depending on the feature the speaker wishes to emphasize. This tendency to classify objects according to shape-based features is fairly widespread, cropping up in many of the languages of the world. Consider the Bantu languages of Africa, for instance, in which nouns are often placed into sixteen or more separate categories on the basis of features of shape, size, and number. Similar systems also occur in Southeast Asia among languages such as Thai, Khmer, and Burmese. Even in English, a similar process is at work with words such as *long, round,* and *short*—though only at the level of vocabulary, not grammar.

Unfortunately, interest in this perplexing topic evaporated almost as quickly as it had surfaced. Other than a few brief articles on the subject, each of them pointing to the need for further work, little has been said about the classificatory systems of northwestern California in general. Yet the area has yielded a wealth of information over the past century, particularly in reference to grammatical categories, contextual application, and the comparative expression of animacy.

Yurok Classifiers

The Yurok classifier system is composed of twenty or so regular semantic elements that combine with numerals as well as some descriptive verbs.[9] Practically speaking, the Yurok speaker must consider the basic categories of the classifier system either when counting or when attributing inherent characteristics to an object, such as its overall size, color, and texture. Most of the categories of this system are based on features of either shape or animacy,[10] as outlined in figure 8.1.

When counting fewer than four objects, or exactly ten, a classifier must be attached to the numerical base as an obligatory grammatical suffix. Consider the base *koh(t)-,* for instance, which signals the presence of a single object, while always combining with a classifier that specifies the shape or animacy of this material thing or life-form. Upon combining with the classifier *-oh,* which signals that the reference is to the class of "round objects," the numeral *kohtoh* is formed, now referring, in this special form, to "one round thing." Here the reference could be to a flower, a stone, an acorn, a berry, or an eyeball, depending on how the speaker applies the form in context. Upon combining with the classifier *-oẘs,* which signals that the reference is to the class of "long objects," the contrasting numeral *kohtoẘs* is formed, referring, in this configuration, to "one flat thing." In this instance, the reference could be to a plank, the floor of

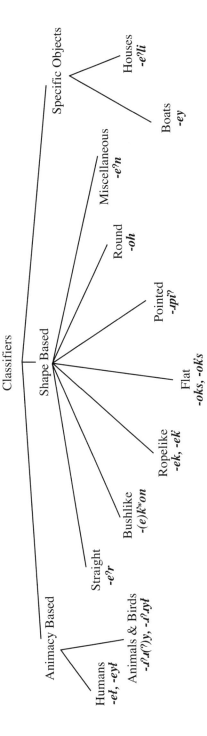

Figure 8.1. Semantic structure of the Yurok classifier system

a wide boat, or a flat expanse of land, depending on how the speaker uses the form. Yet the numerical base *koh(t)-* 'one' does not ever occur by itself—that is, without a classifier to specify the shape or animacy of the object. Other numerical bases that require a classifier include *na?a-* 'two', *nahk-* 'three', *to?on-* 'four', and *wel(owaa)-* 'ten'.

When counting five or more objects, Yurok speakers must use a freestanding classifier, one that is accompanied by a general (nonclassificatory) numeral that specifies the exact number. When speaking of "five objects," for instance, Yurok speakers must also state the shape or animacy of this group of referents. Consider the phrase *meruh tomak̓ʷo?n,* which translates as "five radiant objects." Here the numeral *meruh* signifies the concept of "five," while the classifier *tomak̓ʷo?n* specifies that the reference is to the class of "radiant" or "bushy" objects. In this instance, the classifier occurs with the numerical base *tom(ow)-* (also *toma-*), which combines with the classifier for "radiant" or "bushy" objects *-(e)k̓ʷon,* indicating that the reference is to such objects as plants or bushes. Ultimately, when counting objects of a similar physical type, classification according to features of either shape or animacy is an absolutely obligatory matter for Yurok speakers.[11]

Outside the numerical system, many descriptive verbs also require an obligatory classifier, one that places the referent within a specific category in the overall classifier system.[12] Though not all descriptive verbs require a classifier, those that do are listed in figure 8.2.

Most verbs in this series specify the dimensions of the referent, with special bases for portraying the length, width, height, or overall size. Consider the descriptive base *pel-,* which specifies that the object under consideration is relatively large in overall size. When speaking of many life-forms—including insects, mammals, or birds—this base combines with the classifier *-ɹ?ɹy* to produce the specialized form *plɹ?ɹy,* which limits the scope to the class of "nonhuman animals." So, when speaking of a "large ant," one says *plɹ?ɹy harpuc,* where the noun stem *harpuc* represents the ant and the classifier *-ɹ?ɹy* signals that this referent is specifically a "nonhuman animal." Or consider the contrasting base *ceyk-,* which is used to describe objects that are relatively small in size. When speaking of circular objects, such as stones or flowers, this base combines with the special classifier *-oh* to produce the specialized form *ceykoh,* which limits the scope to the class of round things. So, when speaking of a "small stone," one says *ceykoh ha?aag.* Here the classifier *-oh* specifies that the referent is round, while the stone is represented by the noun stem *ha?aag* 'stone'. Other descriptive verbs specify the color of the referent, with separate forms for

DESCRIPTIVE VERB CLASSES

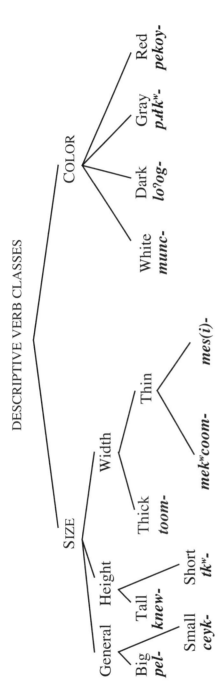

Figure 8.2. Descriptive verb bases that require classifiers in Yurok

objects that are white, dark, gray, or red. Consider the descriptive base *pekoy-*, which indicates that the object of perception is specifically a "red" one. When speaking of red objects with a circular profile, such as stones, hats, and flowers, this base combines with the classifier -*oh* to yield the specialized form *pekoyoh*, which limits the scope to the class of "round things." So, when speaking of a "red flower," one says *pekoyoh ciišep*, where the noun stem *ciišep* represents the flower and the classifier -*oh* signals that this object is specifically round.

The Hupa Classificatory Verb System

The Hupa system of grammatical classification is, in contrast, composed of a series of specialized verb forms that specify the motion or position of certain classes of objects.[13] When describing an object being handled or at rest, the speaker must fit the referent into one of fifteen potential categories, as illustrated in figure 8.3.

In contrast to the situation in Yurok, for which the relative state of motion is of no particular concern, the Hupa speaker is generally forced to consider the spatial and temporal dynamics of a scene when placing an object within a particular category in the classificatory system. Four states of existence are distinguished within the logic of the classificatory system. Each phase, in turn, is divided into a series of specialized spatial and temporal subcategories. Three of these phases are *dynamic,* meaning that they involve a definite element of motion, while one phase is *static,* meaning that it applies strictly to situations in which motion is absent or withdrawn.

Consider the paradigm for referring to a single round object, such as a stone. Here the phase of briefest duration is signaled by a special momentaneous paradigm, which always includes a directional modifier that indicates the specific bearing of the event. When the speaker wishes to refer to a general, ongoing process, an imperfective form is required. A case in point is the form *ya·ʔaʔaW,* which loosely translates as "one person raises a round object upward toward the sky."[14] Here the final unit in the sequence—the verb stem -*ʔaW*—signals the motion of a round object over a relatively short span of time, without reference to either the early, middle, or final phases of the total flow of motion, while the initial element *ya·=* specifies the directional bearing of the event, specifically, a course that reaches up into the air.[15] The next element, a glottal stop (ʔ), is a contraction of the regular third-person form *či-,* designating an agency that is animate, usually a human though sometimes an animal.

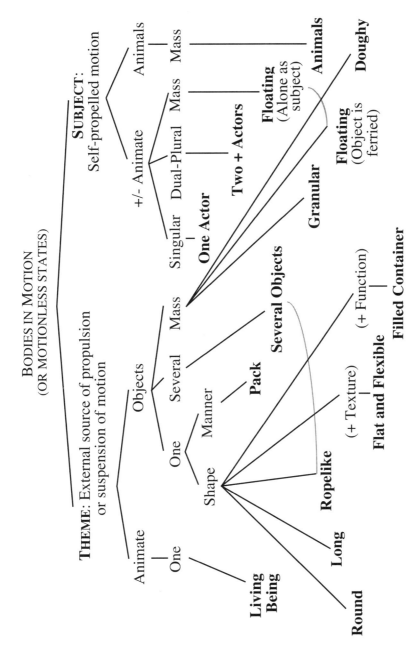

Figure 8.3. Categories of the Hupa classificatory verb system

When the speaker wishes to limit the scope of an event, this shift in perspective demands the use of a contrasting perfective form. Here reference is always to a specific point in the total flow of motion, such as the beginning, middle, or endpoint of the trajectory. Consider the verb form *yaʔwiŋʔa·n*, for instance, which loosely translates as "one person lifted a round object upward toward the heavens." This contrasting form refers not to a general, ongoing performance of the activity but to a single, complete instance of the event, here with focus on the initial stages of the total flow of motion.[16] Again, the classificatory element occurs as the final semantic unit in the sequence, here in the form of the verb stem *-ʔa·n*.[17] Like the stem in the previous form, this element also signals the movement of a single round object, although here the emphasis is on a particular point in the total process. In this case, another marker has been introduced in the middle of the word form, namely, the temporal prefix *win-*. This element usually occurs in perfective forms that focus on the beginning of the action in question, that is, its initial stages. Again, the directional marker *ya·=* indicates the upward path of the event, while the second element is the reduced third-person animate subject form *ʔ-*.

A special continuative paradigm exists for the purpose of marking events of slightly greater duration that take no specific path while traveling through some region of space, in contrast to the momentaneous forms given above. As a rule, continuative verbs do not accept directional marking (in contrast to their momentaneous counterparts, which require it). Continuative forms refer to events that are widely distributed in space and time, following no particular route, while being carried out over a period of considerable, though indefinite, duration. A speaker wishing to refer to the general, ongoing process might say *na·ʔaʔa·*, which loosely translates as "one person carries a round object around." The final element of this sequence, the imperfective stem *-ʔa·*, signals the guided motion of a round object, without reference to either the beginning, middle, or end of the flow of motion. To limit the scope of the event to the middle phases, one says *na·ʔasʔaʔ*, which loosely translates as "one person carried a round object around, not in general, but for a specific time." Here the contrasting perfective stem *-ʔaʔ* signals the movement of a round object, with special focus on a particular point in the flow of the event. Yet in the case of the perfective form, another marker is introduced in the middle of the word, namely, the temporal prefix *s-*. This element usually occurs in forms that focus on the middle phases of an event, without fixing on either the beginning or the end of the process. In both constructions, the first element, *na·=*, signals the absence of a definite directional path. The second element, ʔ-, is again a con-traction from the regular third-person marker čʼi-, which designates an animate agent, usually either a human or an animal.

When the speaker wishes to refer to an ongoing stream of action of poten-tially infinite duration, a special progressive paradigm can be used. Generally speaking, a roughly linear or loosely goal-oriented path is often implied, though no specific directional route is signaled on the surface. Because the reference is always to an ongoing act, progressive forms are always frozen in the imperfective aspect, admitting no perfective, or temporally bounded, counter-part. Consider a scene in which a person handles a round object for an extended period of time, without any particular end to the action in sight. Here there is only one applicable form, namely, the progressive construction čʼiwaʔal, which loosely translates as "one being carries a round object along." Here the final element of the sequence, the verb stem -ʔal, signals the ongoing motion of a single round object over an extended period of time. While the progressive marker w(a)- signals the act of starting out on a process of potentially infinite duration, the subject is specified with the marker ʔ-, again a contracted form of the animate third-person prefix čʼi-.

A special static paradigm exists for the purpose of referring to situations in which motion is absent or withdrawn for a considerable span of time.[18] Here the reference is to a state of motionlessness, for which both the direc-tional status and the duration of the event remain unspecified. In their basic form, static forms are frozen in the perfective aspect, for which the reference is to a single, complete instantiation of the event, with focus on the middle phases of the process, while leaving out both the onset and the endpoint of this ongoing condition. Consider the stative construction saʔa·n, which trans-lates as "a round object rests motionless." Here the final element in the sequence, the perfective stem -ʔa·n, signals the presence of a single round object, with emphasis on a particular phase in the surrounding process. The stative marker s(a)- places focus on the middle stages of this enduring process, without any reference to the onset or conclusion of the state. No particular directional orientation is given in this construction, and any attempt to do so results in an ungrammatical form.

In addition to placing the referent in a particular category—based on features of shape, number, or animacy—the Hupa speaker is also obliged to consider the spatial and temporal status of the surrounding scene, either when handling an object or merely referring to a similar object at rest.

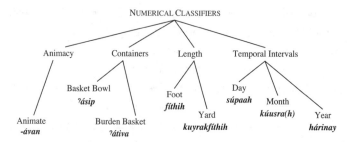

Figure 8.4. Karuk numerical classifiers

Classificatory Elements in the Karuk Language

For Karuk speakers, grammatical classification is not especially obligatory in any single area of the language—in sharp contrast to the neighboring Hupa and Yurok traditions, in which grammatical classification is elaborate and often obligatory. However, some classificatory elements are nonetheless present throughout the structure of the Karuk language.[19]

One system, based on counting and quantification, loosely resembles the numerical system of the Yurok language, though with fewer categories overall. Most of these classifiers reflect culturally significant units of measurement. Some, for instance, are devoted to units of time, including special units for counting days, months, and years. Others are devoted to common containers encountered in everyday life, such as basket bowls and burden baskets. Finally, one special "animate" category is reserved for counting living beings, such as humans and other animals. The basic system is illustrated in figure 8.4.

Functionally speaking, these classifiers run loosely parallel to those of the neighboring Yurok tradition, though without the abstract shape-based categories found in Yurok speech. However, in contrast to the situation in the Yurok language (for which, in practice, every number must be assigned to one of several potential classifiers), most Karuk numerals do not require a classifier. In this sense, Karuk classifiers are not strictly obligatory, so the classifiers only occasionally enter into situations in which the speaker wishes to discuss a series of objects. However, William Bright (pers. comm.), who worked intensively with the Karuk community during the early 1950s, feels that this series may not exhaust the set of numerical classifiers in the language, though he did not have time to elicit any more data on this topic during his early fieldwork.

The other Karuk system of classification consists of a relatively small series of classificatory verbs, which loosely resemble those of the Hupa language, though without the obligatory spatial and temporal categories presupposed by Hupa grammar. The basic series is illustrated in figure 8.5. Throughout the system, animate bodies are systematically distinguished from those that occur in a range of shapes and numerical configurations.

One series is devoted to situations in which an animate subject stays in one location for an extended period of time, with verbs that often translate as "live," "stay," "sit," or "be." Here grammatical number often plays a significant role, with distinct forms for singular, dual, and plural instantiations of a given type of object. For instance, when a single animal or person "lives" or "stays" somewhere for a considerable span of time, one might say *káan* 'there' *ʔávansa* 'a man' *ʔúkrii* 'stayed there'.[20] In this instance, the verb stem *ikrii*[21] signals that the reference is to a single animate subject, while the noun *ʔávansa* specifies that the actor is a "male person." The marker *ʔu-* at the beginning of the form indicates that the subject is in the third person. On functional grounds, this series loosely resembles the Hupa classificatory system, though without the same distribution of categories, for in both languages, speakers must consider the categories of the classificatory systems when discussing the motion or position of certain classes of objects. Yet, unlike the situation in Hupa, there is no general type of situation in Karuk where these categories are obligatory; the Karuk speaker is therefore not forced to select from one of several alternatives.

COMPARATIVE TREATMENT OF ANIMACY

The feature of animacy is marked by at least one major grammatical category in each of the area's languages. In general, this category separates living beings from other referents, which speakers usually classify according to physical properties, such as shape, function, and texture. Otherwise, the criteria for membership in the class of the "animate" differ widely throughout the languages of the region, as do the divisions within the corresponding class of "living things."

Far from representing a purely linguistic concern, devoid of any corresponding cultural significance, the feature of animacy also holds considerable religious interest in the oral traditions of northwestern California. In the core creation lore of the region, all present-day life-forms are said to have emerged from a former race of spirit deities in the ancient past. During this period in the prehistory of the planet, the various forms of life had not yet fully differentiated. Many possessed both animal and human characteristics, holding, for instance, the ability to speak and reason like modern humans, though still possessing

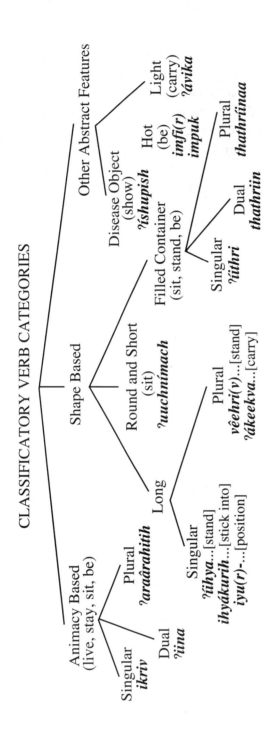

CLASSIFICATORY VERB CATEGORIES

Animacy Based
(live, stay, sit, be)

Singular
ikriv

Dual
ʔiina

Plural
ʔaraárahitih

Shape Based

Long

Singular
ʔiihya...[stand]
ihyákurih...[stick into]
iyu(r)-...[position]

Plural
vêehri(v)...[stand]
ʔákeekva...[carry]

Round and Short
(sit)
ʔuuchnímach

Other Abstract Features

Disease Object
(show)
ʔíshupish

Filled Container
(sit, stand, be)

Singular
ʔiithri

Dual
thathriin

Plural
thathriinaa

Hot
(be)
**imfi(r)
impuk**

Light
(carry)
ʔávika

Figure 8.5. Karuk classificatory verbs

218

animal-like bodies. Then, during the era of the transformation, when the present world was set into motion, a series of splits began to distinguish the various life-forms, especially the increasingly separate realms of animals, plants, and humans. From this common foundation in religious thought, each group takes a similar interest in the relative animacy of the world's creatures. Yet each group has advanced its own interpretation of the meaning ultimately attached to this ancient division among the life-forms.

Hupa: The Motion Criterion

Among Hupa speakers, the feature of animacy is extended, fairly uniformly, to animals and humans alike. This particular scheme of classification is conso-nant with one reading of the local creation lore, one that asserts the underlying unity of the various life-forms, with the notable exclusion of plants from this framework. The capacity for self-propelled motion appears to represent the fundamental criterion for membership within the animate class, despite the fact that this category is sometimes applied to situations in which a living being is either controlled outright or where motion is temporarily suspended. That is, all of the beings included in this category are capable of moving of their own volition under ordinary circumstances, while none of them lack this general capacity for self-propelled motion.

Among Hupa speakers, the animate class embraces an enormous range of life-forms. Typical referents include mammals, birds, reptiles, and insects, alongside worms, fish, monsters, and humans. In this setting, a form such as *ya'witte·n,* which loosely translates as "one has picked up a living being," could equally refer to any of these creatures, regardless of whether the object in question is a person or some other form of life. So, too, for the parallel form *č'iste·n,* which loosely translates as "a living being rests motionless"; this expression could equally refer to a person, a large monster, or an animal protag-onist in oral literature. In each of these forms, it is the stem *-te·n* that signals the presence of a living being, while the remaining grammatical material spells out the spatial and temporal contingencies that surround the situation. The presence of the prefix *ł-* in the first form (*ya'witte·n*) signals a shift from subject to object, indicating that the activity of this creature has fallen under the control of an external agent, which is the subject of the construction. The absence of this prefix (*ł-*) in the second form (*č'iste·n*) indicates that the living being remains the subject, albeit one that remains in an ongoing state and under-goes no actual movement for an extended period of time. While the first form features the inceptive prefix *wi(n)-*, indicating an event that is in its initial stages, the second form features the stative marker *s-*, indicating a situation of great, though indefinite, duration. Because motion is present in the first situation, the directional marker *ya·=* signals that this being moves "up into the air," while the subject marker *č'i-* indicates that the being who guides the movement is more powerful than the object.

In the Hupa language, people are generally classified as living beings, alongside other animals. Typical situations include cases in which one's movement temporarily falls under the control of another being, such as a larger or more powerful person, and cases in which such motion is absent, as in the states of sleep or death. When speaking of a person at rest, one might say *siWte·n* 'I lie motionless', wherein the stem *-te·n* again signals the presence of a living being whose relative state of motion is a topic of conversation. In this construction, the prefix *s-* signals a state that is ongoing or without a definite onset or conclusion, while the person marker *W-* signals that the (first-person) subject is the speaker. When handling a baby, one might say *yehč'e'ittiW*, a construction that loosely translates as "one actor places a living being in a container, such as a basket." Here the stem *-tiW* signals that a living being undergoes movement over a relatively brief span of time, while the spatial marker *yeh=* indicates that this being, a child in this instance, enters into a container, such as a baby-basket. The temporal prefix *'i-* indicates that the event is repeated, as a matter of custom or habit, over an extended, though indefinite, period of time. The third-person marker *č'(e)-* indicates that another being, with greater control, guides the movement of the child.

When speaking of a "kidnapping," the object of the hunt, the victim, is also placed in the category of living beings. Consider the expression *tiŋxottiW*, which loosely translates as "take a living being away." Here the object marker *xo-* indicates that the being in question is specifically human, while the spatial marker *ti-ŋ=* suggests that this being is soon to embark on a journey from which he or she will not return. Though present at an underlying level, the second-person marker *n-* does not appear on the surface, merging instead with the classifier *ł-*, as is regular in Hupa grammar.

Generally speaking, animals are classified as "animate," without enforcing any strict division into various orders of beings. Instead, mammals, birds, reptiles, insects, and worms are uniformly classified as "living beings" without division into subcategories. When handling a pet, for instance, one might say *na·'atte·*, an expression that loosely translates as "one carries a living being around."

Here the continuative stem shape -*te·* signals that this living being is handled over an extended time period. The third-person subject marker *ʔ-* indicates that another being, with greater control, guides the movement, while the spatial marker *na·=* signals that the path is varied and nonlinear, conveying a sense similar to the English preposition "around." More generally, this same expression may also be used to refer to the general, ongoing condition of "owning" a pet.

When removing an insect from a pouch or container, one might say *čeʔnitte·n* 'one has taken out (a) living being',[22] wherein it is the stem -*teʔn* that signals that the object of the event is specifically animate. The spatial marker *če·=* indicates that this activity emerges from a container, such as a medicine bag, while the temporal prefix *ni-(n)* signals that the event reaches a definite conclusion; again, the third-person marker *ʔ-,* in the middle of the form, indicates that another being, with greater control, guides this movement.

Many forces of nature thought to possess the capacity for self-propelled motion are classified as "living beings" in popular idioms. In this sense, evil spirits, which are thought to invade the body of the afflicted, where they cause sickness and discomfort, are often spoken of as if they were living creatures. Based on this assessment, a sucking doctor is known as a *kʸitwe·-če·ʔittiW,* a phrasal noun whose descriptive content loosely translates as "one who removes evil spirits." In this expression, it is the stem -*tiW* that classifies the spirit as a "living thing." The spatial marker *če·=* indicates motion 'out of an enclosure', namely, a human body that has been invaded by illness, while the third-person subject marker *ʔ-* refers to the doctor who, from a position of greater control, guides this activity of removal. The sickness referred to in this expression is known as *kʸitwe·,* a noun of action whose literal meaning is 'what attacks (someone)'. Usually this consists of such disorders as colds, influenza, and pneumonia. The noun derives from the skeletal verbal unit *t-we·* 'to attack something', here with the third-person indefinite subject marker *kʸi-,* which in this context refers to those evil spirits that are known by all to perform such wicked or nefarious acts.

In religious idioms, the earth is sometimes classified as a "living being," perhaps in part because the earth supports the life that thrives on its surface. In creation lore, the earth is said to rest on the back of an enormous turtle, whose movements unfold on too great a time scale to be perceived by humans, apart from the occasional earthquake. When speaking of wrongful acts, especially violations of taboo, one says *ninisʔa·n čʷinʔdaʔwitte·n,* an expression that loosely translates as "one (person) brings a living being to a point of ruin," though a more graceful translation is "someone spoiled the world." Here the stem -teᐧn places the earth in the animate class, while the prefix ɫ- signals that this "creature" occupies the role of object, for another agent controls it. This agent is specified by the second glottal stop (ʔ) in the expression, which is a reduced form of the animate third-person subject, a being with greater control in this situation. The surrounding grammatical elements suggest that a sequence of events brings the object of the activity, here the earth itself, into a state of defilement. Originally based on a metaphor in which dirty matter is flung into the mouth of a living victim, the Hupa adverbial modifier for "defiling something" is composed of the elements č'ʷinʔ 'dirt' and daᐧ 'mouth', which here signal the state of spoliation into which the world is brought. The noun ninisʔaᐧn represents the "world," while the inceptive prefix wi(n)- suggests that this act of spoliation enters its initial phases with the violation of a taboo.

The feature of animacy is sometimes extended to things that once possessed a life force, such as fresh kill or cultural objects fashioned from the flesh of slain animals. When handling the body of person who has recently died, one might say hayah 'there' dahnaʔxʷeʔiɫtiW 'on they lay him back out'.[23] Here the unit ɫ-tiW signals the controlled movement of a living being over a relatively short time span, while the object marker xʷe- indicates that this animate object is human. The spatial marker dah= indicates a suspension of motion over a relatively flat expanse, here a platform, while the iterative marker naᐧ= signals that this event has been repeated, this time returning to some point of origin. The third-person subject marker ʔ- indicates that another being, an external source of agency, guides this activity.

In a related sense, the traditional fisher-skin quiver is usually classified as animate, most likely reflecting its derivation from the flesh of a living creature. When speaking of the quiver, this important object is usually placed in the animate category, as in the phrase c'idaɢ-naʔweᐧ '(a) fisher-skin quiver' č'eʔiniɫteᐧn 'one took out'.[24] Here the unit -ɫ-teᐧn signals that the object of this activity is animate, while the animate subject marker ʔ- indicates that the being that guides this movement possesses greater control in this particular situation. The directional modifier č'eᐧ= signals that this movement emerges from out of an enclosure, namely, the clothing to which it was bound, while the conclusive prefix ni(n)- indicates that this activity reaches its goal, ultimately freeing the quiver from entanglement.

Anything incapable of propelling itself under ordinary circumstances is generally excluded from the class of living things. For this reason, baskets, plants, trees, and stars are generally eliminated from the animate category among Hupa speakers, though this is not the case for all of the area's languages.

Yurok Animacy: Animals versus Humans

For the Yuroks, the realm of the animate is split into two respective classes, one that refers exclusively to humans and another that embraces most of the remaining forms of life. On the cultural plane, this split echoes the mythic division between the realms of animals and humans, which now separates these two orders of life, however similar they may have once been before the time of the transformation. In everyday life, one series of classifiers applies strictly to humans and another one to mammals and birds.

When counting living beings, one must always state whether these creatures are human or nonhuman forms of life. Consider a situation in which one must count a group of people. Here the Yurok speaker is obliged to use the special classifier for human beings, a conceptual category whose presence is signaled with the suffix *-eył*. If there were exactly "four men," one would be obliged to say *coʔoneył pegɹk*, wherein the numerical base *coʔon-* combines with the classifier for humans (*-eył*). Here the noun *pegɹk* signals nothing further about the number of people, translating as either "man" or "men," depending on the number stated elsewhere in the construction. When speaking of a group of "four birds," one is obliged to change the classifier, saying, in this instance, *cɹʔɹnɹʔɹył c'uc'iš*. Here the numerical base *coʔon-* combines with the classifier for nonhuman animals (*-ɹʔɹył*), which assimilates the rhoticized midcentral vowel (*ɹ*) of the classifier. The noun *c'uc'iš* is invariant as to number, meaning either "bird" or "birds," depending on the context.

Similarly, when describing the size or color of a life-form, one is forced to state whether this creature is a human or a nonhuman being. When speaking of a "big person," one might say *pelił ʔooł*, where the descriptive base *p(e)l-* combines with the special classifier for humans *-(e)ł*. Yet when speaking of a "large animal," such as a deer, one is forced to change the classifier to reflect the shift in animacy, saying, in this instance, *plɹʔɹy puuk*. Here the classifier for nonhuman animals *-ɹʔɹy* combines with the descriptive base *p(e)l-* to produce the specialized verb form *plɹʔɹy*, which signals that the reference is to a "big nonhuman animal."

Yet several life-forms are classified according to their shape, not their animacy. Instead of being placed with other nonhuman animals, snakes and worms are, for instance, generally placed in the "ropelike" class. When speaking of a "long snake," one is obliged to state that it belongs to the "ropelike" class, saying, for instance, *knewolekin leyes.* Here the descriptive base *knewol-,* which contributes the sense that the object is "long" or "tall," combines with the special classifier for ropelike objects, *-ek.* The attributive marker *-in* at the end of the verb form signals that the reference is to a specific object that manifests these qualities, namely, the snake, *leyes.* Similarly, when speaking of a "long worm," one might say *knewolekin (ʔ)yekʷł,* wherein the classifier *-ek* again specifies that the reference is to a ropelike object, namely, a worm *(ʔyekʷł).*

Plants, in contrast, are generally placed in a special category for "radiant" or "bushy" things, without a linguistic marker to stress their life force. When speaking of a "small huckleberry bush," one might say *ceykekʷoni nɹhpɹyuup',* where the classifier *-kʷon* signals that the reference is to a bushy or radiant object. The descriptive base *ceyk(e)-* contributes the sense that the object is "small," while the attributive marker *-(n)i* signals that the reference is to a specific object that manifests this qualities, namely, a huckleberry bush.

Animacy in the Karuk Language

Karuk speakers tend to place animals and humans together in the class of "living things," often without explicit attention to the underlying capacity for motion. This particular classification is distinct from both the Hupa situation, in which motion is a fundamental criterion, and the Yurok situation, in which the split between animals and humans is a dominant concern. Echoing still another theme from the local creation stories, the Karuk sense of animacy underscores the common ground shared by the life-forms, which were thought to have been more similar before the era of the transformation.

Many Karuk verbs, for instance, portray activities that are typically associated with "living beings," though without enforcing any strict division into separate orders of animals and humans. A case in point is the verb stem *ikriv* (also *ikrii*), which signals the condition of "living" or "dwelling," where the reference is specifically to just one being. Or consider its counterpart, *ʔiina,* a verb that also signals the condition of "living" or "dwelling," here with reference to two living creatures. In the singular form *ʔukrii,* which translates as "one being stayed (there)," the reference could be to animals or humans, fairly equally. Similarly, in the construction *kunʔiin,* which translates as "the two of them stayed (there)," the reference could be, somewhat ambiguously, to either animals or humans. In this setting, neither subject marker helps to sort out animals from humans. While the singular marker ʔu- potentially refers to either animals or humans in the role of subject, so, too, does the plural marker kun-.

Even in the numerical system, no regular distinction between the realms of animals and humans is enforced. Instead, a single classifier applies, equally, to all "living creatures." Though certainly derived from the noun stem ʔávan, which ordinarily refers to a "man" or "husband," when applied to numerals, this form creates a classifier that specifies the entire class of "animate things." In this setting, the general numeral ʔáxak 'two' gives rise to the form ʔáxak-avan, which signals that the reference is to two "living beings," either animal or human. Similarly, the general numeral kuyraak 'three' gives rise to the form kuyraak-ávan, which also signals that the reference is to two "living beings," whether animal or human. Of course, the same pattern may be extended to any numeral above three. As occurs with many forms in the Karuk language, including some verbs and pronouns, the numerical system creates no regular distinction between the realms of animals and humans.

In creation stories, even baskets and stars are sometimes classified as animate, reflecting their status as spirit deities before the era of the transformation.[25] Before he became a beacon in the night sky, Evening Star, for instance, once lived in this world with his sweetheart, whom he later abandoned after a quarrel, only to be reunited with her through the power of a potent love formula.

When the narrator announces Evening Star's former presence in this world, both he and his sweetheart are cast as "living beings" with the words ʔikxunanáhaanich 'evening star' kunʔíin 'they lived there' mukeechíkyav 'his sweetheart' xákkaan 'with one another'.[26] Here Evening Star and his sweetheart are both placed squarely in the realm of the animate, as reflected in the expression kunʔíin, which literally translates as "the two of them lived there." Based on the verb stem ʔiina, which signals the presence of two living beings, this form also contains the plural subject marker kun-, which also generally refers to animate actors.

During the ancient era of creation, even the storage basket was said to have held the capacity to fish and sing on Coyote's command. When the narrator announces these miraculous deeds, the storage basket's acts are placed squarely within the realm of the animate, with the words sípnuuk 'storage basket' ʔúkrii(v) 'sits' ʔupakurîihvutih 'singing along'.[27] Here the verb ʔúkrii(v), which literally translates as "one being sits," classifies the storage basket as a "living being," based on the verb stem ikriiv, which signals the activity of "one living being." Though the storage basket no longer sits and sings like a living being, during the era of creation it was briefly endowed with these abilities.

Significantly, during this critical period in prehistory, the various forms of life were not yet fully distinct. Baskets, trees, and stars, in the time of creation, were still regarded as "spirit deities," representing the very forces that would eventually breathe life into the world around us. Following the transformation, greater differentiation eventually set in, so that today most of these forms are no longer considered animate. Consequently, their classification as "living beings" is usually restricted to stories set during the time of creation.

COMPARATIVE CLASSIFICATORY SEMANTICS

Even when similar categories occur in several languages, the criteria for membership within any given conceptual class tend to vary widely throughout the area's speech communities, as do many of the metaphorical possibilities. Often a similar conceptual class appears in several of the languages, such as the categories for "round" and "long" objects, which are common in many classificatory systems throughout the world. Other categories are more limited in distribution, such as the specialized category for counting "houses" found in both Yurok and Karuk (Conathan 2004b). Though each system of classification can be applied to tangible physical referents that are readily apparent in the surrounding world, many of the categories also lend themselves to metaphorical extensions. Here the scope of reference can be broadened to encompass a number of figurative senses, some of them highly language specific and others fairly widespread throughout the region.

Round Objects

A special category for "round objects" is present in many of the area's languages, though with widely different semantic implications in each tradition. Generally speaking, the reference is to bodies with smooth contours or those that lack significant accentuation along any single dimension, such as a stone, an eye, or even the sun.[28] The criteria for membership are otherwise fairly language specific, especially where metaphor is concerned.

Among Hupa speakers, for instance, the special category for "round things" typically refers to compact and roughly spherical bodies in three full dimensions. Prototypically, the reference is often to manipulation of a stone, a bundle, or an arrow point, especially as it is controlled in the hands. Consider the expression *noˑnaˀniŋˀaˑn,* where the classificatory stem *-ˀaˑn* signals the presence of a single round object over a fairly short span of time, while the directional marker *noˑ=* indicates that the motion bears downward toward the ground. This expression as a unit loosely translates as "one lowers a round object back down the ground." Depending on context, this construction could potentially refer to an enormous range of referents, including a stone, a bundle, an arrow point, or even a piece of root.[29]

In Yurok speech, in contrast, the special category for "round things" often refers to roughly disc-shaped objects in two primary dimensions—not necessarily the fully three-dimensional objects typical of Hupa grammar. In this sense, the reference, in Yurok speech, is often to flowers, drums, coins, and hats—all roughly circular objects when viewed from above, though certainly neither "round" nor "circular" when viewed from other potential angles.[30] When counting or when attributing a size, color, or texture to any of these objects, the Yurok speaker is obliged to use the special classifier for "round things." When speaking of a "red flower," for instance, one says *pekoyo(h) ciišep,* where the descriptive base *pekoy-* 'be red' combines with the classifier for round objects, *-oh.* However, in addition to describing many disc-shaped objects, the special "round object" class of the Yurok language also embraces some spherical forms—objects that retain a circular profile even when rotated in three full dimensions. In this sense, stones, nuts, berries, heads, hearts, and eyes are also included in the "round object" category (see Haas 1967). Thus, when speaking of "a small rock," one says *ceyhko(h) haˀaag,* where the descriptive base *ceyk-* combines with the classifier *-oh* to signal that the reference is specifically to the class of "round objects." Then, when speaking of a "stout" or "fat" person, a special form is used, effectively placing this human in the "round object" category with the descriptive verb *ploh(keloy-),*[31] meaning "a round thing is big." Here the descriptive base for large objects, *p(e)l-,* combines with the classifier *-oh,* metaphorically placing a person in the "round object" category.

On purely metaphorical grounds, Hupa speakers often extend the reference to the manipulation of a song or dance under the direction of a skilled performer. Consider the expression *noˀwaˀaWil,* which loosely translates as "one person is putting a round object down while going along." This particular form comes from Sapir 2001, where, in its original context, the reference was to the process of bringing a song to a point of termination, as if this song were a round object that one could carefully manipulate in the hands (p. 123). Here the special progressive stem *-ˀaWil* places the referent in the class of round objects, with explicit focus on a steady stream of motion, punctuated with occasional stops and starts. Otherwise, most objects that resist simple categorization elsewhere in the classificatory system can usually be classified as "round" by default, including incorporeal abstractions such as advice, heat, noise, power, spirits, and even pains that cause illness. In Hupa speech, all of these objects may be "packed" or "positioned" like round objects, though in a strictly metaphorical sense. Consider the expression *miq'eh-naW'ay* (see Golla 1996:45), where the classificatory stem -*'ay* signals the presence of a round object over an extended period of time, while the spatial marker *na(·)*- indicates that the event follows no particular directional path as it travels "around" in a wide area. The positional modifier *miq'eh* at the beginning of the construction places the scene in the aftermath of another event, here by implication a prior event in which advice was given. Literally, the expression refers to a round object that the speaker packs around after receiving some advice from someone, though a looser translation is "I heeded the advice, carried it with me as I traveled around." In some expressions, even credit, tradition, or a person's reputation may lie motionless as a "round object" in a metaphorical sense.[32]

Long or Straight Objects

Many of the languages of northwestern California have developed specialized categories for "long" or "straight" things for referring to objects with significant linear extension along a single dimension. In most of the languages, typical referents include sticks, canes, bows, arrows, and quivers, all common cultural implements that loosely fit the bill.[33] Yet the criteria for membership in the class of "long" objects are often highly language specific, especially where metaphor is concerned.

In Yurok and Karuk speech, for instance, trees are often placed in the special class of "long" or "straight" objects. Thus, when speaking of a single redwood, one might say *kohte'r kił* in Yurok, where the numerical base *koh(t)*- combines with the classifier -*e'r* to place the referent in the "straight object" category. In a similar way, Karuk speakers have access to the verb stem *'íihya*, one that refers to the act of "standing like a stick."[34] Naturally, the category is sometimes applied to trees in Karuk, as reflected in the following sentence: *káan* 'there' *'íppaha* 'a tree' *'u'íihyaa* 'it stood'.[35] For Hupa speakers, in contrast, trees and other plants with stalks are generally placed in the special "filled-container" category instead, as reflected in the expression *k'ʸisxa·n*, where the special classificatory stem *-xaⁿn* signals the presence of a "filled container," while the stative prefix *s-* indicates a state or condition that continues to exist over a great but indefinite time span. Though this expression literally translates as "a filled container rests motionless," this particular form often refers to a standing plant, possibly because it is full of sap.

Among Hupa speakers, the "long object" category is widely extended to a range of situations in which a person manipulates a sticklike object in the hands, as well as to related scenes in which such an object comes to take a position of rest. Consider the form *yaʔwintaⁿn,* where the classificatory stem *-taⁿn* signals the presence of a "long object" whose movement has temporarily come under the control of an external agent, while the adverbial modifier *ya·=* species that this movement passes "upward in the air toward the heavens." As a unit, the expression loosely translates as "one picked up a long object." Some of the potential referents are as follows: poles, canoes, pipes, arrows, bows, quivers, flutes, pestles, logs, planks, sweathouse doors, fishing platforms, ridges; tongues, hairs, bones, penises, short ribs; headbands, Jump Dance baskets, platters, dippers, dip nets, or fish traps. The range of reference is similar in other Athabaskan languages, such as Apache and Slave.

Filled Containers

Other categories are restricted to a subset of the area's languages, lacking a close parallel elsewhere in the region. Several of the languages have, for example, developed a special category that separates "filled containers" from other potential vessels. Though baskets generally act as the prototype, many of the meanings are highly language specific.

For instance, many figures of speech in the Karuk tradition are not paralleled elsewhere in the region. Consider the verb root *axyar,* which generally refers to the act of "filling something up," usually a basket or another type of container. Among storytellers, this verb is sometimes applied to situations in which a neck brims over with necklaces, as they are stacked to the limit, as illustrated in the following sentence:[36]

vúra ʔuum taay	*patóoppiikívship*	*thíin*	*ʔaxyár*	*vúra*
(A great) many	one puts on necklaces	throat glands	a container fills	EMPHASIS

"He had lots of necklaces on, and his neck was full up to his throat glands."

The same root also gives rise to the related verb stem *axyaníppan,* which refers to a river filling up to the point of overflowing. Here the root *axyar* (also *axyan*) combines with the specialized directional marker *-(r)ípa(a),* which normally indicates motion that bears "horizontally away from the center of a body of water," sometimes all the way to the shore.[37] As a unit, this stem refers to a body of water that continues swelling as it reaches the shore. Among storytellers, however, this stem is sometimes applied to situations in which a river fills up with salmon, as illustrated in the following sentence:[38]

pa?áama	káan	vúra	kunpaxyaníppaneesh	peeshkêesh	poossaamvárak
The salmon	then	EMPHASIS	they will overflow	the river	(as) it flows down from upriver

"The salmon will overflow the river as it flows down from upstream."

Similar metaphors are possible with other stems in the Karuk tradition that refer to filled containers and their contents. A case in point is the parallel root *?íithri,* which normally refers to a filled container, such as a basket, as it rests motionless in a sitting position. Among storytellers, however, the reference is sometimes extended to the earth's filling up with water during a flood, as illustrated in the following sentence:[39]

peethívthaaneen	?aas	?upiithránik
The earth	water	it (container) filled up

"Water collected on the earth."

Though common in Karuk, similar metaphors are not attested in the neighboring Hupa and Yurok traditions. Among Hupa speakers, the "filled containers" category is applied to plants, utensils, and people to create a series of special idioms (no similar metaphors are attested in Karuk speech). Consider, for instance, the previously discussed Hupa expression *ḱʸisxaˑn,* where the special grammatical marker *ḱi-* signals a subject known by context, in this case a plant, while the classificatory stem *-xaˑn* indicates that this subject belongs to the class of "filled containers." The temporal marker *s-* in the middle of the form specifies that the subject occupies a motionless position for an extended period of time, without a definite onset or endpoint. As a unit, this construction loosely translates as "a filled container rests motionless in one place," though in an idiomatic sense, the reference is to a standing plant full of sap. With an animate subject marker, the reference shifts to a woman resting motionless in a sexually suggestive position, as can be illustrated with the related form *č'isxa·n,* which literally translates as "one being rests motionless (like) a filled container."

Ropelike Objects

A special category for "ropelike objects" is also present in several of the languages, including both Hupa and Yurok. Generally speaking, ropes and strings act as prototypes in both traditions, though the language-specific extensions are often highly distinctive. For instance, among Yurok speakers, snakes and worms hold their primary membership in this class. When speaking of a "long snake," for instance, the Yurok speaker is obliged to state that it belongs to the "ropelike" class, saying *knewolekin leyes.* As previously described, the descriptive base *knewol-,* which contributes the sense that the object is "long" or "tall," combines with the special classifier for ropelike objects, *-ek.* In contrast, among the Hupa, snakes and worms are generally classified as living beings, not as ropelike objects, except in a metaphorical sense.[40]

Among Yurok speakers, the special "ropelike" category is also extended to many forces of nature, including fog, snow, and even streams. A thin stream, for example, is sometimes placed in the ropelike category, presumably on the basis of its meandering course, which resembles the sinuous shape of a loose stretch of rope. When speaking of a "thin stream," for instance, one uses the verb *mesik,*[41] a descriptive construction that is based on the initial *mesi-* 'thin' and the classifier *-(e)k,* which places the flowing stream squarely in the "ropelike" category. For reasons that are not altogether clear, a thick fog or snow may also be placed in the ropelike category. Thus, when speaking of a "thick" fog or snow, one uses the verb *tomik-,*[42] a descriptive construction that is based on the initial *tom-* 'thick', here occurring with the classifier for ropelike objects, *-(e)k.*

Among Hupa speakers, the special "ropelike" category is often applied to a series of objects that have been joined together in some fashion, regardless of their shape. In cases such as this, the shape and texture of the individual members no longer play a role, and the string of objects is only "ropelike" in a metaphorical way. Typical referents include a series of rocks, sticks, bones, faces, pains, marks, tattoo marks, and waves, where there is no special requirement for ropelike physical characteristics. Consider the form *deʔk̓ʸidiliW,* where the two-part adverbial marker *de·=di-* signals that the referent passes into the fire, while the indefinite object marker *ḱʸi-* specifies that the referent must be defined by context. In a literal sense, this form could refer to the act of placing an eel into the fire to cook, though in a secondary way, speakers often use this form to talk about placing a series of separate objects into the fire, one after another. Or consider the form *taʔwilay,* where the directional marker *ta·=* signals that the referent passes "into the water," while the inceptive prefix *wi(n)-* places the focus on the initial phases of the total process. In an idiomatic sense, this expression loosely translates as "one took several objects into the water," though the literal reference is to placing a single "ropelike object" into the water. In practice, speakers use this form to talk about the act of launching a fleet of canoes. With the indefinite object marker *ḱʸi-,* the reference is sometimes extended to coordinated movements of the hands or eyes, working together in tandem. A case in point is the form *yaʔḱʸilay,* where the object marker *ḱʸi-* signals that the ropelike object is actually the subject's arm. In practice, speakers use this form to refer to the act of "raising one's arm."

GRAMMATICAL PATTERNING IN NORTHWESTERN CALIFORNIA

Obligatory systems of classification are especially elaborate in many of the Native languages of northwestern California, reaching their high point in the regular semantic structures of the Hupa and Yurok languages, with some parallel developments in the neighboring Karuk tradition.[43] While the Native peoples of this region have long attached similar cultural significance to many objects and events in their combined experience, each language nonetheless imposes a separate classification onto the world of events reported in story-telling or encountered in everyday life.

These systems of classification enter into very different areas of grammatical pattering, leading speakers of each language to apply the underlying categories to very different types of situations in everyday life. The Hupa system, for instance, is composed of a series of specialized verb forms that specify the motion or position of certain classes of objects. For Hupa speakers, time perspective and directional orientation are intrinsic to the semantics of the categories. The Yurok system, in contrast, is composed of a series of semantic elements that combine with most numerals and some descriptive verbs. Practically speaking, the Yurok speaker must consider these categories of the classifier system either when counting or when attributing inherent characteristics to an object, such as its overall size, color, and texture. And although some classificatory elements occur throughout the structure of the Karuk language, classification is not obligatory in any single area of the grammar. One system, based on counting and quantification, loosely resembles the numerical system of the Yurok language, though with fewer categories overall. The other system consists of a small set of classificatory verbs, which loosely resemble those of the Hupa language, though without the obligatory spatial and temporal categories presupposed by Hupa grammar.

A special category for living beings is present in each of the languages considered in this study, though each tradition holds separate criteria for membership in this parallel conceptual class. Among the Hupas, all things capable of self-propelled motion are classified as animate, a category that is secondarily extended to fresh kill and cultural objects fashioned from the flesh. The Yuroks, in contrast, split the realm of the animate into classes for either human or non-human actors, echoing the mythic division between the realms of animals and humans said to have emerged during the ancient past. Karuks place both animals and humans, together, within the class of "living things," often without explicit attention to the underlying capacity for motion; in creation stories, even baskets and stars are sometimes classified as animate, reflecting their former status as spirit deities, before the era of the transformation. Thus, even where parallel categories occur in several languages, the corresponding conceptual divisions tend to vary widely throughout the neighboring speech communities.

Similarly, a general category for smoothly contoured objects without significant accentuation in any one dimension is present in each of the classificatory systems. Loosely, these categories refer to "round objects." For the Hupas, this category generally refers to a roughly spherical body occupying three dimensions. Prototypically, the reference is to manipulation of a stone, bundle, or arrow point in the hands. Metaphorically, the reference may be to the manipulation of a song, dance, or tradition under the direction of a skilled performer. Any object defying classification elsewhere in the Hupa system may be classified as round, including tradition, credit, and a person's reputation. For the Yuroks, a similar category refers to roughly disc-shaped objects in two primary dimensions, although objects of circular proportion in three dimensions fit equally well within this category.

Similarly, the Hupa and Yurok languages share a category for referring to objects with "ropelike" characteristics. Ropes and strings are prototypes for both groups. Among the Yuroks, snakes and worms hold their primary membership within this class; metaphorically, the category is also extended to such elements of the physical world as streams, which are capable sinuous movement. For the

Hupas, the reference is still further extended to any series of objects joined together in a stringlike fashion. However, snakes and worms are generally classified in Hupa as "living beings" rather than "ropelike objects."

Finally, the Hupa and Karuk languages both share a category that separates "filled containers" from other potential vessels. Baskets, in both traditions, act as prototypes for the category. Yet the metaphorical extensions vary widely among traditions. For Karuks, the reference may be extended to a stream of salmon, a neck full of necklaces, or the earth during a flood. For Hupas, the reference may be extended to a standing plant full of sap, a woman resting motionless in a sexually suggestive position, or a utensil brimming over with food.

9

Cultural Meaning in
Everyday Vocabulary

Single Algonkin words are like tiny imagist poems.

Edward Sapir, Language

No two languages are ever sufficiently similar to be considered as representing the same social reality. The worlds in which different societies live are distinct worlds, not merely the same world with different labels attached. . . . The understanding of a simple poem, for instance, involves not merely an understanding of the single words in their average significance, but a full comprehension of the whole life of the community as it is mirrored in the words, or as it is suggested by their overtones.

Edward Sapir, Selected Writings

In the traditional vocabulary of northwestern California, even common nouns often appear to be constructed somewhat like miniature haikus. That is, by presenting only a small sample of highly suggestive images, these brief, allusion-filled constructions often capture an entire episode of outstanding cultural significance, in a fashion that is somewhat reminiscent of the classic Japanese poetic form. Throughout the region, familiar episodes culled from everyday life tend to act as templates for creating and interpreting often-elaborate descriptive nouns. As a by-product of this creative tradition, many nouns contain detailed references to familiar scenes from the local storytelling traditions. In this setting, even the most common objects of experience are often "named" for those familiar roles they play in everyday life, whether in folklore, mythology, or daily cultural practices. That is, familiar stories are often echoed in the names assigned to animals, plants, people, or places.

Consider, for example, the story of the little bird known in English as the dipper or water ouzel, two colorful labels that convey no particular folkloric significance for most English speakers. Yet for the Hupas and Karuks, a definite story is ascribed to this animal, wherein the Water Ouzel receives an eternity of punishment for once having been a poor father, long ago in the ancient past. At one time, it is said, this selfish bird hoarded the food he caught during his daily hunting expeditions, food that rightfully belonged to his wife and children, who, as a consequence, came to starve. For this original wrong, the Water Ouzel received an eternity of punishment, meted out each day until the end of time.[1] Yet several versions of this tale circulate within the region, so that each group assigns a different fate to this character at the end of the story.

According to the Hupa version of this popular tale, the Dipper is condemned to having sex with stones, though never again with his wife. In the vocabulary of the Hupa language, this image is captured in the common name for this bird, where the matching noun of action *ce·-q'e·t'* loosely translates as "the one who copulates with stones." The central idea in this construction is conveyed by the verb stem *-q'e·t'*, which refers to the act of "copulating with something," while the noun root *ce·* signals the "stone" that stands in as the object of this humorous and perhaps notorious act. At the end of the word, the relativizing enclitic *-i* is present in a submerged fashion, where its only tangible effect is to preserve the shape of the stem, which would otherwise be reduced to *-q'eh*. In semantic terms, this enclitic transforms the verb phrase into an elaborate noun of action by adding the meaning "the one who performs the deed in question." Without this relativizing enclitic, the contrasting form *ce·-q'eh* simply means "it copulates with stones," not "the one who copulates with stones." With this colorful label, the Hupa have attached an element of folklore to an observable fact of nature, one that potentially comes to life anytime a speaker considers the meaning of the name or ponders the significance of the related story. In another sense, the image reflects one aspect of the dipper's natural history, namely, its habit of hopping about on the rocks along the river in an effort to spot its underwater prey, which it then lunges in to capture.

In the Karuk tradition, the Dipper is condemned, not to having sex with stones, but to sucking the moss from the floors of rivers. This image is reflected in the parallel noun of action *ʔasaxvanishʔámvaanich*, which translates as "the little one who eats river moss." Here the Karuks have attached a parallel element of folklore to still another aspect of the dipper's behavior, observable to some extent in the bird's familiar habit of plunging into the water. The Karuk word form is based on the verb stem *-a(m)*, which refers to the act of "eating something," a form that has been modified with the grammatical marker *-va* to signal that the action is plural and that more than one item is consumed over any given stretch of time. Here the agentive marker -*aan* signals that the reference is to "the one who performs this feat," while the resulting verb *amvaan* translates as "the one who eats many things." The noun root *ʔasaxvárish,* at the beginning of the form, signals that "river moss" is the object of the act, with the resulting construction *ʔasaxvanishʔámvaan* translating as "the one who eats river moss." The word form ends with the diminutive suffix -*ich,* which signals that the actor, namely, the dipper, is small in stature. Again, the finale of the popular story is condensed into a single, highly suggestive word form whose meaning is obvious at once to anyone familiar with this episode in the local creation lore.

A similar act, one that likewise finds expression in everyday vocabulary, is attributed to the Sun in the local creation lore. During traditional times, the Sun was regarded as a mythical being who traveled across the heavens each day, casting his radiant light down upon the earth.[2] By night, the Sun was said to sink into the ocean, only to emerge the next morning from beneath the mountains. Yet at one time, the Sun hovered motionless in the sky all day, until night made his entrance at dusk, alongside sleep. Then, in the time of the transformation, the Sun was assigned the chore of walking across the heavens each day, sustaining the life below by bringing the world out of darkness. This particular image is reflected, in parallel fashion, in each of the area's languages.

This image finds its most explicit expression in the Karuk language, in which the sun is sometimes known as "the one who walks in the sky," or *páy nanuʔávahkam ʔahóotihan.*[3] The central idea in this construction is conveyed by the verb stem *ʔáhoo,* which signals the act of "going" or "walking." The durative marker -*tih* specifies that the event continues on for a considerable span of time, while the participial suffix -*han* signals that the reference is to the particular being who is known to perform this act, here, by implication, the sun. The location of the event is then supplied by the adverb *nanuʔávahkam,* which loosely translates as "(in) the sky," though, literally, the reference is to "the entire realm that lies above us." This adverb is based on the spatial root -*ʔávah-,* which refers to a region "above" something, here in relation to a group of people, as denoted by the possessive first-person plural prefix *nanu-,* meaning "us." At the end of the form, the suffix -*kam* signals that the reference is to the "side" that is above us, here, by implication, the realm of the sky. The article *pay* then makes the reference more definite, indicating a specific one known by all to walk in the heavens every day since the beginning of time. Among the Karuks, this particular form is mostly restricted to storytelling and prayer and is rarely used in everyday life.[4]

Among the Yuroks, the sun is similarly known as "the one who travels by day," an image that is captured in the phrasal construction *kecoyn hiigoo,* the ordinary name for the sun. Here the noun *kecoyn* refers to "daytime." This form is based on the related verb *kecoy-,* which by itself means "to be daylight." Here the attributive suffix *-n* transforms this verb into a noun that refers to the period "(when) it is daylight." The word *hiigoo,* in the second part of the construction, is also based on a verb, here the root *hoo,* which usually refers to the process of "going" or "walking." In this case, the presence of the intensive infix *-iig-* contributes the sense that this walking is performed "always" or "eternally."

In the Hupa language, the reference is far more obscure, occurring only in the phrasal construction *de·di-ɢa·l,* which loosely translates as "that one (who is) walking along." Not an everyday form, this special term is usually invoked only in religious narratives and prayer. Here the verb stem *-ɢa·l* signals the act of "walking." This third-person stem shape, cast in the progressive aspect, refers to the act of "moving along" continuously, with no particular end in sight.[5] The demonstrative *de·di* restricts the reference to that particular one that is known by all to walk across the heavens each day since the beginning of time. The rest of the reference, including the location where the act takes place (in the sky) and the time period when the action is performed (in the daytime), is left to the imagination. Here this single act is enough to complete the entire reference, however obscure the connection may appear to an outsider. The pattern is widespread among Hupa speakers, among whom even the protagonists in a creation story are rarely mentioned by name but are instead identified through their deeds.

Despite the scale of the multilingualism, each group tends to maintain its own distinctive name for many objects of routine experience. Surprisingly, the evidence for borrowing, during traditional times, is minimal, insofar as each present-day vocabulary bears testament to a lengthy historical legacy reaching back over many generations.[6] As a consequence, neither the sound patterns nor the associated word meanings run especially parallel as one passes from one speech community to the next, even for identical referents or objects of experience. At the same time, even loan translations (that is, cases in which the content of a word has been translated without a concurrent transfer of linguistic material from the source language) are rare. The pattern is a general one within the region, so that even in terms of oral traditions, each group usually maintains its own distinctive version of the common stories that have long circulated throughout the neighboring speech communities. The local differences of interpretation, which often crop up from one village to the next, also make their appearance in the content of the vocabularies, as seen in the case of the water ouzel.

PORTRAITS OF ACTION

Some of these word forms convey a vivid scene of action, effectively linking the referent with an associated process that must be deciphered on a cultural basis. Yet the languages often assign different images to the same referents, so the neighboring speech communities do not always share the same associations with the referent. That is, once an image takes root in the vocabulary, the associated link between actor and act often reaches no further than the next linguistic boundary. Many of the associations are based on events that can still be witnessed firsthand.

Animal names, for instance, often reflect scrupulous attention to the natural histories of these creatures, whether the focus is on the movements they routinely make or the prey they constantly seek. Consider, for example, the bird known as "the little one that disappears into water" in Karuk, as captured by the word *sinkuníhvaanich,* the common name for the mud hen. Here the verb stem *sin* conveys the sense of "disappearing" or "becoming lost," while the directional modifier *-kú(n)ih* specifies a path that leads "into the water." The plural action marker *-va* signals that the action is repeated in rapid succession, while the diminutive marker *-ich,* at the end of the form, suggests that the referent, the mud hen, is small in size.

Or consider the Hupa name for the stag beetle, in which reference is again made to a familiar scene from everyday life. This inset is called *čʷanʔ-kʸitiɬma·s* in Hupa, where the reference is literally to "the one who rolls excrement along." Of course, that is familiar to anyone who has seen this industrious little bug in action. Here the verb *-t-ma·s* conveys the sense of "rolling something," while the distributive marker *ti-* refers to an action that proceeds "off" or "along" for a considerable distance. The subject of this act is indicated by the indefinite marker *kʸi-,* which refers to an agent whose identity is implicit with the context, here the stag beetle, which is known to perform this act as a character trait. The object of the event, the waste matter that the stag beetle rolls along, is marked explicitly by the noun stem *čʷanʔ,* which refers to "excrement."

Or consider the Yurok name for the screech owl. Known as k^wɹyk^{w}ɹyɹc among the Yuroks, this descriptive noun translates as "the one who whistles," based on this animal's status as a harbinger of evil or grave misfortune.[7] The construction is based on a diminutive form of the noninflective verb stem k^weyk^{w}eyur, the ordinary Yurok verb for the act of "whistling."

Even plants are sometimes named for an associated scene of action, often one that is based on a scene from creation lore or everyday life. A case in point is the flower known as "the little one who sees spring salmon coming" in Karuk, because this plant, which blossoms in early spring, is charged with the important task of heralding the annual return of salmon at about the same time. Called ʔatmahavníkaanich by Karuk speakers, this word is based on the verb root *mah-*, which refers to the act of "seeing," while the suffix *-av(n)ik*[8] signals that the object of the act, the sight this plant takes in, is in motion. Toward the end of the form, the agentive suffix *-aan* signals that the reference is to "the one who" is known to perform this act characteristically, while the diminutive marker *-ich* specifies that this actor is small in size. The object of the event is designated by the noun root ʔáat, which specifically refers to "spring salmon," here occurring in contracted form, at the beginning of the word.

Or consider the plant known among the Hupas as "the one people use to trip others up." In the Hupa language, this image is captured by the word *xoc'ineʔ-mił-yaʔmil*, the common name for the Oregon grape. This descriptive noun is based on the verb stem *-mil*, which refers to the act of "throwing several things." Here the directional modifier *ya·=* specifies that the reference is to throwing several things "up into the air." Sandwiched between the directional marker *ya·=* and the verb stem *-mil* is the reduced form of the animate third-person subject marker ʔ-, which signals that the actor who performs this deed could be any person in general (though not the speaker or the addressee). At the beginning of the form, the possessive noun *xo-c'in-eʔ* specifies that the object of the act is "someone's legs," namely, those belonging to the person who is tripped up in the process. In the middle of the form is the grammatical marker *-mił*, which indicates that the referent is the instrument that is regularly used to perform this act, here, by implication, the vines of the Oregon grape.

MYTHIC IMAGES

Some of the most gripping scenes of action are those that portray a familiar episode from the local storytelling traditions, effectively transferring an image from the realm of folklore to the currency of everyday vocabulary. Here the actor and associated act are thoroughly intertwined, so much so that the mythic act comes to stand for the very object it represents, at least within the collective social imagination of a given speech community.

Once crystallized in vocabulary, these images imbue many objects of routine experience with poignant scenes from creation lore. With a moment's reflection on the meaning of the word, a religious image is potentially called to mind, reinforcing the importance of creation lore in daily social life. Like Aesop's fables, the allegorical acts attributed to animals by the Native peoples of northwestern California often take on either heroic or sinister proportion, depending on whether the deed in question is exalted or condemned. That is, these stories also act as implicit templates for human action.

In the religious traditions of northwestern California, many animals and plants are seen as present-day embodiments of spirit deities, who chose to remain in this world after the time of the transformation, when the majority of these sacred beings fled for the heavens at the fringes of the universe. Some would provide medicines; others protection; still others, who had been infested with some great evil, would cause suffering or disease. The dog, for instance, is widely regarded as a stranded angel who chose to remain in this world after the creation times to watch over people. Originally, Dog could speak, but he elected to forfeit this power when humans entered the world, while still retaining a passive comprehension of the spoken word. If Dog should ever speak again, the end of the world will be at hand. Serving as a guardian or protector of humanity, the dog barks to warn people of danger. Because some of these acts were established in the creation times, many of them represent unbroken streams of action stretching across the fabric of time, where the reference in each case is to a characteristic act that is as true today as it was in the ancient past, when the activity was first set into motion.[9]

Consider, for example, the story of the Mourning Dove. According to the shared creation story, which circulates in each of the speech communities, the Mourning Dove was fond of gambling. One day, as he was winning a round, news came that his grandparent was dying. Yet the Mourning Dove did not want to cut his game short, so he begged to play one more round, and then another, until at last his grandparent finally passed away. Since he never made it to his grandparent's deathbed or to the funeral afterwards, the Mourning Dove was later plagued with enormous pangs of guilt. To make reparations for this original wrong, committed long ago in the ancient past, the Mourning Dove pledged to mourn each summer thereafter, until the end of time, both for the loss of his grandparent and for the funeral he never attended, owing to his enormous love of gambling.

Based on this story, the Yuroks call this bird "the dove (who) always mourns," an image that is captured in the word *megey ʔoʔrowiʔ*, the common name for the mourning dove. This construction is based on the verb stem *mey*, which refers to the act of "mourning" or "weeping," while the intensive infix *-eg-* contributes the sense that this activity is performed "repeatedly" or "eternally." The second part of this construction (*ʔoʔrowiʔ*) is simply the ordinary Yurok word for the dove, one that holds no particular descriptive meaning.

The Hupas and Karuks introduce the notion that this "mourning" reaches its high point during the summertime, a fact that also reflects an aspect of the animal's natural history. In Hupa, the mourning dove is called *xonsił-čʷiw*, or "the one who cries in the summertime." Here the stem *-čʷiw* signals the act of "weeping," while the relativizing enclitic *-i* preserves the shape of the stem, which would otherwise be reduced to *čʷeh*. Semantically, this enclitic signals that the reference is to the "one who weeps." The initial unit, *xonsił*, which literally means "(when) it is hot," specifies the time period in which this activity reaches its height, namely, during the summer months. This form, in turn, is based on the skeletal verbal unit *n-sił*, found in many derivative constructions that refer to the state of being hot. The spatial element *xo-* contributes the sense of "a place in space or time" wherein this quality is manifest, which refers, in this case, to the entire span of "summertime."

The equivalent in Karuk is *pimnanihtanákaanich*, which translates as "the little one who cries in the summertime." Here the verb stem *tá(n)ak*[10] refers to the act of "crying" or "weeping," while the agentive suffix *-aan* specifies that the reference is to "the one who" performs this act, namely, the mourning dove. At the end of the form, the diminutive marker *-ich* shifts the meaning to "the little one who cries." The temporal adverb *pimnáanih* specifies the time when this crying normally takes place, namely, "(during) the summer."

Other images are more local in distribution. A case in point is the story associated with the pygmy owl. In creation lore, this animal is said to chase down deer by entering their ears and thereby confusing the deer until they lose their balance. Among the Hupas, the pygmy owl is called *kʸintiyoʼdi-ǯ*, a form that translates as "the little one that chases it along." Here the central meaning is signaled by the stem *-yoʼd*, which, together with the prefix *n(i)-*, conveys the meaning "to hunt or chase." The fact that this stem has not been reduced to its alternative form *-yoh* indicates that the relativizing enclitic *-i* is present at an underlying level, here converting this phrase into an extended verbal noun that refers to that specific someone who regularly performs the deed in question. The middle prefix *ti-* suggests an action that travels along a roughly linear course. Immediately before this element, the prefix *kʸi-* indicates that the object of the pursuit is a certain someone or something defined purely by context, here the deer that the pygmy owl chases. Finally, the diminutive marker *-ɔ̃* at the end of the form suggests that the actor is either very small or very dear.

The Karuk word for the pygmy owl is based on a very different image. Among the Karuks, this bird is called *ʔipasnáhvaanich,* meaning "the little one who blows or sucks deer," an image based on the bird's purported practice of killing deer by entering their ears and blowing or sucking (Bright 1957:347). This construction is based on the verb *pasnáahva,* which generally refers to the act of drawing breath but in this context suggests the action of either blowing or sucking. The noun *ʔip* at the beginning of the form specifies the object of the act, namely, the deer whose ear is blown into or sucked. The agentive suffix *-aan* indicates that the construction refers to a specific entity who performs this an act characteristically, while the diminutive marker *-ich* suggests that the agent is small in stature. With this image in mind, anyone familiar with the associated mythic act can easily connect these deeds with the proper animal.

Despite strong cultural similarities among the speakers of the area's languages, the bulk of the imagery is highly language specific, without close parallels elsewhere in the region. A case in point is the Hupa word for the spirit deities who were said to have prepared the world for the coming of humanity. Collectively, these beings are known as "the ones who survive," an image that is conveyed in the name for these spirits, *kʸixinay.* This expression is built up around the skeletal verb unit *xi-na·,* which refers to the act of "surviving" or "escaping," here modified with the indefinite subject marker *kʸi-,* which refers to the actor known by context to perform this deed, here including the entire pantheon of prehuman spirit deities. The final *-y,*[11] translating as "those who," transforms the expression into a noun of action that refers to the class of actors known to have performed this feat, literally "those who survive."

Or consider the character known to the Yuroks as "the one who looks after the heavens," based on the isolated story of a figure who fashioned the heavens from netting during the early phases of the creation, later watching over his handiwork from afar.[12] The image finds expression in the common Yurok name for this figure, which takes the form *ǩi ʔwesʔonah megetoɬ,* a construction that is based on the verb *megetoɬ,* which refers to the act of "looking after or protecting something." Here the object of the act, the place this figure protects, is supplied by the noun *(ʔ)wesʔonah,* which broadly refers to everything under the heavens, usually translating as "earth," "universe," or "cosmos."

The Karuks sometimes speak of a supernatural being who is said to look after the yearly acorn harvest. The name for this figure takes the form *thuxriv-ʔishkúruhan* among the Karuks, meaning "the one who carries a net bag by the loop," referring to the pack of acorns that he is said to carry.[13] In this construction, the verb stem *ishkúruh* signals the act of "carrying something by a looped handle," while the marker *-han* specifies that the reference is to "the one who" is known to perform this act characteristically. The object of this act, the pack that is carried by the looped handle, is supplied by the noun *thuxriv,* which refers to a net bag generally used to carry game, though here one that is used to transport acorns.

Other figures are known for the wicked acts they continue to inflict on humans. Among the Hupas, evil spirits said to dwell in the water are known as "the ones who attack things," based on the sense that these incorporeal beings inflict illness on their unsuspecting victims. These spirits are called *ǩʸiłweˑ* by the Hupas; this construction is based on the verb stem *-weˑ,* which, together with the classifier *ł-* before it, refers to the act of "attacking something." The indefinite object marker *ǩʸi-,* at the beginning of the form, restricts the reference to the class of beings that these spirits are known to attack, usually a sick person.

Among the Karuks, practitioners of black magic, who are thought to rob graveyards and devil people under cover of the night, are known as *ikxaramvuráyvaan,* an expression that loosely translates as "the ones who wander by night." This construction is based on the verb *vúrayva,* which refers to the act of "going around" or "wandering," while the agentive suffix *-aan* signals that the reference is to "the one who" characteristically performs this act, namely, those who practice black magic. The temporal adverb *ikxáram* at the beginning of the form specifies that this activity is performed "(by) night."

GEOGRAPHICAL REFERENCES IN VOCABULARY AND CULTURE

Other names are based on geographical associations, effectively linking the referent with a spatial concept that must be understood in cultural terms. Animals, for instance, are often named for the geographical location most intimately connected with their regular presence, such as a favorite hunting ground or nesting area. For similar reasons, culture heroes and monsters are sometimes known for the mythical land where the figure is said to have made its eternal home. Though less dramatic than the portraits of action (discussed in the preceding section), many of these constructions are equally charged with poetic content, often building on references to everyday life or episodes from the local folklore and mythology.

Consider the Hupa name for the great blue heron. Among the Hupas, this animal is known as "the one at the riffles," an image that is captured by the word *xahslin-taw*. The first unit in this construction, *xahslin,* designates the "riffle" and is itself from a verb that refers to a place "where water mounds up." Here the stem *-lin* designates the flowing of water, while the prefix cluster *xa(h)=s-* specifies that this motion bears "uphill," or simply "upward" and away from the base of the river. The second element, *-taw,* is a postpositional root that, when attached to a noun or verb, creates a phrase that means "in the vicinity of this thing or event." Based on this analysis, a fuller, if less natural, translation of the word *xahslin-taw* is "the one who lives at the place where the water mounds up."

Other nouns portray a scene from creation lore, often based on a character's homeland, as attributed in popular stories. Consider, for example, the Duck Hawk, called *ʔáʔiknêechhan* among the Karuks; this expression literally translates as "the little one who lives above." Here the reference is based on this bird's mythical home at the crest of Sugar Loaf Mountain.[14] In this construction, the verb root *ikriv,* meaning "to live" or "to dwell," combines with the diminutive suffix *-ach* to form the underlying base *ikrivach,* which is then contracted to the attested form *iknêech* through regular grammatical processes.[15] At the beginning of the form, the adverbial root *ʔaʔ* specifies that this activity takes place at a location that is "up" or "above" the implicit ground of the Karuk homeland, while the participial formative *-han,* at the end of the form, signals that the reference is to "the one who" characteristically performs this act.

Spatial Imagery in Karuk Vocabulary

Spatial imagery is especially common in Karuk vocabulary. Most of these nouns identify the homeland of the referent, usually in relation to Karuk country. Many animal names, for instance, identify the land where this creature makes its home. Consider, for example, the name for the scorpion, which the Karuks know as the mountain-dwelling counterpart of the crawfish. While the crawfish is called *xanthun* (an unanalyzable noun root that conveys no particular descriptive meaning), the corresponding term for the scorpion is *mahxánthuun,* a related noun created by adding the prefix *mah-* to the name for the crawfish, to indicate its counterpart that lives on the land, in the mountains, away from the rivers.

Other associations are more direct. The otter, for example, sometimes goes by the nickname of *páy sáruk,* which literally translates as "that one downhill." Here the adverb *sáruk* refers to a place located somewhere "downhill," while the article *páy* signals that the reference is to "the one" that lives in this region.

The same pattern also applies to plants, which are often identified by their geographical homeland within the surrounding country. A case in point is the term *mahamtáparas,* which refers to a species known as the "mountain lupine." Or consider the related word *mah'asaxxêem,* which refers to another species known as "mountain moss." Both plants are distinguished from their lowland counterparts with the prefix *mah-,* which designates a region "uphill" and toward the mountains from Karuk country proper.

Even the names of the seasons are sometimes based on geographical associations. A case in point is the expression *káruk vákkuusra(h),* the traditional term for the ninth month of the year, which literally refers to "the month belonging to upriver." Here the noun stem *kúusra(h)* signals a period of one "month," while the directional adverb *káruk* situates the events that take place at this time "a great way upstream." The inanimate possessive marker *va-* indicates that this month, in a sense, "belongs" to the upriver country, where the great religious dances are usually held at this time of year in the homeland of the Karuk people.

Like animals and plants, culture heroes are also known for the land where they are said to have made their eternal home. Consider, for example, the prehistoric race of giants who were said to have terrorized humanity from their distant homes in the mountains above Karuk country. In the Karuk language, the name for this former race takes the form *maruk'áraara,* which literally refers to the "people of the mountains." Here the noun *'áraara* signals that the reference is to a race or "people" of some kind, while the adverb *máruk* places this group in a land that is "a great way uphill" from Karuk country. Among Karuk speakers, even the central myth figure of the region is known for his homeland, far across the waters of the ocean: the Karuk name for Across-the-Ocean-Widower takes the form *ithyarukpíhriiv,* an expression that refers to "the widower across the waters." Here the noun *píhriiv* refers to a "widower," while the adverb *ithyáruk* situates the referent "across the water."

In recent times, tribal names have often been based on geographical associations. In this sense, the Karuks sometimes identify themselves as "the people of the upriver country," a conception that is conveyed in the Karuk expression *káruk vaʔáraar.* This construction is based on the noun stem *ʔáraar(a),* which refers to a "person" or group, while the directional adverb *káruk* situates this community "a great way upstream" from the neighboring tribes. The inanimate possessive marker *va-* signals that this group of people, in a sense, "belongs" to the upriver country, where they have made their home. For similar reasons, the Karuks sometimes refer to their Yurok neighbors as "the people of the downriver country," as reflected in the parallel term *yúruk vaʔáarara.* Here the directional adverb *yúruk* signals that these people are situated "a great way downriver" from their neighbors, including the Karuk speakers.[16] Yet according to William Bright (pers. comm. 2003), both of these tribal names may be of recent origin. In traditional times, it is likely that the Karuks simply knew themselves as "the people," as expressed in the word *ʔáraara,* which also applies to the neighboring Hupa and Yurok speech communities.

Though many Karuk nouns are based on the concept of a geographical homeland, only a handful explicitly identify the path the referent takes while traveling through space. Consider the goldfinch, for instance, which the Karuks know as "the one that shoots down from upstream," based on its habit of scurrying up and down the rivers. The Karuk name is *ishnimvánakach.* Here the verb stem *ishri(m),* or *ishri(v),* which refers to the act of "shooting," conveys the central idea in the construction, while the directional modifier *-vá(n)ak* refers to a trajectory that heads "hither (downriver) from someplace upriver."[17] The suffix *-a* transforms this verb into an abstract noun portraying the act of "shooting down from upriver," while the diminutive marker *-ach* indicates that the creature in question is small in stature. Similarly, the Karuks know the northern lights as the force of nature that "burns downriver from upriver." Here the Karuk name is *ʔiinvárak.* This construction is based on the verb stem *ʔiin,* which refers to the act of "burning," while the directional suffix *-várak* specifies a path that heads "downriver from someplace upriver."

Among the Karuks, even the act of telling stories sometimes holds special directional significance. Consider, for example, the Karuk expression *pikvahrúpukva,* which is the traditional term for singing good luck songs before a hunt. Here the verb stem *pikvah* refers to the act of "telling stories," while the directional marker *-rúpuk* means "(facing) outdoors, down toward the river below." At the end of the form, the plural suffix -*va* indicates that several stories are often told, or sung out loud, on such occasions.

Spatial Imagery in Hupa Vocabulary

In contrast to the Karuks, the Hupas place greater emphasis on the path taken by an object while moving through space, with less emphasis on the location occupied by the referent. A case in point is the Hupa word for their Yurok neighbors, to whom the Hupas refer using an expression that means "the ones who come from downstream": *yida·č'in-ninyay.* This word literally refers to the people who "travel" from their distant homeland downstream to the upstream land where the Hupa live—not merely to the people who "live" downstream. This construction is based on the verb *ninyay,* which refers to a group whose travels bring them to a particular destination. The adverb *yida·*- situates the journey relative to a region "downstream," while the modifier -*č'in* specifies that the whole event emanates from this region as a source, ultimately heading away from it.

In a similar fashion, the Hupa know their distant Tolowa cousins (who live along the coast) as "the downriver people who speak an Athabaskan language," explicitly referring to an activity performed by these people in this downriver homeland, namely, "speaking." The expression referring to the Tolowa Indians takes the form of *yide?-diniŋ?xine·W* among their Hupa neighbors. Here the skeletal verb unit *xi-ne·W* refers to the act of "speaking," while the element *diniŋ* signals that these people are "fellow Athabaskan speakers." Sandwiched between the element *diniŋ* and the verb *xi-ne·W* is a reduced form (*?*) of the animate third-person subject marker, which signals that the actor who performs the deed is someone in general, though neither the speaker nor the addressee. The directional adverb *yide?,* at the beginning of the form, contributes the sense that this speaking is done somewhere "downstream" from Hupa country.

Even the Europeans are known as "the ones who go around across the waters," as reflected in the descriptive noun *yima·n?dil,* the ordinary term for the nonnative peoples starting in the early contact period. This construction is based on a contracted form of the continuative verb *na?dil,* which refers to a group of people who "go around" or "live" together, while the directional adverb *yima·n* refers to their foreign homeland "across the water" in Europe.

The name for the sea lion adheres to a similar pattern. Among Hupa speakers, this animal is called *yida·č'in-te?il,* an expression that literally refers "the one who swims along from downstream." Here the verb root -*il* signals the act of "swimming," while the prefix *t(e)-* specifies that the event continues along in a fairly linear fashion. The directional adverb *yida·* at the beginning of the form situates this act in relation to the country "downstream," while the enclitic *-č'in* indicates that the activity originates in this land, heading upstream away from this source region.

Reflecting the opposite direction of movement, the south wind is known as "the wind that blows along from upstream," because this wind enters Hupa country from the upstream end of the valley. The matching Hupa expression is *yinah č'in-tehs č'e·*. Here the verb stem *-č'e·* refers to the act of "blowing somewhere," while the directional marker *t(eh)-* specifies a fairly linear and continuous stream of motion and the aspectual marker *s-* signals a steady flow of activity, without a definite onset or conclusion.[18] At the beginning of the form, the adverb *yinah-* situates the event relative to the "upstream" country, while the directional marker *-č'in* signals that the activity emanates from this region, ultimately heading "downstream" away from this source.

Among Hupa speakers, culture heroes are often known for the paths these figures took, long ago, during the creation times—not merely the homeland where these sacred beings live today, as is common in Karuk vocabulary. Consider, for example, the central myth figure of the region, Across-the-Ocean-Widower, who was said to have fled to the heavens across the ocean after becoming disgusted with humans as they first entered the world. Among the Hupas, the name of this figure literally translates as "the one who went astray across the water": *yima·n-tiw'winyay*. Here the classificatory stem *-yay* refers to the self-propelled motion of a single actor, while the directional modifier *ti(w)=*[19] specifies a path that leads off into the trails, whereupon the subject becomes lost. The spatial adverb *yima·n* signals that this being became lost in the spirit realm "across" the great cosmic waters thought to circle the earth.

Certainly action plays a major part in many of these spatial portraits. Only a handful of nouns state a geographical region without also stating a related event that takes place at this location. The corners of a living house are, for instance, known for the geographical directions that are regularly associated with them. In traditional times, the entrance to a living house usually faced down toward the river below, while the back of the house faced uphill, toward the mountains above. A case in point is the expression *yo'n-yidaɢ,* the traditional name for the back of the house, which literally translates as "uphill corner (of the house)." Here the adverb *yo'n* refers to the area beyond the fire pit of a house, while the adverb *yidaɢ* signals that this is the wall on the uphill side. The related expression *yoʔn-yinaɢ,* the traditional name for the inner wall of a house, can be literally translated as the "upstream corner (of the house)." Here the contrasting adverb *yinaɢ* situates this corner at the upstream end of the house. For similar reasons, the woodshed outside the house is known as "upstream pocket of the house," or *minʔt'ah-yinaɢ,* because this side usually faces upstream.

Though the Karuks sometimes call themselves the upriver people, the Hupas know their Karuk neighbors as "the people from uphill." The matching Hupa expression is *yidah-č'in.* Here the adverb *yidah-* (a special combining form of the adverb *yidaɢ*) locates these people "uphill" from the Hupa homeland, while the directional marker *-č'in* specifies that this group "comes from" such a place. At the end of the form, the collective human suffix *-n(i)* converts the expression into a noun that refers to the "group of people" who come from this particular directional bearing.[20]

Even time is reckoned in relation to geographical landmarks. At any given time of day, the sun takes a different position in the sky relative to the neighboring mountains, which enclose the valley on the west and the east. From this geographical frame of reference, the morning is known as the time of day when the sun moves into a position from uphill. The matching expression for the morning is *de·di-xʷi-yidah-č'iŋ-wiŋʔaʔ-miɬ.* Here the verb *wiŋʔaʔ* refers to a point in time when a round object (in this case, the sun) enters into a relatively motionless position, while the directional adverb *yidah-č'iŋ* specifies a path that comes from an uphill source, over the mountains. At the beginning of this construction, the demonstrative *de·di-xʷ,* which loosely translates as "here about," situates the event in relation to the implicit sundial of Hoopa Valley, while the element *-miɬ,* at the end of the construction, converts this entire string into an adverbial expression capable of situating another event relative to the time period when the sun reaches this spot in the sky. The expression as a whole translates as "when this way from uphill (the sun) settles into position." The reference, of course, is to morning, when the sun is known to occupy this position in the sky.

By a similar logic, the afternoon is known as the time when the sun takes its position in the heavens "upstream." During this time of day, the sun reaches its apex in the sky, where it is directly above the center of the valley and equidistant from both of the mountain walls that enclose the valley. Here the sun appears to be slightly southeast or "upstream," because the river flows in this direction as it passes through Hupa country. The matching expression for the afternoon is *de·di-xʷi-yinaɢa-wiŋʔaʔ-miɬ,* which refers to a time "when (the sun) settles into position this way upstream." For similar reasons, the late afternoon (or evening) is known as the time of day when the sun takes its place over the mountains, as it heads "downhill." The corresponding expression for the evening is *yice°ni-wiŋ°a°-mił*, which refers to the time "when the sun comes to rest downhill."

Spatial Imagery in Yurok Vocabulary

Only a small handful of Yurok nouns, such as tribal names, are based on geographical associations.[21] For example, the Yuroks refer to themselves as the "downriver people." This conception is reflected in the corresponding descriptive noun *pulekukla(a)°*. Here the suffix *-la°* signals that the reference is to people of some kind, while the directional adverb *pulekuk* specifies that this group lives somewhere "downriver," in this instance, in the traditional homeland of the Yurok people. The corresponding expression for the Karuks is *peckula(a)°* (also *pecikla°*), which refers to the "upriver people." Here the directional adverb *pecku* locates this group somewhere "upriver," in this case, in the traditional homeland of the Karuk people, while the suffix *-la°* again signals that the reference is to a particular group of people.

Several animal names also identify the geographical homeland of the species. Consider, for example, the bird known in Yurok as the "mountain hawk," an image that is captured in the phrasal noun form *hełkik ni knuuu*. Here the noun root *knuuu* refers to the hawk, while the prepositional element *ni* locates these birds at a particular site, here specified by the directional adverb *hełkik*, which signals a distant region in "the mountains." Or consider the name for the "daddy longlegs," which also contains a submerged geographical reference. In etymological terms, the name refers to the one who lives "along the river," as reflected in the word *pulews*, which is based on the directional root *pul*. While this root (*pul*) refers to a region "downriver," the spatial suffix *-ew* adds the meaning "toward" or "along."[22] The name for the surf-fish is one of the few Yurok nouns that specifies both a directional bearing and a related element of motion. The name for this animal is based on the intensive verb form *leg*, which refers to the act of "passing" to a certain point in a regular or repeated fashion,[23] while the directional adverb *hełkus* specifies that this motion reaches an "onshore" destination. The resulting name for the surf-fish is *hełkusleg*, which loosely translates as "(what) often passes ashore."

Like the neighboring Hupas and Karuks, the Yuroks also know the area's central culture hero for his home in the heaven across the ocean, where he is said to have fled long ago, during the ancient past. Among the Yuroks, the expression that defines this character is *wohpekumew,* meaning "the widower belonging to the realm across the water," which is based on the possessive form of the noun *mew,* the ordinary term for a "widower." Here the directional adverb *wohpek^w* locates this figure "across the waters," while the third-person possessive prefix *(ʔ)u-* specifies that he, in a sense, belongs to this distant land where he has made his home.

MISCELLANEOUS CULTURAL REFERENCES

Other words are based on enduring qualities that the referent possesses, such as a smell, a taste, or a tactile property, either attributed in myth or merely given in natural history. A case in point is the snake known in Karuk as "the slippery snake," an image that is conveyed by the word for the Western yellow-bellied racer, *apsunmúnukich.* Here the noun root *ápsuun* signals that the reference is to a "snake," while the adverb *múnukich* indicates that this particular one is known to be quite "slippery." According to local folklore, long ago during the creation times, this snake first acquired the trait of slipperiness when it smoked more than its share of tobacco and began to slip and slide everywhere it attempted to travel. The biological trait of the snake that its name references is thus also imbued with mythic significance.

Sometimes the referent is linked to a mythical relative, often one that is portrayed in familiar creation stories. Consider, for example, the yellow-breasted chat, which is known among the Hupas as "salmon's grandmother," owing to the claim that this bird once hoarded all the salmon at the upstream end of the world, long ago, during the creation times. Across-the-Ocean-Widower later freed these fish, so that the salmon could one day serve as a major dietary staple for the area's Native people. In the Hupa language, this image is captured by the word *łoʻqʼi-čʷoʻ,* the usual term for the yellow-breasted chat. This compound is based on the noun root *łoʻqʼ,* which by itself designates the salmon, while the second noun root *čʷoʻ* signals that the referent is actually the "maternal grandmother" of the salmon. Because the yearly departure of the yellow-breasted chat from the area roughly coincides with the annual return of the salmon in early spring, this colorful label also loosely refers to an observable feature of the animal's natural history.

Other life-forms are linked with a mythical benefactor, who either created them or still owns them today. Consider, for example, the blossom or rose of the redwood tree, which the Yurok know as the "flower" or "thorn" of a ghost.

The two names for the rose of the redwood in Yurok are *saʔał weciišep,* meaning "flower of the ghost," and *saʔał waʔah,* meaning "thorn of the ghost." Both revolve around the root noun *saʔał,* which means "ghost." The noun root *ciišep* refers to the "flower" in the first form, occurring with the possessive third-person prefix *(ʔ)we-* to signal that it belongs to a ghost. Or consider the plant known as "Across-the-Ocean-Widower's stinking armpit" in the Karuk language. This image is conveyed by the Karuk word *ʔithyarukpíhriiv muneevxâat,* the name for turkey mullein. The construction is based on the noun root *nêev,* which signals the "armpit," here occurring with the third-person possessor *mi-* and the adjective *xâat,* meaning "rotten" or "stinking."

THE POETRY OF EVERYDAY VOCABULARY

In the traditional vocabulary of the Hupa, Yurok, and Karuk Indians, even the most common objects of experience are often named for those roles they play in the mythology, folklore, and cultural practices of the region. In this sense, common nouns often capture, in a minimum of well-chosen images, an entire episode or event of outstanding cultural significance.

Far from representing frozen historical derivations devoid of living meaning, many of these descriptive nouns continue to act as repositories for cultural knowledge. Even today, following the large-scale shift to English, children often learn these stories when acquiring traditional vocabulary, either at home or in the classroom—stories that many children are wont to recite, even where the content of the tale is a bit risqué, as in the story of the Water Ouzel, recounted earlier in this chapter.

In this setting, the process of naming things for cultural reasons has probably always been an active, living tradition within this region, granting the speaker the freedom to coin new expressions every now and then, as the communities see fit to accept. The preponderance of descriptive imagery throughout the area's vocabularies attests to a long tradition of naming things after familiar images culled from everyday life. Yet the fact that many of these word meanings remain highly transparent and have not given way to contraction or any attendant loss of meaning also attests to a relatively recent historical vintage and, therefore, the presence of an ongoing, living tradition.

As Jocelyn Ahlers once noted (1996), the process is largely a metonymical one, where one outstanding trait comes to represent the referent as a whole, as this association is crystallized in vocabulary. First, speakers select a characteristic trait associated with the referent, often one that is based on deep-seated cultural associations, such as an ancient act once performed in myth or a sacred homeland known from the creation stories. Then, in a secondary way, this action or spatial quality comes to define the referent on a daily basis, as reflected in common speech.

Social considerations also provide a glimmer of insight into the constant need for new word forms. For in traditional times, strong taboos against speaking the names of the dead sometimes forced villages to discontinue the use of an animal name every so often. Because people were sometimes assigned nicknames based on the name for an animal, many of the descriptive words for animals also came to double as popular monikers for people. As with nicknames everywhere, these terms were usually based on an element of resemblance. Upon the death of such a person, the animal that served as the source for the nickname would require a new descriptive title, to avoid inadvertently speaking the name of a dead person when talking about the animal.[24]

This avoidance of animal names following a death in the community protects the family of the deceased from potential insult, eliminating the nickname of their loved one from future circulation. To whatever extent this process of replacement held sway over the millennia, it certainly must have contributed to the demand for new names.[25]

In addition, on psychological grounds, speakers often claim to remember words by first picturing the associated image, a process that triggers their memory of the sound pattern and semantic representation found in their native tongue. Yet the dominant element in this process is the associated image, which appears to hold considerable psychological reality for speakers.

Drawing on this tradition of descriptive imagery, speakers today have little difficulty assigning new names to things. These new words, like the old ones, generally convey a familiar story or some other outstanding characteristic of the referent, such as an associated action, location, or quality. Although the speaker may not recall the entire episode every time the word is uttered, the name often emerges directly from the local cultural life, which it also preserves, in abbreviated form.

Given that these linguistic groups have long inhabited similar natural and social environments, the diversity of imagery in the area's vocabularies is surprising. Rather than promoting uniformity, this constant interaction among the neighboring speech communities appears to have heightened the sense of creativity.

Part V

From Language Contact to Linguistic Relativity

10

Language Contact, Multilingualism, and Divergent Drift

How does such a network of language, culture, and behavior come about historically? Which was first: the language patterns or the cultural norms? In main they have grown up together, constantly influencing each other. But in this partnership the nature of the language is the factor that limits free plasticity and rigidifies channels of development in the more autocratic way. This is so because a language is a system, not just an assemblage of norms. Large systematic outlines can change to something really new only very slowly, while many other cultural innovations are made with comparative quickness. Language thus represents the mass mind; it is affected by inventions and innovations, but affected little and slowly, whereas to inventors and innovators it legislates with the decree immediate.

Benjamin Lee Whorf, Language, Thought, and Reality

L ike his teacher, Edward Sapir, Benjamin Lee Whorf stressed the historical adaptability of language in advancing his own provisional model of linguistic relativity. For languages, like cultures, are constantly changing, a lesson that was central to Boasian anthropology, in which every society was seen as the product of its own unique history. Certainly, on a synchronic basis, Whorf argued that worldview is pervasively reflected in language use, as can be illustrated, for instance, with the geographical directional concepts that enter the regular grammatical categories of the Hupa, Yurok, and Karuk languages. Though prevalent in the grammatical structure of the area's languages, these spatial categories also hold strong religious meaning and cosmological significance throughout the region, where they play a central role in both constructing and transmitting worldview.

Whorf also argued that languages are capable of gradually accommodating changes in culture and worldview on broad historical grounds (as reflected in this chapter's epigraph). Over time, every language inevitably adopts new words and grammatical categories, while old linguistic concepts often take on new meaning, as speakers discover new ways to apply existing ideas to novel situations. Consider the growth of scientific terminology in English, for instance, as hundreds of words continue to flood the language each year in an effort to keep up with conceptual developments in the various branches of scientific knowledge. Or consider the gradual loss in recent centuries of the pronominal forms "thee," "thy," and "thou," which were once used to assert familiarity among intimates as opposed to distance with superiors, who were addressed with the contrasting form "you." Here humble pronouns played an active role in perpetuating social hierarchy, which speakers recreated through actual performance when asserting either intimacy or distance through their choice of pronouns, as required by the grammar. Yet as overt expressions of hierarchy became increasingly distasteful to the English-speaking masses, so did the opposition between the "familiar" and "formal" in pronoun forms. In response to this shift in worldview, the distinction was eventually collapsed, and the "familiar" forms were gradually dropped from the language, so that words such as *thee, thy,* and *thou* survive today as vestiges of a former age.[1]

In the popular imagination, the concept of linguistic relativity has often been reduced to a matter of determinism, with a one-way arrow pointing from language to worldview, under the assumption that the speaker must accept a single monolithic outlook merely to communicate. Yet, as seen in the chapter epigraph, Whorf's view of linguistic relativity was actually a profoundly dynamic one, based on the assumption that languages change in response to shifts in culture or worldview. Because speakers actively construct worldview in language, this inherently creative process often leaves a lasting impression on the structure of the languages, including grammar and vocabulary. In this sense, every language is a product of an ongoing dialogue between the members of a speech community, who constantly strive to express their daily conceptual concerns in their native tongue, even as these ideas change. Over time, the participants in these exchanges introduce subtle shifts in form and meaning as the language undergoes constant revision in conversation, storytelling, song, or prayer.

As a student of Edward Sapir's, Benjamin Lee Whorf was deeply aware of the fact that languages are notoriously slow to change, often preserving core structural traits, inherited from the original source stock, for centuries or even millennia to come. Cultural changes, in contrast, often proceed more rapidly, something that must have been blindingly obvious to anyone who came of age in the early twentieth century, in a generation that witnessed more change than any generation had ever seen before. Taking the relative rates of change into consideration, Whorf cautioned that languages, especially grammatical structures, typically respond to changes at a slower pace than cultures, so that language and worldview may not always be in sync with one another. Here Whorf suggested that languages often preserve vestiges of former ancestral perspectives, either in grammar or in vocabulary. Even aphorisms such as "A man's home is his castle" preserve vestiges of a former age, as do the names for the figures on a chessboard, such as knights, kings, and queens. Or consider the archaic ring of words such as "thee" and "thou," which smack of Shakespeare, the King James Bible, or an isolated religious sect somewhere far from mainstream society. In this sense, the Native languages of northwestern California also preserve some features inherited from their respective source stocks (see chapter 11).

Certainly every living social institution undergoes change over time, a process that affects both the language and the culture of any given group. Yet identifying the source of change has remained deeply elusive to scholars working in the fields of both anthropology and linguistics, in part because changes cannot always be easily observed. For this reason, many theorists are more comfortable working with synchronic concerns, rather than confronting problems with explicit historical dimensions. Certainly Boasian anthropologists, for their part, strongly emphasized synchronic studies, while recognizing historical dimensions that often went unexplored, if for no other reason than for the lack of solid evidence at the time, given that many of the societies studied by anthropologists were preliterate. Similarly, Saussurean linguists separated synchronic description from comparative or historical studies, largely isolating the two strands of inquiry in practice. Yet in isolation, neither approach offers much insight into the subtle mechanisms that give rise to contemporary changes.

THE UNIVERSALITY OF CHANGE IN LANGUAGE

All languages change over time, a fact that has now been firmly established for every language on which there exists even a scrap of historical evidence. Consider the gradual evolution of English from *Beowulf* to the works of Shakespeare, as attested in classic literature. Or observe the gradual shift from the flowery English of the colonial period, widely attested in many historical documents, to the many modern forms of the vernacular spoken in North America today. Still other changes may be witnessed even in the course of a lifetime, often by the dozens. Consider the gradual loss of voicelessness at the beginning of such words as *whale* and *white,* for example, which were pronounced with a sudden puff of air by many English speakers in Europe and North America just a few generations ago. Though once common among the educated in the twentieth century, this feature is now confined to a handful of old-fashioned speakers on both sides of the Atlantic. In the process, it has lost the element of class or erudition that was once associated with it; the pronunciation sounds old-fashioned or archaic to most speakers today.

However obvious in the case of English, with its extensive literary history, this principle of change applies fairly universally to all known languages,[2] as scholarship in the field of linguistics has long indicated. Early in twentieth century, linguists such as Sapir and Leonard Bloomfield carefully demonstrated the universality of change with comparative evidence from several Native American language families.[3] While working in the field, both scholars had stumbled on languages that bore striking resemblances to often far-flung languages spoken elsewhere on the continent. Not surprisingly, some of these languages, such as Navajo and Apache of the American Southwest, were spoken in adjacent areas, perhaps representing what were once regional dialects that had since become different languages. Others, such as Wiyot of California and Abenaki of the eastern seaboard, were spoken at a far greater distance, with a span of several thousand miles to separate them. Upon further examination, both Sapir and Bloomfield came to hypothesize that these similarities were not a matter of chance but instead reflected descent from a common ancestor at some point in the remote past. Of course, if the original ancestral tongue had not changed over time, it would not have given rise to the family of related languages spoken today, leading to the inevitable conclusion that change is intrinsic to language.

As Sapir and Bloomfield had come to demonstrate, the evidence for historical change is overwhelming, even in the absence of written records. Here the conclusion is based on comparative evidence left behind by languages thought to have emerged from a common source stock deep in the ancient past. Of course, this approach had already been tested on the Indo-European language family, even as early as the eighteenth century, and had come to be known as the "comparative method," because history could often be inferred from evidence left behind by the daughter languages. By comparing similar words and grammatical forms in Latin, Greek, Sanskrit, English, and Old Church Slavonic, the early linguist Sir William Jones was able to announce that all of these languages had emerged from a common stock in the remote past.[4] When this discovery was announced to the Royal Asiatic Society in 1786, the results were shocking, for it indicated that the languages of Europe and India shared deep historical ties, contrary to the popular views of the times. Though the speakers of these languages had adopted different social customs, the languages continued to bear many unmistakable similarities in vocabulary and grammar, even after many thousands of years apart. This suggested the existence of a mother tongue even older than the written histories extending back to the first millennium B.C.E. for several of the languages, including Sanskrit, Latin, Greek, and Hittite.

Once demonstrated for languages that had no history of writing, such as Algonquian and Athabaskan, the comparative method could be extended to other unwritten tongues, either for the purpose of reconstructing common proto-forms spoken long ago in the remote past or for the purpose of making other historical inferences about patterns of migration or the contours of the ancient protoculture. In the case of Athabaskan, for example, Sapir concluded that the original tongue was spoken in the north, where the speakers would have occasion to talk about "snow" on a regular basis, a conclusion based on the survival of an ancient word root originally used for describing snow among people who had migrated into relatively snowless regions.[5] No linguist since then has doubted the universality of historical change, though the mechanisms that produced this change still remained mysterious and elusive.

From Variation to Change

Based precisely on this type of comparative evidence, which has now cropped up in nearly every corner of the planet, linguists, as a group, have long been forced to accept the universality of change in language. Yet, to many scholars, this obvious conclusion at first appeared deeply counterintuitive, even paradoxical. Of course, conventional wisdom insists that language hinges on the nearly mathematical application of regular grammatical rules, which the speaker must uphold merely to be understood. Above all, every language depends on a general consensus within a speech community regarding the meaning and use of particular forms.

If speakers must agree on the meaning of words and the same general rules for creating proper grammatical forms, the following question eventually raises its head: how does change ever arise, without violating these grammatical rules or stretching word meanings beyond comprehension? The question represents the so-called Saussurean paradox of early-twentieth-century linguistics, a problem that was not resolved, or even adequately addressed, until the advent of modern sociolinguistics in the past few decades. Even more baffling was the discovery that these historical changes often follow rules that are every bit as regular as synchronic rules. With this long-standing awareness of the continual diversification of speech within families, linguists, as a group, have long been forced to deal with change, which went against the principles of structural linguistics.

One clue lay in the presence of variation. Of course, even in the smallest speech communities, one encounters significant variation in everything from pronunciation to grammatical rules, however unconsciously speakers choose among these alternatives. Certainly some variation emerges from the creative impulse, one of the fundamental design features of all languages and an instinct shared by all humans. In this sense, even word meanings often vary significantly according to the social circle one keeps, so that elderly speakers may not be comfortable using popular expressions such as "cool" and "dude." Conversely, few younger speakers of English have ever heard of an "ice man" or a "chamber pot," though the terms were still in use just a hundred years ago.

Even on the grammatical plane, languages are constantly creating new affixes or dropping old ones in response to changing conceptual demands within the speech community. In English, for instance, the derivational affix -ly, which converts adjectives into adverbs, historically derives from the freestanding word *like*. In practical terms, this affix allowed old-fashioned expressions such as "swift-like" to be compressed into "swiftly." Of course, expressions such as "quick-like" and "swift-like" remain comprehensible to speakers, but they now carry a decidedly archaic ring. The tense markers of northwestern California probably entered the Native languages by a similar route, allowing speakers to express with a single affix what would have once taken an entire phrase to communicate. The Hupa marker of the future tense (-te·), for instance, bears a striking similarity to the root te·, which is widely found in constructions that refer to spatial extension, such as the prefix te·- 'off, along' or the verb stem -te·l 'be wide'. At one time, these established grammatical forms would have been novel affixes, giving rise to variation within the community, until the older forms were dropped.

Certainly every linguist discovers the often-baffling phenomenon of endless variation when entering the field for the first time.[6] But speakers also encounter variation on a daily basis, often recognizing these subtle differences, even if they do not produce the forms themselves. Consider, for instance, the English sound *th*, known as an "interdental fricative," which is routinely reduced to *d* in colloquial speech, a form that most speakers instantly recognize, even if it is not representative of their own native dialect. Or consider the common word *cool,* whose most literal meaning is "low in temperature," though it has acquired the popular colloquial meaning of "highly acceptable" in recent decades, at first only among the younger speakers. Or consider the verbal suffix *-s,* which most speakers use when marking present tense verb forms for the third person, though it is absent altogether in many colloquial varieties of English, in which all verbs remain unmarked in the present tense, even in the third person. Most speakers are aware of these alternative forms, as well as the sociolinguistic implications for using them in a particular situation. Though all of these forms were once linked with African American speech, the features have now spread to many other sectors of the society, including youth culture.[7]

Of course, once variation is allowed to reenter the picture, the whole Saussurean paradox begins to disappear. Variation within a speech community at any given point in time is often quite comparable to the similar, or even consequent, changes that develop over a greater stretch of time. Unfortunately, the methodology advocated by Saussure's students largely removed variation from the purview of the new science of linguistics, if only for the sake of writing concise descriptive accounts of particular languages without getting lost in all of the minor nuances or idiosyncratic details.[8] Yet far from representing an unusual state of affairs or an inconsequential anomaly, variation is in fact present in all known languages, sometimes on an enormous scale, as sociolinguists have been arguing in recent years.[9]

From Variation to the Concept of Drift

At any given moment of its evolution, language is stratified not only into linguistic dialects in the strict sense of the word . . . but also—and for us this is the essential point—into languages that are socio-ideological: languages of social groups, "professional" and "generic" languages, languages of generations and so forth. From this point of view, literary language itself is only one of those heteroglot languages—and in its turn is also stratified into languages.

Mikhail Milosevic Bakhtin, The Dialogic Imagination

Variation need not be relegated to the periphery; substantial differences in grammar, style, pronunciation, and vocabulary are present in all speech communities, often on an enormous scale. Instead of regarding variation as an aberrant trait or a departure from the "standard" form of the language, linguists can more simply accept that these pervasive differences emerge from very social circumstances to which language owes its existence. For languages are spoken by diverse social groups with a range of interests, and these groups generally use this common tongue to express many competing, or merely contrasting, outlooks on life. As a language takes root in a variety of social settings, the common tongue typically begins to diversify, often on a fairly minute scale at first, as each group begins to leave its own mark on grammar, pronunciation, vocabulary, and style. Again the impetus is often creative, though any resulting variation is quickly linked with the group that originates it, before becoming more widespread. The condition is one that the Russian linguist Bakhtin characterized as *heteroglossia,* in which competing factions continue to give rise to rich internal variation within a community, almost without limit, despite strong pressures to assimilate a standard outlook or linguistic variety (see Bakhtin 1981:263–72, 291–94, 428).

It is variation, of course, that plants the seeds for future change. Sapir, for one, saw variation as a breeding ground for drift, or the often-unpredictable changes that emerge in all languages over time. Early in the history of linguistics, he hypothesized that historical changes often have their roots in exactly the type of variation we have witnessed in English, in which contemporary differences in grammar, vocabulary, and pronunciation are abundant.[10] Perhaps inspired by the Darwinian concept of drift that was popular in his day, Sapir argued that languages (like gene pools) undergo a similar type of change, one that is inevitable but less than fully predictable.[11] Like biological evolution, historical changes in language have their roots in an ongoing process of selection that can, to some extent, be witnessed by paying close attention to current social processes. That is, he surmised that historical changes in language often emerge from contemporary variation, as some forms are dropped and others are retained. Over time, some of these variants become more prominent, while others fade away, as they do in a biological setting; others, of course, survive merely as vestiges.

Because change can emerge from variation, as some forms become more prevalent and others fade, Sapir hypothesized that contemporary stylistic preferences often provide a key to the ongoing process of drift.[12] What is more, he suggested that the drift often has a general "direction" that can be predicted, to some extent, by paying close attention to current trends in the language. Here even the most-subtle variation potentially provides a key to future changes. Consider, for instance, the grammatical marker *whom,* which is used in English to mark what is known as the accusative (or objective) form of an indefinite pronoun, as opposed to the contrasting form *who,* which marks the nominative (or subjective) form. In this sense, the word *whom* is parallel to the pronouns *them* and *him,* which also mark the objective forms. Yet Sapir noticed that most other interrogative forms, such as *how* and *when,* do not distinguish between the nominative and accusative cases—so, in this sense, the word *whom* is highly anomalous in the English language. The distinction is also absent with words such as *which.* Because of this anomaly, or absence of symmetry, Sapir predicted that *whom* would eventually drop out of the language altogether, as had so many other older forms before it. Even in the 1920s, the word *whom* was already in decline, but the fate of the word today has confirmed Sapir's suspicions. Significantly, the word *whom* survives today only among the most educated speakers, and then only in the most formal settings.

Clearly change hinges on variation.[13] But all of this begs the question: where does this variation itself originate? And what principles guide the selection of diverse speech forms? Even if we accept that variation is intrinsic to the social fabric of language, the process of selection remains mysterious. Of course, it had long been understood that what begins as a dialect often evolves into a separate language, given enough time to continue changing, but few theorists had any insight into what gave rise to these changes in the first place. Of course, not all changes are predictable; moreover, once separated, regional dialects continue to differentiate, eventually becoming separate languages. Whereas Sapir had begun to explore the formal mechanisms, with uncanny insight into the future directions the field would take, it is clear that there is more to the picture.

SOCIAL MOTIVATIONS FOR LANGUAGE CHANGE

Another factor contributing to language change is social identity. Simply put, the way one speaks often reflects one's social past, the point of origin for one's deeply ingrained, often unconscious habits of speech. Though first acquired by rote or by reflex within the setting of one's home community, over time these preferences become markers, or "indexes," of one's social past, within the context of the larger world of human relations. Here the connection between one's dialect and one's social background is largely an existential one, pointing from the accent one speaks to the home community, where these habits were acquired, much as a cloud of smoke points to a distant fire even if the fire itself is not clearly visible. Here the strong political overtones of one's accent or social dialect are viscerally felt every time a speaker opens his or her mouth, a process that most people have personally experienced when treading upon alien linguistic turf. Significantly, this variation often correlates with other markers of social status, such as one's home region, ethnicity, and religious background. Of course, none of this is surprising to most speakers, who constantly use dialects and accents to make unconscious judgments about the social status of fellow inter-locutors. Because language is so deeply tied to social identity in the public imagination, speakers often manipulate the form of their speech to actively construct a sense of solidarity with one group or distance from another.

Consider the well-known case of Martha's Vineyard, where a rivalry between social classes has recently given rise to a new "native accent" on this island community off the southern Massachusetts coast. Though the origins of the practice are unknown, longstanding residents of the island slowly began to centralize their vowels in selected word forms as early as the 1930s, when this distinctive trait was first documented. At first, words such as *house* were being pronounced with the tongue slightly higher in the mouth, where the new form could be represented as [həws] as opposed to the standard [haws].[14] Rapidly the form had spread to similar words such as *mouse* and *louse,* in which the vowel began to undergo similar changes. By the 1960s, this once-isolated trait had spread throughout much of the surrounding community, as the sociolinguist William Labov (1963) demonstrated when he first began to investigate the phenomenon on statistical grounds. Yet, surprisingly, speakers were far from uniform in their pronunciation. Instead, most speakers vacillated between the old standard forms and the new centralized forms, showing a variety of graded responses when asked to pronounce certain words, ranging from "no accent" to the strong centralization that was so characteristic of the emergent accent of the island community.

Though few speakers were consciously aware of the alternation, some old-timers noticed that youngsters often increased their centralization after returning home from college. Stimulated by this important insight, Labov probed the speakers' attitudes about their island homeland. Sure enough, the new accent correlated very strongly with the sense of membership within the community. Though the island had been overrun with tourists starting in the late 1940s, the change had reached few of these outsiders, who continued to speak their own imported accents. The new accent was strongest among those islanders who felt a deep sense of identification with the island as their "home-land," especially among those who planned to stay and follow in the footsteps of their parents, grandparents, and beyond. Though subtle, this new accent provided a sharp contrast with the mainland accent imported by the tourists or summer people, who spoke outside dialects without the centralization found solely on the island. Thus, a rivalry between rival social factions—the islanders and the summer people—was being played out with mere accents.

In fact, the spread of this new accent was strongly tied to the onslaught of the outsiders, the summer people, who arrived in droves following the postwar boom of the late 1940s. Though once restricted to a few isolated pockets during the 1930s, the new accent eventually reached the majority of the long-term residents. In this case, an incipient change was strongly correlated with other markers of social identity. Though the change was based on a variation that was already present in the community before the (mass) arrival of the summer people, long-term residents began to select forms that set them apart from the outsiders, which only cemented their own internal sense of group identity. Here the clash between the two factions provided a powerful motivation for condensing the linguistic differences between these rival social parties. Rather than producing a new dialect to collapse the distinction between these groups, the clash only solidified, or accentuated, the differences. In a highly charged political setting, even something as trivial as an accent often seals one's social fate.

Though Sapir had linked change to variation, Labov had demonstrated that the mysterious process of selection is often powerfully socially conditioned.[15] Of course, when a speaker selects one form over others, this choice often bears strong political implications within the surrounding community. However unconsciously speakers select a given form, the choices often speak as loud as the words themselves, by allowing the speaker to negotiate a sense of solidarity with a particular segment of society. Consider the popular story of *Pygmalion,* by George Bernard Shaw, in which a lower-class Cockney becomes a full-fledged lady by shedding her native accent.[16] Or consider the case of the so-called third gender of India: biological males place themselves into a new social category, one that is neither fully male nor fully female, partially by drawing on the semiotic resources of both male and female speech, to send different kinds of messages (Hall and O'Donovan 1996). Though the female forms typically signal solidarity within the third-gender (or *hijra*) community, male forms are often used to signal either distance from or contempt for the referent. On a grander scale, consider the gradual shift in women's speech over the past century and a half. At one time, in the nineteenth century, female speakers were under enormous pressures to "speak like a lady" in the English language. In recent years, following the various feminist movements of the twentieth century, the distinction has been relaxed, so that few young women today feel compelled to speak "like a lady." As the playing field has leveled, women have been granted more freedom to use non-standard forms, like their male counterparts. Here increasing social freedom has been followed by a corresponding linguistic freedom.

The connection between variation and social status is often a loose one, so that most speakers are familiar with at least a few of the varieties typically spoken in their vicinity. In the case of Martha's Vineyard, most islanders were capable of producing both types of forms. As for the *hijras* of India, both styles of speaking, those of males and those of females, still have their place within the community.

Outside Influences on Languages

Certainly, contact with outsiders can precipitate change in a community, as speakers strive to set themselves apart from their nearest neighbors. In the case of Martha's Vineyard, the encroachment of outsiders cemented the sense of local identity, so that the clash between the natives and the summer people eventually solidified the differences between the social dialects of these groups, most notably on the plane of sound. The *hijras* of India, in contrast, have fashioned a new style of speaking that is neither typically male nor typically female but draws on the semiotic resources of both identities to create something new. In the case of men and women in English, the two groups still find ways to set themselves apart linguistically. It is still the rare English-speaking male, for instance, who uses the words *mauve* and *lovely* in a sentence, while female speakers are less inclined to use nonstandard forms such as *runnin'* and *dude* than their male counterparts are. Here mere stylistic preferences serve as powerful markers of in-group status, allowing speakers to negotiate or actively construct a sense of gender identity.

Though contact often precipitates internal changes within a language, sometimes the variation itself enters from outside sources, such as neighboring dialects or languages. Oftentimes, variation simply enters a community from neighboring dialects. In this sense, remote communities often emulate speakers from major cultural centers, whose perceived prestige provides a motivation for adopting the outside forms. Consider the prestige that is still assigned to British English in American speech communities, where words such as *bonnet* and *pullover* continue to stand in as the highbrow words for "hood" or "sweater." Among sociolinguists, this process is aptly called *change from above,* because the new forms are thought, by speakers, to hold great social prestige. Yet even the speech of the lower classes can also carry considerable covert prestige, inspiring a similar kind of awe or reverence within an audience. In the United States, for instance, the ghetto talk of Harlem or Los Angeles is especially popular among the youth, acting as a badge of in-group status far outside the cities. Among sociolinguists, this contrasting type of process is known as *change from below*. Either way, local dialects are constantly influencing each other, and outside influences are crucial to the evolution of language.

Foreign languages also supply a rich source of variation. Most languages, in fact, show evidence of influence from foreign tongues, at a range of time depths. Yet for purely geographical reasons, some languages are fairly immune to the process. Included here are the remote island communities of the South Pacific and the extreme arctic habitats of Alaska and northern Canada, where the climate alone limits contact with the speakers of foreign languages. For the vast majority of the world's languages, however, contact with foreign tongues is a daily affair. In this sense, few languages are without their external influences. Indeed, most of the world's languages are utterly surrounded by speakers of foreign tongues, a pattern that has long been the norm on every continent.

Consider the English language, for instance. Since its arrival in the British Isles in the fifth and sixth centuries C.E., contact with foreigners is observable in nearly every aspect of this language, including its vocabulary, grammar, and, to some extent, phonology. The most obvious influences have occurred at the level of vocabulary, for English has borrowed massively from most of the languages it has encountered (Barfield 1985). Upon their arrival on the island, the Anglo-Saxons began to borrow profusely from Latin and Greek in the context of the early church, at which time scores of new words were introduced, such as *altar, creed, candle, clerk, deacon, hymn, martyr,* and *shrine.* In the ninth and tenth centuries, the Scandinavian Viking invaders brought new words such as *husband, knife,* and *leg.* Even more impressively, new pronouns—including *they, them, their,* and *she*—displaced old pronouns, as the Scandinavian invaders came to influence the very structure of English grammar. Later, with the arrival of the French following the Norman conquest of 1066, hundreds of new words began to enter the vocabulary, especially in the context of the court, where the French were dominant. Included here are words such as *prince, duke, baron, judge, attorney, court,* and *chancellor.* With the words also came new sounds, most of them entering through borrowings from French, such as the initial *v* in *veal* or the special *z* of *azure,* which Old English lacked as distinctive sound units. Still later, with colonial contact, came scores of new words including *moose, skunk,* and *chipmunk* (from Algonquian speakers) and *chocolate, avo-cado,* and *tomato* (from the Nahuatl-speaking Aztecs).

Even when speakers consciously strive to eliminate foreign elements from their speech, profound influences often proceed below the threshold of aware-ness. Consider modern French, for which a panel of experts meets each year to review the influx of foreign loanwords. Though these experts generally strive to remove English words from the vocabulary, they have not succeeded in altering the direction of the drift, which grants limited prestige to some new words that enter from the English-speaking world: the masses continue to use English terms such as *blue jeans* and *le weekend.* Or consider Tatar, a Turkic language spoken by about a million people in present-day Tatarstan. Starting in the 1930s, the former Soviet Republic sought to eliminate Arabic and Persian loanwords from the vocabulary, for two main reasons: to suppress Islamic religious influ-ences and to promote Russian cultural supremacy (Wertheim 2003). The tides have turned, and today nationalists are striving to restore the Arabic and Persian loanwords that had accumulated over the centuries, while eliminating any hint of Russian from their speech. The success has been varied. Purists, of course, make every effort to eliminate Russian influences from their speech, where they are actually aware of it, but many of the forms have now become almost indistin-guishable from the native stock, to all but specialists in the field of comparative linguistics. Despite the efforts of the Russians and the Tatar purists, the Tartar language continues to bear the stamp of its many foreign influences.

Multilingualism as a Source for Variation

Where variation enters a community from the outside, multilingual speakers are often at the vanguard of change, serving as bridges between two or more traditions. The speakers who introduced scores of French words into English following the Norman conquest of 1066 usually spoke both languages well enough to transmit this vocabulary, often in the context of the courts, for the ruling classes were increasingly Norman French. Today, French-based words continue to carry a certain prestige, especially in academic, judicial, or culinary settings (where they were first introduced), while native Anglo-Saxon equivalents continue to have a more earthy sound for most speakers. Compare the French-based words *pork, beef,* and *mutton* with the native Anglo-Saxon equivalents *swine, cow,* and *sheep.* Other native words were lost by the dozens, including *learning-knight,* which was replaced with *apprentice.* English is not unusual in this respect.

Throughout much of the human past, a certain amount of multilingualism has probably always been the norm, if the anthropological record provides any key. Even today, knowledge of several languages is still a survival skill for many throughout the world, where economic circumstances force speakers to learn more than one tongue for the purposes of work, trade, travel, or marriage. Often speakers get by on a limited command of a second language, which is restricted to a certain specialized social setting, including work, trade, or participation in the religious life. In much of the Muslim world, for instance, regional communities often continue to speak their native tongues, including indigenous languages such as Javanese or Turkish. Yet classical Arabic is the language of choice for reciting religious texts, including daily prayers from the Koran. In practical terms, this *diglossic* situation, in which the two languages serve different functions, has resulted in a number of loanwords from Arabic. Turkish, for instance, has absorbed thousands of Arabic loanwords over the centuries, in all spheres of learning from religion to the culinary arts.[17] Even in the United States, many immigrant groups remain fiercely multilingual despite strong pressures to shift to English. Consider the many millions of immigrants from the Spanish-speaking world, some of whom only grudgingly acquire English for the purpose of work or participation in mainstream society. Whereas Spanish is often reserved for in-group encounters, serving as the language of intimacy, English is used with the outside world, serving as the language of the mainstream society. Some speakers have begun to combine the two codes, English and Spanish, creating a form of speech known as "Spanglish," which draws on the semiotic resources of both languages.

The phenomenon is also well known among Americanists. Boas was one of the first scholars to draw attention to the presence of multilingualism in Native American societies, which he took as evidence that some "mixing" may have occurred among many of the languages (like Spanglish today), blurring the boundaries over the course of many thousands of years. In the introduction to his *Handbook of American Indian Languages,* Boas warns, "The possibility of such a transfer of sounds can not be denied. Among the American Indians, for instance—where intermarriage between individuals belonging to different tribes are frequent; where slave women raise their own and their masters' children; and where, owing to the small number of individuals constituting the tribe, individuals who have mastered several distinct languages are not by any means rare—ample opportunity is given for one language to exert its phonetic influence over another. Whether this explanation is adequate, is a question that remains to be decided by further historical studies" (1966[1911]:44).

This very proposition, namely, that a language could have a "mixed heritage," sparked the famous Sapir-Boas debate of early-twentieth-century linguistics. Sapir, for his part, is famous for taking the bold position that, under the majority of conditions, most languages continue to bear the stamp or hallmark of their source stock for enormous stretches of time, perhaps even for many thousands of years. Though this principle was widely accepted at relatively shallow time depths (say, on the order of a few thousand years), scholars had generally main-tained that languages quickly change beyond recognition over any greater span. Of course, if substantiated, Sapir's finding would be of tremendous interest to anthropologists and historians, who could use data on the world's linguistic stocks to reconstruct the human past beyond the reach of written documents. Taking a more conservative stance, Boas simply restated his position that, as a result of contact, any language could have a "mixed ancestry." For many, the position Boas espoused continued to cast doubt on any attempt to reconstruct protolanguages in North America or beyond.

We will return to this question in a moment. Obviously, the answer largely depends on how thoroughly the languages have been affected by contact. Yet, as Sarah Thomason and Terrence Kaufman (1988) have shown, there are many possibilities, ranging from "shift," where the original language is dropped, to "purism," where contact has a minimal effect. For now, suffice it to say that the century-old debate between Boas and Sapir was no longer at a standstill. Yes, languages could borrow words from other tongues or absorb structural features on nearly every front, yet in the majority of the cases the transmission was normal, preserving features of the original mother tongue spoken within a community over the generations. In this setting, Thomason and Kaufman con-vincingly demonstrated that even English is not a "mixed language," in a strict sense, but continues to bears witness to its Anglo-Saxon roots in its grammar, phonology, and vocabulary (1988:263–303).

In the case of northwestern California, the scale of the linguistic diversity brings this whole question into great relief. Because speakers often married mem-bers of neighboring linguistic groups, it is safe to assume that a certain amount of multilingualism was commonplace in the region before the arrival of Europeans, when the speech communities were still vibrant. During the early days of anthro-pology, fieldworkers such as Kroeber and Sapir frequently encountered bilingual consultants, such as Mary Marshall, who spoke both Hupa and Yurok.

Yet in northwestern California, a strong sense of village identity probably prevented such "mixing of tongues," so that a speaker such as Mary Marshall rarely had an opportunity to speak Yurok except when visiting her relatives in Yurok country. Lucy Thompson, who wrote a book about her experiences as a Yurok woman in the early twentieth century, reports that bilingualism was common at the religious dances, where neighboring groups often poured in from distant villages speaking utterly different languages (1916:104–105).[18] Scouts, she says, were posted to ensure that outsiders did not disturb the dances, especially those visitors who lacked sufficient knowledge of the Yurok language to follow the content of the ceremonies.

Types of Contact Situations

Though political considerations generally play a role, the social conditions in which speakers adopt more than one language are far from uniform. In many parts of the world today, speakers adopt the language of the dominant group for economic reasons, usually because it is required for work or participation in the larger society. In the most extreme cases, speakers adopt an entirely new language over the course of one or more generations. Formally known as "language shift," this process is currently affecting many thousands of languages throughout the world, whose speakers feel compelled to drop their ancestral tongues in favor of an international language, such as English, Chinese, Spanish, French, or Arabic. Here the pressures to assimilate the speech habits of a dominant group are considerable, as found by indigenous groups in most modern nation-states, including Native Americans and Aboriginal Australians.

In addition, new languages are sometimes born under circumstances of extreme domination. Where few of the speakers share a common tongue, the community as a whole often settles on a common "pidgin" language, whose vocabulary typically derives from the local prestige language. As children adopt this language as their native tongue, it quickly becomes a "creole" language, with an extensive vocabulary and grammar largely created by the new generation through a process of social interaction. Though many of the ancestral languages do not survive intact, traces of their vocabularies often live on in the language forged by the new generations.

Where the original language survives, it is often profoundly influenced by the speech of the dominant group, as Thomason and Kaufman demonstrated in their watershed book, *Language Contact, Creolization, and Genetic Linguistics* (1988). With casual contact, the influence is often restricted to vocabulary, with the possibility of a simultaneous, though slight, impact on structure. Consider the case of English, whose vocabulary was profoundly shaped by French following the Norman conquest, though with only minor adjustments to its grammar and phonology.[19] With more intense contact, the structure of a language may also be affected, a process that sometimes results in mixing, as the features of two or more languages are blended. Consider the case of Asia Minor Greek, where contact with the politically dominant Turkish has profoundly affected the structure of the language, from phonetics to morphology, syntax, and basic vocabulary. Because many speakers are bilingual, Greek speakers gradually began to introduce features of Turkish into their speech, probably below the threshold of consciousness at first. Under enormous pressures to assimilate, much of the original grammar is quickly replaced, leaving only the vocabulary of the ancestral speech community, as is the case with some English-speaking Gypsies, who retain thousands of native words from their ancestral language, Romani, while adopting a mostly English-based grammatical system.

In global terms, much of the world can be divided into two major types of zones, based on the degree of linguistic diversity that has developed in the area as a whole. As Johanna Nichols demonstrated in her study on large-scale patterns in the ecology of languages (1992), two predominant situations emerge as languages push into new territories, each one giving rise to a different type of zone.

One type of region, known as a "spread zone," consists of a small number of languages that extend out over a fairly broad area. Often the languages emerge from a common source stock, with a single prestige language that serves as the source for innovations at the periphery. Not infrequently, the prestige language is overturned with time. Among small-scale societies, spread zones often occur in arid climates, which are not capable of supporting an abundance of life, such as the steppes of Eurasia and the outback of central Australia. In North America, the Great Basin is a prime example of the phenomenon, with the Uto-Aztecan family spreading out over hundreds of miles. Overall, the scale of linguistic diversity remains quite low, when compared to other types of situations.

The other type of region, known as a "residual zone," sustains many language families while at the same time providing abundant opportunities for contact between unrelated languages. Residual zones typically occur in areas with high annual rainfall and rugged mountain terrain, which support an abundance of life. Here, new languages continue to pour in over the millennia, while the families often remain quite distinct despite the contact. Over time, linguistic diversity generally tends to increase, while these zones often lack a single lingua franca that serves as a common tongue for all of the groups. Instead, the languages are highly localized, which encourages multilingualism. Classic examples include the Caucasus Mountains of the Eurasian continent and island communities of Papua New Guinea, where linguistic diversity reaches epic proportion, with a strong tendency toward general societal multilingualism.[20] In this sense, northwestern California is a classic "residual zone," with speakers of over a dozen languages coming into frequent contact with one another on a daily basis.

Where relations are relatively egalitarian, speakers often adopt a second language for the purposes of trade, marriage, and participation in social events, such as religious rites. This type of situation is fairly common in small-scale societies, where many languages are spoken nearby, such as northwestern California, New Guinea, and the Amazon Basin. Here speakers often adopt a new language for the course of married life, speaking this new language after moving to the natal village of a spouse, while reverting to one's native tongue when visiting one's original home community. Of course, knowledge of several languages confers many other social benefits, including an increased ability to participate in trade, religion, and political life throughout the surrounding region. Over time, these languages often come to exert a profound influence on one another, as speakers introduce new elements of structure and meaning into the neighboring speech communities.

IDEOLOGICAL MOTIVATIONS FOR LINGUISTIC CHANGE

Ideological factors also play an important role in the evolution of languages. Provided that a certain amount of variation is present within a community, the speakers' attitudes toward these alterative forms can powerfully channel the direction of drift.[21] Consider the previously discussed loss of second-person singular forms in modern English, a change that was largely motivated by ideological considerations (Bauman 1983).[22] Until the eighteenth century, English speakers asserted familiarity with singular forms such as *thee, thy,* and *thou,* while the plural forms were reserved for addressing superiors. The pattern is common in Indo-European languages and continues today in virtually all of the remaining languages in the family. Yet for religious reasons, the Quakers and other religious groups objected strongly to the assertion of social hierarchy, which was being reinforced through linguistic practice every time an inferior addressed a superior with a plural form. Of course, Quakers held that ranking is blasphemous on religious grounds, a criticism that was also leveled against the hierarchy of the established church; the Quakers argued that all were equal in God's eyes. Soon these iconoclasts were addressing everyone with the familiar forms, which quickly threw the whole system into utter confusion. In response to this rapid and confusing shift in practice, the distinction was eventually collapsed. Soon the familiar forms were dropped from the English language entirely, surviving today only as colorful archaisms. Yet in most of the remaining languages of Europe, including French, Spanish, and German, the distinction survives, making English one of the few Indo-European languages to have taken the drastic measure of eliminating the familiar forms. Though the Quakers did not single-handedly eliminate the second-person familiar forms from the language, their ideological protest did set the entire process into motion. And, in the end, they succeeded.

Convergent Drift: Increasing Similarity as a Result of Contact

Ideologies also play an important role in contact situations, in which attitudes toward the alien linguistic material play a critical role in channeling the direction of drift. At one end of the spectrum, speakers freely adopt features of the neighboring languages, including everything from phonology and vocabulary to grammatical features, such as affixes or even syntax. This pattern is common where speakers pass between languages on a regular basis, especially where one's identity is not exclusively tied to a single tongue. At the opposite end of the spectrum, speakers attempt to minimize the impact of outside linguistic influences. Yet despite the potential impact of ideological factors, a certain amount of influence is inevitable when two or more languages come into contact. Even where speakers attempt to stop it, the influences often proceed below the threshold of consciousness.

In one extreme form, the distinction between the languages can be temporarily relaxed, producing a situation sometimes known as *syncretism,* where elements of both traditions are freely combined in some settings. Jane and Kenneth Hill (1986) personally observed such a phenomenon in the Malinche volcano region of central Mexico, where Mexicano speakers frequently intersperse their speech with Spanish, often quite liberally. Though most Mexicano speakers are bilingual, the community has not shifted completely to Spanish, because the two languages serve different functions. On ideological grounds, many speakers attribute "distance" to Spanish and "intimacy" to Mexicano. Yet today, speakers have increasingly opted to collapse the opposition in some settings, blending the resources of both traditions. As a result, Mexicano, which descends from classical Nahuatl, has absorbed a number of features from Spanish, including nouns, verb roots, grammatical affixes, and syntactic templates. In an effort to return to the original language (Nahuatl), some speakers have embarked on a well-meaning campaign to remove intrusive foreign elements from their speech, which, ironically, threatens what survives of Mexicano today, with its strong Spanish influence.

Where speakers pass between several languages on a daily basis, convergence often proceeds on a massive scale, especially where a significant segment of the local population is multilingual. Consider the village of Kupwar, in south-central India, where many villagers speak several languages in the course of daily life.[23] The majority of the villagers speak Kannada, a Dravidian language, which is strongly linked with followers of the Jain religion, most of whom hold land and work as craftsmen. Yet the village is also divided into many smaller groups, each with its own in-group language, which is usually spoken in the home or when interacting with other members of one's religion or profession. Muslim landowners, for instance, typically speak Urdu, an Indo-European language. In contrast, lower-class untouchables and landless laborers typically speak Marathi, another Indo-European language, in the home. Finally, low-status rope makers typically speak Telugu, another Dravidian language.

Though every villager speaks a particular language in the home, most males also speak a local lingua franca, known as Marathi, which is common in the surrounding areas, far outside of Kupwar village. In this sense, Kupwar village is highly diglossic, meaning that speakers regularly switch between languages as the situation demands. While Marathi is ideologically neutral for most speakers when interacting with the wider public, one's home language signals solidarity to other members of one's group—or exclusion to outsiders who are within earshot. As a result, most males speak at least two languages on a daily basis, since both languages are central to one's participation in the village social life and one's sense of membership in the wider community.

Though the languages serve different functions in the village, no particular ideology prevents the languages from influencing one another. Without a strong block on this type of interference, the languages have grown more similar over the centuries, under circumstances of intense multilingualism. Most strikingly, these neighboring languages have developed nearly identical syntactical structures in many settings, especially in the types of daily situations that arise when speakers regularly switch between the languages. Because the languages are so similar on the syntactic plane, sometimes only the content words set the languages apart, because the word order is otherwise identical.

Surprisingly, even loanwords are common; these frequently enter the other languages from Marathi. Semantically, all of the languages have developed an elaborate three-way contrast between the masculine, feminine, and neuter genders. Though the pattern is a common one in standard Kannada (a Dravidian tongue), most of the remaining Indo-European tongues of India, such as Urdu and Marathi, adhere to a two-way split between the masculine and feminine, with inanimate objects falling into one or the other of the categories. Among the Kupwar villagers, no particular area of grammar has been spared. In this highly multilingual speech community, contact has affected everything from phonology to grammar and vocabulary.

At the opposite end of the spectrum, speakers sometimes strive to eliminate foreign elements from their speech. Here social identity usually plays a role, as previously discussed in the cases of French and Tatar, who wished to distinguish themselves, respectively, from their English and Russian neighbors, while claiming their own sense of national identity. Certainly these purist efforts have had some effect, though they rarely block the outside influences completely.

For a more extreme case, consider the Vaupés region of the Amazon Basin, where neighboring villages strive to uphold a rule of linguistic exogamy.[24] The area is home to a considerable amount of linguistic diversity, including some twenty-five languages that fall into three recognized families. Here the ideal marriage joins members of two separate linguistic groups, so that each parent represents a different language, one's "father tongue" and "mother tongue." In this setting, the woman typically moves to the husband's village, where she primarily speaks her husband's language, except when interacting with speakers of her father's tongue, who may also be present in this new village. The children, in turn, grow up around several languages, including one's "mother tongue" and "father tongue" in addition to the languages imported by other mothers in the village, or the neighboring languages of the adjacent villages, which are often two hours to an entire day apart. For all of these reasons, most speakers are highly multilingual throughout the Vaupés region, with many speakers passing between four or five languages on a fairly regular basis. When interacting with neighbors, for instance, the two interlocutors generally exchange greetings in their respective father languages, before settling on a common tongue known equally well to both parties.

Mixing, however, is highly unacceptable among the residents of the Vaupés region, for the marriage rules provide a powerful reason for maintaining the boundaries between the languages. Here the "father language" acts as a marker of one's paternal line, meaning that one must seek a partner outside this group. For most males, this language is spoken throughout life as a badge of membership within one's natal village. For females, the "father language" marks one as a potential mate to those outside this group, while the "father language" of a woman's husband becomes a badge of membership within his village after marriage. In this setting, mixing languages potentially opens the door to incest, because the languages act to separate the family lines, which must be kept distinct for the sake of marriage. As a consequence, the languages have not, as a rule, converged toward a common type. In particular, borrowing has been minimized at the level of vocabulary and grammar. On the plane of sound, however, languages have grown more similar, possibly as the result of the rise of lingua francas following the period of European colonization.

Though the pattern is not as striking as for the previous examples, the Native languages of northwestern California have also grown more similar as a result of intense contact and widespread multilingualism. Unlike Kupwar village in India or the Malinche volcano region of central Mexico, the village communities of northwestern California practice virtually no code switching, while no lingua franca facilitated communication on a regionwide scale. As in the Vaupés region of the Amazon Basin, however, a powerful social ideology prevented mixing, though some influences continued below the threshold of consciousness.

Though of diverse origins, the Native languages of northwestern California have adopted many common semantic traits as a by-product of long-term contact. Many of these traits are strongly linked with the expression of cultural concepts, such as the geocentric spatial categories, which also hold considerable religious meaning throughout the region. Others, such as the tense systems and the haiku-like word structures, are tied to storytelling. Even the classificatory systems of the area's languages are often used to convey cultural concepts, as when the feature of animacy, for instance, is extended to various types of actors in the context of storytelling. Because these similarities are mostly restricted to the semantic plane (see O'Neill 2002:87–88), Lisa Conathan has recently dubbed the phenomenon *functional convergence,* an apt description for a process that has largely left the grammatical and phonological structures intact (2004b:180). That is, though phonological convergence is virtually absent throughout the region (see Guide to the Orthographies), the languages also remain distinct on the grammatical plane (O'Neill 2002).

The structural relationships between language, culture, and worldview, as envisioned under this model of "convergent drift," are diagrammed in figure

10.1. Here three languages from three distinct source stocks (L_1–L_3) have come to assume many common semantic traits within the setting of a common culture area (C_0).

In this figure, the symbol "L_{NWCA}" represents the common linguistic traits found throughout the Native languages of northwestern California, when taken as a whole. Despite the structural differences, many striking resemblances occur in nearly every area of conceptual patterning. When taken to its logical conclusion, this model predicts massive convergence on the linguistic and cultural fronts. If nothing else were happening, this type of diffusion would eventually level out the differences between the neighboring linguistic traditions, an outcome that actually emerges in some types of contact situations, as illustrated in the case of Kupwar village above. When applied to northwestern California, however, this model is simply unrealistic.

Divergent Drift: Accentuating Local Linguistic Boundaries

Contact between neighboring groups rarely results in complete convergence. More often, conflict, punctuated with outright warfare, is the all-too-common outcome, a familiar pattern that can be witnessed on every continent. Because languages often function as markers of social identity, contact sometimes accentuates local linguistic differences between neighboring groups. That is, rather than strictly promoting convergence, contact between neighboring social groups often provides a powerful motivation for asserting local differences. In this way, language often provides an unconscious mechanism for asserting the local sense of identity, as Labov demonstrated on the plane of sound with data from Martha's Vineyard.

The process also operates on the cultural plane. Consider the process of "schismogenesis," a concept that Gregory Bateson introduced to anthropologists in his classic ethnography *Naven* in 1936. While conducting a study on the Iatmul tribe of New Guinea, Bateson found that neighboring factions often took opposite sides on any potential schism. The process was a generative one, so that new social forms could actually be predicted by observing existing differences among the groups, which is rather like watching Democrats and Republicans take opposite sides on any new political debate in American society. Decades later, Claude Lévi-Strauss applied this approach to his own brand of structural analysis, finding that neighboring groups often invert common motifs that circulate within a region (1976:173). Though not one of Lévi-Strauss's examples, a classic case of this phenomenon can be observed in the Near East,

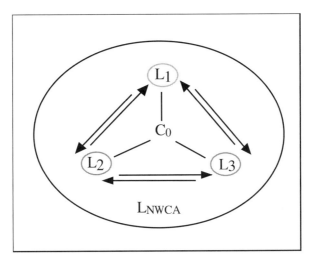

Figure 10.1. Convergent drift

where Jews and Muslims hold conflicting versions of the story of Abraham, the first monotheist. According to the Judeo-Christian telling of the story, God commands Abraham to sacrifice his beloved son, Isaac. The neighboring Muslim version, which emerged in the seventh century C.E., agrees in most details, except for the part about the beloved son, who is Ishmael rather than Isaac in the Islamic tradition. The process is a pervasive one in human relations, as I discuss in chapter 11.

When languages come into contact, speakers sometimes consciously strive to maintain the boundaries between their own traditions and those of their neighbors. This pattern is common where speakers identify with a single primary language, even if they speak another language in some situations.[25] In an extreme form, this tendency results in an ideology of purism, in which speakers seek to eliminate foreign elements from their speech, despite the fact that these efforts are rarely completely successful. The observations of Hill and Hill (1986) concerning Mexicano (previously discussed) provide one example. In the American Southwest, consider the case of the Arizona Tewas (Kroskity 1993), who have sought to keep their language separate from their Hopi-speaking neighbors, as well as the Spanish-speaking missionaries with whom they have had contact for centuries.

Even ecological considerations sometimes exert an influence on language ideologies. Based on her work with the Tohono O'odham of southern Arizona,

Jane Hill (2000) uncovered a fundamental correlation between the distribution of material resources and attitudes about neighboring linguistic varieties. Where local resources are fairly secure, speakers tend to maintain tight-knit social networks in the immediate area, while resisting external linguistic influences. Linguistic and material resources are managed in a similar fashion, so that speakers maintain strong ties within the group and have no strong need for outsiders. Where resources are widely distributed and less secure, speakers tend to cast a wider social network, while remaining more open to external linguistic influences, including the dialects of neighboring groups. Extending Hill's thesis, Conathan proposes a general ideology of localism, meaning that speakers are more likely to maintain sharp linguistic boundaries where their material resources are fairly secure (2004b:151), as in the abundant material world of Native northwestern California. Yet, as Conathan also remarks, beneath the surface the languages are free to borrow from one another, as is often the case on the semantic plane, where speakers may not be as conscious of the subtle influences in meaning alone.

In the village communities of Papua New Guinea, ideological factors have dramatically shaped the general linguistic situation. Clearly ecological factors have also played a role (see Nettle and Romaine 2000:80–90). Though the rainforest ecology supports a continuous harvest throughout much of the year, most of the island is broken up into fairly small political units, who form shifting alliances for the purposes of trade or warfare. However, the nature of the gardens largely prevents aggregation into larger groups, as does the constant threat of diseases such as malaria, which quickly reach epidemic proportions in larger populations. Because most of the languages are spoken by fewer than five thousand people, the island as a whole is home to some eight hundred or so languages. Many of the languages have fewer than five hundred speakers. In this setting, most of the languages are specific to a particular local group, such as a village or valley. Many languages are confined to a single village, though others span several. Because the groups live in close proximity to one another, multilingualism is common throughout the region, especially among males, who gain considerable prestige through mastering several languages, usually for the purpose of trade, politics, or war. Yet women often learn a neighboring language as well, especially when marrying a husband from an adjacent area.

Here a thorough knowledge of the village language is critical to maintaining social identity, because language is strongly tied to participation in the life of the surrounding community. Because multilingualism is so widespread, many

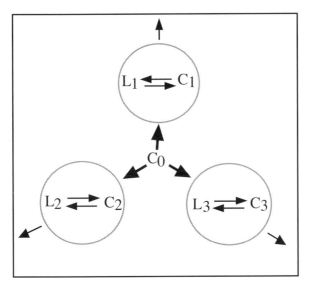

Figure 10.2. Divergent drift

of the languages have undergone convergence in most areas, with sweeping similarities rising up at nearly every level, from phonetics and syntax to vocabulary and grammatical patterning. Yet rather than completely leveling out the differences, pervasive multilingualism has in fact had the opposite effect. That is, speakers strive to maintain boundaries between the languages for the political purpose of maintaining separate social identities. As Gillian Sankoff notes, contact has actually "heightened consciousness of and pride in difference" (1980:10).

The structural relationships between language, culture, and worldview, as envisioned under this model of "divergent drift," are diagrammed in figure 10.2. Separated by many sharp linguistic boundaries, each speech community (L_1–L_3) begins to diverge on cultural and conceptual grounds as well (C_1–C_3), despite the fact that all of these groups have settled on many parallel cultural traits (C_0).

Certainly the languages of northwestern California have developed many common semantic traits as a by-product of ongoing social contact. Yet, like those of the village communities of Papua New Guinea, the languages of northwestern California also remain profoundly distinct on a number of fronts. Though the languages have adopted a shared geographical orientation to the spatial world, these directional concepts receive separate elaboration in each of the grammatical traditions, reaching great height in Karuk, where a profusion of fine-grained directional distinctions are marked on the verb in an oftentimes-obligatory fashion. At the same time, the religious meaning assigned to each directional region also varies from one language to the next. Though the area's grammars generally divide the past into a wide range of tense categories, each language puts forth a different classification of the realm of time as a whole, while ascribing different episodes to many of the common mythic periods shared by all. In terms of the tendency to classify objects according to features of shape or animacy, each grammatical system does so according to its own set of semantic criteria, ultimately projecting a unique classification onto the surrounding world of experience. And while the languages of the region tended to "name" things by attaching elaborate descriptive imagery, each tradition imports its own choices of interpretation into this richly symbolic semantic sphere; while the Hupas invest heavily in portraits of action, the Karuks place a greater emphasis on spatial imagery. Even in the realm of sound, the Hupa and Karuk languages each hold true to their own distinctive phonological plans, neither one ceding much to the pressures of assimilation (see Guide to the Orthographies). The Karuk language, for example, lacks glottalized stops altogether, though this feature is all but universal in the surrounding languages of the area. In a similar vein, Hupa is one of the most phonologically conservative of all the Athabaskan tongues, perhaps in part as a result of its unusually intense history of contact with speakers of foreign languages.[26]

11

Contact, Extremism, and Linguistic Relativity in Northwestern California

Propinquity breeds inversion.

Aram Yengoyan

Contact between neighboring social groups often heightens the local sense of identity. The phenomenon is a familiar one to anthropologists and linguists the world over, who often encounter people who have settled on similar cultural or linguistic practices, as a by-product of social contact. Yet as these neighboring social groups begin to settle on a common way of life, the parallel social institutions often undergo a process of inversion, as community members strive to maintain boundaries between their own traditions and those of the people who live nearby. Almost as soon as these neighboring peoples assimilate a common trait, minor departures usually begin to crop up at the local level, setting the groups apart on a symbolic, though often unconscious, basis.

Recall the story of Abraham, discussed in chapter 10, in which Jews and Christians both hold that Isaac was the favored son, while Muslims claim just the opposite, namely, that Ishmael occupied that role. Though set apart on this one key point, the two versions of the tale agree in many of the remaining details. Or consider the status of Coyote among the neighboring village communities of northwestern California. Among the Karuk villagers, Coyote plays a central role in creation lore as, ever teetering in suggested status between the sacred and the profane, he establishes many of the features of the present world, including some ceremonies and even the downward flow of the rivers. Yet among Hupa speakers, Coyote is often portrayed as a buffoon or troublemaker at the fringes of culture and is not usually elevated to the status of even a minor religious figure.

MARKING IDENTITY WITH LANGUAGE AND CULTURE

However profound or seemingly inconsequential, these subtle social differences play an absolutely crucial role in the construction of group identity, which is rarely fixed but instead negotiated according to the situation at hand.[1] Consider the Middle East, where throughout much of history, Jews, Muslims, and Christians have all regarded themselves as God's favorite people, based on ties to the legacy of Abraham, either through Isaac, Ishmael, or Christ. (That is, for Christians, the story of Abraham is echoed in the sacrifice of God's own son, in the person of Christ, who is also in the line of Isaac.) Here subtle variation in the common story makes all the difference, and bitter conflicts continue to erupt under the banner of each of these religions.

Similar processes are at work in northwestern California. For instance, the Hupas, Yuroks, and Karuks all agree that a series of heavens lay beyond the horizon and that there the great religious dances have been performed every night since the beginning of time. Yet these neighboring groups often hold nearly opposite conceptions about specifically where these dances are performed within the total conception of the universe. As I discuss in chapter 5, the Hupas place the White Deerskin Dance in the downstream spirit realm, while the Yuroks place the same dance in the spirit heaven upstream. In this sense, neighboring communities often take opposite sides on any potential schism, thereby claiming a monopoly on the truth.

By the same token, perceived similarities are often a cause for unification, sometimes giving rise to a more embracing sense of identity, based on wider parallels. Since the rise of Islam in the seventh century c.e., for instance, Muslims, Jews, and Christians have all regarded themselves as "fellow people of the book," meaning that all subscribe to similar tales popular in the Near East for millennia, as echoed in the Koran, the Torah, and the Bible. Yet the balance is always a precarious one, so that Muslims, Jews, and Christians have sometimes fought bloody wars against one another based on the assertion of separate identities, only later to align, at times, based on their perceived similarities. Despite the overwhelming parallels, including the belief in a common God, the differences among these groups remain vital to the sense of identity as Jews, Muslims, or Christians. Individuals, of course, must decide for themselves how to negotiate a sense of identification with their own religious community, which is often signaled in actual performance, through the use of various visible markers of group status, such as the yarmulke, the veil, or the cross. While public symbols of faith sometimes bring acceptance within the group, members of each community have also been martyred for openly displaying their beliefs.

Similar trends are at work in northwestern California, where many of the central themes run closely parallel throughout the region, such as the popular stories about the culture hero known as Across-the-Ocean-Widower. Like Abraham, this ancient figure institutes many of the sacred religious traditions of the region. Each group, for instance, sets his origin at the Yurok village of Kenek, at the center of the universe, where he spontaneously springs into existence and begins to prepare the world for the coming of humans. With him arise the prehuman spirit deities, alongside forces of good and evil. From there, the neighboring traditions begin to part ways. Recall the story of how death enters the world, discussed in chapter 1. All three of these language-speaking communities agree, for instance, that the original inhabitants of the earth did not experience death but that mortality was introduced only as a result of some primal misdeed, committed long ago. For the Hupas and the Karuks, Across-the-Ocean-Widower plays a central role in this episode, as one of the most powerful characters in the creation pantheon. For the Yuroks, the origin of death is attributed to other, more minor characters, including Mole and Jerusalem Cricket. Yet, in an even more significant way, each group set the origin of death in the homeland of one of the neighboring groups (though not in their own territory). Generally, the village communities preferred to emphasize their similarities, as part of a concerted effort to avoid interpersonal conflict on a daily basis. Offending a neighbor in a serious matter—even the most minor breaches of politeness—could be punished with stiff fines. Nevertheless, at times, wars broke out between the neighboring speech communities, with one famous one occurring between Hupa and Yurok villagers shortly before the California gold rush of 1849 (Sapir 2001:515–30).

Though there are many ways to signal membership in a community, language remains one of the most powerful markers of group identity found in human society, partly because of the strong ideological overtones associated with speaking in a particular fashion. In the Middle East, for instance, Arabic is strongly linked to Islam, as the sacred language of the Koran, in which, according to Muslims, the words of God are recorded exactly as delivered to Muhammad through the angel Gabriel in the seventh century c.e. Likewise, Hebrew is closely tied to the history of the Jewish people, especially the modern nation of Israel, where it is currently spoken by some six million souls, most of them practitioners of the Jewish faith. When it comes to speaking in a public setting, knowledge of either one of these tongues typically marks the speaker as a member of a particular religious community, either Muslim or Jewish, according to the form of one's speech. In the highly charged political environment of the Near East today, the consequences are often severe. Yet in actual practice, both parties sometimes adopt the language of their neighbors, either to express sympathy with their rivals or to gain provisional membership within the opposing society, as has been required of many Jews when living under Arab rule over the centuries. Similar processes are at work among in northwestern California, where language acts as an emblem of one's village identity.

Among the Native peoples of northwestern California, the village has always been the primary unit of analysis, as far as social identity is concerned. The typical village consisted of somewhere between fifty to slightly over a hundred people, who all lived together on a level area along a river, while sharing a series of neighboring households. Everything from daily subsistence activities to local political leadership revolved almost entirely around life in this home village. Additionally, geographical factors isolated the villages to the extent that a trip into alien linguistic turf often took a commitment of several days' time. Yet since the ideal marriage was to a partner from a distant village, in practice children often grew up in the company of bilingual parents.

Apart from a few bilingual areas between the adjacent territories of the neighboring speech communities, however, most of the villages were home to a single dominant language, which served as a powerful marker of in-group status. To speak this language outside of its homeland was generally considered improper, meaning that imported spouses generally needed to master the language of their new village before gaining full acceptance into this community. By the same token, knowledge of another language was an advantage when trading, seeking a marriage partner, or participating in religious ceremonies nearby. On ideological grounds, each village cherished the distinctiveness of its ancestral language, regarding this language as an artifact of creation stretching back to the beginning of time.[2] According to one report, collected by Edward Sapir, the neighboring peoples were warned not to bother Hupa speakers in times of war, because of the power this language was said to hold. This power stretched back to the time of creation, when the Hupa language was first established, presumably alongside other contrasting forms of speech.[3] Because strong religious and political ideologies were associated with the languages, maintaining distinctive linguistic traits served as something of a social imperative, allowing speakers to forge symbolic ties with their home community, while setting themselves apart from neighboring groups nearby. Because knowledge of the other languages was commonplace in traditional times, the task of setting one's language apart may have been all the easier to accomplish, however unconsciously all of this may have been carried out.

Certainly there is some evidence of linguistic convergence in northwestern California, as is to be expected, given that the Native peoples of this area gradually settled on a common way of life after arriving in the region along separate routes of migration. That is, in response to the same kinds of underlying cultural concerns, the languages have grown more similar in many respects. For instance, as Bright and Bright noted in their famous 1965 survey (see also Kroeber 1925:14–16), all of the languages have settled on a common geographical orientation to the spatial world, where mountains and rivers provide the basic frame of reference for establishing spatial relationships in the surrounding world.

Yet the convergence is far from absolute. On the contrary, in spite of the pressures to assimilate the habits and ways of neighboring peoples, the local speech communities remain profoundly distinct on a number of fronts. By and large, the potentially unifying effects of contact have not penetrated the structural kernel of any of the languages, as often happens in other contact situations, such as Kupwar village (Gumperz and Wilson 1971), where several unrelated languages have grown remarkably similar in a matter of mere centuries. Instead, despite the scale of social contact and societal multilingualism, the Native languages of northwestern California have maintained highly distinctive grammars, vocabularies, and even phonologies (O'Neill 2002), most likely as a marker of in-group identity within a village setting. Unlike Kupwar villagers, who usually have reasons to identify with two or more village languages, the Native peoples of California generally identified with only a single dominant language within the context of daily village life. Like Papua New Guinea or the Vaupés region of the Amazon Basin, northwestern California is home to a large number of indigenous speech communities that have striven to maintain their differences on the linguistic plane, though some amount of convergence has also taken place, largely below the threshold of consciousness.

If the languages of this region have resisted the convergence, it is not because the speakers were unfamiliar with the neighboring linguistic traditions. On the contrary, daily social circumstances afforded members of each group with frequent opportunities to interact with speakers of the neighboring languages. To begin, intermarriage was common (see Waterman and Kroeber

1934), so growing up around speakers of several languages was not unusual if one's parents came from far-away places, as they often did. Generally, the wife moved to her husband's village after marriage, so females were often especially multilingual. As a consequence, children often grew up in the presence of bilingual mothers, often being exposed to a number of unrelated languages even from their earliest days. Within the context of an extended family, a person's full circle of relations often encompassed several neighboring speech communities, providing frequent opportunities to visit and converse with speakers of many unrelated languages. In addition, trade relations were strong among the various speech communities. In this setting, for very practical reasons, many people were passively familiar with the neighboring dialects and languages, especially those of the smaller groups, such as the Chimarikos.[4] Many others were thoroughly multilingual, speaking several languages fluently throughout the course of life. Taken together, various factors provide a glimmer of insight into the social circumstances that may have conditioned some of the interinfluence among the area's languages.

The situation in northwestern California is similar to one that the Russian literary critic Mikhail Bakhtin (1981:61–68, 431) once described as "polyglossia,"[5] in which multiple languages come into association with a single national culture. Of course, there was no national culture in precontact northwestern California, but speakers of a dozen or so languages participated in an extensive culture area. The speakers of these languages adopted a common way of life while retaining many distinctive features of language, culture, and worldview at the village level.[6] Like Bakhtin's (1981:263–72, 291–94, 428) concept of "heteroglossia" in language and society, within which endless variation continues to emerge despite efforts to impose a uniform standard, this study suggests that the principle of "linguistic relativity" is inherent to the human condition, emerging from ongoing differences among neighboring social groups who strive to maintain their differences, often on an unconscious basis.

Convergence, through the traditional notion of diffusion, is certainly a predictable outcome of ongoing social interaction. However, there is also evidence that this long-term contact has, in some cases, produced increasing opposition, or extremism, among the groups of northwestern California, perhaps partly as a reflection of various reactions to a common theme or cultural element. Yet once set into motion, these differences also serve as markers of identity, setting the neighboring communities apart in often publicly accentuated ways.

The results of this contact are rife with implications for the principle of linguistic relativity, whereby the speakers of different languages are led to different observations about the world around them in accordance with conceptual patterns of their grammar or vocabulary. Of course, where local differences persist, the principle of linguistic relativity retains a viable influence, reflecting differences of worldview that have been built up over many generations within the conceptual structure of the language. And where convergence is evident, the speakers have often clearly settled on a common worldview or outlook on life.

VOCABULARY

Even the most common objects of experience are often named for those familiar roles they have long played in the storytelling traditions of an area's people (see chapter 9). In this sense, even the most basic noun tends to capture an entire episode of outstanding cultural significance through allusion. Yet despite the cultural parallels and the scale of the multilingualism, each group tends to maintain its own distinctive name for many objects of experience, as with the dipper, or water ouzel, which the Hupas refer to as "the one who copulates with stones," and the Karuks call "the little one who eats river moss." As discussed elsewhere, both names allude to culminating scenes from a creation story told in markedly different ways among the two speech communities.

The bulk of the imagery is highly language specific. That is, the evidence for borrowing among neighboring languages is minimal, so that neither the sound patterns nor the associated word meanings run especially parallel as one passes from one speech community to the next.

Many nouns are based on a familiar scene of action that must be deciphered in cultural terms. The names assigned to animals, for instance, often reflect careful attention to the natural histories of these creatures, and even the names of plants are sometimes based on scenes from everyday life, as with the flower that the Karuks know as "the little one who sees spring salmon coming." Some of the most gripping nouns of action are those that depict a poignant scene from the local oral traditions, effectively transferring an image from folklore to everyday vocabulary: recall the Yurok name for the screech owl, known as "the one who whistles," based on its status as a harbinger of misfortune.

These nouns of action are especially abundant in the vocabulary of the Hupa language, outstripping not only the neighboring Yurok and Karuk languages but also many of the related tongues in the Athabaskan family.[7] Consider the following basic Athabaskan noun stems that have gradually been replaced with explicit portraits of action in Hupa, as with "rain," discussed in chapter 2. To start, consider the old noun root *ta·,* the basic word for "water" in many Athabaskan languages. Though no longer attested as a free form in modern Hupa, the root survives in compound forms such as *ta·sił* 'steam' or as a directional modifier in verbs such as *tahč'isyay,* which means "one being came out of the water." The Hupa have replaced this old noun with the word *taʔna·n,* which literally refers to "liquid that one slopes (to drink)." Even the old Athabaskan word for an "arm," which can be reconstructed as **ɢan,*[8] has been replaced with the expression *xokʸa·ŋʔay,* a noun of action that literally refers to that part of the body "which extends away from (a person)." Or consider the old root for "people," especially fellow Athabaskan speakers, which can be reconstructed as **dine.*[9] In Hupa, this term has been replaced with an explicit noun of action, *kʸiwinyaʔn-ya·n,* which literally refers to the "ones who eat what is eaten (acorns)." Even today, a noun of action is gradually supplanting the general Athabaskan word for a "pet," so that few Hupa speakers use the word *łiŋʔ* when speaking of a dog, as other Athabaskans do. Instead, the Hupas prefer the word *no·kʸine·yo·d,* which literally refers to an animal "that hunts things down."

Many nouns also contain explicit references to the surrounding geography, based on images that generally must be deciphered in terms of familiar cultural associations. The names assigned to animals, for instance, are often based on the geographical site most intimately connected with its presence, such as a familiar hunting ground or nesting site. Recall the Hupa name for the great blue heron, "the one at the riffles." Other names depict scenes from local oral traditions, as with the race of giants known among the Karuks as "the people of the mountains."

Spatial imagery is especially abundant in Karuk, as illustrated in the names for the goldfinch, "the one that shoots down from upstream," and the otter, "that one downhill" (see chapter 9). Similarly, the war dance called *káhʔiravárak* in Karuk literally translates as "upriver world renewal ceremony (performed while) coming down from upriver." Even the occasional personal name features a geographical reference in Karuk, including Itkaratiháyav, which literally translates as "good looking into the river."

Given that these neighboring speech communities have long inhabited similar natural and social worlds, the diversity of imagery in their vocabularies is surprising. Rather than promoting uniformity, this constant interaction among the neighboring speech communities appears to have heightened the local sense of creativity. To speak a particular language, in this setting, is to share in a series of associations cast from the vocabulary of any of the languages out into the experience of the surrounding world.

CLASSIFICATION

As established in chapter 8, specialized systems of classification are especially elaborate in many of the Native languages of northwestern California, reaching their high point in the semantic structures of Hupa and Yurok, with some parallel developments in neighboring Karuk.[10] However, the language-specific systems of classification remain highly distinctive despite centuries of contact and multilingualism.

The Yurok classifier system far outstrips the neighboring traditions of the Hupa and Karuk languages in terms of the total number of categories,[11] most of which are based on features of either shape or animacy (see figure 8.1).

Though parallels certainly exist elsewhere in the Algic stock (see Conathan 2004a), the Yurok language has developed one of the most elaborate classifier systems in the entire group, one that is rivaled only by neighboring Wiyot, another member of the family and also situated in northwestern California.[12] In many of the Algonquian languages, for instance, a small series of productive medials can be used to place either the subject or the object of the verb within a particular conceptual class, often based on features of shape or substance. Consider the classificatory medial -aaskw- of the Plains Cree language, which refers to wood or wooden solids (see Wolfart 1996:427). In intransitive forms such as *kinwaaskosiw,* which loosely translates as "one being (here a tree) is long," the reference is to the subject, in this case a tall tree. Yet in transitive forms such as *niimaaskweew,* which loosely translates as "he takes along (wooden) weapons," the reference is to the object, here a weapon made of wood. Similar medials exist for other classes of objects, including -aapisk-, which refers to solids with stonelike properties, and -aapeek-, which refers to ropelike referents. Though similar in spirit to the classifiers of the Yurok language by virtue of the fact that classification sometimes proceeds on the basis of shape, these categories need not be considered by speakers of Plains Cree when counting or when attributing inherent characteristics to an object, such as size, color, or texture. In the case of Yurok, therefore, a characteristic Algic trait has been carried to an unusual extreme.

Likewise, in counting, the Yurok classifier system is especially elaborate, having developed a specialized series of classifiers for measuring units of time, length, wealth, and even some significant forms of property, such as boats and houses.[13] One classifier, for instance, allows the speaker to measure the length of a dentalium shell by comparing it to the size of a human finger joint.[14] Here the specialized classifier -epir can be added to a numerical base to form a special series of numbers for counting the size and value of dentalium shells, one of the primary measures of wealth in the traditional world of Native northwestern California. If the shell spans the length of a single finger joint, the numeral takes the form of *kohtepir,* which signals a measure of "one finger joint." Larger shells warrant the use of higher numbers, including *na?apir* 'two finger joints' and *nahksepir* 'three finger joints'. Because shells rarely grow any longer, the series ends with the span of three finger joints. Another series of classifiers is reserved for counting boats or houses, two of the primary forms of property in the traditional world of Native northwestern California. Here the classifier *-e?li* signals that one is counting houses, while the classifier *-ey* specifies that the reference is to boats. When speaking of "three boats," for instance, one uses the numeral *nahksey,* while the form shifts to *nahkse?li* when speaking of "three houses." Finally, one specialized classifier is devoted to counting time by the number of days, allowing the speaker, for instance, to refer to a span of "three days" with the specialized numerical form *nahksemoył.* Larger units of time are, however, counted without the use of specialized classifiers. Months, for instance, are placed in the "round object" class, perhaps because the most salient marker of this interval—namely, the moon—has a circular profile. When speaking of a span of a "single month," for instance, one says *kohtoh hegor,* where the numerical base *koh(t)-* combines with the classifier *-oh* to signal that the reference is to the class of round objects.

In contrast to Yurok, the Hupa classification system, like those of other Athabaskan languages, is composed of a series of specialized verb forms that specify the motion or position of certain classes of objects. These categories (see figure 8.3) run closely parallel to those found in other languages in the Athabaskan family, such as Apache of the American Southwest and Slave of northwestern Canada.

In contrast to the situation in Yurok, where motion is of no particular concern, speakers of Athabaskan languages are generally forced to consider the spatial and temporal dynamics of a scene when placing an object within a particular category in the classificatory system (cf. Witherspoon 1971 and Basso

1990:1–14). Consider the Hupa verb *ya·ʔatiW,* where the final unit in the sequence, the momentaneous stem *-tiW,* signals the presence of a long object over a relatively short span of time while the initial element (*ya·=*) specifies the directional bearing of the event, specifically, a course that reaches up into the air. This expression, as a unit, translates as "one person raises a long object upward toward the sky." Similar structures exist in virtually all of the Athabaskan languages, such as the parallel Slave construction *nágoįtį,*[15] where the classificatory stem *-tį* signals the presence of a living being while the directional marker *ná-* specifies that the event bears down toward the ground. This particular expression literally translates as "it moved a living being down," though a fairer English translation is "it gave birth." For further comparison, consider the parallel Chiricahua Apache construction *hàyó·ʔą́,*[16] where the classificatory stem *-ʔą́* signals the presence of a round object, while the directional marker *ha-* specifies that the motion heads "out of an enclosed space." This expression literally translates as "one being took out a round object," though in this context the reference is to a stone axe.

When it comes to linguistic classification, the Hupas have preserved the hallmark traits of the Athabaskan classificatory system without developing structural characteristics parallel to those of the neighboring languages, such as the numerical classifiers or descriptive verbs of neighboring Yurok.[17] In this sense, the Hupa language is curiously conservative. Unlike Kupwar village in India, where four languages from two different families have adopted a similar scheme of classification over a matter of mere centuries, the Hupa language has resisted convergence on the plane of grammatical classification despite the scale of the social contact and multilingualism.

For speakers of Karuk, in stark contrast to both Hupa and Yurok, classification is not especially elaborate in any single area of the language. However, classificatory elements are scattered throughout the structure of the Karuk language (see figures 8.4 and 8.5). On functional grounds, these categories loosely resemble some of the classificatory systems of Hupa and Yurok, though without the same distribution of categories. More significantly, these categories are not obligatory in Karuk as they are in Hupa and Yurok.

As discussed in chapter 8, even when similar conceptual categories appear in several of the languages, such as the categories for "round" and "long" objects, the criteria for membership within a particular class and the metaphorical extensions of a concept vary widely throughout the area's languages. Thus, although a special category for "living beings" is present in many of the area's languages, each language holds different criteria for membership in this class. Among Hupa speakers, the capacity for self-propelled motion is generally required for animacy, representing another instantiation of the general Athabaskan focus on motion or action. Unlike the situation in Karuk, in which such objects as baskets and stars (which were once animate, in creation times) are classified as animate, in Hupa such objects are not considered living beings—although Hupa speakers extend the category of animacy to objects fashioned from the flesh. Among Yurok speakers, the realm of the animate is split into human and nonhuman actors, whereas Karuk speakers place animals and humans together in the class of "living things," often without explicit attention to the underlying capacity for motion.

Many of the languages also feature a specialized category for "round things" (as discussed in chapter 8), a concept that makes its appearance in many unrelated classificatory systems throughout the planet, with a possible innate basis in panhuman psychological considerations. Whereas the Yurok category "round objects" generally refers to disc-shaped bodies in two dimensions, the similar category among Hupa speakers usually refers to spherical bodies, although metaphorically the reference is sometimes extended to manipulation of song, dance, or tradition.

Though common in languages with classificatory systems, specialized categories for "long" or "straight" things have also emerged among many of the Native languages of northwestern California. As with other categories, the criteria for membership in this class are often highly language specific. For Yurok speakers, legs, ferns, and bridges are often included in the special category for "straight" objects. Trees can also be placed in the class of "long" or "straight" objects in the Yurok and Karuk languages, although for Hupa speakers, trees are generally placed in the "filled container" category, possibly because they contain sap. Among Hupas and Karuks alike, to place a person in the "long object" category suggests a certain stiffness or lifeless immobility. Hupa speakers extend the category to situations that loosely involve the manipulation of a long object, either in motion or at rest.

Less widespread are special categories for "filled containers" (which Hupa and Karuk speakers extend metaphorically beyond the baskets that are the prototype for the category) and "ropelike objects" (which Yurok speakers use to categorize snakes and worms as well as streams, but Hupa speakers extend to any series of objects joined together, including waves, while excluding snakes and worms).

STORYTELLING AND THE REALM OF TIME

As I establish in Part III, the Native peoples of northwestern California have adopted a common framework of cosmology, wherein all events in the universe are situated within a parallel series of mythic epochs. In the Native conception of the universe, the world as we know it was set into motion perhaps only a handful of generations ago, when a former race of spirit deities sprang spontaneously into existence. Almost as soon as life had begun, a pantheon of myth figures began to embark on those journeys, missions, and often ironic misdeeds that would soon shape the world to come. A flood followed, and there arose a sense that a new type of creature, the human being, was soon to arrive within this world. At this crucial turning point in the history of life on earth, these ancient myth figures set out to prepare the world for the onslaught of a portentous new era, whose events, by and large, they could only partially foresee. An urgent sense of impending doom, perhaps, prodded them to institute the dances and rites that are still practiced today among the Native peoples of the region, with a lineage that reaches back to these most ancient moments in the creation.

Tense Marking and Oral Literature

Though the Native peoples of northwestern California have settled on a common sense of the mythic past, the linguistic representation of time often shifts quite dramatically as one passes from one community to the next. In many of the languages, tense marking plays an important role in storytelling, by allowing the narrator to set a scene in a well-defined period in either the past, the present, or the future. Some of these tense-based categories run loosely parallel throughout the region. Consider the concept of a "future tense," for instance, which is evident in the many languages that have developed a special grammatical distinction between a "near" and "distant" future. Or consider the concept of a "locative" past, which makes its uncanny appearance in both the Hupa and Yurok languages. Yet other categories are restricted in distribution to a single tradition, without occurring elsewhere in the region. Consider the concept of a "distal future," carried out at another location, which finds expression in only a small handful of languages throughout the world, including the Yurok language of northwestern California. Or consider the Karuk marker of the "ancient past," in which a single suffix can be attached to any verb to place the scene in question in the creation times.

Many of these tense-based categories appear to have entered the area's languages fairly recently, perhaps, in part, under pressure to express concepts from the local oral traditions. Structurally speaking, many of these tense markers occur as separate syntactic "particles" that only loosely accompany the verbs they modify, without being more fully incorporated into the verb paradigm as specialized grammatical elements marked directly on the verb itself. Generally, the past is far more heavily subdivided than the future, perhaps partially because the future receives less attention in the local oral traditions, where the focus is on the ancient times of the creation.

Though the Hokan tongues typically express tense-based distinctions with specialized grammatical suffixes, the Karuk language has developed a series of preverbal particles, which loosely resemble the tense markers of neighboring Yurok (Conathan 2004b:70–71). Consider, for instance, the preverbal particle *mit(a),* which marks the "remote past" for Karuk speakers when the reference is to events that are greatly removed from the living present. Or consider the related preverbal particle *ʔip(a),* which marks the "near past" in Karuk when the reference is to an event of some immediacy that just took place in the evolving context of the storyline. Because preverbal particles are common among the Algic tongues and rare among the remaining members of the Hokan stock, the Karuk language may have developed these particles under the influence of the neighboring Yurok language. Though similar in terms of general structure, however, few of the Karuk tense markers exactly correspond to categories found in the neighboring Yurok tense system. That is, rather than borrowing the tense-based concepts wholesale, Karuk speakers appear to have adopted the general idea from their Algic neighbors, developing the trait in language-specific ways.

Similarly, a number of specialized tense categories have developed in the Hupa language, though this is not a characteristic Athabaskan trait. In most Athabaskan languages, the status of an event relative to some fixed point in time, such as the living "present," is usually a matter of secondary importance, despite the intensive focus on the internal dynamics of temporal processes. Where tense is expressed in the Athabaskan tongues, it is usually accomplished periphrastically, with the help of auxiliary verb phrases. In northwestern California and southern Oregon, however, Athabaskan speakers have developed a series of specialized tense markers that occur as enclitic elements immediately following the verb. One series of markers, for instance, derive from a general metaphor of spatial extension, in which the future is placed at an imaginary "distance" from the living present. While the grammatical marker *-teˑ* signals the "general future" for Hupa speakers, the related form *-teˑl* signals a "near future" that is close at hand. Both tense markers are related to the verb prefix *te·-,* which signals that an event moves "off" or "along" a goal-oriented path in a roughly linear fashion. Both markers are related to the verb *ni-te·l,* meaning "to be wide." Because cognate future forms occur in the Tututni language of southern Oregon and Mattole of the northwestern California coast, it is possible that this feature evolved in the context of the general regional culture complex. Though of uncertain derivation, a special marker of the "remote" past has also been developed in the Hupa language. Because a similar category occurs in the Karuk language, the Hupa may have developed this special "remote past" marker under the influence of Karuk speech, although the two markers in no way resemble each other on the plane of sound alone.

Though common in northwestern California, temporal marking reaches its local high point in the grammatical structure of the Yurok language, in which many distinct markers exist for the purpose of situating a scene within a particular time period (see figure 6.7). Some of these resemble markers found elsewhere in the Algic stock, especially among the Algonquian languages (though even in the context of its parent stock, Yurok preverbal particles reach an unusual extreme).[18]

Many of the categories are concerned with the past, as is the case in the neighboring Hupa and Karuk languages. One category, the "general past," refers to former conditions that once existed, while another marker, the "locative past," situates an event at a given place whose time frame is already understood by the audience. The remaining categories are unparalleled in the Hupa and Karuk languages: signaling that an element of motion is involved, providing information about the time schedule on which an event unfolds, placing focus on the earliest phases of activity, and so forth, even to the point of posing a past scenario that never existed. Several markers in this Yurok system of temporal marking also refer explicitly to the present, whereas in the neighboring traditions of the Hupa and Karuk speakers, the temporal ground of the current moment goes unmarked, whether real or imaginary.

As in the neighboring Hupa and Karuk traditions, the future receives less attention than the past in the Yurok tense system. One category, the "general future," is associated with statements of expectation. Parallel markers also exist in the Hupa and Karuk languages. Again as in Hupa, another Yurok tense category, the "near future," is primarily concerned with events that are close at hand. The remaining categories are without parallel in the neighboring languages.

Comparative Semantics and Linguistic Relativity

Though each language is capable of evoking the same basic periods in the common folklore and mythology of the region, the languages could hardly be more diverse in their representations of these parallel episodes in the history of the world. For Karuk speakers, the era of creation can be invoked with a single suffix, one that can be applied to any form in the story line. Yet in Karuk creation stories, most forms remain relatively timeless in scope, with bounded forms only occasionally cropping up to place selected scenes squarely in the ancient past. Similarly, most forms in Hupa narrative remain "tenseless." The Hupa storyteller, however, has no recourse to a special marker of the ancient past but instead usually invokes the era of the creation by mentioning the deeds that took place during this time. As is the case in the neighboring Hupa and Karuk traditions, most forms in Yurok creation lore remain unrestricted in temporal scope. Yet some constructions in Yurok narrative are specifically marked to suggest events that continue to exert a lasting effect on the living present.

During the ancient era of creation, the myth figures frequently speculated about the human world that was soon to emerge in the future. In Karuk creation stories, predictions about the "distant future" of the present era are often reported with future forms that also feature the durative marker -*tih*. In Yurok creation stories, in contrast, ancient events with lasting implications are generally stated with intensive constructions also marked for future reoccurrence. This combination of categories suggests an act that began in the past though it would continue into the distant future, reaching from the myth times into the living present. In contrast, Hupa storytellers often cast these past pronouncements in the "near future," granting a certain immediacy to the predictions made by the characters in the story. From another perspective, these past pronouncements imply that the mythic past is not far removed from the present world. Among Hupa storytellers, other pronouncements are stated with progressive forms. Sometimes these are placed in the general future, suggesting a continuous stream of activity that is maintained from the most ancient times onward.

Sometimes a key episode recounted in oral literature represents a crucial turning point in the history of life on earth. Here the deed performed by this figure during the ancient past becomes its hallmark trait or defining characteristic for all time thereafter. Karuk storytellers often use durative markers to extend a scene from the ancient past into the living present, such that the activity in question can still be witnessed in the world around us today. When

Coyote, for instance, proclaims that the rivers ought to flow downstream, it is with a durative form that Coyote wills this state of affairs onto the world. Hupa storytellers mark similar episodes with customary forms, in which the reference is to the recurrence of an event over a long time, gaining a timeless validity as it continues to recur, as with the lunar eclipse described in chapter 7. Yurok storytellers report similar episodes with intensive forms, which stress the repeated nature of an act that is carried forth from the ancient times, as when Dove pledges to mourn the loss of his grandfather.

THE SPATIAL WORLD

As established in Part II, the speakers of the Hupa, Yurok, and Karuk languages have all settled on a common geographical orientation to the surrounding spatial world. In each of these languages, mountains and rivers act as the primary points of reference when establishing spatial relationships in the surrounding world of experience, rooting spatial thought, in a fundamental way, in these pervasive features of the geography.

Refinement of Geographical Expression

This geographical orientation reaches its high point in the structure of the Karuk language, in which directional concepts such as "upriver" and "downriver" achieve unusual precedence in everyday vocabulary and obligatory grammatical patterning. To some extent, the Karuk language shares this intensive focus on directional categories with the remaining members of the Hokan stock, especially those of northern California. A case in point is the Yana language of northeastern California, in which eight distinct grammatical markers distinguish motion "to" and "from" the points of the compass (Sapir 1949:552). Like Karuk, the Yana language forces speakers to distinguish between the source and goal of motion when talking about events that pass along the surface of the earth. Or consider the neighboring Atsugewi of northeastern California, which has developed over fifty grammatical affixes for the purpose of specifying abstract spatial relationships, none of which is geographical in nature (Talmy 1972:410–27). Closer to home, consider the Shasta language of northwestern California, in which a smaller inventory of grammatical affixes mark directional features such as "upstream" or "uphill" (Silver 1966:144–52). Whether these Hokan languages are genetically related or have merely come to share these traits as a by-product of long-term contact in the early prehistory of Native California, the Karuk

language is extreme even in this context. Nowhere is the geographical refinement of the Karuk language equaled, either in California as a whole or among
the Hupa and Yurok languages.

In the semantic structure of the Karuk verb, each geographical region is
carved into two contrasting frames, one heading toward this region as a goal and
another returning from this region as a source (see figure 4.1). Each potential
path is marked with a separate directional suffix, representing a shift in perspective that every speaker must make in order to speak the language properly.
Consequently, the Karuk speaker is obliged to distinguish four distinct directional paths from any given point of reference along a mountain or river. To speak
the language properly, the Karuk speaker must always indicate whether a body
is approaching or moving away from any point of reference the speaker might
wish to establish along a mountainside or river current. In addition, the Karuk
language routinely distinguishes three degrees of relative distance with respect to
the surrounding countryside, ranging from "a little way" to "quite some distance"
(see table 4.1). For Karuk speakers, these adverbs complement the categories
marked directly on the verb itself, completing the reference by signaling the relative distance. Moreover, in Karuk storytelling or conversation, a single scene is
often surveyed from two contrasting perspectives at the same time. While the
verb signals the source region, an adverb specifies the goal of the event.

Though possible by means of circumlocution elsewhere in the region,
such refinement of geographical reference is not a strict grammatical requirement in any of the remaining languages. Nor do these fine-grained distinctions
achieve the same kind of frequency in oral literature or daily communicative
practices once one ventures outside of Karuk country. For instance, in the
Hupa and Yurok languages these geographical concepts are only moderately
woven into the semantic structure of the verb paradigm. As a result, Hupa
and Yurok speakers are not obliged to observe many of the subtle distinctions
required of the Karuk speaker on an obligatory, grammatical basis. Nor is the
distinction between the source and goal of motion as systematic as it is in the
Karuk language, though such distinctions are available elsewhere in the language, through a process of circumlocution. Consider the Yurok language, for
instance, in which only a handful of stem internal semantic elements signal
the direction of motion along mountains and rivers. Few of these markers are
productive, meaning that directional marking is rarely critical to the construction of well-formed verbs. Instead, most of these markers occur only in fixed,

Table 11.1. Geographical adverbs of the Hupa and Yurok languages

	Hupa	Yurok
Uphill	*yidaɢ*	*heɬkew, heɬkik(s)*
Downhill	*yice'n*	*'oslook^w*
Upstream	*yinaɢ*	*pecku, pecow, pecu(s), hipec, pecik*
Downstream	*yide'*	*pulekuk, pulek^w, pulik*

Source: Robins 1958:134–36 (for Yurok data).

historically derived combinations, while rarely entering into novel verb formations. Similarly, Hupa speakers can call on several prefixes that specify motion along the slopes of mountains and, by extension, several other types of inclines. Yet river-based directional concepts are only partially woven into the structure of the verb system.

In contrast to the situation in Karuk, Hupa and Yurok speakers are not obliged to state the distance of a directional course along a watercourse or mountain slope. Among Hupa speakers, for instance, spatial adverbs merely indicate the bearing of an event, without any division into trajectories that head either "near" or "far" into the surrounding countryside. Similarly, the geographical adverbs of the Yurok language show no systematic division into terms that specify the extent of a path, with the possible exception of the riparian sphere, where several uncertain divisions at least seem possible. The geographical adverbs of the Hupa and Yurok languages are given in table 11.1.

Unlike their Karuk neighbors, Hupa and Yurok speakers rarely state both the source and goal of motion in a single phrase or construction. That is, double directional expressions are exceedingly rare in Hupa and Yurok speech, despite their prevalence in Karuk. Instead, the direction of motion is generally stated in only one grammatical system at a time, usually indicating only the general bearing of the event. Among Yurok speakers, double directional constructions are almost completely absent, because geographical elements are usually expressed by adverbs alone and are rarely marked by stem internal elements at the same time. Hupa speakers, in contrast, make sparing use of this possibility, usually using an adverb or an affix to state directional bearing.

Each language also restricts the types of events that can be modified to express multiple directional paths. Extended to the widest range of events among Karuk speakers, the possibilities for directional marking are severely restricted in Hupa, in which most verbs fall into discrete grammatical classes, with only a small fraction of these permitting modification for directional bearing. Directional marking is even less pervasive in Yurok, in which geographical categories are rarely critical to the construction of well-formed verbs. Many verbs do accept directional modification on an optional basis, and there is even evidence that a few directional markers have been incorporated into the verb complex to function as geographical directional markers. Consider, for instance, the stem-initial element *sloy-*, which sometimes signals motion that bears "downhill." For instance, when a person is walking down a slope, one might say, *sloyecok̓*, a form that loosely translates as "I go downhill." In its original sense, the initial *sloy-* carried the more abstract sense of "sliding under an external force, such as gravity," as with the verb *sloytketoy* 'to sweep' or the related noun form *sloytketo?* 'brush', where *sloy-* contributes the sense that the broom slides across a surface. In contrast to the neighboring languages, geographical marking is only loosely woven into the Yurok verbal complex, suggesting a recent arrival in the rugged mountain terrain of northwestern California.

Geographical Adverbs

Though extended to the widest range of situations in Karuk, geographical marking reaches an extreme at some point in each of the neighboring linguistic traditions, one that is not duplicated elsewhere in the region. Among Yurok speakers, for instance, geographical concepts reach their expressive high point in the realm of independent adverbs, with each directional region being represented by a series of closely related forms that hold roughly the same meaning. Most of these roots enter into several related forms of loose functional equivalence. In terms of the sheer number of forms, the Yurok adverbial system is unparalleled among the neighboring languages. Yurok speakers have developed an extensive set of geographical adverbs in the context of northwestern California, or perhaps while inhabiting a similar ecosystem before arriving in their current situation along the California coast, though such a system is not characteristic of the Algic stock. Even the adjacent Wiyot language, another member of the Algic stock, contains few reflexes of geographical adverbs, possibly because their ancestors did not live directly along a river. Though concepts such as "upstream" and "downstream" are rarely indicated with stem-internal semantic elements in Yurok, similar distinctions are often made with freestanding adverbs.

Time Perspective and Diagonal Terms

Among Hupa speakers, directional marking is sensitive to the time schedule on which an event unfolds, a matter that is rarely a consideration when speaking any of the neighboring languages. Every directional marker in the Hupa verb system falls into one of several grammatical classes, each one holding loose temporal implications, as they often do in the other Athabaskan tongues. Consider the following directional markers, which have been reconstructed as part of the original Proto-Athabaskan verbal system:

*dəx	'(located) on top' (stative aspectual marker)
*yəx	'into house' (inceptive aspectual frame)
*ŋaanʔ	'across' (conclusive aspectual frame)

Though nongeographical in nature, each directional modifier in this set is associated with a different type of aspectual marker, similar to those found in Hupa.[19] In Hupa, however, this tendency, once a part of the original Proto-Athabaskan verbal system, has been specifically extended to geographical markers. Elsewhere in the Athabaskan family, geographical directional marking is mostly performed by adverbs, not verb prefixes, while this geographical marking is not generally constrained by verbal aspect, as it is in Hupa (see Leer 1989). Consider, for example, the geographical adverbs given below, which have been reconstructed as part of the original pre-Proto-Athabaskan directional system:[20]

**niʔ-	'upstream'
**daʔ-	'downstream'
**cənʔ-	'down to the shore' (> downhill)

Because these directional roots originally occurred as independent adverbs outside the verbal system (where aspect is marked), no particular temporal category was originally associated with these Proto-Athabaskan geographical stems. In some languages, such as Navajo of the American Southwest, the river-based directional concepts have all but disappeared from use (Leer 1989:596–600).

In the Hupa language, however, some geographical directional markers have been absorbed into the verb paradigm, where they have come into association with specific aspectual frames, such as those associated with nongeographical marking elsewhere in the family. Some of these directional modifiers place explicit focus on the onset of the act or on the middle phases of motion.

Like their Karuk neighbors, Hupa speakers also recognize a series of diagonal courses that rest halfway between any two sets of geographical landmarks. The Hupa language offers up a precise fourfold division of the diagonal directional paths that rest between the neighboring mountains and rivers—in contrast to the situation in Karuk, in which only two such paths are distinguished.

Cosmological Inversion

Even where there is general agreement, as in the shared system of spatial orientation among the Hupas, Yuroks, and Karuks (see figure 3.1) or in the traditional conception of the universe (see figure 5.1), this basic commonality is splintered into a number of reflections throughout the area's village communities. Consider, for example, the "upstream" spirit heaven, which one finds by starting at the mouth of the Klamath River and traveling from there up against the current of the swirling cosmic river thought to circle the earth, until one comes to the mythical spirit realm "upstream." In the Yurok conception, this is the land where the culture hero Across-the-Ocean-Widower now resides and leads the other spirit deities in a nightly performance of the White Deerskin Dance. The Hupas, as discussed in chapter 5, may have a similar placement of the upstream heaven—but in the Hupa conception, it is the Jump Dance that is performed there.

MAINTAINING LINGUISTIC DIFFERENCE

Home to a staggering diversity of languages, northwestern California was once the center of a thriving culture area embracing speakers of many unrelated tongues. Converging upon the area from separate regions, the various linguistic factions eventually settled on a common way of life. Though closely united in matters of myth, ritual, and religion—not to mention family structure or political organization—the Native peoples of this region spoke a number of radically different languages, representing three distinct families. Yet sharp linguistic boundaries between the neighboring village communities tended to enforce strict differences of interpretation among the groups. Sustained contact over many generations only produced many successive waves of drift, some convergent and others divergent, as similarities and differences continued to accumulate among the neighboring communities. As a result of these competing social trends, some of them increasing the overall similarities and others producing greater diversity, linguistic structure and cultural outlook achieve a nearly kaleidoscopic variability among the Native village communities of this region.

Rather than strictly producing homogeneity, long-term contact has also intensified many of the underlying differences present among the area's languages, sometimes accentuating proclivities inherent to the original source stocks. Though of diverse origins, the languages of northwestern California have indeed developed many common semantic tendencies, as a by-product of their ongoing social contact. Taken together, geographical directional systems, mythic tense categories, classificatory schemes, and descriptive nouns portraying mythical acts are all characteristic of the area's languages. Yet despite the constant, daily pressures to assimilate the habits and ways of neighboring peoples, the area's languages remain profoundly distinct on a number of fronts. This study suggests that the principle of linguistic relativity is inherent to the human condition, emerging from ongoing intellectual differences among neighboring speech communities.

Despite a history of intense social contact, the languages of northwestern California have maintained highly distinctive grammars, vocabularies, and even phonologies (O'Neill 2002). By and large, the potentially unifying effects of contact have not penetrated the structural kernel of these three neighboring languages, as often happens in other contact situations, such as Kupwar village, India, where four languages from two families have grown remarkably similar over a matter of centuries, with convergent phonologies, syntactic structures, and semantic elements (Gumperz and Wilson 1971). And if the languages of this region have, by and large, resisted the type of convergence found in similar contact situations, it is not because the speakers were unfamiliar with the neighboring linguistic traditions. On the contrary, daily social circumstances afforded members of each group with frequent opportunities to interact with speakers of the neighboring languages. The Native peoples of northwestern California, like those of Papua New Guinea or the Vaupés region of the Amazon Basin, have striven to maintain their difference on the linguistic plane, though some amount of convergence has also taken place, largely below the threshold of consciousness. Despite a long history of social contact, including widespread multilingualism, each of the languages maintains its own characteristic signature or stamp, whether on the grounds of structural composition or general semantic organization.

Epilogue

Intellectual diversity is a basic and irreducible condition of human social existence. No two persons are ever entirely alike in thinking, speaking, or cultural understanding, however similar their social backgrounds. Every language is, in a sense, a summation of the creative achievements of its speakers throughout the ages. Each new wave of expression contributes to the growing sum, yet every language is always a work in progress, as it is constantly reshaped and renewed by the constant dialog among its speakers.

The social diversity of Native northwestern California is certainly striking at first glance, especially when considered on both the linguistic and cultural planes at once. As in much of North America before European contact, a surprising number of languages have long been spoken in a stretch of land that could be walked in a matter of days. Yet despite the scale of the linguistic diversity, the social traditions found within these "culture areas" often run closely parallel, though usually with significant difference at the local level.

Throughout much of the history of our species, it has not been unusual to be exposed, even fairly early in life, to a diversity of languages, all coexisting in the same geographical setting. Examples outside California include the native groups of northeastern Australia, the Amazon Basin, New Guinea, and the Caucasus Mountains of the Eurasian continent. In spite of constant pressures to assimilate the habits and ways of neighboring peoples, each group fiercely maintains its own sense of identity, whether in terms of religious beliefs, literary practices, or the conceptual patterns of language. It is a great tragedy that the world is losing many of its native languages, each one representing an enormous intellectual legacy developed continuously over countless generations, though often lost, so easily, over a matter of mere decades.

Notes

INTRODUCTION

1. Andrew Garrett is currently in the process of entering Kroeber's Yurok narratives into a computerized database, so that Yurok word forms and grammatical elements can be systematically linked to instantiations of these forms that appear in texts. Copies of Kroeber's Yurok narratives have been available on microfilm since the mid-1990s.

2. It is from this article that the phrase "The Sapir-Whorf hypothesis" originates.

CHAPTER 1. LANGUAGE AND CULTURE IN NORTHWESTERN CALIFORNIA

1. See Sapir 1921:213–14; Bright and Bright 1965; Haas 1967; Lucy 1992a: 85–88.

2. Hoijer (1951) was the first scholar to discuss this pervasive focus on action or "motion" in the Athabaskan languages.

3. Another member of the Algic stock, known as Wiyot in the scholarly literature, is spoken slightly to the south in coastal northwestern California, though both Yurok and Wiyot are very distantly related to the more close-knit Algonquian branch of the family and are perhaps no more closely related to one another despite their present-day proximity in northwestern California. Some of the more well known languages within the Algonquian branch of the Algic stock include Cheyenne and Arapaho in the Plains; Blackfoot in Montana and the Canadian Rockies; Cree and Ojibwa in central Canada; and Micmac, Delaware, and Abenaki along the Eastern Seaboard.

4. Historical data from Garrett 2001:275.

5. Data from Haas 1958:161.

6. Data from Haas 1958:161.

7. Data from Haas 1958:165.

8. The tripartite stem structure of Yurok and Wiyot was first identified by Ives Goddard (1975). Years later, Paul Proulx (1985a, 1985c) provided further evidence, based on fresh fieldwork with the gifted speaker named Florence Shaunessy. More recently, Andrew Garrett (2004) has continued to explore the tripartite structure of the Yurok stem, even shedding new light on the structure of the Proto-Algic verb.

9. See Bloomfield 1946 for a basic structural plan that largely holds for Yurok and Wiyot as well.

10. Data from Wolfart 1996:424–26.

11. Data from Wolfart 1996:424–26.

12. For this unusual form, which is not attested elsewhere in the Yurok corpus, see Proulx 1985a:124.

13. Garrett (2004) argues that Yurok noninflected stems actually preserve an ancient feature of Algic linguistic structure, representing an ancient state of affairs that was perhaps more widespread before the complex polysynthetic processes built up.

14. However, on a historical basis, many of the monomorphemic word forms in Yurok can be broken down into their constituent etymological roots. For instance, the term referring to the coyote, *segep*, likely contains an intensive form of the root *sep*, which by itself means "prairie," occurring, for instance, in the ordinary word for the prairie, *sepolah*. Elsewhere in the region, the coyote is known as "the one who goes about on the prairies," so the meaning adheres to the expected pattern.

15. Data from Sapir 2001:1017.

16. Wiyot, another member of the Algic stock, also tends toward minimalism of morphological expression, though the two languages are perhaps no more closely related than either is to the Algonquian branch as a whole. Both Yurok and Wiyot may have independently diverged from Proto-Algic as many as several thousand years ago.

17. Extending some sixty miles upstream past its confluence with the neighboring Trinity.

18. A pattern quite unlike the Athabaskan brand of polysynthesis (discussed above), in which affixes tend to occur in highly idiomatic clusters whose meaning cannot be clearly separated.

19. Data from Bright 1957:182 (T5.95), 236 (T35.36), and 351.

20. The sketch to follow is my synthesis based on the many published ethnographies on northwestern California as a culture area, particularly Kroeber 1925:1–97 for the Yuroks, Goddard 1903 for the Hupas, and Kroeber 1925:98–109 for the Karuks. Kroeber's discussion of the Karuks is partly based on his experience among the neighboring Yuroks, whom he took to represent the entire region (1925:108), though I have checked Kroeber's presentation against both William Bright's ethnographic sketch of the Karuks (1978:180–89) and the early work of John P. Harrington (1932a, 1932b). Sapir's brief comment on the cultural similarities among the Hupa, Yurok, and Karuk Indians can be found on page 214 of his famous *Language* (1921). Many of my insights also draw from my own experiences in the region, mostly from 1998 through 2001.

21. Sadly, this traditional mode of subsistence passed out of existence within decades after the onslaught of Europeans, starting in the mid-nineteenth century. Yet many elders are still very knowledgeable about the traditional ways.

22. Redwood is preferred on the coast, where it is abundant among the coastal villages of the Yuroks; cedar is more common inland (Goddard 1903:13), where redwood does not grow. The wood was split into planks with elk-horn wedges.

23. For living arrangements among the Yuroks and, by extension, the neighboring peoples of northwestern California, see Kroeber 1925:78–80. For living arrangements among the Hupas, see Goddard 1903:13–18.

24. For dentalia-shell currency among the Yuroks and, by extension, the neighboring peoples of northwestern California, see Kroeber 1925:22–26. For dentalia-shell currency among the Hupas, see Goddard 1903:48–50.

25. For traditional leadership among the Hupas, see Kroeber 1925:132–33; Goddard 1903:57–60.

26. For village organization in northwestern California, see Kroeber 1925:8–15; for the Hupas specifically, see Goddard 1903:12–18.

27. For the traditional religious life among the Yuroks, Karuks, and Hupas, respectively, see Kroeber 1925:53–75, 103–107, and 134–37; for the Hupas, see also Goddard 1903:74–88.

28. For a full version of this story, as told by McCann, see Goddard 1904:220–25.

29. For a full version of this tale, as told by Little Ike's Mother, see Kroeber's *Karok Myths* (Kroeber and Gifford 1980:32–36).

30. For the full version of this tale, as told by Lame Billy of Weitpus, see Kroeber 1976:47–54.

31. The Yurok name for this village is Oplego, according to Kroeber (1976:50).

32. Chimariko, a now-extinct member of the putative Hokan stock, was once spoken some twenty miles upstream of the Hupa village of Taʔkʸimɬ-diŋ. Early publications suggested that Hupa was a lingua franca in the region (Powers 1976 [1877]:72–73), though follow-up fieldwork has not supported this old rumor. Instead, many Chimariko villagers may have been shifting to Hupa at the time of contact with Europeans (Conathan 2004b:23).

33. There is evidence that a few villages may have been bilingual (Conathan 2004b:110); these all lie on the borders between the neighboring speech communities.

34. This report comes from Sam Brown, who in turn, learned the story from his great-aunt (or, more precisely, his maternal grandmother's sister). To elaborate, he maintains that the Hupa language is capable of reaching out into the water; this is perhaps a reference to casting a curse that spreads into the very depths of the earth. From the story "A War between the Hupa and Yurok" (Sapir 2001:515–30).

35. Put in modern terms, the journey from one speech community to another is something like the drive from Oregon to southern California—say, from Portland to Los Angeles. Even to this day, one-lane back roads are notoriously treacherous in places, as visitors often learn the hard way.

CHAPTER 2. LINGUISTIC RELATIVITY AND THE
PUZZLE OF NORTHWESTERN CALIFORNIA

1. On a very minor scale, many tiny differences in grammar and vocabulary also distinguish the various dialects of English currently spoken around the planet, as summed up in the well-known expression "England and the United States are separated by a common language."

2. Humboldt is famously paraphrased as saying, "Language makes infinite use of finite means" (1988[1836]:91). Thus, even at the outset, it should be clear that these scholars viewed language not solely as an outright limitation on human thought but also as a creative tradition in which it is imperative that individual speakers strive to find their own voice.

3. This statement, in turn, echoes an established European intellectual tradition inherited, by way of Franz Boas, from the likes of Vico, Herder, and Humboldt, generations before.

4. In other words, there is regular contrast between plain and aspirated stops, which create a phonemic contrast in these languages. Yet in English the distinction is allophonic.

5. In phonemic script, this word is written *do·* 'not', though it is actually very different from the English *d* sound, which is fully voiced.

6. Though both Hupa sounds are actually voiceless, on phonetic grounds Athabaskan scholars normally write the plain sound *t* with a *d* and the aspirated sound *t^h* with a *t* when representing these languages in phonemic script. Here scientific accuracy is sacrificed for the sake of convenience.

7. The voiceless Welsh *l* is produced with more friction than the voiceless English *l* in words such as *clean.*

8. In the terminology of semiotics, a cultural perspective has been "naturalized." After being internalized, it is no longer subject to inspection, much as people do not question other habits, from food preferences to dialect or even their social class.

9. In advancing this particular reading of Whorf's ideas, I have been influenced by Slobin's concept of thinking for speaking, in which grammatical concepts have recently been shown to exert a subtle influence on perception and memory as speakers begin to report their observations in a particular language (Gumperz and Levinson 1996:70–97).

10. This is a process that has been central to Western conceptions of discourse since the time of Socrates. Recently, Bahktin (1981) has once again popularized the so-called dialogic imagination, which would have pleased Socrates, the ancient master of both dialogue and discourse. Yet, unfortunately, the concept of dialogue was not specifically addressed in Whorf's writings, though he may have considered the idea to be implicit. His teacher, Edward Sapir, certainly saw language as a social phenomenon and constantly wrote about the importance of process, not rigid, unchanging structures. Sapir, ever the advocate of the individual, was equally committed to differences in worldview found within communities.

11. Sapir was also famous for speculating about this possibility (1921:15–23), an idea that he likely encountered when reading the works of Humboldt and Herder, who wrote about this theme several generations before.

12. Like Whorf's writings, Saussure's lecture notes fell into the hands of his students and colleagues shortly after his death and were quickly revised for publication without consultation with the deceased author. Recently, some of Saussure's personal handwritten notes have been brought together and published (Saussure 2006), and his thoughts were indeed more nuanced than is reflected in the lecture notes collected by his students. Most important for the purpose of this discussion is that he did in fact entertain the possibility that language may influence thought, claiming "it is not thought that creates the [linguistic] sign, but the sign that fundamentally guides thought" (2006:27–28).

13. Of course, Sapir would have debated him endlessly on this point, as Sapir was one of the pioneers of sound-symbolism in language, arguing that sounds often carry or suggest a loose affective value (see Sapir 1949:61–72).

14. Boas never suggested that the Eskimos have more than a handful of words for snow, perhaps no more than we have in English. The myth of numerous Eskimo words for snow inexplicably arose in the popular imagination without much basis in Boas's writings. Certainly his case does not rest on this one overanalyzed example; there are thousands of others just as interesting. And in mentioning Eskimo snow terms, Boas actually meant to demonstrate that this so-called primitive language actually put forth a somewhat abstract classification of reality on a par with English despite the supposedly wide evolutionary gap between the two speech communities—part of Boas's general project of showing that cultures could not be ranked in terms of simple evolutionary schemes.

15. This massive vocabulary, of course, owes in part to the centuries-old tradition of borrowing from every source its speakers encountered, beginning with Latin and Greek almost as soon as the Anglo-Saxons first stepped foot in England during the fifth century A.D.

16. This can be demonstrated even by returning to Old English, in which there are no terms for modern science and technology.

17. For a close examination of a child whose exposure to language was severely restricted until the age of thirteen or so, see Curtiss 1977.

18. For the current state of knowledge on language, brain, and disability, see section 4 of Crystal 1997.

19. A child deprived of language never learns to speak if this deprivation continues past the age of puberty. Yet language blossoms rapidly and unstoppably once a child is exposed to a speech community, even if this exposure occurs at a fairly late age, though before puberty. A telling example is the case of Nicaraguan sign language; a group of deaf children quickly developed a language of their own, complete with grammatical structure such as word order and tense markers, without much input from their parents or teachers. For recent literature on the subject, see Senghas and Coppola 2001; Senghas, Kita, and Ozyürek 2004.

20. This approach prefigured the postmodern concern for restoring the "Native voice" in anthropology by almost a century.

21. See Sapir 1949; Whorf 1956; Duranti 1997; Foley 1997; Gentner and Goldin-Meadow 2003.

22. The principle could just as well have been called the "Humboldtian effect," after another early theorist on the subject of language and thought. Countless other scholars, including Vico, Herder, Vygosky, and Sapir, also deserve credit here.

23. As a result of Sapir's statement, many scholars now see language and culture as separate, if not unrelated, issues or, at least, as different academic specialties too disparate for any one scholar to command. However, as we shall see, the matter of culture cannot be so easily dismissed, especially where issues of cognition enter the picture. Nor does this offshoot position represent the entirety of Sapir's thought on the subject. There are exceptions, however; notable cognitive linguists such as George Lakoff and Eve Sweetser have both paid a great deal of attention to cultural phenomena when analyzing semantic processes in the world's languages. While George Lakoff (1987) applies cultural principles to synchronic processes, such as the classifier system of the Dyirbal language of Australia, Eve Sweetser (1990) applies similar principles to diachronic processes in the Indo-European languages.

24. Consider the Indo-European languages, a well-documented case study in this type of linguistic drift; many common reflexes of the original mother tongue continue to stand after many thousands of years, often in very different cultural settings.

25. For a recent article on the subject, see Ahler 1996, in which the author claims that the stock of basic nouns has been reduced to about four hundred in modern-day Hupa. Nearly all of the remaining nouns are based on verbs, many of them placing an explicit focus on action. For additional examples, see chapters 9 and 11 of this volume.

26. Many of these theoretical positions can be traced back to Humboldt, including the "universalist" positions that are said to devastate any sense of "linguistic relativity." This supposedly revolutionary position, which many attribute to Chomsky, is actually one of the oldest stances ever proposed in linguistics; it can be traced back as far as Leibniz.

27. Recently, the popular writer Steven Pinker has, for instance, spoken of a common "mentalese" shared by all humans (1994:81–82), which is then secondarily translated into whatever language the speaker happens to know. Yet even this position, which closely resembles that of Humboldt's, leaves room for a subtle secondary influence of language on thought.

CHAPTER 3. GEOGRAPHICAL SPATIAL ORIENTATION

1. This observation was initially based on Kroeber's work with the Yuroks, though it proved to be true of the neighboring languages as well. For a more recent survey, see Hinton's chapter entitled "Uphill, Downhill: The Vocabulary of Direction" in Hinton 1994:49–59.

2. For example, English riparian terms such as *upstream* and *downstream* are sometimes extended to the modern highways that now run parallel to the rivers.

3. Consider the contemporary English expression "going south," which sometimes functions as an oblique reference to the erogenous zone below the waistline.

4. Here reduced to *-Won* by normal phonological processes.

5. The Hupa word for the hand (*xolaʔ*), in turn, derives from the inalienable noun stem *-laʔ* '(something's) hand', here occurring with the third-person possessive prefix *xo-*, which adds the meaning "belonging to a person."

6. If these Yurok terms do not derive their sense from the flow of water down along the coast, away from the mouth of the Klamath, then they represent the only truly cardinal concepts in the region. Waterman (1920:194), however, suggests that these terms derive their sense from a stem that means "behind." This would imply that they refer to the region that swings around from behind the curve of the disc-shaped earth of the traditional culture.

7. That is, the absolute directionals of northwestern California, unlike those of Tenejapa Tzeltal, cannot be linked to the compass directions labeled by English speakers.

8. For a fuller description, see Levinson 2003:112–46.

CHAPTER 4. LINGUISTIC SYSTEMS OF SPATIAL REFERENCE

1. An exception is the language of the Shasta Indians, whose homeland began upstream along the north fork of the Klamath and whose traditional culture belonged to a somewhat different type. However, the Shasta language may be distantly related to Karuk, both of which share this focus on geographical spatial reference, though the speakers of the two languages do not share exactly the same cultural life. In this sense, the languages are closer to one another on the plane of conceptual patterning than on the plane of daily cultural practice.

2. These fine-grained distinctions are certainly possible for speakers of the neighboring languages, as they are for English speakers, through a process of circumlocution.

3. The term therefore implies "away from" the river below.

4. Whereas the verb stem *ikvirip-* in the first form often refers to relatively fluid activities, such as salmon swimming through the water, the second stem, *ʔárih-*, often refers to more-rapid-fire events, sometimes even translating "jump." The contrastive use of these stems may also partially reflect the variable ease in traveling downhill as opposed to uphill. That is, the climb up a mountain is a laborious affair, while the descent unfolds at a more rapid pace because the force of gravity is on one's side for the return.

5. Note that the meanings of *-kara* and *rípaa* are reversed on the table given on page 95 of Bright 1957, though Bright gives the correct meanings on the following pages as he provides further examples of these directional suffixes. See page 97 for the correct meaning of *-kara,* "horizontally toward the center of a body of

water." See page 101 for the correct meaning of *rípaa*, "horizontally away from the center of a body of water."

6. The imperfective stem *-na·W*, which also belongs to this same paradigm of motion, refers, in contrast, to instances that lack a definite onset or conclusion, as may be illustrated with the forms *xaʔsina·W* 'one being goes up the slope' and *xohč'ina·W* 'one being comes down the slope'.

7. This form is attested only in Proulx's important article entitled "Notes on Yurok Derivation" (1985a:125). His insights were primarily derived from his work with Florence Shaughnessy, shortly before her death. She was a fluent Yurok speaker and also served as the principal informant to several other investigators, including Robins and Berman, though neither of them noted this particular geographical directional prefix.

8. This unusual form appears in the field notes of Proulx, based on his work with Florence Shaughnessy (Proulx 1985a:122). It does not appear elsewhere in the Yurok corpus.

9. Compare with *hoonecoḱ* 'I climb, walk uphill', in which the reference is to mountain slopes, not river currents. This contrasting form appears in Proulx 1985a:125.

10. The directional marker *-č'iŋʔ* loosely translates as "heading toward (a region) as a goal," while the complementary modifier *-č'iŋ* carries the opposite meaning, namely, "coming from (a region) as a source."

11. This form appears in a religious text, filled with the otherwise colorful expressions of ritual speech (Goddard 1904:227). Reconstruction mine.

12. This form occurs in the story entitled "Coyote's Homecoming," told by Nettie Reuben (Bright 1957:168).

13. Here the directional marker *-rúpuk* '(heading) outdoors' probably derives from the related marker *-rupu* 'heading downriver'. In traditional times, the exits to homes usually pointed down toward the rivers below. The Hupa directional marker *č'e·=*, for example, which generally refers to motion that reaches out of an enclosure, conveys a similar meaning. The form *č'eʔninyay*, which literally translates as "one came out of an enclosure," also sometimes refers, more generally, to the process of exiting the house, descending the riverbank close by, and heading all the way down to the river below.

14. Here the grammatical marker *-ahi* indicates that this object has been made to rest in this position as the result of a previous action.

15. Sometimes the direction a person faces while resting motionless is overtly stated in Hupa speech. However, the reference is often to events that also feature an element of motion, not to purely motionless states. A case in point is the form *č'inehsday*, which refers to the act of "sitting down," a verb that sometimes occurs with an adverbial phrase that indicates the direction the person faces while getting into that position. Take the related phrase *yideʔ-dinaŋ č'inehsday*, for instance,

which means "one person sat down facing downstream." To further illustrate the point, consider the form *ya'wiŋ'ay,* which refers to the state of pointing upward, while sometimes occurring with an outside adverbial modifier, as illustrated in the phrase *yide'-dinaŋ ya'wiŋ'ay,* which loosely translates as "one sat up, pointing downstream."

16. This form, which does not occur elsewhere in the Yurok corpus, is cited from Proulx 1985a:125 (based on Proulx's work with Florence Shaughnessy).

17. Data from Proulx 1985a:123.

18. Each form in this paragraph occurs in the third person, as indicated here by a shift of the stem consonant from its unmarked aspirated form to a glottalized variant. For Yurok speakers, third-person forms often apply equally to animals, humans, and forces of nature.

19. This form is cited from Proulx 1985a:129.

20. Data from Proulx 1985a:115–16.

21. This form appears in Proulx 1985a:116, though it does not occur elsewhere in the Yurok corpus.

22. Most directional suffixes are neutral with respect to time perspective, accepting any temporal marker without restriction. Yet in some isolated cases, two spatial markers also carry a secondary metaphorical temporal significance, though generally only in scenes that involve little or no literal movement through space (see Bright 1957:96–103). Consider the directional suffix *-sip(riv),* which usually specifies motion that passes "up to the height of a person." When applied to the dimension of time, this marker also carries a special initiative meaning, allowing the speaker to focus on the initial stages of an event that involves no actual vertical motion, including activities such as running or swimming. Or consider the related directional suffix *-ish(rih),* which usually specifies motion that passes "down from the height of a person." When applied to the realm of time, the marker also holds a special resultative significance, allowing the speaker to focus on the final or concluding stages of such activities as becoming quiet or settling into a sitting position. The secondary temporal significance attributed to these suffixes may ultimately rest on an analogy to the volitional acts usually associated with these directional frames. In their primary setting, these markers refer to scenes in which human agents move physical objects on a roughly level surface against the force of gravity. When the object is lifted from a position of rest, the event initiates a new sequence of motion in both space and time. Yet when the object is lowered to the ground, the motion comes to a natural halt, in both spatial and temporal terms.

23. All of the forms cited in this paragraph can be found in a short story entitled "Coyote Eats His Own Excrement," told by Nettie Reuben (Bright 1957:200).

24. Historically, the marker *ya·=* derives from an old Athabaskan noun stem that once referred strictly to the sky, though this is no longer attested in modern Hupa. The marker *xo-da·=* derives historically from the root *da·,* which refers to the

mouth of a living being or stream. Upon entering the verbal system as directional markers, both take the temporal marker *win-*, which generally indicates motion that starts out toward a goal without necessarily reaching this destination, here either the sky or the mouth of a stream.

25. This final series of forms, concerning the spatial and temporal dynamics of water flows, occurs only in the notes of Paul Proulx (1985a:115), though the other forms in this paragraph are very widely attested throughout the Yurok corpus.

26. Data from Proulx 1985a:114–15.

CHAPTER 5. GEOGRAPHY AND COSMOLOGY

1. The sketch presented here is my synthesis based on the many published reports on Hupa, Yurok, and Karuk ethnography. The basic portrait owes much to Waterman's *Yurok Geography* (1920:189–93), though many of the details reported in this work do not hold true of the neighboring Hupa and Karuk communities, which were outside the scope of Waterman's study. Many of the basic details of Hupa cosmology can be gleaned from a close examination of Goddard's *Hupa Texts* (1904); Sapir's follow-up fieldwork in the summer of 1927 (Sapir 2001) furnished further evidence on the subject. My primary source for the Karuks is Bright's *Karuk Language* (1957), especially the lengthy selection of narrative texts (pp. 162–307).

2. This map was inspired by T. T. Waterman's early depiction of Yurok cosmology (Waterman 1920:192). Yet, since that is a single culture map, intended only for the Yuroks, figure 5.1 (which also applies to the Hupas and Karuks) is necessarily more general.

3. As reported by Waterman (1921:191). However, this term has not been verified by any of the subsequent investigators, and its historical derivation remains unclear.

4. Waterman (1921:191) reports this form as *ɹkɹgɹ'*, though Andrew Garrett (pers. comm., 2006) speculates that this place-name may be based on a third-person singular form of the verb *krgok* 'he lives', here occurring with a rhotic variant of the locative *ʔo* 'where'. However, since Waterman provides no gloss, it is difficult to narrow down the precise verb stem, and Garrett notes that the second word (*kɹgɹʔ*) could also be based on any short iterative verb beginning with a *k* and containing a rhotic vowel, giving countless other possibilities for the possible derivation and meaning of this form.

5. As reported in the posthumous work of Sapir (2001:897), based on his fieldwork in the summer of 1927, especially with his key consultant Sam Brown.

6. As reported by Sapir's consultant Sam Brown in his short but detailed narrative, "The Afterworld" (Sapir 2001:303–304).

7. For a full version of this tale, as told by William Lewis, see Goddard 1904: 252–64.

8. See, for instance, the tale entitled "Coyote Goes to the Sky" (Bright 1957: 190–91), in which Coyote climbs into the realm of the sky and then passes from the

upstream to the downstream ends of the world while dancing. See also the story entitled "Coyote Gives Salmon and Acorns to Mankind" (Bright 1957:204–205).

9. See, for instance, the story entitled "Coyote Trades Songs and Goes to the Sky," as told by Mamie Offield (Bright 1957:193–94).

10. First Salmon fled to a neighboring land called *kowecik,* not quite as far upriver as the upstream spirit heaven where the White Deerskin Dance is constantly performed (Waterman 1920:191). Another aspect of this story is reported in the tale entitled "Wohpekumew and the Salmon" (Robins 1958:162–63).

11. For a full version of this tale, told in the Hupa language, see the narrative entitled "A Story of the South Wind" (Sapir 2001:433–36).

12. See, for instance, the story entitled "Coyote's Journey" (Bright 1957:170–75), in which Coyote travels upriver to the Klamath Lakes to obtain money.

13. For a full version of this tale, see the narrative entitled "Eel-with-a-Swollen-Belly Creates Shrines," as reported in Lang 1994:54–61.

14. For more information on the folklore surrounding the world's downstream limit, see the narrative entitled "A Story of the South Wind" (Sapir 2001:433–36).

15. See, for instance, the tale entitled "Coyote Goes to the Sky" (Bright 1957: 190–91).

16. As reported in Sapir 2001:897. See also Goddard 1904:215–19 for an account of how the spirit beings came to occupy each of the various heavens, including the northern one, after leaving this earth. For an account of Emma Frank's vision of this northern heaven, see Sapir 2001:238–50.

17. Called *č'indin-tah-diŋ* ('land of the dead') among the Hupas (Sapir 2001: 892). For a detailed description of this land, as narrated by Emma Frank, see Sapir 2001:251–56.

18. For a Karuk description of this land, see the story entitled "A Trip to Indian Heaven" in Lang 1994:63–95.

19. For a full version of this tale, as told by Lillie Hostler, see Goddard 1904:360–68.

CHAPTER 6. THE LINGUISTIC CLASSIFICATIONS OF TIME

1. Whorf's early claim that Hopi is somehow a "timeless" language is flawed. The claim is made in an article in which he says, "After long and careful study and analysis, the Hopi language is seen to contain no words, grammatical forms, constructions or expressions that refer directly to what we call 'time,' or to past, present, or future, or to enduring or lasting, or to motion as kinematic rather than dynamic" (1956:57). Because this article was published after his death, these words probably represent Whorf's private musings on the topic rather than being a polished public statement of a position he had the time to work out. In his later writings, however, Whorf certainly argues that the Hopis have a sense of time—just one that is different from the commonsense view of time conveyed in many English expressions.

2. For this insight, I must thank William Bright, who was kind enough to inform me of this situation, which is not obvious strictly from reading the narrative texts.

3. From the story "Coyote Eats His Own Excrement," narrated by Nettie Reuben (Bright 1957:200).

4. From the narrative "The Story of Bear," told by Nettie Reuben (Bright 1957:240).

5. From the story "Coyote's Journey," narrated by Julia Starritt (Bright 1957:172).

6. From the story "Victory over Fire," narrated by Mamie Offield (Bright 1957:246).

7. From the story "Duck Hawk and His Wife," narrated by Mamie Offield (Bright 1957:222). Glossing mine. Here the verb ʔuttássunihtihanik is based on the stem tásunih-, one that generally refers to a vertical barrier, such as the face of a steep mountain or the cliff behind a waterfall. This stem is based on the root tas-, which usually refers to the act of building a fence, here occurring with the directional marker -unih 'down from a height'. The event is placed in the ancient tense with the marker =anik, suggesting that this barrier had been constructed, perhaps by the gods themselves, before Bear demolished this handiwork. As a unit, the construction translates as "a barrier (existed) in ancient times."

8. From the story "How Deer Meat Was Lost and Regained," narrated by Mamie Offield (Bright 1957:232). Glossing mine.

9. The marker -uraa can mean either "up to a considerable height" or "(heading) uphill" (see Bright 1957:95).

10. From the story "Coyote's Journey," narrated by Julia Starritt (Bright 1957:176). Glossing mine.

11. There is evidence that the derivation is slightly more complex in the paradigm of linear extension, in which the directional marker ni- occurs instead with the inceptive marker win-, while the cluster ni-win merges to form the reduced form nin- (Sapir 2001:942). Yet these forms still loosely belong to the conclusive paradigm, in which the reference is to processes that head toward a goal. In the case of extension, the reference is to an event that stretches along toward this end from a definite beginning point. In this setting, the prefix ni- indicates the end point, while the prefix win- suggests the onset of the event.

12. From the story "Formula of Medicine for Going among Rattlesnakes," narrated by a consultant known as McCann (Goddard 1904:317). Reconstruction mine.

13. As a rule, a long vowel is shortened in a closed syllable.

14. From the story "The Young Man from Serper" (Robins 1958:164). Word-level glossing mine.

15. From the story "The Mourning Dove" (Robins 1958:155). Word-level glossing mine.

16. From the story "Coyote and Crane," narrated by Mary Marshall (Sapir 2001:1017).

17. From the story "The Mourning Dove" (Robins 1958:156). Word-level glossing mine.

18. From the story "The Mourning Dove" (Robins 1958:156). Word-level glossing mine.

19. From "The Story of the Klamath River Song" (Robins 1958:160). Word-level glossing mine.

20. From the text "The First Salmon Rite at Wełkʷew" (Robins 1958:172). Word-level glossing mine.

21. From the story "Coyote Tries to Kill the Sun" (Sapir 2001:1023). Word-level glossing mine.

22. From the story "The Fox and the Coon" (Robins 1958:164). Word-level glossing mine.

23. From the story "The Mourning Dove" (Robins 1958:155–56). Word-level glossing mine.

24. From the story "Coyote and Crane," narrated by Mary Marshall (Sapir 2001:1019).

25. From the story "The Mourning Dove" (Robins 1958:155). Word-level glossing mine.

26. From the story "Coyote and Crane," narrated by Mary Marshall (Sapir 2001:1018).

27. When applied to nouns, the intensive marker often signals a characteristic act that is routinely associated with a specific actor. A case in point is the noun *megey ʔoʔrowiʔ*, the ordinary Yurok term for the mourning dove; the descriptive content of this noun literally translates as "the dove (who) always weeps." This phrasal noun is based on the intensive form of the verb stem *mey,* which ordinarily means "to mourn." The unanalyzable noun root *ʔoʔrowiʔ* merely identifies the referent as a "dove," specifically, one that "always mourns," as suggested by the intensive verb construction *megey.* At a more submerged level, the intensive infix *-eg-* also enters several other derived noun forms, where it draws attention to other defining characteristics. A case in point is the name for the buzzard, *lɹgɹʔl,* a form that likely derives from the intensive form of the verb *lol-,* which ordinarily means "to fly." Consider the related form *loʔl,* which simply means, "it flies." Following a shift to the vowel *ɹ,* the expression carries the meaning "the one (that is) always flying."

28. From the story "The Mourning Dove" (Robins 1958:157). Word-level glossing mine.

29. From the story "Medicine Formula to Get Wealthy" (Sapir 2001:1025).

30. From the story "Medicine Formula to Get Wealthy" (Sapir 2001:1026).

31. From the story "The Owl" (Robins 1958:162–63).

32. The process is a somewhat iconic one, in that repetition on the plane of sound signals a parallel repetition on the plane of meaning. Data in the paragraph are from an article entitled "The Semantics of Intensive Infixation" (Garrett and Wood 2002:113–15).

33. When applied to noun stems, reduplication also signals a repetition of act or process normally associated with the basic form of the stem. Consider the noun stem *ɬkɹmɹkikɹ,* which normally refers to a "single knot of rope." When reduplicated, the meaning becomes multiple "knots in a rope," while the form shifts to *ɬkɹm-ɬkɹmɹkikɹ* (data from Spott and Kroeber 1942:216).

34. This form appears only in the work of Proulx (1985a:127), as do the remaining forms in this section featuring the productive medial *-ekik* 'water flows'. The remaining forms are widely attested in the Yurok corpus.

CHAPTER 7. THE LINGUISTIC CONSTRUCTION OF TIME IN NARRATIVE

1. Even in the semantic structure of the Karuk verb, only one of the markers, the perfective, specifically refers to scenes whose temporal scope is definitely bounded.

2. From the story "Victory over Fire," narrated by Mamie Offield (Bright 1957:246). Glossing mine.

3. From the story "Coyote Trades Songs and Goes to the Sky" (Bright 1957:194). Word-level glossing mine.

4. From the story "Why Towhee Has Red Eyes" (Bright 1957:238).

5. From the story "*Yima·n-tiwʔwinyay*—Creator and Culture Hero," narrated by Emma Lewis (Goddard 1904:96). Glossing and reconstruction mine.

6. From the ethnographic narrative "The Brush Dance," told by Sam Brown (Sapir 2001:153).

7. Here the adverb *hikon,* which means "long ago," may be connected semantically and, ultimately, historically, with the spatial markers *hikoc* and *hikoh,* which both refer to the region "across the water." Of course, this sacred sector of the cosmos is where the myth figures were said to have fled in the ancient past, to remain there for all eternity.

8. From the story "The Mourning Dove" (Robins 1958:155). Word-level glossing mine.

9. From the story "The Mourning Dove" (Robins 1958:155). Word-level glossing mine.

10. From the story "Wohpekumew and the Salmon" (Robins 1958:162). Word-level glossing mine.

11. From the story "Coyote and Crane," narrated by Mary Marshall (Sapir 2001:1021).

12. From the story "Coyote's Journey," narrated by Nettie Reuben (Bright 1957:162). Word-level glossing mine.

13. From the story "Coyote's Journey," narrated by Chester Pepper (Bright 1957:172). Word-level glossing mine.

14. From the story "Coyote Eats His Own Excrement," narrated by Nettie Reuben (Bright 1957:200). Word-level glossing mine.

15. From the story "Coyote as Lawmaker," narrated by Nettie Reuben (Bright 1957:200). Word-level glossing mine.

16. From the story "Coyote Gives Salmon and Acorns to Mankind," narrated by Mamie Offield (Bright 1957:204). Word-level glossing mine.

17. From the story "The Creation of Eels," narrated by Nettie Reuben (Bright 1957:242). Word-level glossing mine.

18. From the story "The Cause of the Lunar Eclipse," narrated by McCann (Goddard 1904:195–96). Analysis and reconstruction mine.

19. From the story "War Medicine," told by Henry Hostler (Goddard 1904: 332–35). Analysis and reconstruction mine.

20. From the story "The Mourning Dove" (Robins 1958:157). Word-level glossing mine.

21. From the story "The Fox and the Coon" (Robins 1958:164–65). Word-level glossing mine.

22. From the story "Wohpekumew and the Salmon" (Robins 1958:162). Word-level glossing mine.

23. From the story "The Owl" (Robins 1958:162). Word-level glossing mine.

24. From the story "The Greedy Father," narrated by Lottie Beck (Bright 1957:216). Word-level glossing mine.

25. From the story "The Origin of the Pikiawish," narrated by Nettie Reuben (Bright 1957:248). Word-level glossing mine.

26. From the story "The Tan Oak," narrated by Nettie Reuben (Bright 1957:226). Word-level glossing mine.

27. From the story "The Mourning Dove" (Robins 1958:157). Word-level glossing mine.

28. From the story "Wohpekumew and Salmon" (Robins 1958:162). Word-level glossing mine.

29. From the story "The Owl" (Robins 1958:162). Word-level glossing mine.

CHAPTER 8. CLASSIFYING EXPERIENCE THROUGH LANGUAGE

1. Heraclites is famous for saying that one can never step into the same river twice, meaning the river changes its constitution each second, because it is in a constant process of flowing. In a similar fashion, a word is never uttered in the same context twice! Nor does it ever mean exactly the same thing every time, ever thwarting the lexicographer's attempts to define all its senses as time progresses and new meanings accumulate.

2. See Kay and Anglin 1982 for one key study on overextension and underextension in the acquisition of vocabulary.

3. See Eleanor Rosch's groundbreaking early work on color, when she still went by the name of Eleanor Heider (Heider 1971, 1972a, 1972b).

4. Rosch (formerly Heider) even demonstrated that new terms, such as the English *green,* can be fairly easily introduced, especially when the terms represent focal color that stands out to all people, even if this particular perceptual referent does not have a regular name. See Heider 1971, 1972a, 1972b.

5. In this sense, every language gives rise to a tremendous sense of internal linguistic diversity, based on individual differences in vocabulary, style, or the deployment of grammatical rules.

6. In English, however, there is no gender-neutral pronoun in the third person; instead, throughout much of the history of the language, masculine pronouns have been used as a default strategy for referring to people in general, until this practice was protested during the equal rights movements of the 1960s and 1970s. To fill this conceptual gap, many speakers have turned to using *their* as a gender-neutral personal pronoun even in the third person. Yet, as prescriptive grammarians are quick to point out, this creates a mismatch in number, as a plural pronoun used in a singular setting.

7. Haas wrote this article as a response to Bright and Bright 1965.

8. Even at the outset, a number of broad parallels can be pointed out, mostly reflecting fairly widespread, even universal, semantic tendencies found throughout the world. For instance, most of the categories found in northwestern California are based on features of shape, number, texture, or animacy, as the classificatory elements serve to place an object of discourse into one or more related categories, such as "round," "long," "living," or "ropelike." Of course, similar categories find expression in most grammatical systems of classification, including many of the Native languages of Africa, Australia, and the Americas.

9. My understanding of the Yurok classifier system is primarily based on Robins 1958, which has a fairly complete inventory of specific numerals and adjectival verbs that are regularly used with certain classes of objects, such as "animals and birds" versus "human beings" or "round" versus "trees and sticks." To complete the analysis, I have identified the individual classifier morphemes, to some extent following the basic analysis presented in Haas 1967, and then I have tracked the distribution of these classifiers with the objects. Along the way, I encountered some surprises, or exceptions to the basic system of analysis presented by previous investigators, such as Haas and Robins. For example, according to Robins's data (but not his analysis), red human hair is actually placed in the category for "animals and birds," not "human beings," as expected. This may be due to the fact that the color red is strongly associated with the feathers of woodpeckers in the traditional religious regalia found in northwestern California; that is, red human hair is perhaps likened to red bird feathers in the semantics of the Yurok language. As another example, pregnant women are placed in the class for "pointed objects." A stout person, in contrast, is placed in the "round object" category, as is the case in the neighboring Hupa language.

10. Though parallel semantic elements are present elsewhere in the Algic stock (see Conathan 2004a), the Yurok classifier system is by far the most elaborate scheme in the entire linguistic group, even outstripping the neighboring Wiyot language of northwestern California. In many of the Algonquian languages, for instance, a small series of affixes can be used to place the subject of an intransitive verb or the object of a transitive verb within a particular grammatical class, usually on the basis of shape.

11. Again, like Dyirbal speakers in Australia, the Yurok speaker also has the option of using the general or miscellaneous category in the classifier system, thereby avoiding mention of any specific shape-based characteristics.

12. By attributing qualities such as color, shape, or size to nouns, all of the verbs in this series perform a function similar to adjectives in English and other Indo-European languages.

13. My understanding of Hupa classificatory verbs is based primarily on Goddard 1904, Golla 1970, and Sapir 2001.

14. Taking the imperfective form as its starting point, the momentaneous paradigm can also be modified to refer to a continuous engagement in the general process, where the actor repeats the momentary act while moving along. Take the basic imperfective form *ya·ʔaʔaW,* which (as previously discussed) loosely translates as "one being raises up a round object," before receiving modification. Here the related progressive form *yaʔwaʔaWil* signals the ongoing process of "raising up a round object again and again while going along." Specifically, this progressive form refers to the act of picking this object up over and over again, at different sites, while moving along, whereas the original form refers only to a general performance of the act, usually at one specific site. The progressive variant features two elements not present in the original imperfective form, namely, the progressive prefix *w(a)-* and the progressive suffix *-il.* Starting with the momentaneous verb *tahč'aʔaW,* the same grammatical machinery produces the progressive variant *tahč'iwaʔaWil,* which means "one being moves a round object into the water, repeatedly, while moving along their way." From the basic momentaneous form *no·ʔaʔaW,* the related progressive form *noʔwaʔaWil* can be produced; it translates as "one being puts a round object down here and there, while moving along their way."

15. This directional prefix is derived from an old Athabaskan noun stem meaning "sky," otherwise unattested in modern-day Hupa, having been absorbed into the verb complex long ago.

16. If the same object is lowered into the water, another verb series applies. Yet this shift in directional perspective introduces a subtle change in the time frame from which the event is viewed. Leaving the scope of the event unbounded, one says *tahč'aʔaW,* an expression that loosely translates as "one lowers a round object into the water." Yet to focus on a single, complete instantiation of the event, with reference, perhaps, to a particular stage in the total process, one says *tahč'isʔa·n,* an expression that translates as "one has lowered a round object into the water." Again, the first form features the imperfective stem *-ʔaW,* while the second form features the contrasting perfective stem *-ʔa·n.* In both cases, the direction of motion is signaled with the spatial marker *tah=,* which specifies movement that passes into the water, rapidly disappearing beneath the surface. Here the perfective form contains the temporal prefix *s-,* a marker that primarily occurs with verbs that refer either to enduring states or to ongoing processes, or the middle stages of an event. In this setting, the shift in directional orientation introduces a corresponding, and obligatory, shift in time perspective, here with focus on the middle

stages of the process. If, however, the same object is lowered to the ground, still another pair of forms comes into play. However subtle, this shift in directional perspective introduces still another change in the time frame from which the event is considered. To leave the temporal scope relatively unbounded, one might say *no·ʔaʔaW,* an expression that loosely translates as "one lowers a round object to the ground." Yet to fix on a single, complete instantiation of the event, with focus on the final phases of the process, one says *noʔniŋʔa·n,* which loosely translates as "one lowered a round object to the ground." Again, the first form features the imperfective stem *-ʔaW,* while the second form features the contrasting perfective stem *-ʔa·n.* In both cases, the directional marker *no·=* signals motion that bears downward, usually toward the ground, where the event, unable to go any farther, reaches a point of termination. Here the perfective verb contains the temporal marker *nin-,* a prefix that is primarily found with verbs that refer either to end points or to the final stages of events.

17. The fact that the stem retains its full form—and is not reduced to the contracted form *-ʔaŋ*—indicates the underlying presence of the relativizing enclitic *-i,* which introduces still another degree of certainty to the event portrayed in the construction. If the form were *yaʔwiŋʔaŋ,* the reference would be slightly less definite, yet still referring to a particular instance. In contrast to the heavy stem form, this form could be placed in the future, as in the construction *yaʔwiŋʔan-te·,* which translates as "one will have raised up a round object."

18. Every static form also gives rise to a derived transitional paradigm, which places focus on the point of entrance into a motionless state. Unlike ordinary static forms, these derived transitional constructions allow the regular contrast between perfective and imperfective time perspectives. Consider a scene where a round object enters into a motionless state. Here the Hupa speaker must choose between two contrasting transitional constructions. To leave the scope of the event open-ended, one might say *ʔeʔeʔaʔ,* an expression that loosely translates as "a round object always comes to rest motionless (in one position)." Here the transitional stem *-ʔaʔ* signals the point of entrance into an ongoing state of motionlessness, while the customary marker *ʔ(e)-* signals the recurrence of this process. Yet to fix on a single, complete instantiation of the event, with focus on the initial phases of the total process, one says *wiŋʔaʔ,* which loosely translates as "a round object came to rest motionless (in one position)." Here the inceptive marker *win-* signals the point of entrance into this motionless state.

19. My understanding of the Karuk language is largely based on a close reading of Bright 1957. Though that book contains no definitive statement on classificatory elements in the language, there are many references to classificatory semantics scattered throughout the grammar and the lexicon. Because that volume also contains a healthy collection of narrative texts, I was able to comb these narratives in search of examples of these categories as they are actually put to use in discourse. Bright's book continues to stand as one of the most complete descriptions of a Native American language ever put forth.

20. From the story "The Bear and the Deer" (Bright 1957:226).

21. This regular variant of the verb stem *ikriv* 'a single being lives, sits, or stays' occurs before a juncture.

22. From the story "Formula of Medicine to Protect Children in Strange Places," narrated by Emma Lewis (Goddard 1904:301). Analysis mine.

23. From the narrative "How to Gather and Prepare Acorns," told by Sam Brown (Sapir 2001:194).

24. From the story "The Chimariko Attack a Hupa Village," narrated by Sam Brown (Sapir 2001:518). Analysis mine.

25. Also reflecting their status as agents in these constructions, a possibility that is not otherwise extended to inanimate objects.

26. From the story "Medicine for the Return of a Sweetheart," narrated by Nettie Reuben (Bright 1957:251). Analysis mine.

27. From the story "Coyote Goes to a War Dance," narrated by Julia Starritt (Bright 1957:186). Analysis mine.

28. This concept makes an appearance in many unrelated classificatory systems around the world, with a possible basis in panhuman psychological considerations. Here the sun and moon may simply represent common "round objects" in human experience, along with the eyes of most animals. A Yurok example is given on page 294, in the context of counting months in terms of moons. For an example from Hupa, consider the expression *yiceʔn-wiŋʔaʔ-miɬ,* a construction that loosely translates as "when a round object comes to rest downhill," referring to the time of day when the sun appears to have taken up a position in the western side of the sky. This form is based on the transitional stem *-ʔaʔ,* a form of the stative stem *-ʔaˑ* that specifically signals a point of entry into a motionless position. The inceptive marker *win-* specifies that the object has just entered this state of resting motionless, while the directional adverb *yiceʔn* indicates that the object lies downhill. At the end of the construction, the postpositional *-miɬ* converts the entire expression into a phrase that refers to the specific time of day "when" this event takes place— that is, to the time of day when a round object comes to rest motionless somewhere downhill.

29. When in a position of rest, many body parts are also placed in the "round object" class. Typical referents include the head, heart, eyes, and belly. Consider the construction *Wikʸan-saʔaˑn* 'my heart', where the classificatory stem *-ʔan* signals the presence of a single round object, in this instance, the speaker's heart. As a unit, this form refers to the body part that, from the speaker's perspective, "rests there inside of me as a round thing."

30. Compare any of these objects with a sphere, which continues to look round regardless of the angle of observation.

31. As reported in Robins 1958:93. Analysis mine.

32. Consider the expression *ʔaˑɬ-saʔaˑn* (Golla 1996:21), which corresponds to the English concept of "credit," while literally translating "a round object that lies there with itself." Or consider the related expression *Wisʔaˑn* (Golla 1996:78), which

corresponds to the English concept of someone's "reputation or way of thinking," though the expression literally refers to a "round object that lies there as my possession." Finally, consider the expression *miɬ-na·saʔa·n* (Golla 1996:99), which corresponds to the English concept of "tradition," though the construction literally refers to "a round object that continues to rest alongside something" (such as the Hupa people, with their unique traditions). All of these expressions are based on the stative verb *si-ʔa·n*, a form that literally refers to "a round object that rests motionless in one place."

33. According to Haas (1967:359), legs, ferns, and bridges are also included in the special category for "straight things" among Yurok speakers.

34. This is also reflected in the related stem *ihyásip(riv)* 'to stick up'.

35. From the story "Coyote's Journey," narrated by Julia Starritt (Bright 1957:176). The sentence loosely translates as "a tree stood there."

36. From "The Story of Crane," narrated by Nettie Reuben (Bright 1957:242).

37. See Bright 1957:101 for a discussion of the semantics of the directional marker *-rípaa*. Note that the stem *axyar* regularly shifts to *axyan* in combining forms (Bright 1957:329). Otherwise, the plural action marker *-n(a)* at the end of the form signals a repetition of the action, a process of continued swelling in waves.

38. From the story entitled "The Origin of the Pikiawish," narrated by Chester Pepper (Bright 1957:248). Here the construction *kunpaxyaníppaneesh*, which loosely translates as "they will overflow the river," also contains the subject marker *kun-*, the iterative prefix (i)p-, and the future marker *=eesh*.

39. From the story entitled "The Flood," narrated by Mamie Offield (Bright 1957:262). Here the root *ʔíithri* occurs with the third-person subject marker *ʔu-* and the iterative prefix *ip-*, while the whole construction is couched in the ancient past with the addition of the tense marker *=anik*.

40. Thus, a form such as *yaʔwitteˑn*, which loosely translates as "one has picked up a living being," could equally refer to any of these creatures, including both snakes and worms.

41. As reported in Robins 1958:222.

42. As reported in Robins 1958:257.

43. Neighboring groups—such as the Wiyots, Tolowas, and Shastas—also share in this orientation, with considerable refinement of expression within the classificatory sphere.

CHAPTER 9. CULTURAL MEANING IN EVERYDAY VOCABULARY

1. For a full version of this tale, narrated by Lottie Beck and recorded in the Karuk language, see "The Greedy Father" (Bright 1957:215). See also Kroeber and Gifford 1980:247–48.

2. For the full Yurok version of the popular tale, see Kroeber 1976:414–16.

3. From the story "Sun and Moon," narrated by Dick Richard's father-in-law (informant F) (Kroeber and Gifford 1980:60, 375).

4. The everyday form is *kúusra(h)*, which means both "sun" and "moon." (This form is also used as a classifier when counting the months of the year.)

5. Contrasting with the alternative stem shape *-ɢahɨ*, the underlying presence of the marker *-i* is suggested, here voicing the final consonant (*l*) while referring, on a semantic plane, to a particular instantiation of this action, one associated with a definite actor, here the sun.

6. Mary Haas (1978) was one of the first scholars to note the paucity of shared vocabulary in the Native languages of northwestern California.

7. For a Yurok tale describing the owl's status as one who foretells the coming of evil, see the story "The Owl" (Robins 1958:162).

8. This suffix also occurs as *-avrik*, though in diminutive forms, *r* often shifts to *n* as a kind of diminutive consonant symbolism (see Bright 1957:77).

9. Admittedly, the association could also evolve in reverse, the name arising from the characteristic activities of the animal, which are only later mythologized; what is important for the purposes of the present analysis is that the name alludes to a familiar scene from the local oral literature.

10. The ordinary form of this stem is *tárak*, though in diminutive forms, the *n* becomes *r* (see Bright 1957:77).

11. The final *-y*, meaning "the one who," is a variant form of the relativizing enclitic *-i*, described elsewhere in this chapter. The form shifts from *-i* to *-y* following a vowel.

12. For a full version of this tale, see Kroeber 1976:131.

13. Gifford originally heard this name as "Sukrivish Kuruhan" when collecting Karuk oral literature during the mid-twentieth century (see Kroeber and Gifford 1980:145, 377). Bright later corrected the orthography to match his work on Karuk linguistics (Kroeber and Gifford 1980:377).

14. This bird is said to ferry lost souls to the heavens (see Harrington 1932a:31), while it also dwells high above in the mountains, swooping down ever so suddenly from considerable heights.

15. In diminutive forms, *r* often becomes *n* through a process of consonant symbolism, while the sequence *iva* regularly contracts to *ee* (Bright 1957:33–34, 77).

16. In casual speech, this term is often contracted to *yurúkvaarara*.

17. The ordinary form of this suffix is *várak*, though in diminutive forms, the *r* shifts to *n* (see Bright 1957:77).

18. This directional marker often takes the form *ti-*, though it is lengthened to *te·-* before the aspectual marker *s-* (Sapir 2001:835) and further modified to *teh-* in syllables closed with voiceless fricatives such as *s-* (Sapir 2001:872).

19. This directional marker ordinarily takes the form *tiŋ=*, though here the final *ŋ* shifts to *w* through a process of assimilation, since the following consonant is also a *w*. This marker, which means "lost" or "astray" when applied to verbs, ultimately derives from the noun *tin*, meaning "trails." Originally, the reference (with verbs of motion) was to becoming lost among the trails.

20. The suffix *-ni* does not appear on the surface, though it has a tangible effect on the meaning of the form by adding the sense that the reference is to a

"group of people." Instead, its short vowel is eliminated by a regular rule, and the double -*n-n-* is simplified (Sapir 2001:530).

21. Data in this paragraph from Berman 1982:210–12.

22. The final -*s* can be added to many directional terms without making a clear difference to the meaning when the subject of the clause is either implicitly or explicitly in the third person (see Robins 1958:137).

23. The stem is *laay-*, meaning "to pass," which gives rise to the inflected stem *legaay-* and the noninflected stem *leg* with the addition of the infix -*eg-*.

24. Pliny Earle Goddard first suggested this possibility as a means of explaining the great abundance of descriptive imagery in Hupa vocabulary. Recently, William Bright (2003) has suggested that the same principle may also apply to the Yuroks and Karuks, who observed similar religious taboos during traditional times. My own analysis agrees with Bright's.

25. In precontact times, one could be fined for speaking the name of a dead person, if the surviving relations decided to pursue a case against the offender (see Goddard 1903:73–74).

CHAPTER 10. LANGUAGE CONTACT, MULTILINGUALISM, AND DIVERGENT DRIFT

1. Outside of the grammar, the opposition between the familiar and the formal still survives in a less obligatory way. In formal settings, a superior is often addressed by title and last name; in less formal settings, familiars exchange first names.

2. Of course, "dead" languages are to some extent exempt, as these are known only through historical records and have no viable speech community. Yet even dead languages are often used creatively or are mangled beyond recognition.

3. While Bloomfield (1925) concentrated on the Algonquian groups of the Plains and Northeast, Sapir (1931) drew his evidence from the Athabaskan languages of the American West. Soon both scholars discovered many striking similarities between these often-far-flung languages, in terms of both grammatical patterning and related items of vocabulary. These similarities were so regular and so predictable that both scholars came to surmise that these patterns reflected the modern-day reflexes of common ancestral forms.

4. Possibly emerging from an ancient homeland somewhere near the present-day Black Sea (see Renfrew 1987). Of course, today, the distribution is worldwide, largely owing to English, Spanish, French, and Russian, all members of the Indo-European family.

5. Consider the Navajo verb *naasas*, which means either "I scatter seeds" or "I sprinkle some sand or grains" (Sapir 1949[1936b]). Here the underlying verb stem -*sas* appears to refer to the act of scattering fine particles. Yet after comparing this form with similar words in the other Athabaskan languages, Sapir discovered that this root is strikingly similar to the pan-Athabaskan stem for "snow," which had been virtually lost in Navajo, due to the shift in habitat. Though the form could be

reconstructed as *yáxs in Proto-Athabaskan, the initial consonant of the stem had undergone a regular phonological change in Navajo, shifting from *y* to *s* under the influence of the verbal prefix *ł-*, as occurred with countless other stems in the language. Though emerging from a common Proto-Athabaskan tongue that had once been spoken deep in the remote past, the original words and grammatical forms had, over time, undergone various types of change in the daughter languages.

6. Today, most linguists have come to expect a certain amount of variation in every speech community, based purely on internal factors, such as age, sex, social class, ethnic identity, profession, and place of origin. Probably the most obvious type of variation occurs when passing from one region to another, where speakers suddenly confront dialects that differ substantially from their own. At the same time, the speakers of these alien dialects often practice cultures that also differ in subtle ways, as can be witnessed, for instance, when passing from the north to the south within the United States. Because of these strong associations with the surrounding way of life, for many the mere sound of another dialect triggers memories of the cultural practices of these neighboring speakers, so that the dialect comes to "stand for" these other people and their ways.

7. Closer to home, considerable variation usually arises from one generation to the next or between the sexes, who often learn to use the language in very different ways. Here one encounters variation not spoken in one's immediate surroundings. But because speakers grow accustomed to hearing these accents on a daily basis, these differences are less noticeable to some than regional dialects are, despite the similar scale of the diversity. Consider the case of gender: men and women tend to speak in markedly different ways in all societies, a general condition that linguists have now come to expect in all speech communities. In this sense, the linguist need not venture further than the typical household to discover sex-based variation among male and female speakers. Significant variation also tends to surround other badges of group membership.

8. To some extent, this may reflect the long tradition of prescriptive grammar. Pedagogues, for instance, have always relegated variation to the realm of the colloquial or flat-out unacceptable. On a mission to eradicate variation, early grammarians advocated for a single uniform code shared by all "educated" speakers.

9. Of course, the same is true of culture as well. See Bateson's *Naven* (1936) for an early recognition of variation on the cultural plane.

10. Yet it was decades before the insight was absorbed into the mainstream.

11. Sapir argued against any sense of "progress" in language, suggesting that the notion of "improvement" over time is like viewing biology as a grand conspiracy to produce the Jersey cow (1921:124): "When it comes to linguistic form, Plato walks with the Macedonian swineherd, Confucius with the headhunting savage of Assam" (1921:219).

12. For Sapir's discussion of this general problem, see Sapir 1921:147–70.

13. Creativity, of course, is a rich source of variation in all languages. For speakers constantly use languages to express novel thoughts, which are usually

refined in a public setting by engaging in dialog with other members of the community. As the Russian literary critic Bakhtin (1981:272, 292–94) often remarked, the speaker can hardly open his or her mouth without expressing a point of view, generally one that must resonate with a sense of worldview shared by other participants in an ongoing exchange. Otherwise, the words fall on deaf ears. Yet, far from passively receiving the speaker's thoughts by merely decoding the conventional meanings assigned to words or grammatical categories, the listener actively shapes the flow of ideas in any given encounter. By contributing still another perspective, the listener often counters or even expands claims made by the speaker, before the roles are again reversed in the context of the ongoing exchange. For Bakhtin, like Socrates before him, dialog is the central reality of language, which often opens the door to change, as old ideas are revisited and revised in the actual flow of speech.

As Bakhtin's friend Voloshinov (1986[1929]:22–23, 99–103) came to argue, the meaning of an utterance is inevitably anchored in a particular "theme," or a common stock of assumptions shared by the participants in an encounter. From this perspective, words and grammatical concepts are constantly taking on new shades of meaning every time speakers apply them to real-world situations. Consider the exclusive use of the pronoun *we* in the framing of the U.S. Constitution, where the reference was not extended to women, slaves, or Native Americans (who had few rights for centuries to come), as is spelled out in the remainder of the document. Or to take another example, consider the racial use of mere color terms such as *black, white,* and *red* in American society before the civil rights movement made their use unacceptable in public settings. In both cases, ordinary words and grammatical concepts propagate powerful social ideologies, partly by extending their range of meaning beyond their literal dictionary sense, within a well-defined social context.

When it comes to speaking in a social setting, language and worldview are always closely linked, even if one is discussing the finer points of quantum physics with arcane terminology only understood by a handful of other scientists. As ideas change, so do languages.

14. This new centralized vowel, ə, has the same sound as the reduced vowel that ordinarily appears at the beginning of words such as *apostrophe,* as pronounced in the standard dialect.

15. This insight would have no doubt pleased Sapir, for he saw language as an instrument for the expression of social ideologies, through and through.

16. In the United States, speakers of regional dialects face a similar stigma when immigrating to other parts of the country, where one's native accent must be dropped when participating in the daily life of the surrounding community.

17. Yet after Turkey became a secular republic following World War I, Turkish nationalists made a concerted effort to purge the language of these foreign influences.

18. Though the early Boasian anthropologists were keenly aware of multilingualism in Native American societies, its broader implications have largely gone unexplored, especially where theories of linguistic relativity are concerned.

19. For instance, in addition to borrowing thousands of words, the English language has also borrowed some sounds and grammatical forms from French, including fundamental suffixes such as *-tion* and *-able,* as well as voiced fricatives.

20. While the Caucasus Mountain region is home to some forty languages, the region as a whole bears the distinction of being the area of greatest per capita linguistic diversity on the planet. Papua New Guinea, in contrast, is home to some eight hundred or more languages, all coexisting on this fairly large island.

21. Consider the loss of sexist terms such as *chairman, fireman,* and *policeman* from modern English, in which, just a few generations ago, these terms were nearly universal. As sexism became unacceptable, these words have been replaced with their modern gender-neutral equivalents, namely, *chair, firefighter,* and *police officer.*

22. The following analysis relies heavily on Bauman 1983 and Silverstein 1985.

23. The analysis is based on Gumperz and Wilson 1971.

24. This sketch is based on several sources, including Sorensen 1967; Jackson 1974 and 1983; and Grimes 1985. For a more recent survey, see Aikhenvald 2002.

25. Note that Kupwar villagers, in contrast, usually have reasons to identify with two village languages: first their home language and then the out-group or general village.

26. For evidence of Hupa phonetic conservatism, compare Hupa with Navajo. Whereas the Hupa stop inventory remains unchanged, holding true to the original Proto-Athabaskan plan (PA in the following chart), most Navajo stops have moved forward in the oral tract, and some have undergone affrication.

Hupa Phonetic Conservatism

*PA	Hupa	Navajo
$*g^y$	g^y	dz [plain]
$*k^y$	k^y	ts [aspirated]
$*k^{,y}$	$k^{,y}$	ts' [glottalized]
$*G$	G	g [plain]
$*q$	x	k [aspirated]
$*q'$	q'	k' [glottalized]

CHAPTER 11. CONTACT, EXTREMISM, AND LINGUISTIC RELATIVITY IN NORTHWESTERN CALIFORNIA

1. See Ochs 1993 for a study on how identity is co-constructed with parents in early childhood.

2. This process is part of a widespread pattern in Native American societies, in which language is often closely linked with place, family, and creation mythology on both ideological and emotional grounds (see McCarty and Zepeda 1999; Basso 1996).

3. This report comes from Sam Brown, who in turn, learned the story from his great aunt (or, more precisely, his maternal grandmother's sister). To elaborate, he maintains that the Hupa language is capable of reaching out into the water, perhaps a reference to casting a curse that spreads into the very depths of the earth. From the story "A War between the Hupa and Yurok" (Sapir 2001:515–530).

4. Chimariko, an extinct member of the Hokan stock, is spoken about twenty miles upstream of the central Hupa village of Taʔḵimł-diŋ. Early publications suggested that Hupa was a lingua franca (Powers 1976[1877]) in the region, though follow-up fieldwork did not support this old piece of information. Instead, many Chimariko villagers may have been shifting to Hupa at the time of contact with Europeans (Conathan 2004b:23).

5. Bakhtin (1981:61) describes polyglossia as follows: "Language is transformed from the absolute dogma it had been within the narrow framework of a sealed-off and impermeable monoglossia into a working hypothesis for comprehending and describing reality. . . . But such a full and complete transformation can only occur under certain conditions, namely, the condition of thoroughgoing *polyglossia.* Only polyglossia fully frees consciousness from the tyranny of its own language and its own myth of language."

6. In a similar vein, Conathan has recently uncovered evidence of extensive regional variation or emergent dialects within many of the area's languages (2004b: 113–38).

7. Though characteristically Athabaskan, action focus reaches an unusual extreme in the Hupa language (see chapter 6), in which most basic nouns have been eliminated and replaced with elaborate verbal constructions that portray salient cultural activities associated with particular actors. As is the case in other Athabaskan tongues, time perspective among the Hupas remains an obligatory category of analysis even in the spheres of noun classification and directional marking, representing still another reflex of this pervasive focus on the subtleties of action in the surrounding universe. Representing still another reflection of the pan-Athabaskan predilection for process orientation, both the myth figures and time periods are largely understood according to the actions that define them.

8. The only surviving reflex of this root in modern Hupa is found in the word *xoɢanтaɢ,* the word for "the shoulders," which literally refers to "(area) between one's arms." Here a vestige of the old root -ɢan combines with the third-person possessive marker *xo-,* while the postpositional root -taɢ signals that this region lies "between" the arms.

9. The sole surviving attestation of this root in modern-day Hupa occurs in the form Diniŋʔxine·W, the traditional name for Hupa Indians, where the original reference was to "those who speak an Athabaskan tongue."

10. Neighboring groups—such as the Wiyots, Tolowas, and Shastas—also share in this orientation, with considerable refinement of expression within the classificatory sphere.

11. This is discernable in terms of both the number categories and their distribution in the language, in which they play a role in both counting and adjectival description.

12. Special numerical classifiers exist for some of the following types of objects in Wiyot (as reported in Conathan 2004a): spherical things, flat things, long things, round things, hairlike objects, strings of dentalia, measures of dentalia, days, months, years, salmon, blankets, heads, herds of deer, and deerskins.

13. Data in this paragraph from Robins 1958:87–93. Kroeber (1911) also notes the existence of specialized classifiers for counting strings of dentalia, deerskins, and woodpecker scalps, though the data on these classifiers are scanty.

14. More generally, length can also be quantified with the specialized classifier -*mɹyš*, which specifically signals a span of an "arm's length" (see Robins 1958:89).

15. Data from Rice 1989:877.

16. Data from Hoijer 1945:18.

17. Yet the Hupas have developed a single series of numerical classifiers that set humans apart from all other types of objects, including other animals. In spirit, this system loosely resembles the Yurok classifier system, which maintains a sharp division between animals and humans. Yet apart from this one series, the Hupas have not developed a more elaborate system of numerical classifiers, such as those found in the neighboring Yurok language.

18. Consider the following preverbal particles from Plains Cree (Wolfart 1996: 408): future, *ka* or *kita*; past, *kii* (with the special form *ooh* or *ohci* occurring in negative clauses set in the past). The resemblance to the Yurok tense system is striking.

19. Data from Leer 1989:596–97.

20. Data from Leer 1989:590–95, 616.

References

Ahlers, Jocelyn C. 1996. Metonymy and the Creation of New Words in Hupa. In *Proceedings of the Twenty-second Annual Meeting of the Berkeley Linguistics Society: Special Session on Historical Issues in Native American Languages,* ed. David Librik and Roxanne Beeler, 2–10. Berkeley, Calif.

Aikhenvald, Alexandra Y. 2002. *Language Contact in Amazonia.* Oxford: Oxford University Press.

Bakhtin, Mikhail Milosevic. 1981. *The Dialogic Imagination: Four Essays.* Trans. C. Emerson and M. Holquist; ed. M. Holquist. Austin: University of Texas Press.

Barfield, Owen. 1985 [1953]. *History in English Words*. Great Barrington, Mass.: Lindisfarne Press.

Basso, Keith H. 1990. *Western Apache Language and Culture: Essays in Linguistic Anthropology.* Tucson: University of Arizona Press.

———. 1996. *Wisdom Sits in Places: Landscape and Language among the Western Apache.* Albuquerque: University of New Mexico Press.

Bateson, Gregory. 1936. *Naven: A Survey of the Problems Suggested by a Composite Picture of the Culture of a New Guinea Tribe Drawn from Three Points of View.* Cambridge: Cambridge University Press.

Bauman, Richard. 1983. *Let Your Words Be Few: Symbolism of Speaking and Silence among Seventeenth-Century Quakers.* Cambridge: Cambridge University Press.

Bergvall, Victoria L., Janet M. Bing, and Alice F. Freed, eds. 1996. *Rethinking Language and Gender Research: Theory and Practice.* London: Longman.

Berlin, Brent, and Paul Kay. 1969. *Basic Color Terms: Their Universality and Evolution.* Berkeley: University of California Press.

Berman, Howard. 1982. A Supplement to Robins's Yurok-English Lexicon. *International Journal of American Linguistics* 48:197–222.

———, ed. 2001. Yurok Texts. In *The Collected Works of Edward Sapir,* vol. 14, *Northwest California Linguistics.*

Blevins, Juliette. 2005. Yurok Verb Classes. *International Journal of American Linguistics* 71:327–49.

Bloomfield, Leonard. 1925. On the Sound-System of Central Algonquian. *Language* 1:130–56.

———. 1946. Algonquian. In *Linguistic Structures of North America,* ed. Harry Hoijer, 85–129. New York: Viking Fund.

Boas, Franz. 1966 [1911]. Introduction to *Handbook of American Indian Languages,* ed. Preston Holder. Lincoln: University of Nebraska Press.

Bright, Jane Orstan, and William Bright. 1965. Semantic Structures in Northwestern California and the Sapir-Whorf Hypothesis. *American Anthropologist* 67:249–58.

Bright, William. 1957. *The Karok Language: Grammar, Texts, and Lexicon.* University of California Publications in Linguistics 13. Berkeley.

———. 1978. Karok. In *Handbook of North American Indians,* vol. 8, *California,* ed. R. F. Heizer. Washington, D.C.: Smithsonian Institution.

———. 2003. Animal Names in Native Northwestern California. Paper presented at Conference on Animal Names in Venice, Italy.

———. 2005. Animal Names in Native Northwestern California. In *Animal Names,* ed. Alessandro Minelli, Gherardo Ortalli, and Glauco Sanga, 357–67. Venice: Istituto Veneto di Scienze, Lettere ed Arti.

Brown, Penelope, and Stephen Levinson. 1993. 'Uphill' and 'Downhill' in Tzeltal. *Journal of Linguistic Anthropology* 3 (1): 46–74.

Buckley, Thomas. 2002. *Standing Ground: Yurok Indian Spirituality, 1850–1990.* Berkeley: University of California Press.

Conathan, Lisa. 2004a. Classifiers in Yurok, Wiyot, and Algonquian. In *Proceedings of the Thirtieth Annual Meeting of the Berkeley Linguistics Society: Special Session on the Morphology of American Indian Languages,* ed. Marc Ettlinger and Mischa Park-Doob, 22–33. Berkeley

———. 2004b. *Linguistic Ecology of Northwestern California: Contact, Functional Convergence and Dialectology.* Doctoral dissertation, Department of Linguistics, University of California at Berkeley.

Crystal, David. 1997. *The Cambridge Encyclopedia of Language.* Cambridge: Cambridge University Press.

Curtiss, Susan. 1977. *Genie: A Psycholinguistic Study of a Modern-Day "Wild-Child."* New York: Academic Press.

De Angulo, Jaime, and L. S. Freeland. 1931. Karok Texts. *International Journal of American Linguistics* 6:194–226.

Dixon, R. M. W. 1972. *The Dyirbal Language of North Queensland.* Cambridge Studies in Linguistics 9. Cambridge: Cambridge University Press.

Dixon, Roland, and A. L. Kroeber. 1919. Linguistic Families of California. *University of California Publications in American Archaeology and Ethnology* 16:47–118.

Duranti, Alessandro. 1997. *Linguistic Anthropology.* Cambridge: Cambridge University Press.

Fishman, Joshua A., ed. 1999. *Handbook of Language and Ethnic Identity.* Oxford: Oxford University Press.

Foley, William. 1986. *The Papuan Languages of New Guinea.* Cambridge: Cambridge University Press.

———. 1997. *Anthropological Linguistics.* Oxford, U.K.: Blackwell.

Foster, Michael. 1996. Language and the Culture History of North America. In *Handbook of North American Indians,* vol. 17, *Languages,* ed. Ives Goddard, 64–110. Washington, D.C.: Smithsonian Institution.

Garrett, Andrew. 2001. Reduplication and Infixation in Yurok: Morphology, Semantics, and Diachrony. *International Journal of American Linguistics* 67:264–312.

———. 2004. The Evolution of the Algic Verbal Stem Structure: New Evidence from Yurok. In *Proceedings of the Thirtieth Annual Meeting of Berkeley Linguistics Society,* ed. Marc Ettlinger, Nicholas Fleisher, and Mischa Park-Doob, 46–60. Berkeley.

Garrett, Andrew, and Esther Wood. 2002. The Semantics of Yurok Intensive Infixation. In *The Proceedings from the Fourth Workshop on American Indigenous Languages,* ed. Jeannie Castillo, 112–26. University of California–Santa Barbara Papers in Linguistics.

Gentner, Dedre, and Susan Goldin-Meadow, eds. 2003. *Language in Mind: Advances in the Study of Language and Cognition.* Cambridge, Mass.: MIT Press.

Goddard, Ives. 1975. Algonquian, Wiyot, and Yurok: Proving a Distant Genetic Relationship. In *Linguistics and Anthropology: In Honor of C. F. Voegelin,* ed. M. Dale Kinkade, Kenneth Hale, and Oswald Werner, 249–62. Lisse, Belgium: Peter De Rider Press.

———, ed. 1996. *Handbook of North American Indians,* vol. 17, *Languages.* Washington, D.C.: Smithsonian Institution.

Goddard, Pliny Earle. 1903. Life and Culture of the Hupa. *University of California Publications in American Archaeology and Ethnology* 1(1):1–88. Berkeley.

———. 1904. Hupa Texts. *University of California Publications in American Archaeology and Ethnology* 1(2):89–368. Berkeley.

———. 1905. The Morphology of the Hupa Language. *University of California Publications in American Archaeology and Ethnology* 3:1–344. Berkeley.

Golla, Victor Karl. 1970. *Hupa Grammar.* Doctoral dissertation, University of California–Berkeley.

———, comp. 1996. *Hupa Language Dictionary.* Arcata, Calif.: Hupa Tribal Education Committee and Humboldt State University.

Grimes, Barbara F. 1985. Language Attitudes: Identity, Distinctiveness, Survival in the Vaupés. *Journal of Multilingual and Multicultural Development* 6(5):389–401.

Gumperz, John J., and Stephen C. Levinson, eds. 1996. *Rethinking Linguistic Relativity.* Cambridge: Cambridge University Press.

Gumperz, John J., and Robert Wilson. 1971. Convergence and Creolization: A Case from the Indo-Aryan/Dravidian Border in India. In *Pidginization and Creolization of Languages,* ed. Dell Hymes, 151–67. Cambridge: Cambridge University Press.

Haas, Mary R. 1958. Algonkian-Ritwan: The End of a Controversy. *International Journal of American Linguistics* 24:159–73.

———. 1967. Language and Taxonomy in Northwestern California. *American Anthropologist* 69:358–62.

———. 1978. The Northern California Linguistic Area. In *Language, Culture, and History*, by Mary Haas, 353–69. Stanford, Calif.: Stanford University Press.

———. 1980. Notes on Karok Internal Reconstruction. In *American Indian and Indoeuropean Studies: Papers in Honor of Madison S. Beeler*, ed. Kathryn Klar, Margaret Langdon, and Shirley Silver, 67–76. The Hague: Mouton.

Hall, Kira, and Veronica O'Donovan. 1996. Shifting Gender Positions among Hindi-Speaking Hijras. In *Rethinking Language and Gender Research: Theory and Practice*, ed. Victoria L. Bergvall, Janet M. Bing, and Alice F. Freed, 228–66. London: Longman.

Harrington, John P. 1930. Karuk Texts. *International Journal of American Linguistics* 6:121–61.

———. 1932a. *Karuk Indian Myths*. Bureau of American Ethnology 107. Washington, D.C.

———. 1932b. *Tobacco among the Karuk Indians of California*. Bureau of American Ethnology 94. Washington, D.C.

Heider [Rosch], Eleanor. 1971. Focal Color Areas and the Development of Color Names. *Developmental Psychology* 4:447–55.

———. 1972a. Probabilities, Sampling, and the Ethnographic Method: The Case of Dani Colour Names. *Man* 7:448–66.

———. 1972b. Universals in Color Naming and Memory. *Journal of Experimental Psychology* 93:10–20.

Hill, Jane H. 2000. Languages on the Land. In *Archeology, Language, and History*, ed. J. Terrell, 257–82. Westport, Conn.: Bergin and Garvey.

Hill, Jane H., and Kenneth C. Hill. 1986. *Speaking Mexicano: Dynamics of Syncretic Language in Central Mexico*. Tucson: University Of Arizona Press.

Hinton, Leanne. 1994. *Flutes of Fire: Essays on California Indian Languages*. Berkeley, Calif.: Heyday Books.

Hoijer, Harry. 1945. Classificatory Verb Stems in the Apachean Languages. *International Journal of American Linguistics* 11 (1): 13–23.

———. 1951. Cultural Implications of Some Navajo Linguistic Categories. *Language* 27:111–20.

———. 1954. The Sapir-Whorf Hypothesis. In *Language in Culture*, ed. H. Hoijer, 92–105. Comparative Studies of Cultures and Civilizations 3. Memoirs of the American Anthropological Association 79. Chicago: University of Chicago Press.

———. 1956. The Chronology of the Athapaskan Languages. *International Journal of American Linguistics* 23:230–32.

Humboldt, Wilhelm von. 1988 [1836]. *The Diversity of Human Language-Structure and Its Influence on the Mental Development of Mankind*. Trans. Peter Heath. Cambridge: Cambridge University Press.

Jackson, Jean. 1974. Language Identity of the Columbian Vaupés Indians. In *Explorations in the Ethnography of Speaking*, ed. Richard Bauman and Joel Sherzer, 50–64. New York: Cambridge University Press.

———. 1983. *The Fish People: Linguistic Exogamy and Tukanoan Identity in Northwest Amazonia*. Cambridge: Cambridge University Press.

Kari, James, ed. 1990. *Ahtna Athabaskan Dictionary.* Fairbanks: Alaska Native Language Center.

Kay, D. A., and J. M. Anglin. 1982. Overextension and Underextension in the Child's Expressive and Receptive Speech. *Journal of Child Language* 9:83–98.

Keeling, Richard. 1992. *Cry for Luck: Sacred Song and Speech among the Yurok, Hupa, and Karok Indians of Northwestern California.* Berkeley: University of California Press.

Kinkade, Dale M., Kenneth Hale, and Oswald Werner, eds. 1975. *Linguistics and Anthropology: In Honor of C. F. Voegelin.* Lisse, Belgium: Peter De Rider Press.

Krauss, Michael E. 1973. Na-Dené. In *Current Trends in Linguistics,* vol. 10, *Linguistics in North America,* ed. Thomas A. Sebeok, 903–78. The Hague: Mouton.

Kroeber, A. L. 1911. The Languages of California North of San Francisco. *University of California Publications in American Archaeology and Ethnology* 9:414–26. Berkeley: University of California Press.

———. 1925. *Handbook of the Indians of California.* Bureau Of American Ethnology 78. Washington, D.C.

———. 1976. *Yurok Myths.* Berkeley: University of California Press.

Kroeber, A. L., and E. W. Gifford. 1949. World Renewal: A Cult System of Native Northwest California. *Anthropological Record* 13. Berkeley.

———. 1980. *Karok Myths.* Ed. Grace Buzaljko. Berkeley: University of California Press.

Kroskity, Paul V. 1993. *Language, History, and Identity: Ethnolinguistic Studies of the Arizona Tewa.* Tucson: University of Arizona Press.

Labov, William. 1963. The Social Motivations of Sound Change. *Word* 19:273–309.

———. 1972. *Sociolinguistic Patterns.* Philadelphia: University of Pennsylvania Press.

———. 1981. Resolving the Neogrammarian Controversy. *Language* 57:267–308.

Lakoff, George. 1987. *Women, Fire, and Dangerous Things: What Categories Reveal about the Mind.* Chicago: University of Chicago Press.

Lakoff, George, and Mark Johnson. 1980. *Metaphors We Live By.* Chicago: University of Chicago Press.

Lang, Julian. 1994. *Ararapíkva: Creation Stories of the People, Traditional Karuk Indian Literature from Northwestern California.* Berkeley: Heyday Books.

Leer, Jeff. 1989. Directional Systems in Athapaskan and Na-Dene. In *Athabaskan Linguistics: Current Perspectives on a Language Family,* ed. Eung-Do Cook and Keren D. Rice. New York: Mouton de Gruyter.

Levinson, Stephen C. 1992. *Language and Cognition: Cognitive Consequences of Spatial Description in Guugu Yimidhirr.* Working Paper 13. Nijmegen, The Netherlands: Cognitive Anthropology Research Group, Max-Planck Institute for Psycholinguistics.

———. 2003. *Space in Language and Cognition: Explorations in Cognitive Diversity.* Cambridge: Cambridge University Press.

Lévi-Strauss, Claude. 1976. *Structural Anthropology,* vol. 2. Trans. Monique Layton. Chicago: University of Chicago Press.

Lucy, John. 1992a. *Language Diversity and Thought: A Reformulation of the Linguistic Relativity Hypothesis.* Cambridge: Cambridge University Press.

———. 1992b. *Grammatical Categories and Cognition: A Case Study in the Linguistic Relativity Hypothesis.* Cambridge: Cambridge University Press.

Lucy, John A., and Richard A. Schweder. 1979. Whorf and His Critics: Linguistic and Non-linguistic Influences on Color Memory. *American Anthropologist* 81:581–615.

McCarty, Teresa L., and Ofelia Zepeda. 1999. Amerindians. In *Handbook of Language and Ethnic Identity,* ed. Joshua Fishman, 197–210.

Milroy, Lesley. 1980. *Language and Social Networks.* Baltimore, Md.: University Park Press.

Mithun, Marianne. 1999. *The Languages of Native North America.* Cambridge: Cambridge University Press.

Nettle, Daniel, and Suzanne Romaine. 2000. *Vanishing Voices: The Extinction of the World's Languages.* Oxford: Oxford University Press.

Nichols, Johanna. 1992. *Linguistic Diversity in Space and Time.* Chicago: University of Chicago Press.

Ochs, Elinor. 1993. Constructing Social Identity: A Language Socialization Perspective. *Research on Language and Social Interaction* 26 (3): 287–306.

O'Neill, Sean. 2002. Northwest California Ethnolinguistics: A Study in Drift. In *Proceedings of the 50th Anniversary Celebration of the Survey of California and Other Indian Languages,* ed. Lisa Conathan and Teresa McFarland, 64–88. Department of Linguistics, University of California. Berkeley.

Orwell, George. 1950. Politics and the English Language. In Orwell, *Shooting the Elephant and Other Essays,* 75–92. New York: Harcourt, Brace.

Pinker, Steven. 1994. *The Language Instinct.* New York: W. Morrow and Company.

Powers, Stephen. 1976 [1877]. *Tribes of California.* Berkeley: University of California Press.

Proulx, Paul. 1985a. Notes on Yurok Derivation. *Kansas Working Papers in Linguistics* 10 (2): 101–43.

———. 1985b. The Semantics of Yurok Terms Referring to Water. *Anthropological Linguistics* 27:353–62.

———. 1985c. Proto-Algic II: Verbs. *International Journal of American Linguistics* 51:59–94.

Reichard, Gladys Amanda. 1925. *Wiyot Grammar and Texts.* University of California Publications in American Archaeology and Ethnology 22. Berkeley.

Renfrew, Colin. 1987. *Archeology and Language: The Puzzle of Indo-European Origins.* London: Cape.

Rice, Keren. 1989. *A Grammar of Slave.* Berlin: Mouton de Gruyter.

Robins, R. H. 1958. *The Yurok Language: Grammar, Texts, and Lexicon.* Berkeley: University of California Publications in Linguistics 15.

Romaine, Suzanne. 2000. *Language in Society: An Introduction to Sociolinguistics.* 2nd ed. Oxford: Oxford University Press.

Rosch, Eleanor. 1975. Cognitive Representations of Semantic Categories. *Journal of Experimental Psychology: General* 104:192–233.

———. 1977. Human Categorization. In *Advances in Cross-Cultural Psychology,* vol. 1, ed. N. Warren, 1–49. London: Academic Press.

———. 1978. Principles of Categorization. In *Cognition and Categorization,* ed. E. Rosch and L. Lloyd, 27–48. Hillsdale, N.J.: Lawrence Erlbaum.

Sankoff, Gillian. 1980. Political Power and Linguistic Inequality in Papua New Guinea. In Sankoff, *The Social Life of Language,* 5–27. Philadelphia: University of Pennsylvania Press.

Sapir, Edward. 1913. Wiyot and Yurok, Algonkin Languages of California. *American Anthropologist* 15:617–46.

———. 1915. The Na-Dene Languages: A Preliminary Report. *American Anthropologist* 17:534–58.

———. 1916. *Time Perspective in Aboriginal American Culture: A Study in Method.* Canada, Department of Mines, Geological Survey, Memoir 90. Anthropological Series 13. Ottawa: Government Printing Bureau. Reprinted in Sapir 1949, 389–462.

———. 1921. *Language: An Introduction to the Study of Speech.* New York: Harcourt Brace.

———. 1924. The Grammarian and His Language. *American Mercury* 1:149–155. Reprinted in Sapir 1949, 150–59.

———. 1925. Pitch Accent in Sarcee. *Journal de la Société des Americanists, Paris* 17:185–205.

———. 1927a. An Expedition to Ancient America. *University of Chicago Magazine* 20:10–12.

———. 1927b. The Unconscious Patterning of Behavior in Society. In *The Unconscious: A Symposium,* ed. E. S. Dummer, 114–42. New York: Knopf. Reprinted in Sapir 1949, 544–59.

———. 1929. The Status of Linguistics as a Science. *Language* 5:207–14. Reprinted in Sapir 1949, 160–66.

———. 1931. The Concept of Phonetic Law as Tested in Primitive Languages by Leonard Bloomfield. Reprinted in Sapir 1949, 73–82.

———. 1933. La Réalité psychologique des phonèmes. *Journal de Psychologie Normale et Pathologique* 30:247–65. Reprinted as "The Psychological Reality of Phonemes" in Sapir 1949, 46–60.

———. 1936a. Hupa Tattooing. In *Essays in Anthropology Presented to A. L. Kroeber,* ed. R. Lowie, 273–77. Berkeley: University of California Press.

———. 1936b. Internal Linguistic Evidence for the Northern Origin of Navaho. *American Anthropologist* 38:225–35. Reprinted in Sapir 1949, 213–24.

———. 1949. *The Selected Writings of Edward Sapir in Language, Culture, and Personality.* Ed. David Mandelbaum. Berkeley: University of California Press.

———. 1994. *The Psychology of Culture: A Course of Lectures,* ed. Judith Irvine. Berlin: De Gruyter.

————. 2001. *The Collected Works of Edward Sapir,* vol. 14, *Northwest California Linguistics,* ed. Victor Golla and Sean O'Neill. Berlin: De Gruyter.

Saussure, Ferdinand. 1972. *Course in General Linguistics.* Translated and annotated by Roy Harris, edited by Charles Bally and Albert Sechehaye, with the collaboration of Albert Riedlinger. Peru, Ill.: Open Court Trade and Academic Books.

————. 2006. *Writings in General Linguistics* Trans. Carl Sanders and Matthew Pires; ed. Simon Bouquet and Rudolf Engler. Oxford: Oxford University Press.

Senghas, A., and M. Coppola. 2001. Children Creating Language: How Nicaraguan Sign Language Acquired a Spatial Grammar. *Psychological Science* 12 (4): 323–38.

Senghas, A., S. Kita, and A. Ozyürek. 2004. Children Creating Core Properties of Language: Evidence from an Emerging Sign Language in Nicaragua. *Science* 305 (5691): 1779–1782.

Silver, Shirley. 1966. *The Shasta Language.* Doctoral dissertation, Department of Linguistics, University of California at Berkeley.

Silver, Shirley, and Wick Miller. 1997. *American Indian Languages: Cultural and Social Contexts.* Tucson: University of Arizona Press.

Silverstein, Michael. 1976. Shifters, Linguistic Categories, and Cultural Description. In *Meaning in Anthropology,* ed. K. Basso and H. Selby, 11–55. Albuquerque: University of New Mexico Press.

————. 1985. Language and the Culture of Gender: At the Intersection of Structure, Usage, and Ideology. In *Semiotic Meditation,* ed. Elizabeth Mertz and Richard Parmentier, 220–59. New York: Academic Press.

Sorensen, A. P. 1967. Multilingualism in the Northwest Amazon. *American Anthropologist* 69:670–84.

Spott, Robert, and A. L. Kroeber. 1942. *Yurok Narratives.* University of California Publications in American Archaeology and Ethnology 16:177–314. Berkeley.

Sweetser, Eve E. 1990. *From Etymology to Pragmatics: Metaphorical and Cultural Aspects of Semantic Structure.* Cambridge: Cambridge University Press.

Talmy, Leonard. 1972. *Semantic Structures in English and Atsugewi.* Doctoral dissertation, Department of Linguistics, University of California–Berkeley.

Teeter, Karl V. 1964. *The Wiyot Language.* University of California Publications in Linguistics 37. Berkeley.

Thomason, Sarah Grey, and Terrence Kaufman. 1988. *Language Contact, Creolization, and Genetic Linguistics.* Berkeley: University of California Press.

Thompson, Lucy. 1916. *To the American Indian.* Eureka, Calif.: Cummins Print Shop.

Voloshinov, Valentin Nikolaevich. 1986 [1929]. *Marxism and the Philosophy of Language.* Trans. L. Matejka and I. R. Titunik. Cambridge, Mass.: Harvard University Press.

Waterman, T. T. 1920. Yurok Geography. *University of California Publications in American Archeology and Ethnology* 16 (5): 177–315.

Waterman, T. T., and A. L. Kroeber. 1934. Yurok Marriages. *University of California Publications in American Archaeology and Ethnology* 35:1–14. Berkeley.

Wertheim, Suzanne. 2003. Language Ideologies and the "Purification" of Post-Soviet Tartar. *Ad Imperio* 1:347–69.

Whorf, Benjamin Lee. 1956. *Language, Thought, and Reality: Selected Writings of Benjamin Lee Whorf.* Ed. John B. Carroll. Cambridge, Mass.: MIT Press.

Witherspoon, Gary. 1971. Navajo Categories of Objects at Rest. *American Anthropologist* 71 (1): 110–27.

Wolfart, H. W. 1996. Sketch of Plains Cree: An Algonquian Language. In *Handbook of North American Indians,* vol. 17, *Languages,* ed. Ives Goddard, 390–439. Washington, D.C.: Smithsonian Institution.

Young, Robert W., and William Morgan, Sr. 1992. *Analytical Lexicon of Navajo,* with the assistance of Sally Midgette. Albuquerque: University of New Mexico Press.

Index

Acorns, 26–28, 32–33, 57, 208, 244, 292, 318–19n8, 323n16, 327n23

Across-the-Ocean-Widower (character in storytelling), 30, 124, 127, 131, 142, 162, 166, 182, 183, 185–86, 188–89, 194, 246, 249, 252–53, 287, 306. *See also* Hupa vocabulary; Karuk vocabulary; Yurok vocabulary

Ahlers, Jocelyn, 253

Algic stock, 8–9, 21–24, 293, 298–99, 304, 309n3, 310n8, 310n13, 310n16, 324n10

Algonquian family, 8–9, 21–23, 133, 261, 270, 293, 299, 309n3, 310n16, 324n10, 330n3

Amazon Basin, linguistic area, 275, 278–79, 289, 307–308. *See also* Contact; Drift; Language ideology; Multilingualism

Animacy, 11, 207–208, 217–19, 233, 279, 304, 324n8; in Hupa, 11, 21, 155, 215, 219–23, 296; in Karuk, 224–26; in Yurok, 11, 208, 210, 223–24, 293. *See also* Linguistic relativity

Aspect, verbal, 138; Hupa, 21, 104, 139, 146–60, 163–67; Karuk, 140–43; Yurok, 167–75. *See also* Hupa language; Karuk language; Tense; Yurok language

Athabaskan family, 4–5, 19–21, 38, 62, 182, 229, 248, 261, 284, 292, 294–96, 298, 305, 309n2, 310n18, 312n6, 317n24, 325n15, 330n3, 330–31n5, 333n26, 334n7, 334n9

Autonomy, theoretical position on the relationship between language and culture, 57–60

Bakhtin, Mikhail, 53, 263–64, 290, 332n13, 334n5

Basket (character in storytelling), 225–26, 233; classification in languages, 157, 216, 220, 222, 225–26, 229–30, 233–34, 296; status in traditional culture, 27

Bateson, Gregory, 280, 331n9

Bauman, Richard, 49, 275, 333n22

Bear. *See* Grizzly Bear (character in storytelling)

Berman, Howard, 9, 316, 330n21

Bilingualism. *See* Multilingualism

Boas, Franz, 7, 35, 41–43, 47, 51–52, 55–56, 271–72, 312n3, 313n14

Bright, William: ethnolinguistic area, 56; Karuk ethnography, 310n20, 330n24; Karuk fieldwork, 6, 216; Karuk linguistics, 6–7, 13, 74, 83, 86, 91, 216, 243, 247, 310n19, 315–16n5, 317n22, 320n2, 326n19, 328n37, 329n8, 329n10, 329n13, 329n15, 329n17; linguistic relativity in northwestern California, 10–11, 289, 309n1, 324n8

Canoe, 32–33, 85, 89, 100, 109, 157, 188, 229, 232

Čʼeˑʔindiɡoʔdiŋ (Hupa village), 167, 185

Characters in storytelling: *See* Across-the-Ocean-Widower; Basket; Coon; Coyote; Crane; Dog; Duck Hawk; Eel; Evening Star; First Salmon; Fox; Frog; Grizzly Bear; Jerusalem Cricket; Mole; Money; Moon; Mourning Dove; Owl; Sun; Towhee; Water Ouzel

Chilula language, 19

Chimariko language, 32, 290, 311n32

Chomsky, Noam: language universals, 314n26; linguistic creativity, 59